Displays!

Displays!

Dynamic Design Ideas for Your Library Step by Step

SUSAN P. PHILLIPS

McFarland & Company, Inc., Publishers

Jefferson, North Carolina, and London

LIBRARY OF CONGRESS CATALOGUING-IN-PUBLICATION DATA

Phillips, Susan P., 1945–
Displays! : dynamic design ideas for your
library step by step / Susan P. Phillips.
p.   cm.
Includes bibliographical references and index.

ISBN 978-0-7864-4024-5
softcover : acid free paper ∞

1. Library exhibits—Handbooks, manuals, etc.
I. Title.
Z717.P475   2012   021.7–dc23   2011046868

BRITISH LIBRARY CATALOGUING DATA ARE AVAILABLE

Front cover image: The Edgar Allan Poe Display

Manufactured in the United States of America

McFarland & Company, Inc., Publishers
Box 611, Jefferson, North Carolina 28640
www.mcfarlandpub.com

To my sons,
Brian and Jeff Silsbee,
two of my very best ideas.

In loving memory of my sister,
Mary Ellen Palmieri,
who braved her final battle
with courage and dignity.

Acknowledgments

Many thanks to:

Morgan Dorsey, class of 2010, for her dedication to this project. I appreciated her contributions of photographs and other materials featured in the display Egypt on the Nile. She served as the photographer for these displays: Egypt on the Nile, And the Winner Is, The Jersey Shore, Get Lit at the Library, Olympic Fever, Fit or Fat: Are You Fed Up? Frida, Garden Gate, Autism Aware, Generations, Season's Readings, ...Isms, Lovers in History, 1776, Sci-Fi, Cinco de Mayo, Gallery of Rogues, Will Power, Legends: Women Who Have Changed the World, Land of the Rising Sun, A Wild Wilde Ride, and Bastille Day. She also made creative design contributions to Connections: The Social Network, Frida, The Jersey Shore, The Great Ships of Sail, Bastille Day, A Wild Wilde Ride, Maya Mysteries, Olympic Fever, Far Out: Surviving the 1960s, Land of the Rising Sun, Going Green, Season's Readings, Land Down Under, Edgar Allan Poe, Lovers in History, ...Isms, Cinco de Mayo, Reel Women, Mostly Mozart, Yosemite in Focus, Autism Aware, Gallery of Rogues, Sci-Fi, And the Winner Is, Get Lit at the Library, Legends: Women Who Have Changed the World and Fit or Fat: Are You Fed Up?

Dr. Allen Richardson, professor of religious studies at Cedar Crest College, who provided the photograph of the members of the college community who accompanied him on a pilgrimage to Egypt seen in the display of the same name. He also lent the cat in that display, the photographs of Paris in Bastille Day, the field telephone featured in The Great War 1914–1918, the model, ship interior illustration and signed postcard seen in *Titanic!*, the ancient miniature ceramic head in Cinco de Mayo, the antique violin in Mostly Mozart, the nautical text, whistle, sextant and telescope seen in The Great Ships of Sail, the Buddha and 19th century gong in Land of the Rising Sun, all of the realia in the 1776 display and most of the religious icons featured in ...Isms.

Lauren Panepinto, who photographed the Plain People and made contributions to the Edgar Allan Poe and Sci-Fi exhibits. Lauren also patiently edited the majority of the text of this book.

Special thanks to:

• Pat Badt, professor of art, Cedar Crest College, for the Japanese tea items featured in Land of the Rising Sun.

• Carol and Arturo James for their family photos and memorabilia from Mexico featured in Cinco de Mayo and for their support of this project.

• Joan and Mike Allen for the loan of their Byar's Choice carolers featured in The Jersey Shore—and for a lifetime of generosity and friendship.

• Laura Cole, 2008, for photographing these displays: FDR Remembered, Ladies of the Court, The Wright Stuff and Gutsy Girls. She also created the Eiffel Tower featured in Bastille Day.

• Megan Ammons, class of 2009, for her contribution to Reel Women and her photographs of these displays: The Great War 1914–1918, Maya Mysteries, 1776 and Bastille Day.

• Charlie Crimi for the loan of musical items from his extensive collection of rock memorabilia featured in Rock & Roll, and for the loan of his mint container and books from his personal collection for the *Titanic!* display.

• Cathy Meyett, class of 2011, for her original Play-Doh flower featured in Autism Aware and her photograph in Far Out: Surviving the 1960s.

• Shay Andrews, class of 2011, for the photographs of *Titanic!*, The Great Ships of Sail, Connections: The Social Network and Reel Women.

• Jen Decky, class of 2011, for her photographs in Land Down Under and Edgar Allan Poe.

• Mark Scasny, of Staten Island, New York, for permission to feature his extensive collection of World War I memorabilia and for his thorough descriptions of items featured in The Great War 1914–1918.

• Mike Frederick for sharing his artwork in the display Autism Aware.

• Anne Bivans for the generous use of her photographs featured in the display Yosemite in Focus.

• Susan Freeh for the loan of the textile shown in Maya Mysteries.

• Rachael Roeckel, class of 2009, for the loan of the political buttons seen in Far Out: Surviving the 1960s and Election Central.

• Rachel Brown, class of 2009, for the loan of her lava lamp seen in Far Out: Surviving the 1960s.

• Rachel Edgar, class of 2009, for the loan of the bust used in 1776 and for her photography of Mostly Mozart and Yosemite in Focus. Rachel also served as editor for a sizeable portion of this book.

• Ana-Kay Rhoden, Elizabeth Sunderhaus, Crystal Morlock, Camelle Clarke, Nyssa Kudravy, Carolyn Kirch, Kris Ellis, Grace Beverly, Kaili Quinn and Angela Smith for their help in creating many of the displays.

• Elizabeth Sterling and Steph Spiker for the loan of items from their collections for Land of the Rising Sun.

• Barbara Cantalupo, Ph.D, associate professor of English, Penn State Lehigh Valley, and founding editor of the Edgar Allan Poe Review, for the loan of the excellent source Edgar Allan Poe: An Illustrated Companion to His Tell-Tale Stories by Henry Lee Poe and a copy of the Edgar Allan Poe Review.

• Judith Malitsch, assistant professor of Biological Sciences, Cedar Crest College, for the loan of the skull and bones featured in the Edgar Allan Poe display.

• Michele Groncki for her photograph of Election Central.

• Lynnette Horne, class of 2011, for her photograph of Edgar Allan Poe.

• Susan Cox for the loan of items from the Marsha Root Walsh Alumnae Museum of Cedar Crest College and Maureen Yoachim, manager of the Barnes & Noble bookstore at Cedar Crest College, for the loan of college memorabilia featured in the Generations display.

• Rebecca Callan, costume director of Cedar Crest College, for contributions made to Far Out: Surviving the 1960s, Legends: Women Who Have Changed the World, Generations, A Wild Wilde Ride and 1776.

• JoEllen Christensen for scanning and editing many of the photographs featured throughout the book. I thank her for her enduring friendship, daily counseling, honest critiques and valued assistance in creating the display Generations.

• Elouise Schreffler for the loan of the tie-dye shirt, the Barbie and Ken dolls and the trolls featured in Far Out: Surviving the 1960s, as well as the sombrero in Cinco de Mayo—and, especially, for her generosity of spirit and friendship.

• My sisters Eileen Griffin, Barbara Famulary and Mary Ellen Palmieri, whose love and support were much appreciated over the six years it took to create two library display books.

• Mary Silsbee for her contributions of autism materials and her advice and counsel for the display Autism Aware.

• My granddaughters Callie Marie Silsbee, for the loan of the maracas featured in Cinco de Mayo, and her sister, Emme Charles, who will no doubt inherit them and make her own music.

• And, finally, to my husband, Dennis, for his support and counsel throughout this project and for the use of a host of his worldly possessions prominently featured throughout this book. I appreciate the loan of the much treasured and hard earned trophy, won by his prized 1995 Polo Green Metallic Corvette C-4, which is featured in And the Winner Is. He also contributed to these displays: A Brush with History: Portraits of the Presidents, Ladies of the Court, Sci-Fi, Land Down Under, Far Out: Surviving the 1960s, Olympic Fever and Lovers in History. Denny took the original photograph of the ruin at Xuantunich, in Belize, which is featured in Maya Mysteries. He also photographed In Stitches, A Brush with History: Portraits of the Presidents and Rock & Roll.

Table of Contents

Preface

It has been my pleasure to design almost 400 library displays in my academic career. I have endeavored to create colorful, eye-catching exhibits that generate interest and excitement. I have tapped into the talents, passions and interests of my friends, colleagues and family, incorporating items from their collections and relevant books on the topic.

In my position as lending services supervisor at the Cressman Library of Cedar Crest College, I managed a large staff of student assistants. My day to day responsibilities were sometimes rather mundane, but these students were anything but. It was my privilege to know and mentor them, to see them evolve over their college years, and to help launch them into the professional world at the end of their tenure at the college. Since 1988, I have tapped into their talents to assist me in the creation of effective library displays.

When the opportunity to write books on library displays was presented to me I knew I could count on my students to accompany me on this journey. They found appropriate fonts for signage, assisted with research, cut hundreds of letters and searched for images ranging from space aliens to the Eiffel Tower. They crafted French fries, windmills and paper flowers, they carted bones from the Biology Department and religious icons from Social Sciences. They brought treasures from their homes and willingly shared collectibles from lava lamps and porcelain geishas to Egyptian jewelry and vintage political campaign buttons. They showed interest in new display possibilities and commented candidly on the finished products! And, they made it all a joy.

This second volume of library displays was a true labor of love. It provided the perfect forum for artistic expression and forced me to use every last ounce of creativity. *Displays! Dynamic Design Ideas for Your Library Step by Step* offers 45 colorful displays mounted at minimal expense. It includes a comprehensive introduction to the subject, gives the genesis of the idea, offers specifics as to the information included and its source, and provides ideas on how to expand or alter the concept for larger exhibit spaces. Seventy-seven additional display ideas are offered in the resource pages of this book followed by an extensive bibliography.

I endeavored to include a wide range of subjects. They range from Mayan ruins to the Jersey shore, from the land of the rising sun to the land down under, from William Shakespeare to Edgar Allan Poe, from women in film to the ladies of the court, from the mystery of autism to the greening of the environment, from surviving the sixties to the evolution of the social network, from the demise of the *Titanic* to a world at war, from the NASCAR speedway to the natural wonders at Yosemite, and, finally, to the shocking prospect of a world without people.

It is my hope that this book will serve as a guide, provide you with some fresh ideas for your display cases and lessen the burden sometimes associated with keeping these spaces relevant. I am confident this source will help you become more aware of the treasures in your midst that could be appreciated and admired as the focal point of one of your upcoming displays.

Good luck!

1 Globe Trotting

Land of the Rising Sun

In a mad world, only the mad are sane. —Akira Kurosawa, film director

Japan comprises a group of islands located 100 miles east of the mainland of Asia. The ancient Japanese settlers knew of the location and existence of Korea and China but were unaware of any land lying to the east of the islands. These early inhabitants thought that their land was the first to be touched by the rising sun. The Japanese call their land *Nippon,* meaning the "land of the rising sun." Europeans learned of Japan from the Chinese, who mispronounced the name as *Zipango.* Eventually, that word evolved into *Japan.*

Japan encompasses an area of 145,902 square miles and is slightly smaller than the state of California. With a population of about 128 million people, however, it is four times more crowded. Japan experiences almost as many climates as the U.S., from subtropical to temperate. The northernmost part of Hokkaido is the same latitude as Montreal, Canada, while the southernmost tip of Kyusha is parallel with Pensacola, Florida.

Toyko is the capital and other major cities include Yokohoma, Osaka, Nagoya, Sapporo, Kobe and Fukuoka. The country is made up of rugged, mountainous islands. More than 70 percent of Japan consists of mountains and those mountains include more than 200 volcanoes. Mt. Fuji, the tallest mountain in Japan, is an active volcano. The country experiences 1,500 earthquakes every year.

Japan's imperial past has given way to a modern, thriving democracy. The country has become highly urbanized and industrialized. Japan's export markets are vast, and, as a result, the economy is generally strong. Japan ranks first among major industrial nations in per capita gross national product. Still, many of its citizens live in substandard housing and lack such basic necessities as indoor plumbing. Poverty has become a major problem that threatens the basic social fabric of this nation.

The crowded conditions within the country influence how the Japanese people live. Land prices are very high, so most Japanese cannot afford individual homes. Some live in small apartments called danchi, originally built as government housing, beginning in the 1950s. This space is divided into very small sleeping and living rooms and has an even smaller kitchen and bedroom. One third of these dwellings measure a mere 11 feet by 11 feet. Today, many danchi are owned by large corporations that encourage employees to live among their colleagues, sometimes rent-free, in order to foster a sense of family within the company.

Until recently, Japan led the world in the production of automobiles. However, in the face of declining global consumption, nearly everything that Japan exports, from electronics and machinery to steel and ships, is in less demand. This economic reality has forced factories to close or to cut shifts. In recent years, companies have terminated a large number of irregular or part-time workers due to the global recession. People in their 20s and 30s who cannot find work have become a fixed feature of the economy and higher education continues to elude the children in low-income families.

The aggressive military mentality that

Land of the Rising Sun. A 19th century gong, an authentic Japanese tea set and an elegant pair of colorful geishas flank a bronze Buddha framed by the flag of Japan.

existed in Japan in the early and mid–20th century has given way to a streamlined and well-trained Self-Defense Force designed to minimally defend the homeland. Although possession of nuclear weapons is not explicitly forbidden in its constitution, Japan, as the only nation to have experienced the devastation of nuclear attacks, has expressed its loathing of nuclear arms and its determination not to acquire them.

The Japanese people are sports enthusiasts. Although sumo is considered Japan's national sport, baseball is very popular and draws many spectators. Soccer is also played and enjoyed widely in this country followed by the martial arts and karate. Over the past century, Japan's population of approximately 128 million has undergone tremendous growth largely due to scientific, industrial and sociological changes. The work force currently totals 67 million. Currently the life expectancy in Japan is 77 years for males and 84 for females.

Japan is the tenth most populous country in the world. In 2005, the population declined for the first time in the country's history. After decades of sustained growth, Japan is facing a sharp decline in its population as the number of deaths outpaces the number of births. Longer life expectancy and low birth rates means that the declining Japanese population is graying at a higher rate. This is an alarming situation for Japan, especially during this universal time of global recession. Private industry has gone so far as to offer a range of financial incentives for couples to have additional children.

Everyday life in Japan includes the act of bowing, which is an honored tradition. The bow helps keep the peace, establishes and affirms relationships and serves as a ritual within given situations and people. The bow equates to the North American handshake. The depth of the bow depends on the association between the parties involved. This act can range from simple shallow nods to kneeling bows where heads touch the floor. The person who is lower in status should bow first and lowest. Bowing has morphed into an art form in the business community. New hires are often trained in the correct bowing techniques to employ toward coworkers and customers. Men bow with their hands at their sides and women bow with their hands just touching in front. Heels remain together for this gesture. The bow is also in evidence in the world of sports such as karate, kendo, judo, sumo and bowling. This ritual is not without risks, however. Known for proper protocol, the city of Tokyo has 24 recorded instances of people either being killed or receiving serious skull fractures while bowing to each other in the traditional greeting.

The language spoken in Japan is Japanese and the religions include Shintoism, Buddhism and Christianity. Shintoism and Buddhism have been coexisting for several centuries and have, to a certain degee, complemented each other. Most Japanese view themselves as Shintoist, Buddhist or both. The role religion plays in everyday life in Japan is minimal. Most people adhere to religious rituals at ceremonies surrounding births, weddings and funerals. The Japanese may visit a shrine or temple on their New Year and participate in local festivals called matsun, most of which have religious backgrounds. For more information about the religions of Japan visit http://www.asianinfo.org/asianinfo/japan/religion.htm.

As a result of their respect for and appreciation of education, the rate of literacy in Japan is an unbelievable 99 percent! There are four different writing systems in the country: romaji, katakana, hiragana and kanji. The first full-length novel, *The Tale of Genji,* was written in 1007 by a Japanese noblewoman, Murasaki Shikibu. The story tells of the life of Genji and his many romances against the backdrop of Japan's court society. After the death of Shikibu's husband, the author served in the imperial court. It is thought that the novel was based on her true-life experiences at court.

The word Geisha means "person of the arts" and, surprisingly, the first geisha were men! Although geisha were trained to perform dance, music and poetry, many were viewed simply as courtesans. Young girls were sold into the geisha life by their families until the mid–20th century and were often subject to the ritual of *mizu-age,* whereby

their virginity was sold to the highest bidder. Those practices no longer exist and today's geisha are seasoned veterans, much like a favorite aunt or a grandmother.

In Japanese homes, raised floors give a hint as to when it is proper to take off shoes or slippers. At the entrance to the home, the floor will usually be raised about 6 inches, indicating that you should remove shoes and put on slippers.

The Japanese Tea Ceremony is an honored ritual in Japan. The host spends days reviewing minute details to make sure the service will be flawless. There are various styles of tea ceremonies. The ceremony takes place in a specially designed room called the *chashitsu.* The room is usually within a teahouse and is located away from the residence in the garden.

For a colorful glimpse into Japanese culture get a copy of *A Year in Japan* by writer/illustrator Kate T. Williamson. This charming travelogue combines journals and whimsical drawings from the author's trip to Japan. Williamson provides a glimpse into the intricacies of the culture to which the average tourist would not be privy. Visit these sites for a lengthy list of interesting facts about Japan: http://www.facts-aboutjapan.com/interesting.html; http://www.state.gov/r/pa/ei/bgn/4142.htm, and http://lcweb2.loc.gov/cgibin/query/r?frd/cstdy:@field(DODCID+jp0012).

Credits

Our cataloger often points out books of interest that might make an effective display for our exhibit space. She mentioned that our collection of Japanese literature and culture had beautiful covers. When I perused these areas of the stacks I realized how effective these books would be with a simple graphic, the flag of Japan, as a background.

Cedar Crest College has had an Anime club on campus for many years. This organization promotes the Japanese culture and has shared many of those customs with the members of our college community. Students interested in this type of animation, which originated in Japan, enjoy graphic novels and comic books called *manga.* Our library has been the recipient of many of these works, which are available to our students in the reserve collection.

I am grateful to Pat Badt of the Art Department and Dr. Allen Richardson of the Social Sciences Department at Cedar Crest for items lent for this display.

Assembling the Display

1. The flag of Japan was created using white poster board for the background and red poster board for the circle. This was attached to a background of black felt and pulled forward. The font was created using Polo Brush sized at 180. This is available to download free at http://www.1001freefonts. com. The lettering was printed on white card stock and cut into rectangles then arranged around the image of the sun.

On the top left is a document titled the "History of the Japanese Kimono." This information can be found if you visit http://www. japanesekimono.com/kimono_history.htm. Under that document was the quotation that introduced the display. Last was information about the Japanese pagoda, which can be found if you visit http://crystalinks.com/pagadoas.html. Items on the left were printed on white card stock and mounted on red and black poster board.

2. On the top right was poem titled "In the Autumn Fields." Written by Ki no Tsurayuki (872–945). Calligraphy depicting the word *autumn* was inserted above the text. That image can be found if you visit http://www.webvider.com/kanji/index1-001.html:

In the Autumn Fields

In the autumn fields
Mingles with the pampas grass
Flowers are blooming
Should my love too, spring forth
Or shall we never meet?

Under that was a summation of the Japanese Tea Ceremony, which is available at http://www.asianartmall.com/teaceremonyarticle. htm.

Items on the right were printed and mounted like those on the left.

3. On the bottom shelf was a Japanese Buddha, two geisha dolls, an embroidered belt, a box with wooden picks, a cast iron teapot and red cloth napkin, a wooden tray with loose green tea and tin, paper embossed with a blossom, a bowl for preparing the tea, wooden picks for sweets, a whisk, a wooden spoon, a tile with the image of a geisha, miniature shoes, several postcards, a Japanese Pilgrim book and blessings and a Daruma figure. The Buddha, geisha dolls and tea tray were elevated on Styrofoam blocks covered with black velvet. A 19th century gong hung from the grate covering the light on the top left of the display.

Books featured in the display were *The Japanese Tea Ceremony: Cha-no-yu* by A.L. Sadler, *A Year in Japan* by Kate T. Williamson and *The Silent Cry* by Kenzaburo Oe.

Bigger and Better

You may want to feature an alternative and powerful Japanese flag called the ensign flag in your display. For that graphic visit http://www.printableworldflags.com/large-flags/Japan_Naval%20Ensign_Flag-441.gif.

Should your space be larger you could include other items relevant to the culture. Add some cherry blossoms on a branch and have that serve as your background. Display a kimono and shoes if available, coupled with some paper lanterns hung from above.

Have your display serve as an instructional guide for creating origami. There are many good books and online sites that would be helpful. Try this site: http://www.origami-instructions.com/simple-origami. htm. Enlarge the images and have them prominently displayed. Organize a workshop at your library to create a variety of shapes to be included in a display on this art form. For video origami instruction visit http://www.metacafe.com/watch/2805074/how_to_make_an_origami_gift_box.

Include some bento boxes which house the packed meals the Japanese would take to lunch. A miniature screen, scrolls or journals created through the art of bookbinding and calligraphy could be featured. Buddhas are both unique and fascinating. Feature a collection of various size Buddhas and house some in appropriate altars. Add some low candles and vases of flowers.

For additional ideas for displays on the

Far East, see my first book, *Great Displays for Your Library Step by Step.* Displays included are A Thousand Cranes (p. 76), Chinese Calligraphy (p. 127) and Indian Arts (p. 137).

Maya Mysteries

Myriad threads intertwine in the tapestry of the Maya cultural tradition; their colors blend subtly to represent many themes. We cannot achieve a full understanding of the processes by which Maya civilization came into being by pulling out a few bright threads. True insight depends on the laborious unraveling of many historical strands.

—John S. Henderson

The country of Belize is said to be the center of the ancient Mayan world. Formerly known as English Honduras, this country has a long history of stability, democracy and tranquility. It is located on the eastern, or Caribbean, coast of Central America. Belize shares borders on the north and part of the west with Mexico and on the south with Guatemala. The mainland is about 180 miles long and 68 miles wide. With a population of approximately 200,000, Belize is also home to the second largest barrier reef in the world. It totals over 168 miles in length. The landscape of Belize is diverse and distinctive, a unique travel adventure like no other. It is the most ecologically protected and environmentally varied country in the world. The beaches and keys are amazing sites that invite exploration.

The history of this country dates back 4,000 years, when the mighty Mayan empire ruled the land. It was during the Classic period of A.D. 250 to A.D. 900 that the population is thought to have exceeded one million people. It was at this time that the kingdom began to decline. This downward spiral would continue until the 18th century, when the Europeans came into power. The influences of the Spanish, Scottish, Garifuna and British can be seen in the cultural montage that comprises the disposition of the people of Belize.

It is archaeology which provides the primary means to learn of the existence and behaviors of people of the past. Many of the most impressive remains of the Maya civilization have been unearthed in Belize. Archaeological remains of these ancient people include pottery, skeletons, monuments, tall palaces, temples, and ceremonial centers. In the late 1970s and early 1980s there was a concerted effort to increase and diversify the archeological explorations. These investigations have yielded revolutionary findings. Scientific teams recovered cultural remains, then photographed, sketched, classified, recorded, analyzed and reported on newfound sites. Methods of preservation were set into motion and many of the artifacts were sent to institutions abroad. Archaeologists have since returned to the location of these findings and gleaned additional information from the data collected by the pioneers.

Caracol is the largest Maya archaeological site in Belize. In A.D. 650, the urban area of Caracol had a radius of approximately 10 kilometers around the site's epicenter. It appears that escalating warfare was largely responsible for the city of Caracol's abrupt extinction. Drs. Arlen Chase and Diane Chase, archeologists at the University of Central Florida, have found this to be the case in their digs which have taken place since the end of the 20th century. Burn marks on buildings and an increase in war imagery on late monuments and pottery are good indicators of this aggression. For photos and print information about their project, visit http://www.caracol.org.

The ancient Maya were unique in that they were the only fully literate native Americans. They have been proven to have been the most innovative scientists in the New World. Gifted astronomers and chronologists existed among the Maya. Using monuments, buildings, and crossed sticks to provide fixed sight lines, Mayan astronomers made careful observations of the sun, moon and Venus and may have studied the movements of the planets Mars, Jupiter, Mercury and Saturn. Not only did they develop tables for predicting lunar eclipses, they came very close to measuring the exact length of a lunation. Their accurate astronomical calculations enabled them to develop a precise calendrical system, one that served both practical and ritualistic purposes and exerted a tremendous influence over every other aspect of life. They computed the length of the tropical year at 365.2420 days, incredibly close to its actual length of 365.2422 days. They measured the synodical revolution of Venus as 584 days compared to the actual figure of 583.92. The Maya were aware of this error and periodically adjusted their calculations to correct it (Clancy, 24).

The world's finest architecture, painting, sculpture, poetry and epic literature were produced by these people. Although historians have spent decades endeavoring to comprehend these accomplishments and their place in the Maya cultural tradition, questions about the civilization abound.

The study of the hieroglyphics of the Maya reveals a highly sophisticated language, complete with puns, jokes, lies, conceit and tall tales of the reigning royals. The images that emerge in early Mesoamerican writings include wars and heroes of battle, pageantry and barbarity, diplomacy and infidelity. Maya glyphs have been difficult to decipher because some are pictographic, which means that their images represent entire words or names, while others are syllabic and represent syllables and linguistic sounds (phonetics) (Netzley, 85). The difficulties surrounding the decipherment of Maya hieroglyphs stem from e fact that they are unrelated to any European or Oriental linguistic roots. There are no precedents to assist scholars in unraveling the meaning of Maya inscriptions. Only recently has it become clear that the hieroglyphs contain a mixture of all but alphabetic elements, and the relatively new discovery of phoneticism as a major aspect of Maya writing has opened a particularly promising avenue for future research (Clancy, 27).

The Museum of Belize was built as a colonial prison in the mid–1800s. It currently houses a permanent exhibit of ancient Maya pottery and chronicles the history and culture of Belize City and the Maya. For information about the Maya and the history of Belize go to http://www.belizenet.com/history/ and select from the chapter list.

Credits

In December 2007 my husband and I took our first cruise to the western Caribbean. The itinerary included a stop in the port of Belize City, Belize. Since neither of us had visited a Mayan ruin, we were eager to sign on for the offshore excursion to Xuantunich, a major Mayan ceremonial center located on a natural limestone ridge. As luck would have it the outing included an outdoor lunch stop at a restaurant called Hodes Place and entertainment provided by a local Marimba band. Fantastic.

I was not prepared for the poverty we saw during our two-hour expedition through the countryside. Although there were scattered pockets of middle-class housing to be seen, I was struck by the shacks which served as shelter, windows without panes, schools devoid of plumbing, clothes hung on clotheslines mounted under the houses, and a plethora of rusted roofs and abandoned cars. The only saving grace for me was that the children appeared to be well nourished. Fruit trees were abundant and the bounty of the sea was readily available.

There was a visible nobility among the faces of the people of Central America. Although they didn't lay claim to many material possessions, it was apparent that there was a keen sense of family and pride in their noble heritage. Oh, and, they always found a way to incorporate this phrase into the conversation they had with tourists: "Belize it or not!"

In 2009 a film about the end of world premiered. Titled *2012*, it cashed in on the Internet-stirred fears of an end-of-the-world prophecy for December 21, 2012. This prediction was often attributed to the Mayans, whose calendar ended on that date.

Assembling the Display

1. The black felt background was chosen to provide a contrast to the photograph of Xuantunich, which was enlarged to measure 28"w × 20"h and mounted on bright

Maya Mysteries. This photograph of the Mayan ruin at Xuantunich in Belize is flanked by tropical greens. A framed textile, crafted in the color and spirit of this ancient civilization, adds warmth and texture.

green poster board. Green silk palm fronds, which were attached with pins, flanked this image. The font Thailandesa sized at 200 was used to create the lettering. This was printed on card stock and traced onto poster board and glued to the photograph.

2. On the top left was a document entitled "History of the Maya in Belize," which can be found if you visit http://www.belizenet.com/history.html. Under that was the quote that introduced this display. A photograph of the Maya ruin taken from midway up the structure was last. A descriptive caption of Xuantunich was affixed to the bottom of the photo. Items were mounted on green or black poster board. Photographs of the ruin are available if you visit http://mayaruins.com/xunantunich.html.

3. On the top right was a Maya calendar which can be found through an online image search. This was double mounted on green and red poster board. Under that was an explanation of the calendar, which was affixed to black poster board. This can be found if you visit http://www.webexhibits.org/calen

dars/calendar-mayan.html. Last was a graphic of Hunab Ku, a Maya glyph representing the "black hole "of our galaxy. This was mounted on green poster board.

4. At the bottom center was a colorful framed textile made in the color and spirit of the ancient Maya. To the right of that was a Maya royal couple which were originally part of a chess set. They were set on Styrofoam that was covered in black velvet. Palm fronds, stones of varying sizes and moss were strewn throughout the books on the base of the display. Information about Maya textiles was placed at the bottom of the textile. For background on these textiles go to http://www.mayanculture.com/preservation.html.

Books featured in the display were *Maya: Treasures of an Ancient Civilization* by Flora Clancy, *A Forest of Kings: The Untold Story of the Ancient Maya* by Linda Schele and David A. Freidel, *The Ancient Maya* by Lila Perl, *The Mayan Civilization* by Shirley Jordan, *Your Travel Guide to Ancient Mayan Civilization* by Nancy Day, and *The Blood*

Of Kings : Dynasty and Ritual in Maya Art by Linda Schele.

Bigger and Better

You may want to feature the art of the Maya, which was a reflection of their lifestyle and culture. *Maya: Treasures of an Ancient Civilization* by Flora S. Clancy, et al., is an excellent resource on that topic. For online sources visit http://www.crystalinks.com/may anarch.html.or http://www.utexas.edu/cou rses/wilson/ant304/projects/projects98 /gaffordp/art.html.

Your display could center around the sophisticated written language of the Maya. An excellent source for this would be *Maya Hieroglyphic Writing: An Introduction* by J. Eric S. Thompson. For online sites visithttp:// www.omniglot.com/writing/mayan.htm, http:// www.famsi.org/mayawriting or http://www. ancientscripts.com/maya.html. Create a wall of glyphs that tell a story.

Should you decide to focus on Maya deities, be sure to visit http://members.aol.com /hmupuni/deity.htm for some great images.

Olympic Fever

The main issue in life is not the victory but the fight, the essential is not to have won but to have fought well.
—Pierre de Coubertin, founder, International Olympic Committee

The ancient Olympic Games began simply as a tribute to Zeus, the father of the Greek gods and goddesses. The festival was held in Olympia, a rural sanctuary in western Greece. The opening of the Games was marked by the lighting of a flame at the altar honoring this deity. Eventually the festival grew to include a running competition. The participants were all males, representatives of every corner of the Greek world. They spoke the same language and shared the same religious beliefs. Along with the ancient athletic contests was a separate festival in honor of Hera, wife of Zeus, where unmarried females engaged in competitive foot races.

The ancient games are said to have begun in the year 776 B.C. when Koroibos, a cook from the city of Elis, placed first in the stadion race, a footrace about 600 feet in length. Up to 40,000 people crowded into the stadium to pay homage and watch the race. Footraces dominated the early competition, but eventually wrestling, boxing and the pentathlon were added. The latter event included a stadion race, the long jump, discus and javelin throws as well as wrestling. Among the most popular competitions was the pankration, a no-holds-barred combination of wrestling and boxing. There were some unusual contests added over the years such as the race in armor, the competition for trumpeters and the apene race in which the chariot was pulled by mules rather than horses. It is unclear when nudity became the standard for the early athletes. One hypothesis was that a runner from Megara lost his shorts and completed the stadion race naked. Another possibility concludes that it was the Spartans who introduced nudity in the 8th century B.C., as it was their tradition. By the late 8th century, nudity was standard for all the male athletes.

The competition reflected a political transformation in Greece. The rise of the city-state was widespread and there was a sense of competition among the residents of these different regions to assert their superiority. All wars and fighting ceased during the competition. The military exercises required of young males produced physically fit citizens. These games provided an outlet for the soldiers' vigorous training and a victory brought honor to the athlete's home city.

The scope of the Olympic Games grew, drawing contestants from throughout the Macedonian and Roman empires. There was only one prize for winners in the early Games, a crown of olive leaves. The athletes enjoyed the support of their countrymen and were rewarded upon returning to their hometowns. Paralleling some issues that have surfaced in the modern games, cheating, bribery and boycotts have been documented in some of the earlier Games.

Although athletes came from all social classes, including slaves, not all of the participants were unknowns. Phillip II of Macedon and his son, Alexander the Great, were competitors. Pythagoras the mathematician served as team doctor for Kroton, a city of Greek settlers on the Italian coast.

The Olympic Games continued until A.D. 394 when Roman Emperor Theodosius I abolished them as part of a series of reforms against pagan practices. It wasn't until the mid 19th century that the idea of the modern Games surfaced. Pierre de Coubertin was a French pedagogue and historian who recognized the growing interest in the ancient Olympics due to revivals in both Greece and the United Kingdom and archaeological finds at Olympia. He organized an international congress in 1894 and proposed the establishment of the International Olympic Committee. It was agreed that the first IOC-organized Games would take place in Athens, Greece.

The Games were reintroduced to the world in 1896 and have remained a regular event held every four years in different cities around the globe. In 1994, however, the winter games were held in Lillehammer, Norway, and two years later the summer games were staged in Atlanta, Georgia. This two-year rotation continues to this day.

Many important symbols have been associated with the Olympic Games. The five rings that appear on the official flag were introduced in 1914. The colors—yellow, green, blue, black and red—represent the five continents of Africa, the Americas, Australia, Asia and Europe. The flag is raised in the host city where it remains until the completion of the events. It is then flown to the next Olympic site. The Olympic torch symbolizes purity, the drive for perfection and the struggle for victory. It played a major role in the ancient Games and was reintroduced in 1928. It is currently carried by many select individuals with great fanfare to the host city, where the flame is kept burning until the close of the competition.

The inspiring Olympic anthem was written by Academy Award–winning composer John Williams for the 1984 Games, which

Olympic Fever. The magic and history of the Beijing games began on 8/08/08—a sure sign of good luck for the Chinese, who garnered a total of 100 medals. The sports equipment featured adds some authenticity to this celebration of the summer games.

were held in Los Angeles. Williams has composed music for four of the sets of Olympic Games held in the last 26 years. The music is a prelude to the colorful March of Nations where athletes from each country parade into the arena to the sound of their country's anthem and proudly display their nation's flag.

Many recent Games have been highly politicized. The world saw the rise of Nazi Germany (Berlin, 1936), Middle East conflicts (Melbourne, 1956, and Munich, 1972), Black Power (Mexico, 1968) Apartheid (Montreal, 1976) and the Cold War (Helsinki, 1952, Moscow, 1980, and Los Angeles, 1984).

Over two hundred years ago Napoleon Bonaparte remarked that China is like a sleeping dog: Do not dare wake her, for when she wakes the world will tremble. The shaking started for the global sports community on August 8, 2008. Sports, culture, politics and the environment were intrinsically interwoven at the Beijing Olympics. The entire world was center stage via a host of stellar athletes who gathered in the summer of 2008 for several weeks in eastern Asia. China had been embroiled in a storm of criticism prior to hosting these sporting events. Politics were particularly prominent as the issue of greater religious tolerance, press freedom, and autonomy for Tibet spurred protests and created global headlines. The Games became a lightning rod for China's record on human rights and environmental degradation and its arms and oil dealings with Sudan. China earned the right to host the summer Olympics primarily by agreeing to grant greater religious and cultural freedom to Tibet.

As a first-time Olympic host, China was eager to be viewed positively. They wanted to be seen as capable and friendly and more than the manufacturer of cheap goods exported for First World spending. They wanted to be more than an emerging consumer of precious commodities such as oil and air and water. More than anything, China wanted to be viewed as a global player (Vecsey, H1).

Beijing is a city of huge importance to China and the world. Originally named Dadu, or Great Metropolis, it has been the primary capital of China since the thirteenth century. Formerly called Peking, it is the political voice of a country that often inspires controversy. To much of the world, this northern city *is* China. Major political upheavals have played out on the world's foremost stage, Tiananmen Square. Although there are dozens of other large cities within China, Beijing has been the prime focus of media attention in modern times. Beijing lacks the landscape, climate and agricultural output of the picturesque Yangzi valley. Its proximity to Inner Asia, especially Mongolia and Manchuria, proved valuable during periods of rebellion. Twenty-first century Beijing is the center of finance and more open to foreign influence.

Liu Jingmin served as vice-mayor of Beijing and executive vice president of the Beijing Organizing Committee for the Games of the XXIX Olympiad. Early in 2001 he stressed that there were nine tasks necessary to prepare for the Olympics. These priorities were environmental protection, traffic control, restructuring of energy, communication and networks, the high-tech industry, construction of gymnasiums, the cultural sector, security and safeguards as well as fund-raising. All of these issues have been addressed by the Chinese government.

Construction of the Bird's Nest Stadium began in 2003 and is a true architectural feat. A consortium formed by Herzog & Meuron (Switzerland), Ove Arup (UK) and China Architecture Design & Research Group, managed to beat out the competitors with a design for a stadium that would resemble a bird's nest. Chinese architect Ai Weiwei, who contributed to the design, called it "an object for the world." The son of a poet who lived in the U.S., Ai has been critical of the Chinese system. He felt, however, that the stadium reflected the ambitions and dreams of the people at the time. If they fail or disappoint they still speak volumes about the Chinese at this period of history. It is how they wish the world to perceive them.

The stadium structure was surrounded by a membrane which is curved and double-layered, featuring decorative soundproofing, wind-proofing, rain-proofing and even UVA protection. The membrane was designed to provide better acoustics and help with the lighting within the stadium, diminishing glare and shadowing and thereby allowing for a highly effective competition environment. The structure became green when soldiers and workmen installed 7,811 square meters of mobile turf in a 24-hour period. The red lights and gray steel structures of the project combine to create a unique addition to Beijing's nightscape.

Money appeared to be a nonissue for the Chinese as they prepared to host the Beijing games. It has been documented that they spent 40 billion dollars in Games-related construction from the time the contract was awarded in 2001 (Wolff 48). Prior to these Games, the Chinese would never have permitted foreign firms to contribute to or influence their architecture and especially the lasting structural designs that remain in Beijing after the Olympics. The Chinese are content that they achieved their goal, met the world halfway and accomplished the slogan of the festival: "One World, One Dream."

The magic and history of the Beijing games began at 8:00 P.M. on 08/08/08 with a phenomenal demonstration of the Chinese mastery of both technology and performance art. The significance of the number 8 was a certain sign of good luck for the Chinese athletes, who harvested fifty gold and one hundred total medals. This number represented a 40 percent increase over their achievements in the Athens games. The world witnessed amazing athletic performances by 204 nations competing over 16 record-breaking days that served to forever alter the history books. Countries like Bahrain, Togo, Sudan, Mauritius and Afghanistan won their first Olympic medals. American swimmer Michael Phelps stunned audiences by winning 8 gold medals in world record times and collecting a career total of 16 medals, more than any other athlete to that date. The random killing of volleyball coach Hugh McCutcheon's father-in-law by a deranged national was the only thing that marred the memories made in Beijing.

The closing ceremonies rivaled the majesty, scope and precision of the opening ceremonies. Once again China tapped into its richest resource, its people, to showcase their evolution from an ancient Chinese culture to their arrival in the modern world.

A double decker red bus carrying British soccer sensation David Beckham signaled the transfer of the Olympic torch from Beijing to London 2012 and the next summer games. The electronic Chinese farewell would long be remembered as the Brits make preparations for a proper garden party.

For information about the Olympic Games or Beijing visit http://www.english club.com/esl-articles/olympic-games.htm or http://en.beijing2008.cn/en.shtml.

Credits

When my sons were young, the Olympic Games were a much anticipated event in our household. After the boys viewed televised track and field events, hurdles would appear in the backyard, and the sibling competition would begin. This would be followed by soccer challenges, tennis competitions and some rather impressive long jumps. These games instilled within my sons a fervor to excel athletically and a spirit of good-natured rivalry that continues to this day. I looked forward to these Olympic events because I knew I was seeing an excellence which had a positive influence on my children. The competition taught them to work harder, practice longer, and strive for their best performance on the field and off.

Assembling the Display

1. The flag of China was created using red poster board. The stars were found through a Google image search, printed on card stock and traced onto yellow poster board framed in black poster board. They were attached with pins and pulled forward. The Olympic rings were cut from blue, yellow, black, green and red poster board and glued onto the flag. The font Domo Aregato was created in Word Art. It was sized at 96 and enlarged to 200 percent on the photocopier. This was traced onto black poster board and then framed with yellow poster board. The letter *J* was created freehand and the top of that letter was the Olympic flame. The flame was created using yellow, gold, orange and red poster board. The letters were attached with pins and pulled forward. This free font can be found if you visit http://www.1001 freefonts.com/domoaregato.php or http://ww w.1001freefonts.com/domoaregato.php.

2. On the top left of the display was a photograph of the Olympic stadium, which was fondly referred to as the "bird's nest" due to its unique design. This image was found through an online search. Under that was the following quote by George Orwell (1950):

> Serious sport has nothing to do with fair play. It is bound up with hatred, jealousy, boastfulness, and disregard of all rules and sadistic pleasure in witnessing violence—in other words it is war, minus the shooting.

Next was the Olympic motto: "Citius, Altius, Fortius" (faster, higher, stronger). Under that was a brief history of the Olympic Games, which can be found if you visit http://www.museum.upenn.edu/new/olympics/olimpicorigins.shtml.

All the items on the left were printed on card stock and mounted on red and yellow poster board.

3. On the top right was the official slogan of the Beijing '08 games: "One World, One Dream." Next was a description of the design and creation of the Beijing Olympic medals. To the right of that document were replicas of all three medals. For this information visit http://en.beijing2008.cn/67/83/article214028367.shtml.

The quote by Pierre de Coubertin which introduced this display followed. Under that was a photo of a sculpture which was entered into the 2008 Olympic Landscape Sculpture Contest Exhibition at the Michael Fowler Centre in Wellington, New Zealand.

All items on the right were printed and mounted like those on the left.

4. On the base of the display were shin guards, a fencing mask and glove, table tennis paddles and balls, a field hockey stick and ball, a pair of cleats, a soccer ball and a swim cap.

Books features in the display were *Olympia: Gods, Artists & Athletes* by Ludwig Drees, *Beijing's Games: What the Olympics Mean to China* by Susan Brownell, *The Ancient Olympics* by Nigel Spivey, *Olympics* by Chris Oxlade and David Ballheimer, *Olympic Dreams: China and Sports 1895–2008* by Xu Guoqi, and *China's Great Leap: The Beijing Games and Olympian Human Rights Challenges* by Minky Worden.

Bigger and Better

Your display may feature the Olympic Games in London 2012 or the Winter Games in Sochi in 2014. There are many Websites chronicling the progress these cities are making to design and create a spectacular sporting complex for the events. The London Aquatics Centre construction began in mid 2008 and is an incredible architectural concept. Be sure to visit these sites for Olympic updates: http://www.olympic.org/uk/games/index_uk.asp and http://sochi2014.com/ and http://www.london2012.com.

There are some great ideas for graphics for the London 2012 Games. Any of those at http://www.logoblog.org/wp-images/london-olympic-logos/london-olympic-logos-2.jpg could be worked into an effective Olympic display. Should your space be larger you can include some of these items (in addition to the sports equipment featured in Olympic Fever). Feature a tennis racquet and balls, a volleyball, weights, a quiver, arrows and a bow, badminton racquet and shuttlecocks, a basketball, a softball and bat, sailing gear, a canoe paddle, an oar and swim goggles. Visit this site for specifics about the individual sports held at the Summer Games: http://www.pocanticohills.org/olympics/summerolympics2.htm.

Should you feature the Winter Games, be sure to include skis and a ski pole, winter hat and gloves, ice skates, hockey stick and puck, goggles and a snowboard. Line the case with fiberfill and toss a few snowflakes around. The graphic designed for the Sochi Olympics is clean and simple and would be easy and effective as the background for your display. Visit http://turin.gazeta.ru/files/549282/sochi2014_1.jpg.

Be sure to include some historical background on the city of Sochi. This fashionable resort area was frequented by Joseph Stalin, who had his favorite dacha, or second home, built in the city. Approximately 25 percent of city dwellers in Russia have seasonal homes in resort areas in this country.

There is much optimism about the Olympics in the city of Sochi. The Russian government has committed to a $12 billion investment package, shared 60–40 between the government and private sector.

Egypt on the Nile

The Kingdom of heaven is within you; and whosoever shall know himself shall find it. —Ancient Egyptian proverb

The above proverb is one of the many and powerful teachings found in the temples and tombs in the city of Luxor and throughout Egypt. Although not originally bound as a monograph, these inscriptions could be viewed as the first "Holy Book" known to man. Proverbs were vital to these ancient people who were on a religious journey of self knowledge and a quest for an understanding of the universe. Dogma taught that the divine attributes of both the heavens and the creator existed within men and were therefore articulated in their teaching.

Nearly five thousand years ago, a king known as Narmer united the lands in the northern sector of the River Nile for the first time. The people in this new kingdom revered him and believed him to be a god. Narmer's rule was followed by thirty dynasties of Egyptian kings who oversaw the formation of one of the most impressive civilizations the world has ever seen. Some legends suggest that the king responsible for uniting Egypt was named Menes, so the speculation remains as to whether Narmer and Menes were really one and the same (Sands, 9–11).

Archeologists have uncovered traces of people who established communities along the Nile thousands of years before the reign of the pharaohs. Remains of pottery, jewelry and flint tools indicate a highly sophisticated society. Evidence suggests that farming and the domestication of animals existed as well as a system of trade or bartering. Once the fertility of the region was determined, wars were fought to maintain control of the fruitful strips of land which flanked the river Nile. Excavations of villages near Luxor indicated a high level of literacy among the population.

In 2010, Egyptian archeologists discovered a set of tombs belonging to the workers who built the great pyramids, shedding light on how the laborers lived and ate more than 4,000 years ago. Evidence shows that the men who built the last remaining wonder of the ancient world ate meat regularly, worked in three-month shifts and were given the honor of being buried in mud-brick tombs within the shadow of the sacred pyramids on which they worked. If the pyramids had been built by slaves, the workers would not have been able to build their tombs beside their king's. This new evidence dates back to Egypt's 4th Dynasty (2575 B.C. to 2467 B.C.).

Ancient Egypt was a gift of the Nile, since the river's flooding served to bring a renewed life into the valley at summer's end each year. It was a rich oasis in the midst of the massive expanse of the Sahara Desert. This was not always the case, however. Early inhabitants endured a much less arid climate. Also, the river was not always a meandering body in a wide floodplain during late summer and it frequently brought erosion which affected older archeological deposits, so few early remains have been preserved (Shaw, 17).

The ebb and flow of the river, which resulted in both flooding and famine, defined many aspects of life in ancient Egypt. Building pyramids and waging war were more productive activities during the flood stages, whereby planting and harvesting needed to be done when the weather was favorable and prior to the return of the floods.

The pyramids at Giza are the most famous of all of the monuments in ancient Egypt. The design of those early pyramids was primitive when compared to those erected later. The size of the structure was in direct proportion to the stature of the person entombed. Each of the pyramids was part of a larger burial system that allowed for transport of the king's remains accompanied by a funeral procession and a temple or mortuary for the burial traditions (Sands, 16).

More than two million blocks were used in the building of the Great Pyramid, each weighing over two tons. Various theories exist regarding the manner in which the pyramids were constructed. Here are some of the theories:

1. Stones would have been dragged up huge ramps of earth and set in place.
2. Logs were slid under the large stones to make mobility easier. The blocks would

Egypt on the Nile. A large basalt cat on a marble base anchors this display. Palm trees flank a papyrus scroll hung in the shadow of an ancient pyramid.

have been attached to large ropes with people pushing the blocks forward.

3. Pathways of mud brick would have been coiled around the perimeter of the pyramid and the stones moved in place by animal-drawn sledges.

4. Pulleys would have been assembled to move the stones into place.

Of course there is always the theory that suggests aliens, with their advanced technology, landed to assist the ancient Egyptians in this monumental task! For information regarding the building of the great pyramids go to http://www.bbc.co. uk/history/ancient/egyptians/ great_pyramid_01.shtml or http:// unmuseum.mus.pa.us/blpyram. htm.

The temples at Abu Simbel were among the most impressive monuments known to man. These structures were originally noted in 1813 when J.L. Burckhardt came over the mountain and saw the façade of the great temples as he prepared to journey down the Nile. The temples housing Ramses II and Nefertari became a tourist destination for Victorian travelers as a result of Burckhardt's rave reviews. The temples were in danger of submersion in Lake Nasser due to the construction of the Aswan High Dam during the 1960s. The Egyptian government received the support of UNESCO and launched a campaign to salvage the structures. As a result, the two temples were dismantled and moved over 60 meters up a cliff from where they originally existed 3,000 years prior to that time. When reassembled, they were positioned in the exact same relationship as they originally had held to each other and the sun. Antiquity experts were called to correctly rejoin the stones, but evidence still exists on the interior which indicates where the blocks were cut. For more information about the temples at Abu Simbel visit http://www.touregypt.net/abusimbel.htm.

Like many other ancient peoples, the ancient Egyptians dated important political and religious events not according to the number of years that had elapsed since a single fixed point in history (such as the birth of Christ in the modern western calendar) but in terms of the years since the accession of each king (regnal years). Dates were, therefore, recorded in the following format: "day 2 of the first month of the season *peret* in the fifth year of Nebmaatra." It is important to be aware of the fact that, for the Egyptians, the reign of each new king represented a new beginning, not merely philosophically but practically, given the fact that dates were expressed in these terms (Shaw, 7–8).

The early Egyptians were fascinated with cats. Cats were not only the most popular pet in the house, they were also acknowledged to be sacred and esteemed deities unlike any other creature. Historians suggest that the cat was domesticated around 2000 B.C. in Egypt and that most modern cats are descendants of the cats of ancient Egypt. It is assumed that wild cats hunted poisonous snakes, rats and mice which threatened the food supplies in the homes and the village granaries. The felines kept the vermin in the villages at bay. As a result, a unique symbiotic connection between man and these animals evolved. Tomb paintings with cats shown as a part of family life began to appear during the New Kingdom (1540 to 1069 B.C.), about 500 years after the first efforts at feline civilization. The most significant evidence for domestication comes from the cemeteries of mummified cats (about 1000 B.C.)

Credits

In January of 2008, 33 members of the Cedar Crest College community, led by associate professor Dr. Allen Richardson, embarked on a trip to Egypt which included a five-day cruise down the Nile. The focus of the a trip was the exploration of ancient Egyptian religions. Several students on my staff were a part of this pilgrimage and the excitement surrounding the venture was palpable. They eagerly shared their photos and sentiments upon their return. Clearly, they were forever changed by this cultural experience and would never view the world and its religions in quite the same way.

Ancient Egyptian royalty made the news in February 2010 in an article featured in the *Journal of the American Medical Association.* Egypt's Supreme Council of Antiquities studied five generations of pharaohs from 2007 to 2009. The eleven mummies, including King Tutankhamen, date from 1410 B.C. to 1324 B.C. The boy king reigned for nine years and died at the age of nineteen. Writers have suggested foul play in Tut's early demise, but the new analysis found malaria genes and indicated a family plagued by bone necrosis. Scientists concluded that Tut had a club foot and other bone loss, and that he probably died of a broken leg along with the ravages of a malaria infection. The study relied on a $5 million genetic analysis lab built under the Cairo Museum housing many of King Tut's artifacts, with funding from cable television's Discovery Channel.

Certainly, ancient Egypt remains topical and would be a vital subject worthy of a display in your library.

Assembling the Display

The camel-colored felt background provided the backdrop for the 24½"w by 24"h pyramid which was cut from 2 pieces of dark brown poster board and attached with pins and pulled forward. A 4" diameter circle cut from orange poster board was attached in the same manner and represented the desert sun.

The font Arabolical, available at http://www.dafont.com, was sized at 375, printed on card stock and traced onto black poster board. Palm trees were found through a Google image search, printed on card stock and traced onto black poster board. The letters and palm trees were attached with pins and pulled forward. The trees flanked the papyrus scroll that featured Egyptian figures and hieroglyphics in gold and black tones. Under that was the following ancient Egyptian proverb, which was printed on card stock and mounted on black poster board: "If you search for the laws of harmony, you will find knowledge."

On the top left was a photo of the members of the Cedar Crest community standing in front of the sphinx and pyramids. Under that was a row of hieroglyphics found through a Google image search. These were printed on paper stock and attached with double-sided tape on both sides of the display. Under that was a photo of King Tut's tomb followed by a description of this archeological find and a photograph of Howard Carter, who unearthed the boy king's tomb in 1922.

All items within the display were mounted on black poster board and attached with double-sided tape.

2. On the top right was a photo of the tomb at Abu Simbel. Under that was historical information about the structure and an Egyptian scene found through a Google image search inserted at the top of the document. Below that was information on the tomb of Ramses IV and a photo of actual hieroglyphics painted on the wall.

3. Styrofoam forms were covered in a black silk fabric and placed on the base of the display. A large basalt cat on a marble base was centered on the form. Sculpted letter openers, carved from camel bone, flanked the cat. A bird sculpture sat at the bottom of the case flanked by Egyptian bookmarks. Jewelry surrounded both forms and dotted the bottom of the case.

Books featured in the display are *The Oxford History of Ancient Egypt* Edited by Ian Show, *Hatshepsut: From Queen to Pharaoh* by Catharine H. Roehrig, *Ancient Egypt, the Land and Its Legacy* by T.G.H. James and *The Egyptology Handbook: A Course in the Wonders of Egypt* by Emily Sands.

Bigger and Better

The base of your display space could be lined with sand and you could feature three pyramids of varying sizes. If your artistic ability, or that of your staff, permits, make a sarcophagus out of a large rectangular box. Add a facial image of a pharaoh and place it over an appropriately draped fabric of silk or velvet.

Your display could pay homage to King Tut, about whom many books have been written. Obtain a poster or create a burial mask and have that be the focal point of your display. Consult *Tutankhamen* by Christiane Desroches-Noblecourt for its incredible photographs, or *Discovering Tut-ankh-Amen's Tomb* by Shirley Glubok for its easily comprehended language. Feature background information on Howard Carter and refer to the three volumes that he wrote on this discovery.

2 Mother Nature

Garden Gate

It is utterly forbidden to be half-hearted about gardening. You have got to love your garden whether you like it or not.
—W.C. Sellar and R.J. Yeatman, *Garden Rubbish*, 1936

Ideally, your garden should make as important a contribution to the quality of your home life as your house does. Therefore, its design requires the same level of attention as that allocated to your interior spaces. Like your house, the garden can be a source of pride and relaxation. It can mirror your passions, hobbies and tastes.

From an economic standpoint, monies spent on landscaping and garden design have proven to be a wise investment for homeowners. The curb appeal created by a good landscape design is the first impression a perspective buyer has of your property. You can be assured of visitors' interest in your home and property by creating excitement in the front yard that can be seen as they make the approach to your door. It has been estimated that for each dollar spent on landscaping, a three-dollar return is common upon the resale of that home.

No matter where you live, you will want your garden to provide a buffer against the rush, noise and influx of too many people—to be a sheltered spot where recreation and relaxation are possible. This private retreat can be achieved through thoughtful planning and appropriate design.

The beauty and interest your garden design creates for passersby can also be viewed as an asset to your community. Some examples of ways to accomplish this are to plant a blend of plants with exciting textures, color or form contrast, along with some interesting structural features—all effective ways to draw

attention to the landscape. Be certain to consider the garden's ultimate effect on your home. Planting shade trees near the house, for instance, may have the benefit of reducing the cost of cooling your home. Some plants, on the other hand, are invasive, can be destructive and should be planted a distance away from the house. Certain types of vines are capable of destroying rain gutters, and overhanging tree limbs can threaten your roof in a storm.

Successful design for your property requires some preliminary steps such as those employed by landscape architects. The first step is to determine the wants and expectations you have for your garden. Next, make an objective assessment of your property. Then, gage the possibilities for improving, such as what should be upgraded, replaced or allowed to remain untouched. Once you have zeroed in on a style, you are ready to start the process. First, consider the hardscapes you wish to incorporate (such as terraces, walkways, etc.) then the plant choices followed by the design arrangement.

Keep in mind that creating a winning garden design takes time. The nature of a garden is to evolve as it matures, changing character as plants grow larger and broaden. While this evolution is in process, your needs and priorities may be subject to change. There may be a point where professional advice will be warranted. You may need to consider installing your design in stages that comply with your budget. Remember that it's

Garden Gate. Clusters of colorful flowers peek from behind a miniature garden gate. The angel figurine provides a touch of serenity to this celebration of the coming of spring.

best to plant key trees and shrubs in the first phase so they will be growing as you complete other work. If possible, mature, established trees should be incorporated into the plan rather than removed.

The term garden can be defined in many ways. It can mean a discrete planting area such as a border or a vegetable patch. More broadly defined it can encompass an entire property as the object of an overall landscape design. A vegetable or cutting garden can be located on a remote part of the property. Gardens can be created adjacent to the house, making a functional outdoor room of sorts. Many properties include a series of gardens linked by a network of pathways. Linking parts of your property with the house has the added benefit of providing additional living space. The outside and inside combine to form one small world. Certain areas in your garden can be designated as places to entertain, play, meditate or relax. With a

good design, the serenity provided by your home will extend to your surrounding gardens. Areas designated for relaxation should be cool and inviting. It is a good idea to position trees and shrubs so that shade is cast on the house, patio or deck space in the summer months. This can have the added benefit of reducing the cost of cooling your home.

The nature of your neighborhood can be the impetus for your decisions regarding your garden design. You may find it necessary to block a neighboring property's sight line or capture a view in the distance. Both the style of your home and your area's history can provide guidance in the choices you make with regard to establishing a garden. Your garden might be designed to accommodate less tangible impulses. You may want to create a certain mood or stimulate fond memories. Or you might decide on plantings that have the added dimension of attracting colorful birds or butterflies to your garden.

Foremost on your list of concerns may be to establish year-round interest in your planting areas. Conservation of energy, capital and natural resources may be at the top of your list of priorities. Your plan may consider ways in which to decrease the amount of time allocated to laborious tasks such as mowing, watering, fertilizing, weeding and pruning. Poll family member for preferences and expectations of the garden space. Consider what would amuse the children. Does the family cook expect to find fruit, herbs and vegetables in the garden? Should pets be a consideration?

Survey your property by objectively driving by and making notes. Is the house in clear view? Does harmony exist between the design of the house and the existing garden? Go to neighboring yards for yet another perspective on your property. In addition to providing a new view, it will help determine any necessary screening you may need to consider. Look out various windows of your home to help you focus on possible sight lines for your design. Areas visible from picture or kitchen windows are obvious areas for garden development. You may decide to enlarge or install windows or doors to provide better garden views.

Focal points occur when sight lines intersect in the garden. Visible vignettes most often lie within the property, but can actually appear beyond it—perhaps in the form of a beautiful pond or a graceful tree. A leisurely stroll through your garden will determine existing or potential focal points. These will be stopping points and the sight lines leading to them will become walkways. Gates erected at transition areas and steps created near sloping paths are sure to enhance your stroll through the garden.

A good rule of thumb when planning a garden design is to keep it simple. Too much ornamentation, too many important points, too many types of plantings may combine to create an impression of disarray, even confusion. A winning design will provide a unifying structure for the elements it encompasses—from inviting entertainment areas to shady spots and fragrant herb gardens. Be mindful of the principles of proportion, which will help to create the mood in your garden design. A garden can feel cramped if

ensconced within inordinately tall vertical elements such as buildings, walls or fences.

Just like the flowers in a border are generally arranged by height, your house serves as a determinant of scale relating to the plantings in your garden. Surrounding trees and structural choices should be in proportion to the size of your home. You will find that scaled-down ornaments add depth to a garden and never overpower it.

Remember that the farther an object is from the viewer, the larger it must be to have a proper presence. A perennial garden located at the rear of your property needs to be a least half as wide as the distance between the deck and your garden to have a real visual impact. Peruse the size of every element and plant in your garden to assure that correct balance has been achieved. True harmony occurs when forms, textures and colors properly relate.

If elements and plants are too much alike there is a tendency for them to blend together and the overall effect will be less distinctive. Try setting up contrasting groups of plantings that will complement each other. Choosing plants for their texture will yield a particularly good result in a single color garden or shady foliage areas. Remember to avoid straight lines when creating your garden. They are never found in nature, lack imagination and, for all practical considerations, are impossible to maintain.

You can be assured that plants will fail, preferences will change and the weather will remain unpredictable. The more thought you put into what you want and what you liked about last year's garden design, the better the result for the year to come. Careful record keeping and honest assessment will prevent many of the disappointments inherent in the first-year garden. Your only obligation is to enjoy the beauty with your friends and family and to pass on the wealth of knowledge you gained through the garden design process.

There are literally dozens of types of gardens. If you are interested in an alpine garden, an autumn garden, a garden of bulbs, a night garden, a garden of grasses, etc., be sure to get a copy of Peter Loewer's *Gardens by Design: Step by Step Plans for 12 Imaginative Gardens.* Another great reference resource for all aspects of gardening is *The Complete Garden*

Guide, a Time-Life publication. Your local public library will offer many other worthwhile titles related to this all-consuming pastime.

Credits

Each year I resolve to create a proper garden—one which would cause drivers passing by to tap their brakes ever so slightly so they might have the opportunity to "take it all in." I yearn for people to inquire as to the variety of perennials I have selected and my secrets to these flowers' phenomenal size and vibrant colors. Surely they will marvel at the color palate of the various annuals that I have chosen to be interspersed among them!

Each year I dutifully make multiple trips to the area garden centers, where I eavesdrop, inquire, elicit responses, copy customer selections, engage in gardening banter—all in the hopes that it will finally make sense and insure that my garden really comes together. Clearly, all the other shoppers seem to exude a certain confidence as they visualize the garden they are about to create. True gardeners ... how is it they just seem to know?

This year we had a large grove of evergreen trees installed in the hopes of privatizing our property in the years to come. Alas, another planting area crying for my attention, challenging my creativity, surely another battle ... lost! Help!

Assembling the Display

1. The background of this display was light blue felt. The wooden sign read "Garden Gate" and had a green background with gold lettering and was centered above the flower garden. Fiberfill was placed around the sign to create the Illusion of clouds.

2. On the top left was the quote that introduced this display. Under that was a document titled "Herbs to Grow from Seed." This information can be found if you visit http://www.backyardgardener.com/herb/. These items were printed on white card stock and mounted on yellow and green poster board.

3. On the top right was the following anonymous quote:

> When weeding, the best way to make sure you are removing a weed and not a valuable plant is to pull on it. If it comes out of the ground easily, it is a valuable plant.

Under that was document titled "How to Grow a Tomato Plant." This can be found if you visit http://www.gardenersnet.com/vegetable/tomato.htm.

4. The multicolored silk flowers were set in two large blocks of Styrofoam covered in green felt. Silk ivy covered the Styrofoam and a 30" piece of vinyl fencing served as the garden gate. A 14" garden angel was placed on the left and river rocks were strewn throughout the base of the display. A miniature bird was set beside a larger rock on the bottom right.

Books featured in the display were *Herbs* by James Underwood Crockett, *Growing Food in Solar Greenhouses* by Delores Wolfe, *Gardening When It Counts* by Steve Soloman, *Herb Gardening with Derek Fell: Practical Advice and Personal Favorites from the Best Selling Author and Television Show Host* by Derek Fell and *The Herb Gardener: A Guide to All Seasons* by Susan McClure.

Bigger and Better

Should your space be larger, incorporate some birdhouses and a birdbath. Use an obelisk or compass structure as a focal point. Mount a trellis and attach roses, trailing hydrangea or flowering vines. Add some tree branches and a butterfly net and arrange colorful silk birds and butterflies throughout the tableau. Include a miniature garden chair with a popular book, gardening hat, sunglasses and a beverage complete with lemon slice. Title it "Garden Glories."

With the struggling economy in mind, design a silk vegetable garden and give hints as to which varieties are easiest to grow or yield the best results. For helpful information visit http://www.fruitsandveggiesmorematters.org/ or http://www.pbs.org/wgbh/victorygarden/. The latter site features the victory gardens so prevalent during World War II. Title it "Vegetable Victory."

For display ideas with garden/floral themes see my first book, *Great Displays for Your Library Step by Step*. On page 161 you will find a display titled "In the Garden." "Flowers in Books and Drawings" can be found on page 169.

Yosemite in Focus

Yosemite Valley, to me, is always a sunrise, a glitter of green and golden wonder in a vast edifice of stone and space.
—Ansel Adams, American photographer (1902–1984)

The Sierra Nevada range is America's longest continuous mountain range and an amalgamation of extremes. It includes our highest peak outside of Alaska, the deepest canyon and the longest wilderness. The sequoia trees, native to this region, are the largest living things on earth. Three national parks cover 1.6 million acres and eight national forests include 8.1 million acres. The majestic Sierra Nevada mountains measure 400 miles long and approximately 50 miles wide, discounting foothills. The mountains encompass 12.8 million acres in parts of eighteen counties in California and two in Nevada.

Yosemite National Park was the first state and national park in the United States. Located within the Sierra Nevada mountain range in northern California, it encompasses 1,170 square miles, or 748,542 acres. The park was named after an Indian tribe that lived in the area for thousands of years. These Native Americans spoke the Miwok language and settled into the Ahwahnee Valley. The word Ahwahnee means "a deep grassy valley." A mysterious disease forced the departure of the Yosemite tribe from the Ahwahnee Valley and the area remained devoid of human life for many years. After several generations, approximately two hundred members of the Yosemite tribe returned to the fertile Ahwahnee Valley.

Early settlers heading westward found the mountain range to be an impediment to both communication and progress and had little interest in the region. All that changed dramatically two years before California received her statehood. The discovery of gold in 1848 in the nearby mountains brought thousands of fortune hunters to the Sierras. Soon great numbers of cattle were herded into the area. These animals quickly altered the balance of nature. They ate the acorns and grasses and forced the Yosemite tribe to move higher and higher into the mountains. The Yosemite tribe began to prey upon the newly imported cattle and horses and raided the settlements for food. The response from Washington, D.C., was to send a group of men called commissioners to Mariposa, in the heart of the Yosemite area. Under the command of James Savage the battalion's task was to attempt to subdue the Yosemites, establish a treaty and relocate them to the Fresno River.

In 1859 James Hutchings, of San Francisco, visited the valley with the artist Thomas Ayres. A noted landscape artist, Ayres was the first to introduce accurate images of the natural wonders of the Yosemite Valley to the public. Photographer Charles Leander Weed arrived the same year, followed shortly by his renowned colleague Carleton Watkins. Watkins, in particular, had the technical expertise and artistic sensibility to bring the grandeur of Yosemite to those who would be instrumental in preserving its great beauty.

In June 1864, Congress granted Yosemite Valley and the Mariposa Grove of Big Trees to the state of California in a proclamation signed by President Abraham Lincoln. The act made Yosemite the first public park placed under the administration of a state. Galen Clark, who discovered the Mariposa Grove of Big Trees, was appointed the first guardian of the park. He worked tirelessly to protect and preserve the wilderness but was keenly aware of the changes necessary to permit future tourism. Clark worked to make the valley more pleasant by dynamiting part of a recessional moraine—glacial debris—that dammed the Merced River. This action resulted in dryer valley floor, comprising pleasant meadows, and reduced the mosquito population. Clark then cleared forest litter to allow open pathways through the groves of "Big Trees" and established roads which granted reasonable access for public recreation.

Scottish-born naturalist John Muir wrote

Yosemite—In Focus. Photographer Anne Bivans shares a breathtaking shot of Mirror Lake in one of America's great national parks. More amazing photos of her travels can be found at http://www.anne99.blogspot.com/.

many articles about his beloved Yosemite and was an advocate for expansion of the park beyond the valley. He persuaded numerous dignitaries to visit the park, including transcendentalist thinker Ralph Waldo Emerson This poet's heartfelt enthusiasm for Yosemite was conveyed to others upon his return to the East. In 1903 President Theodore Roosevelt, an ardent conservationist, spent three days in Yosemite with Muir. Their discussions regarding conservation became the basis of the Antiquities Act of 1906, which was the vehicle by which the National Park Service was created.

In 1890, largely through John Muir's efforts, Yosemite National Park was established around the original Yosemite Grant. It was Muir's leadership and interest in the natural environment that led him to establish the Sierra Club and shape the ideas that helped to drive the modern environmental movement. In 1905, the state of California transferred its original grant to the federal government in order to unify the administration of the park. On August 25, 1916, President Woodrow Wilson signed the act creating the National Park Service, a new federal bureau in the Department of the Interior responsible for protecting the 35 national parks and monuments then managed by the department, with provisions for those to be established at a future time.

A natural wonder formed by ancient glaciers from the granite cliffs of the western Sierra Nevada range, Yosemite Valley reveals the power and splendor of nature's hand. In the magnificent, incomparable valley of John Muir, alpine forests surround the celebrated sites of Half Dome, El Capitan, Bridalveil Fall, Yosemite Falls, and other stone formations. Yosemite Valley has long been the muse for writers, artists and photographers and continues to inspire.

One might sum up Yosemite with mathematical totals of acreage, trees, birds, waterfalls, trails, and the like. But the human experience and expectations are widely disparate. Tour groups invest but a fraction of a day and hikers meander the backcountry for weeks at a time. Outdoor studios are established as painters' easels and photographers' tripods dot the meadows. Scientists study the environment, the geology, and the forests. Visitors to the park strive for wide-ranging outcomes, among them relaxation, adventure, and even revelation. Of all of America's national parks, Yosemite is truly exceptional—a singular place onto which is mapped the myriad expectations and desires of its countless visitors.

The story of the national parks is not just about their majestic scenery or even the complex stories of the enigmatic individuals who found and then endeavored to save these places. It is also about the persons who accompany us to these destinations, and the passions generated by those who clearly value our parks and vow to assure that they will continue to thrive for our children and our children's children. For more information about Yosemite please visit http://www.the-atlantic.com/unbound/flashbks/muir/muir.htm or http://www.smithsonianmag.com/people-places/yosemite.html.

NATURE PHOTOGRAPHY

I didn't want to tell the tree or weed what it was. I wanted it to tell me something and through me express its meaning in nature.

—Wynn Bullock

Photographing the natural world is nothing more than providing a voice offstage. Although the person behind the camera is the operator of the image-making apparatus, they are not present in the picture, and rightly so. The wonders of nature are center stage, the main event.

Nothing seems easier, to the inexperienced photographer, than photographing a landscape. All the photographer needs to do is point and click. But the reality is that the resulting photo rarely captures the image the photographer meant to convey. Ansel Adams, who spent a lifetime capturing nature, said that nature photography is the supreme test of a photographer—and often the supreme disappointment. Scores of variables must be considered, such as the time of day, the change in weather, the smallest shift in viewpoint.

Clearly, the human eye and the camera do not see the same thing. The human eye sweeps across the landscape and toward the horizon and back, sending hundreds of different visual messages to the brain. Together they add up to a composite impression. But the camera takes just a single sector of the total view. Unless the segment is well chosen, it will fail to convey the sense of spaciousness that is perceived by both the eye and the brain. A picture that includes only distant countryside, for example, defeats the very concept of distance that the photographer wants to illustrate. This is because it offers no point of reference, no contrasting object in the foreground or middle ground. The eye without the camera picks out such reference points by shifting alternately from near objects to far ones (Time Life Books, 190).

A good landscape photographer must focus on his goal, which is to document the look of the land in both an impressive and evocative way. He studies the splendor of the mountain ranges, the intimacy of the forest glades, the freshness of grasses and the vibrancy of wild flowers. He searches for the unusual effects of light or atmosphere—sunshine streaming through flora or lying radiant on the ripples of a lake, the pattern of shadows cast by grooves in a newly plowed field, or haze enveloping a valley as dawn nears.

Modern digital single-lens reflex cameras enjoy many advantages over film cameras. While the initial cost of a quality camera may be slightly higher, the long-term expenses will be much less since film and processing costs are eliminated. Having the ability to immediately see the images shot with a digital camera is a huge benefit. Problems with exposure, light, composition and sharpness are obvious immediately and adjustments can be made on the spot.

Digital technology is really a learning tool. The ease of its use encourages the photographer to take more shots and therefore to master the required techniques more quickly. There is the added benefit of convenience, portability and ease in travel. Airport X-ray machines can play havoc with film, but they have no effect on the digital camera.

Correct exposure is vital to shooting first-rate outdoor images. The properly exposed digital image avoids overexposed bright areas and the pixels capture just enough light so that the colors are true. Although exposure with this technology is easier, the photographer must still master the fundamentals. It is critical to understand the aperture values and shutter speeds and how they work together. When combined with various software programs, digital images can produce incredible prints.

The success of nature photography is highly dependent on the photographer's understanding of crucial light in creating exceptional images. Photographers must capture the light that illuminates the subject. Data about the light, regarding intensity and color, is then captured by pixels. This information is processed to reconstruct an image of the subject. Certain types of light, such as the soft light of a hazy day or the crimson light of dawn, can actually serve to generate mood. Even poor light for photography has the ability to be modified and turned into beautiful light.

For the photographic purist, crisp, sharp focus is one of the standards by which any photographic image is measured. Digital is no exception. Most sources recommend the use of a tripod to eliminate tiny movements when attempting to focus in nature.

Good composition is recording the subject in the most effective way. It is the thoughtful placement and arrangement of primary and secondary objects, lines, shadows, shapes and colors within the image. It includes using lenses well to affect the size of the foreground and background elements with respect to each other, to use effective zones of depth of field, eliminating distractions from the image, and even choosing shooting angles to use the light to best advantage or to control the background (Gerlach, 119).

Powerful images are created in many ways. During a shoot at night darkness provides a blank canvas and a flash or campfire allows you to paint with light. Don't be afraid to generate a sense of action through motion blurs. Make abstract images that will challenge perceptions. Look for extreme angles and forgo shooting at eye level. Shoot into the sun to backlight your subjects. Find new, untapped locales and forget the trophy shot that everyone wants to take. Rearrange elements in your scene to create visual interest. Embrace adversity—storm clouds can add

drama to your composition. And finally, rules are made to be broken, so take some risks!

Clearly, the more you know about nature, the better your images will be. However, you don't need a degree in science to have excellent results. Nature photographers savor the outdoors. Their quest for the perfect wildflower or the shot of the winged bird in flight offers an escape from the routines of everyday life and can provide the incentive to rise with the sun and drive into untamed areas for that perfect opportunity. Many a world traveler began their journey in the simple pursuit of preserving nature in that extraordinary photograph that fills first the heart and then the frame.

For some great tips on digital nature photography online visit http://www.out doorphotographer.com/how-to/shooting/be-a-photography-rebel.html or http://www.scra pjazz.com/topics/Photography/Lessons/66. php.

Credits

Anne Bivans has been a member of my book club for quite some time. A couple of years ago she forwarded a blog and photos of her trip to Nantucket to the members of the club. It was evident then that she had a great eye for composition and a true appreciation of nature. A year later, she followed that blog with one of her travels to the Sierra Nevada. I was hooked! I knew that I wanted to feature her photography in a display on Yosemite at the Cressman Library. Happily, she agreed!

Anne loves hiking Pennsylvania trails and visiting national parks. She enjoys photography because it enables her to combine her love of nature and the outdoors with her love of art and beauty. Anne uses a Canon EOS Digital Rebel and a Canon Power Shot A570 IS. She hopes that by sharing photographs of the beautiful places she visits she can inspire others to experience nature and to protect our natural resources. Her hiking pictures can be found at http://www.anne 99.blogspot.com/. Born in Bethlehem, Pennsylvania, Anne is a graduate of Moravian College and currently resides in Whitehall, Pennsylvania. She is employed as a software developer in the Lehigh Valley.

Assembling the Display

1. The font Logger, sized at 350, was used for the word *Yosemite*. This was available as a free download at http://www.simplythebest.net. The letters were printed on card stock, traced onto black poster board and painted with various shades of brown acrylic paint. The font Wrexham, sized at 250, was used for the phrase *In Focus*. This was available free at http://www.dafont.com. The photographer's name was created using Franklin Gothic Demi font sized at 300. All letters were created by printing on card stock and tracing onto black poster board. These were then glued to bright green poster board.

The image of Mirror Lake was sized at 20" × 26" and was mounted on foam board with pins. Fresh pine branches were attached with pins to the left of the photo and to the left and right of the Yosemite sign. Silk cattails provided a balance on the right. Twigs were arranged and flanked the top and bottom of the poster.

Books on display on the top shelf were *Landscape Photography* by Tim Fitzharris, *Digital Nature Photography*: *The Art and the Science* by John and Barbara Gerlach, *Field Notes from Yosemite* by Teresa Jordan and *Yosemite: An American Treasure* by Kenneth Brower. Twigs, pine cones and greens flanked the books.

2. On the top left was a photo of "Waterfall at Yosemite Falls." Under that was a document titled "Ten Tips to Create Unique and Powerful Images." This information can be found if you visit http://www.outdoorphotographer.com/how-to/shooting/be-a-photography-rebel.html. Next was a photo and description of Liberty Cap and the 375-foot Vernal Falls. All photos on the left were printed on presentation paper and mounted on black poster board. The document on photography tips was printed on white card stock and glued onto black poster board.

3. On the top right was a picture of the photographer, Anne Bivans, sitting on Dewey Point. Under that was her biography, which is included in the credits section of this chapter.

Next was a photograph of a rainbow over a spraying waterfall followed by this quote by John Muir:

> But no temple made with hands can compare with Yosemite. Every rock in its walls seems to glow with life ... as if into this one mountain mansion Nature had gathered her choicest treasures....

Under that was a photo of a view of wildflowers with Half Dome in the distance.

Items on the right were printed and mounted like those on the left.

4. On the base of the display case were pine branches, a log, twigs and stones. On the top left of the log was this quote by photographer Anne Bivans:

> Yosemite is spectacular; I have never before experienced such grandeur on such a majestic scale. In Yosemite, cliffs and waterfalls plunge thousands of feet, two thousand year old trees tower over two hundred feet, and the wild rivers thunder into the valley below.

Books featured on the base of the display are *John Muir: Life and Work* edited by Sally M. Miller, *Yosemite Place Names* by Peter Browning, and *Yosemite in Time* by Mark Klett, Rebecca Solnit and Byron Wolfe.

Bigger and Better

There is no limit to what you could include in a display on nature photography. Just take a walk in the woods and your props surround you!

There are so many talented amateur photographers, you could practically feature a display on photography semiannually. You might want to have a contest and coordinate that with a program on digital photography. You might limit the entries to flora or fauna. You could have a "Teen Challenge" or one called "Senior Snapshots" for your retired patrons. Your contest could be called "In a Flash" and include photographs created using a flash.

You could title your display "Sacred Places" and have patrons submit photos of locales in nature that generate special feelings. The photographers could submit a paragraph or two about their subject. You could have patrons vote with coins to select the winning photo, the proceeds going to your local park for clean-up, additional landscaping, etc. Tie this into an April Earth Day event. Your contest could be limited to black and white images and could be titled "Ebony and Ivory." You could have 35mm photographers compete against digital photographers.

If you mount a display on Yosemite, there is a publication by Arcadia Press from the Images of America Series titled *Yosemite Valley*. It chronicles the evolution of the Yosemite Valley through a collection of magnificent photos. Included are some early images which illustrate the daily life of the Yosemite Indians. Many of these photographs are courtesy of the Yosemite Museum Scenes and depict Native American dances, crafts, costumes and culture that illustrate the unique and challenging existence of these rugged mountain dwellers.

Ken Burns and Dayton Duncan wrote a wonderful book which became a PBS documentary shortly after I mounted this display. It is called *The National Parks: America's Best Idea: an Illustrated History*. The photographs are breathtaking and would be an excellent source for your display.

If you would like a alternative display idea on John Muir or National Parks, see p. 165 my first book, *Great Displays for Your Library Step by Step*. An idea for a display on photography titled Exposed can be found on p. 173.

Land Down Under

Australia: the island continent; the largest nation on earth to occupy an entire land mass; as big as the United States; larger than Europe; reaching from the cool end of the temperate zone into the tropics and across three time zones; ancient, isolated—these are the threads from which Australia's story of nature and people has been woven.
—Ian Brown, *Flying High Australia* (19)

A mere two centuries ago the European colonizers believed that they had found a lush, forested land "down under." Alas, it was an illusion. For beyond the humid fringe the trees became small and scattered, then vanished entirely. In the expansive interior only shrubs and dwarf trees could survive. The new land was one of stark contrasts, presenting many challenges. Traditional tales recounted by the indigenous Australians tell of the creation of the continent and many of its unique landscape features. These Aboriginal stories accentuate the close spiritual relationship between the people and the land.

The first Aborigines colonized Australia 50,000 years ago. They came across from New Guinea via a land bridge. Aboriginal people thrived on the continent and made unique advances long before the European explorers arrived. The native Australians, inventors of the aerodynamic boomerang and a spear thrower called the woomera, were the first society to grind edges on stone cutting tools and the earliest civilization to use those tools to grind seeds.

Although there is evidence that the Chinese explorers knew of a land in the south as early as the Sui dynasty (A.D. 589–618), it wasn't until 1422 that their ships had actually mapped a part of Australia. They landed expressly in search of metalliferous ores. The first documented discovery of the southern land mass was by the Dutch commander Willem Jansz, in 1606. The early Dutch explorers had named the continent New Holland. They decided there was not enough of value with regard to spices or precious metals to warrant further exploration. The main English and French explorers arrived in the late 1700s. James Cook charted the eastern coast of the continent, followed by the French, who explored much of the western shore.

Matthew Flinders was a skilled navigator and chart maker. In a career that spanned twenty years, he circumnavigated and named Australia. He survived shipwrecks and disaster only to be imprisoned by the French and held in captivity for seven years. Flinders wrote a book on his experiences titled A Voyage to *Terra Australis*, which is considered the seminal work on Australian exploration. The charts contained in that text were so

Land Down Under. A tricolored background showcases kangaroos bounding over tall Australian grasses. A koala and her joey symbolize the fauna native to the island continent.

accurate they were used for many years after his death. Flinders' data proved finally that Australia was not a series of islands but rather one large island, and, indeed, a continent. He died in 1814, at the age of 40, the day after the book was published.

So, the question remains, was this new land really the world's largest island, or its smallest continent? Since it sits on its own tectonic plate and has completely unique flora and fauna, Australia is considered a continent. Still, it is sometimes referred to as an island continent because it is entirely surrounded by water and separate from any other land mass.

When contemplating the land down under, people often conjure up images of the continent's center, or outback—complete with sheep stations, the red center and sunburnt plains. Consequently, Australians often describe their homeland as flat and dry. Although the population of Australia is a fraction of that of the United States, about 15 percent, in area it matches the 48 contiguous states—minus Illinois. The country has the lowest population density in the world—only two people per square kilometer.

It is the vast coastline to which the inhabitants of Australia are drawn. Not only is this the locale where the great majority of the 21 million people live, the shoreline has a powerful influence on the population's philosophies of life, the activities they pursue and their eventual accomplishments. Given the island setting, it's no surprise that the people of Australia excel at water related sports and competitions.

GREAT BARRIER REEF

The Great Barrier Reef, located off the east coast of Queensland in northeast Australia, is the only living organic collective visible from space. It is one of the wonders of the natural world. Over the years, human activity has created pollutants and the reef has suffered damage. Of particular concern are the wetlands, which have diminished in size by over 50 percent since the European settlement. Protecting this environment has been challenging. Access to many areas is limited or prohibited. Restrictions on activities such as boating, fishing, reef walking, snorkeling and tourism are enforced.

The Great Barrier Reef area abounds

with wildlife, including dugong and green turtles, many varieties of dolphins and whales, more than 1500 species of fish, 4000 types of mollusk and over 200 species of bird life. One of the primary aims of the Great Barrier Reef Coastal Wetlands Protection Program is developing measures for the long-term conservation and management of priority wetlands. The reef's future lies in educating younger generations to respect rather than exploit wildlife, instilling strong moral values to safeguard the natural heritage.

THE CORAL

Coral reefs are one of the greatest natural attractions on the planet. Clear warm seas and sun-drenched shallows are two of the main ingredients for coral reef development. If these conditions are present, abundant plant growth occurs which provides the basic fuel for coral and other organisms. The coral reefs have abundant life forms. In addition to the community of plants and animals seen on or above the surface of the reef, there are thousands of unseen organisms. Communities of microscopic organisms live on the reef's surface, under sand, and in the water column directly above.

There are many different types of coral. Some are slow growing and live to be hundreds of years old, and others are faster growing. The colors of coral are created by algae. Only live coral is colored; dead coral is white.

One of the great dangers to the habitat is the Crown of Thorns starfish. Since the 1960s it has been destroying the coral which comprise the reef. The starfish outbreak can take one to 15 years and can negatively affect the sea and bird life.

FLORA AND FAUNA

There are about 280 species of mammals, 800 of bird, 300 of lizard, 140 of snake and two of crocodile residing on the continent of Australia. Of the mammals, almost half are marsupials. The rest are either placental mammals or monotremes, and most of them are unique to Australia.

Australia's best-known animals are the kangaroo, koala, platypus, wombat and spiny anteater. Isolation enabled the Australian continent to become a haven for marsupials. However, recent reports indicate that koalas have suffered a sharp population decline due to increased development, bushfires and global warming and could vanish within decades. Estimates of koalas on the Australian continent range from 43,000 to 80,000, well under previous estimates of more than 100,000.

Among Australia's marsupials are grazing animals, tree climbers, amphibians, earth burrowers, and the counterparts of cats, dogs, rats and mice. There are about 50 species of kangaroo, some as tall as a man and others as diminutive as cats. Estimates of the number of kangaroo on the continent range around 40 million, more than when Australia was first settled.

Of the bird species found in Australia, 400 are unique to the continent. Isolation also allowed for the development of strange birds—as strange as the kangaroo and the koala. They range from tiny honeyeaters to the flightless but stately emu, which stands nearly two meters tall. There are 55 species of brilliantly colored parrots in Australia. More species of venomous snakes exist there than on any other continent and the spiders are also among the world's most deadly.

Following a rain, wildflowers turn the arid and savanna grassland areas of Australia into carpets of color. Native forests are limited mainly to wetter coastal districts and rainforests are primarily in Queensland. The somber tones of the eucalypts give the face of Australia its distinctive appearance. Eucalypts inhabit the continent, from the snow country of the south to the tropics of the north, salt-laden estuary banks and harsh deserts. Some species hug the ground while others tower more than 150 meters.

Australia is a highly developed country with a prosperous multicultural society. It has achieved excellent ratings in areas such as health care, life expectancy, human development, public education, economic freedom and the assurance of civil liberties and political rights. Major cities in Australia rank among the world's most desirable in terms of cultural offerings and quality of life.

Credits

In the early 1990s my husband traveled solo to Australia. Mementos of his journey can be spotted throughout our home.

Pictures of koalas, a framed vintage newspaper masthead, coasters and coffee table books are fond reminders of the time he spent exploring the natural beauty of this southern continent. His was an expedition of incredibly varied vistas which resulted in much self-reflection. His experience in Byron Bay, Australia's most easterly point, was the hallmark event of all of his travels to date. Although I haven't had the pleasure of an actual journey to the land down under, it was my hope that a display featuring this continent would be lush, colorful, energetic, informative and, it is hoped, of interest to many of you.

Assembling the Display

1. A light blue felt background was affixed to the back of the display case. A strip of yellow poster board 8" high was cut to fit the width and attached 8" from the top of the case with pins. An 8" strip of green poster board was attached under the yellow strip. Tall grass was cut from black and tan poster board and attached with pins under the green poster board.

Images of kangaroos in motion were found through a Google search, printed and enlarged on the photocopier to three different heights, the largest 7½" high. They were traced onto black poster board, attached with pins and pulled forward. Various size birds in flight, found through an image search, were printed on white card stock, attached with pins to the blue felt and then pulled forward.

The font Berlin Sans FB Demi, available in Microsoft Word, was sized at 375 to create the title. The word Under was italicized. These were printed on card stock and traced onto black poster board. They were attached with pins and pulled forward.

2. On the top left was information about the Sydney Opera House, which can be found if you visit http://www.sydneyoperahouse. com/about/house_history_landing.aspx.

An image of the opera house, found through a Google search, was inserted in the top center of the document. Under that was this stanza of a poem by Dorothea Mackellar, written in 1904, titled "My Country":

> I love a sunburnt country,
> A land of sweeping plains
> Of ragged mountain ranges
> Of droughts and flooding plains.

Next was information about the Great Barrier Reef. An image depicting the reef was inserted into the top center. For specifics about this area off the coast of Australia visit http://www.barrierreefaustralia.com/the-great-barrier-reef/great-barrier-reef.htm.

Items on the left were printed on white card stock and mounted on blue poster board.

3. On the top right was this quote by geologist and priest J. Milne Curran, 1898:

> Australia has a history far more ancient than any written by men—to read this history is one of the objects of geology—records preserved in the great stone-book of nature.

Under that were a variety of interesting facts and statistics about Australia which can be found if you visit http://www.australia.com/about/facts.aspx?ta_cid=sem0910:09:en:us:002.

A replica of the country's flag, found through a Google image search was inserted in the top center. Last was the quote that introduced this display.

Items on the right were printed and mounted like those on the left.

4. On the base of the display was a large stuffed koala holding a joey. The koalas were elevated on a stack of books covered by green felt. In front of these marsupials is information about the species that can be found if you visit https://www.savethekoala. com/koalas.html. Green silk fronds were placed behind and in the paws of the koalas and interspersed among the books. A framed old Australian newspaper masthead was placed at an angle in front of the stuffed animals and a coaster with Aboriginal art was centered in front of it. Moss, stones and shells lined the base of the case.

Books featured in the display were *Surprising Lands Down Under* by Mary Ann Harrell, *Australia: A New History of the Great Southern Land* by Frank Welsh, *In a Sunburned Country* by Bill Bryson, *The Future Eaters* by Tim Flannery, *Australia: Flying High* by Klaus D. Francke and Ian Brown, *The Explorers: Stories of Discovery and Adventure from the Australian Frontier* edited by Tim Flannery, *Sydney: The Story of a City* by Geoffrey Moorhouse and *Wild Shores of Australia* by Ron Fisher.

Bigger and Better

Your display on Australia could feature various sizes of lighthouses which dot the coastline of the continent. Use nautical flags to spell out the title of your choosing. You may consider calling it "Harbor Lights," "Preserve & Protect" or "Beacon of Light." Use an assortment of shells, fish nets, coral and sand. Include sailboats and a model ship in distress and position it up against some rocks. Feature information about shipwrecks in the coastal waters, which can be found if you visit http://www.cultureandrecreation. gov.au/articles/shipwrecks/.

If you would prefer to focus on the Sydney Opera House, there are many posters from which to choose. For a selection visit http://www.allposters.com/-st/Opera-House-Posters_c7894_.htm. Include scores, DVDs or CDs of some of the major operas, facts about the architect of the opera house, the structure and a time line on the construction of the complex. For this information visit http://www.cultureandrecreation.gov.au/articles/sydneyoperahouse/. Create fireworks as a backdrop for your opera house and install the display for New Year's or Australia's National Day, which is celebrated on January 26.

Use the term "aboriginal art" in a Google image search and it will yield fascinating results. Some of these primitive images might inspire your creativity or be the catalyst for a contest among your students or patrons. Feature sea life in the display and incorporate silk eucalyptus into the design. Add a boomerang or two!

For display ideas featuring artifacts from another continent and country see "Tribal Treasures" on page 105 and "Indian Arts" on page 137 of my first book, *Great Displays for Your Library Step by Step.*

3 Women of Note

Reel Women

You don't have to act with me, Steve. You don't have to say anything and you don't have to do anything. Oh, maybe just whistle. You know how to whistle, don't you, Steve? You just put your lips together and ... blow.
—Lauren Bacall (Slim) in *To Have and Have Not* (1944)

Hollywood has long looked to the literary world for material adaptable to film. Some of the most compelling works of fiction are the product of female writers. Early novelists Louisa May Alcott, Jane Austen, Charlotte Brontë and Harriet Beecher Stowe penned works that later evolved into film classics. Twentieth century writers such as Edith Wharton, Ayn Rand, Alice Walker and Amy Tan have afforded insights into varying aspects of the moral fiber of American society.

Some of the most enduring novels, such as *Uncle Tom's Cabin* and *Little Women,* have been retold and re-created on film numerous times. Harper Lee's Pulitzer Prize–winning work, *To Kill a Mockingbird,* scored well both at the box office and at the 1962 Academy Awards. The novel, published two years prior to the awards ceremony, appears on school reading lists and remains popular fifty years later.

Many of Hollywood's most profitable films were based on novels by American women. Pearl Buck's Nobel Prize–winning epic, *The Good Earth,* told the tale of a simple Chinese family whose lives were forever changed by greed. The 1937 film garnered a host of Oscars. Other successful books-to-film include two works by Edna Ferber, *Giant* and *Showboat,* Marjorie Kinnan Rawlings' *The Yearling* and Katherine Ann Porter's *Ship of Fools.*

Margaret Mitchell's beloved novel of the Old South was set in and around the Civil War. This epic novel, *Gone with the Wind,* is widely considered the best Hollywood film of all time. Producer David O. Selznick took a gamble and it paid off. He paid Mitchell $50,000 for the film rights. This was a tremendous sum for a first-time author in the late 1930s. The Pulitzer Prize–winning book was transformed into an Academy Award–winning film by a fledgling studio with a mere seven prior productions to its credit. By the time of the film's release, the nation was reeling from a lengthy depression and the prospect of an impending war. Mitchell wrote a poignant account of a more genteel time and of "a Civilization gone with the wind." Her Scarlett O'Hara was a universally appealing character who triumphed over a host of challenges including death, war, and poverty.

Film historians have found that men play a disproportionate amount of leading roles and heroes on the big screen. Males were usually depicted as employed professionals, as opposed to the great percentage of women, who were shown as unemployed housewives. Throughout much of film history, women have been portrayed as manipulative, sexually repressed or sexually overt. There was a shortage of sisterhood depicted onscreen and films with women interacting with other women in a constructive manner.

Almost 20 years after *Thelma & Louise* was released, it remains culturally significant and politically powerful. This movie's screenplay, written by Callie Khouri, has been used

Reel Women. A colorful marquee provides a sense of the theatrical to this display celebrating women involved in all aspects of the film industry.

as an affirmation of female empowerment and self-assertion and also as a caution of the perceived dangers of female involvement in violent behavior. By portraying women as both victims and perpetrators of violence, *Thelma & Louise* broke radical new ground in conventional American representation, threatening those critics who objected to its breach of the standard of violence as a male privilege. Miss Khouri addressed the sustained interest in this groundbreaking film after two decades: "[It] seems to hold it own place and be either revered or despised with a lasting intensity. I think, in general, it is more often remembered fondly, and for some, profoundly. I don't know how any writer or filmmaker could hope for more than that" (Cook, 189).

Today we see more sensationalized sexual roles for women, a trend that began in the 1970s. Women are also seen as waifs, a tendency that originated in the 1960s. Women's marital status is known more often than their male counterparts in film and female characters are frequently defined by their relationship with a man.

Film noir is commonly identified as a particular period in the development of the thriller in the 1940s and 1950s during which certain highly formalized inflections of plot, character and visual style dominated, at the expense of narrative coherence and comprehensible solution of a crime, the usual goal of the thriller/detective film (Kaplan, *Women in Film Noir,* 27). There are a number of features of film noir that produce a specific location for women and somewhat vague ideological effects. There is the investigative construction of the narrative and plot devices such as voice-overs or flashbacks—sometimes both. There are numerous points of view expressed throughout the film. The heroine is repeatedly characterized as unstable. There is a clear emphasis on sexuality in the style of the female photography.

Dr. Martha M. Lauzen is founder and executive director of the Center for the Study of Women in Television and Film at San Diego State University. Her 2008 study titled *The Celluloid Ceiling* analyzed the percentages of women involved in directing, producing, writing, editing and cinematography on the top 250 domestic grossing films. Surprisingly, the opportunities for female directors are in decline. In 2007, only 6 percent of directors were women, down from 11 percent in 2000. Women were most likely to work on romantic comedies or romantic dramas, documentaries and animated features . They were least likely to work on science fiction, horror and action-adventure features (Lauzen, 3). One of the first successful pioneers in women's directing was Dorothy Arzner. She managed to survive the transition from silent to sound films and sustained a career lasting thirty years. Arzner, a true pioneer for women in directing, dressed in manly fashion and worked frequently with noted actresses, whose talents she showed to their best advantage.

The actress Ida Lupino was determined to exercise control over her career and became the only woman director working in the 1950s. She attributed much of her success to the fact that she formed her own production company where directing was an economic necessity. The Filmmakers, as the company was known, wanted to make affordable, high-quality films, often about provocative topics with a special feminine sensibility. This endeavor created many jobs for aspiring young actors. Lupino was also involved in the writing process for the films she directed. She wasn't permitted to control anything other than "B" films throughout her film career and eventually made her way to directing various television series.

Following Lupino into the director's chair were Nora Ephron (*Sleepless in Seattle*), Nancy Meyers (*Something's Gotta Give*), Amy Heckerling (*Fast Times at Ridgemont High*), Martha Coolidge (*Lost in Yonkers*), Kathryn Bigelow (*K–19, the Widowmaker*), and Mimi Leder (*Pay It Forward*). Relative newcomers included Kimberly Pierce (*Boys Don't Cry*), Patty Jenkins (*Monster*), and the first Academy Award–nominated woman director, Sofia Coppola (*Lost in Translation*). Notable actresses turned directors were Penny Marshall (*Big*), Jodie Foster (*Little Man Tate*), Barbra Streisand (*The Prince of Tides*), Angelica Huston (*Bastard Out of Carolina*) and Elaine May (*The Heartbreak Kid*). International notables were Lina Wertmuller, Jane Campion, Gillian Armstrong and Leni Riefenstahl.

Studies on the employment figures of women in films have yielded some interesting results. Despite the fact the three major studios were headed by women in the past decade, new opportunities for females did not follow. Major studios were still unwilling to assign a $50 million movie to a woman, and the independent sector concurred. An exception was made for Kathryn Bigelow, who was allotted a $90 million budget for *K–19: The Widowmaker,* which grossed a disappointing $65 million worldwide. Her most recent film, *The Hurt Locker*, won the Academy Award for Best Picture of 2009, putting her back in the good graces of the motion picture industry.

About 40 percent of characters in film are female, so the opportunities for acting are more available to women. Salaries have been a different story. Julia Roberts helped women achieve parity in earnings when she crossed the $20 million barrier in 1999. Approximately 22 percent of producers are women and about 17 percent are working as editors. Female writers represent 10 percent of the current workforce.

Laura Ziskin, producer of two Academy Award presentations and fifteen full-length films, including the successful Spider Man franchise, has suggested that it was the men who built the cities, made and defined the culture, interpreted the world. At no time in recorded history have women been culture makers. Movies are arguably the most influential, important medium in the world. They have a tremendous cultural impact. Because women are now making movies, women's ideas, philosophy and point of view will seep into the culture. And that's never happened in history (Gregory, 377).

Despite the inroads that women have made behind the scenes in the film industry, there is still much progress that needs to be made.

Credits

Cedar Crest College offers a course titled "Women Go to the Movies" taught by Carolyn Segal, PhD. This class is a real favorite of the students, and the films on the course syllabus ultimately found their way to the reserve collection I monitored in the Cressman Library. It has been interesting to see the reaction of the students viewing or reviewing these films on reserve. Inevitably there would be a dialogue at the time of discharge as the students attempt to absorb and analyze the film's content and their interpretation of it.

Most of the films included in this display were on the syllabus of the above-mentioned course and feature strong roles for women.

Assembling the Display

1. The font Cooper Black was sized at 425 to create the title "Reel Women." This was printed on card stock and traced onto black poster board. The letters were glued to a 10" × 46" piece of white poster board. Lines were drawn above and below the lettering with a black Sharpie pen. The top of the marquee was made of black poster board, the same dimension as the white but with a 2 ½" center peak. The design came from a Google image search. The image was enlarged several times and the individual pieces cut out and traced. Red, orange and yellow design pieces were cut from poster board and glued to the black area. Circles traced from a quarter were cut from silver and gold poster board and framed the design. The smaller circles that framed the top center design were traced from a dime onto gold poster board. A 4" × 35" × 46" trapezoid was cut from black poster board and attached to the bottom of the white signage. This created the underside of the marquee. Tiny squares of gold poster board were glued in angled rows to create the effect of under lighting beneath the marquee. The three sections were taped together and attached to the felt with pins and pulled forward.

2. On the top left was a document titled "Hollywood's Women Directors Hit Celluloid Ceiling," which can be found if you visit *http://www.buzzle.com/editorials/7–4–2002–21795.asp*. Under that was the quote that introduced the display. Next was a document titled "Women Go to the Movies," which included synopses of 5 films featuring women. For the list "100 Best Female Char-

acter Roles in Film" visit *http://www.film site.org/femaleroles.html*.

Items on the left were printed on white card stock and mounted on orange and/or black poster board.

3. On the top right was this quote from *As Good as It Gets* spoken by Helen Hunt (Carol) to Jack Nicholson (Melvin):

> When you first came in for breakfast, when I first saw you, I thought you were handsome.... Then, of course, you spoke.

Next was a document which analyzes "The Femme Fatale" in film noir. Information on that topic can be found in the monograph *Women in Film Noir* by E. Ann Kaplan or online if you visit *http://www.filmsite.org/fem mesfatales.html*. Under that was this quote from Julie Hagerty (Elaine,) in the film *Airplane:*

> There's no reason to become alarmed, and we hope you enjoy the rest of your flight. By the way, is there anyone on board who knows how to fly a plane?

Items on the right were printed and mounted like those on the left.

4. On the base of the display was a miniature gold-plated statuette elevated on a Styrofoam circle covered in velvet. Behind that was a gray 10 ½" movie reel. In front of that was a black evening bag with rhinestones, a string of pearls, a bottle of perfume and a white fabric flower. Two movies tickets found through a Google image search were placed alongside the bag. Two 7" movie reels spray-painted silver flanked the DVDs in the display.

DVDs featured in the display were *Girl Interrupted, Million Dollar Baby, Thelma & Louise, Chocolat, Mean Girls* and *It Happened One Night.*

Books featured in the display were *Action Chicks: New Images of Tough Women in Popular Culture* edited by Sherrie A. Innes, *Blockbusters: A Reference Guide to Film Genres* by Mark Graves and F. Bruce Engle, *Women Who Run the Show* by Mollie Gregory, *Women in Film Noir* edited by Ann Kaplan, *A History of Film* by Jack Ellis and *Frankly, My Dear: Gone with the Wind Revisited* by Molly Haskell.

Bigger and Better

You will want to mount this display in March for Women's History Month. You may want to limit YOUR Reel Women to just award-winning actresses. Call it "Famous Film Legends" or "Screen Sirens." You could choose to focus on women directors. Use *Women Directors and Their films* by Mary G. Hurd as a resource. For information about this topic visit *http://www.afterellen.com/ blog/ace/six-women-directors.*

Should you decide to create a display on the lack of more genuine opportunity for women in the film industry, call it "Celluloid Ceiling" and refer to Martha Lauzen's study by the same name that analyzes the lack of women working in behind-the-scenes roles in the film industry. This can be found if you visit *http://magazine.women-in-film.com/ Portals/0/Article_Images/lauzen/2007ceiling /2007_Celluloid_Ceiling.pdf.*

Choose top films about women and call it "Best of the Best." Include favorites such as *Now, Voyager; Annie Hall; Bonnie & Clyde; Rebecca; The Color Purple; Boys Don't Cry; Erin Brockovich; Little Women; Imitation of Life; The Joy Luck Club* and *Monster.*

Create a display titled "First in Film" and refer to this Website: *http://www.listology. com/content_show.cfm/content_id.14956.* Another idea for a movie-related display titled "From Page to Screen" can be found on page 35 of my first book, *Great Displays for Your Library Step by Step.*

Legends: Women Who Have Changed the World

Don't call me an icon. I'm just a mother trying to help.—Diana, Princess of Wales

The legendary women featured in this display share a common bond. They overcame obstacles and transcended popular conceptions of their gender in what had largely been a man's world. For some such women, the hurdles included breaking social boundaries and racial barriers. It is important that we acknowledge all of these women for accomplishing something truly monumental; for challenging the status quo; for establishing the perfect time in which to rebel; and for delivering a message for which the world may have been unready.

The impact of the women's movement on the ability of females to accomplish their goals has been profound. The awareness it forced the reduction of discrimination in areas such as literature, science, politics, fashion, entertainment and sports. All of the women featured in this display were pioneers, conquering new frontiers of achievement and showing us how the modern world has been altered and shaped by and for women. Here are some of the women who, in just a lifetime, managed to change the world.

AMELIA EARHART

Born in 1897 in Atchinson, Kansas, Amelia lived in various towns in America's heartland during her childhood years, largely due to her father's position as a railroad attorney. After going to school in the East, she ultimately joined her family, who had relocated to California. There Amelia worked odd jobs to pay for flying lessons. Recognizing this passion, her mother and sister helped finance her first airplane, a Kinner Airstar. Following a Red Cross first aid course, Amelia worked as a nursing assistant caring for wounded soldiers in Toronto during World War I. She later trained to become a doctor, but left to pursue her real passion, aviation.

Amelia was nicknamed "Lady Lindy" because her posture, build and features resembled those of Charles Lindbergh. She was befriended by Eleanor Roosevelt, who obtained her student pilot's license just so Amelia could be her flight instructor.

Although she didn't pilot the plane, Amelia was the first woman to fly over the

Atlantic in 1928, along with pilot Wilmer Stultz and mechanic Louis Gordon. Newspapers heralded this passage, and from that point on Amelia was a public figure. Three years later she married the sponsor of the flight, publicist George P. Putnam. In the course of their marriage, he published two of her books, *The Fun of It* and *Last Flight*.

In 1932 Amelia set out from Newfoundland on a solo crossing of the Atlantic with Paris as the destination. Icy weather necessitated that she land the craft in Ireland. As a result of this accomplishment, she was given many prestigious awards both in the U.S. and on the Continent. Amelia later flew solo across the Pacific, the first person ever to do so.

As her popularity grew, Amelia branched out and developed a line of clothing "for the woman who lives actively." It was manufactured by several New York companies and marketed in exclusive stores in major cities. In 1935, she joined the faculty at Purdue University as a career consultant. Purdue's purchase of a Lockheed Electra enabled Amelia to fulfill her dream of circumnavigating the globe.

Amelia's last remaining challenge was about to be realized. Accompanied by copilot Fred Noonan, she set off from Miami on June 1, 1937, and flew to South America, Africa, India and Asia. On July 2 they faced the final trans–Pacific flight of 11,000 km. Their journey was almost complete when confusion arose as to their location. Although weather was not a particular issue, the coast guard lost contact with the aircraft. Four thousand people were involved in the search and rescue mission, which lasted 16 days. No trace of the plane was ever found. As a result, the disappearance and death of this national heroine remains the subject of conjecture and enduring conspiracy theories.

As a final tribute to his beloved wife, George Putnam authored Amelia's biography, titled *Soaring Wings,* in 1939.

Mother Teresa

Born in Skopje, now the Republic of Macedonia, in 1910 to a well-to-do Albanian family, Agnes Gonxha Bojaxhiu was destined to become Blessed Teresa of Calcutta. The family's financial situation was compromised by the sudden and shocking death of Gonxha's father, probably due to his political involvement. By age 12 she had developed an interest in overseas missions and believed that her vocation was in helping the poor in India. She left home at age 18 to join the Sisters of Loreto, a community based in Dublin,

Legends. This stylized Art Deco design of a woman in profile provides the graphic image for a display featuring an array of remarkable women who lived amazing lives.

Ireland. Due to the language barrier, she made very little impression on the congregation and was considered "ordinary."

Named Sister Mary Teresa in 1929, she was elevated to Mother Teresa eight years later. Her first assignment was teaching history and geography at St. Mary's High School in Calcutta, where she stayed about 15 years. While aboard a train to Darjeeling, en route to a retreat, divine intervention guided Mother Teresa to leave her teaching post and begin working with the poorest of the poor.

After undergoing medical training, the Vatican granted Mother Teresa permission to establish a new congregation, named the Missionaries of Charity, in 1948. The members took the usual vows of poverty, chastity, and obedience in addition to a vow to help the poorest poor—free of charge. The congregation focused on the mentally ill, unwanted, unloved, orphaned, uncared for, and, eventually, it endeavored to give dignity and love to lepers and those who were old and terminally ill. Today these missionaries serve the underprivileged around the world.

Mother Teresa's achievements were recognized globally when she won the Pope John XXIII Peace Prize in 1971 and the Nehru Prize for her promotion of peace and understanding in 1972. She was awarded the Nobel Prize for Peace in 1979. Here is an excerpt from her acceptance speech: "He died on the cross ... for you and for me and for that leper and that man dying of hunger and that naked person lying in the street not only of Calcutta, but of Africa, New York, and London, and Oslo—and insisted that we love one another as he loves each one of us" (*Women,* 128–129). Subsequently, she won the 1985 Presidential Medal of Freedom, the 1992 UNESCO Prize for Peace Education and the 1997 U.S. Congressional Gold Medal.

In March of 1997 she stepped down as head of her order. She died of a heart attack on September 5 of that year. Just before her passing Mother Teresa proclaimed that her heart belonged entirely to Jesus. In 2003 she was beatified by Pope John Paul II. Dressed in a plain white sari with a blue border and simple cross at the shoulder, Mother Teresa—and the congregation she oversaw—simply endeavored every day to change the world.

DIANA, PRINCESS OF WALES

Born on July 1, 1961, in Sandringham, England, to the Viscount and Viscountess Althorp, Lady Diana Frances Spencer grew up destined to marry a prince. Diana's family were aristocrats with close ties to the British royal family for decades. As a child, Diana showed a flair for the arts, especially music and dancing. Later she was sent to finishing school in Switzerland. Upon her return to England she worked as a kindergarten teacher.

Diana met the criteria established by royals for marriage to commoners. She was well-bred, Protestant, unmarried and uninvolved in another relationship. With great pomp and circumstance, 19-year-old Diana married 32-year-old Prince Charles, heir to the British throne, at St. Paul's Cathedral in London on July 29, 1981. The heir apparent, Prince William, was born the following June and Prince Harry, "the spare," in 1984. Diana quickly rose in popularity throughout England and around the world. She was unaffected by the adulation and very much at ease in front of the photographers who pursued her ceaselessly. Beautiful and poised, Diana publicized the plight of the homeless and disabled, children in need and those afflicted with HIV and AIDS.

When Charles resumed his relationship with former paramour Camilla Parker-Bowles during his marriage to Diana, his wife's name became linked with other men. On December 9, 1992, Charles and his wife separated and Diana announced that she would be leading a more private life. On occasion she appeared with the royal family at important events. In 1996 Charles and Diana divorced, agreeing to have equal custody of the children. She was now known as Diana, Princess of Wales, and given a home at Kensington Palace. Although she resigned from some charities as a result of her change in station, she remained dedicated to those with whom she had a long association. Diana was an active campaigner for a ban on the manufacture and use of land mines and brought global attention to the problem.

On August 30, 1997, while on vacation in Paris, Diana and boyfriend, Dodi Fayed, along with the driver of the car and her bodyguard, fled the paparazzi who were in hot pursuit. The car was involved in a high-speed accident in a tunnel located under the River Seine. Three of the occupants died. Only Diana's bodyguard, who had worn a safety belt, survived.

Three million people lined the route of the funeral cortège. According to the wishes of her family, the Princess of Wales was laid to rest on an island in a lake at Althorp. Her brother, Earl Spencer, spoke these words at her funeral: "Of all the ironies about Diana, perhaps the greatest was this: a girl given the name of the ancient goddess of hunting was, in the end, the most hunted person of the modern age."

COCO CHANEL

Gabrielle Bonheur "Coco" Chanel began life in 1883 in Saumur, France. She was orphaned at a very young age, but went on to become one of the most revolutionary fashion designers of all time. She changed the look of fashion to such an extent that she was the only couturier in *Time* magazine's 100 most influential people of the 20th century. By taking masculine clothes and giving them a feminine twist, Coco influenced women's clothing and women's rights movement.

Known as "Mademoiselle" to close associates, Coco got her name from a popular song that she sang in Parisian cafés while still in her teens. Although her singing career was brief, through it she became involved with wealthy men who eventually became financial backers. She opened her first millinery shop in Paris, in 1912, where she pioneered her own flapper style of hat. Coco was a strong businesswoman with a flair for marketing.

The "little black dress" was not a novelty. Many designers offered them. The dress that Coco created in 1926 was considered stylish enough for *haute couture*. Many of her designs evolved out of necessity because she could not afford expensive designer clothes. The jersey suit became a Chanel classic and is still being produced. Her timeless, comfortable and loose fitting clothing had a great appeal for her clients.

Coco served as a nurse in World War I. The Nazi occupation meant that the fashion business in Paris was cut off for some years. Coco's affair with a Nazi officer resulted in

her diminished popularity and exile to Switzerland. Chanel No. 5 perfume was launched in 1923 and started a trend for fashion designers to produce signature scents. Prince Wertheimer became Coco's partner in this venture. It is rumored that he was also her lover. The Wertheimer family continues to control the Chanel perfume company today. Her 1954 comeback restored Coco's previous ranking in the fashion industry. She introduced pea jackets and bell bottom pants for women. She also made a foray into stage and movie costume design.

Coco Chanel died in 1971 while still a vital presence in the industry. Her successor, Karl Lagerfeld, has been chief designer of Chanel's fashion house since 1983.

The legacies these women left are the fruits of a life well lived. They proved that their existence mattered and that their milestones made a difference. They are characters; icons; compassionate women of beauty, strength, fortitude, passion and courage.

Credits

Many years ago, at an American Library Association (ALA) convention, I picked up a poster from publisher New World Library. It was titled *Legends* and featured a black and white image of Audrey Hepburn. Although the poster is long gone, the idea of featuring a display on formidable females lingered. However, I have included the book featured on the poster in this display.

As a former staff member at one of the remaining women's colleges in the United States, I often endeavored to find ways to celebrate women and promote women's issues through displays. Over the years I have featured displays on breast cancer awareness, artist Mary Cassatt, children's book illustrator and Cedar Crest alum Jane Dyer, women and computers, vintage hats and handbags, women and fitness, pioneering women, Pocahontas, women who dared, mothers & daughters, Mary Shelly and Mary Wollstonecraft and first ladies. There are several displays on women in my first library display book. The biggest challenge in creating this display was deciding which women should be featured. Obviously, due to practical limitations, many worthy women are not included.

Assembling the Display

1. The inspiration for the graphic used is this display can be found if you visit *http://www.worthpoint.com/worthopedia/vintage-art-deco–lady-enamel-compact-rare*. The image was enlarged on the photocopier. Elements were then cut out and traced onto poster board. Blue, black and silver poster board were used to create the circular image. The flower was cut from hot pink poster board and the stem from blue poster board framed in silver. The star was silver. This was attached with pins and pulled forward on a background of black felt.

The font Copasetic was sized at 400 and used to create the title of the display. This was printed on card stock and traced onto silver poster board. The font can be downloaded free if you visit *http://www.dafont.com* The lettering and silver stars were attached with pins and pulled forward.

These books were featured on the top shelf: *Wise Women: A Celebration of Their Insights, Courage, and Beauty* by Joyce Tenneson, *Film-star Portraits of the Fifties: 160 Glamor Photos* by John Kobal, *Legends: Women Who Have Changed the World, Through the Eyes of Great Women Writers* by John Miller and Angelica Huston. A pink silk begonia was placed on the shelf.

2. On the top left was a biography of Diana, Princess of Wales. This can be found if you visit *http://womenshistory.about.com/od/diana/p/princess_diana.htm*. A photo of Diana was found on a Google image search and printed on white paper, mounted and placed above the document. Under that was the quote that introduced this display.

Next was information about the life and times of Coco Chanel. This can be found if you visit *http://womenshistory.about.com/od/chanelcoco/a/coco_chanel.htm*. A photo of the designer was found through a Google search and printed on paper, mounted on silver poster board and placed under the biography. Last was this quote by Katharine Hepburn:

> If you obey all the rules, you miss all the fun.

Biographical information on the left was printed on white card stock and mounted on silver or black poster board. Quotations were printed on white card stock and mounted on hot pink and black poster board.

3. On the top right was a biography and photo of Amelia Earhart. This can be found if you visit *http://www.ameliaearhartmuseum.org/AmeliaEarhart/AEBiography.htm*. A photo of Amelia found through a Google image search was printed on white paper, mounted on silver and black poster board and placed above the document. Under that was this quote by feminist writer Betty Friedan:

> It is easier to live through someone else than to become complete yourself.

Next was biographical information about Mother Teresa, which can be found if you visit *http://www.americancatholic.org/features/teresa/WhoWasTeresa.asp*. A photo found though a Google image search was printed on paper, mounted on black poster board and placed above the document. Under that was this quotation by famous photographer Margaret Bourke-White:

> Work is something you can count on, a trusted, lifelong friend who never deserts you.

Items on the right were printed and mounted like those on the left.

4. On the base of the display was a Styrofoam head and vintage black felt hat with a rose and white silk flower and black veil. Eyelashes were crafted from black poster board and attached with pins. This form was elevated on a Styrofoam disk covered in black velvet. Black fabric lined the base. A silver evening bag, long black silk gloves, a jeweled watch, a string of pearls, a vintage French franc, a silver star and a pair of hot pink pumps were on the base of the display.

Books featured were *Notable Moments by Women in Music* by Jay Warner, *Women Who Changed the World: Fifty Inspirational Women Who Shaped History*, and *Fearless Women: Midlife Portraits* by Nancy Alspaugh, Marilyn Kentz and Mary Ann Halpin.

Bigger and Better

Should your display space be larger you may want to include historic legends such as Cleopatra, Mary Magdalene, Boudicca,

Hildegard of Bingen, Eleanor of Aquitaine, Joan of Arc, Isabella I of Spain, Catherine de Medici and Catherine the Great. See *Women Who Changed the World: Fifty Inspirational Women Who Shaped History* for short biographies on these and other notable figures.

Late 20th- and early 21st-century notable women who could be featured in a display on this topic are astronaut Sally Ride, TV personality Oprah Winfrey, former Supreme Court justice Sandra Day O'Connor and current justices Ruth Bader Ginsburg and Sonia Sotomayor, secretary of state Hillary Rodham Clinton and former secretaries of state Madeline Albright and Condoleezza Rice.

Not feeling crafty? Check out this poster available for purchase on the topic of women legends: Visit *http://www.alleducationalsoftware.com/xs38418.html.*

You could focus on women in music. Title it "Females on Fire" and feature rock, rap or cutting edge musicians. For ideas on graphics about this topic visit any of these: *http://www.gilli.net/wgm/images/FOFEST.comwhitelogo-sm.jpg; http://stuff.nowim.org/front_page/NOWIM_Logo.jpg; and http://ethnocenter.org/files/WMLogo.jpg.*

If you are thinking of a display on literary or sports legends, or leading ladies, create a collage of photographs of these women and position them around your title. Attach some with adhesive foam tape squares, which will provide some interest and depth to the graphic.

For an idea on a display on the subject of "women worldwide" see page 134 of my first book, *Great Displays for Your Library Step by Step.*

Frida

There have been two great accidents in my life. One was the trolley, and the other was Diego. Diego was by far the worst.—Frida Kahlo, artist

The artist known as Frida Kahlo was born Magdalena Carmen Frieda y Calderón on July 6, 1907, in Coyocoán, Mexico City, Mexico. The daughter of a German-Jewish photographer and an Indian-Spanish mother, she grew up in a home known as Casa Azul, or the Blue House. Most biographies state that at age six, Frida was stricken with polio which affected the development of her right leg and kept her bedridden for nine months. However, author Hayden Herrera, in a documentary for the Biography series, suggests that spina bifida was known in the family and, in an effort to keep that information confidential, the family may have preferred that the polio diagnosis be made public. Despite Frida's gender and the existing mores, her father encouraged her to participate in male dominated sports such as swimming, soccer, and even wrestling in an effort to strengthen her leg and speed her recovery.

Frida enrolled at the National Preparatory School in 1922. She lied about her age, choosing the year of the Mexican Revolution, 1910, as her birth year. She may have been self-conscious about being older than the other students, including a boyfriend. One of its few female students, she was known within the school community for her jovial nature. It was at NPS that she developed friendships with some of the boys, who took pains to devise and execute many pranks. She stood apart from the teen crowd in her wardrobe choices, which comprised traditional colorful Mexican clothing and jewelry. It was during her years at NPS that she first came in contact with the famous Mexican muralist, Diego Rivera, who had been commissioned to paint a mural for the school auditorium.

On September 17, 1925, at the age of 18, Frida was riding a bus in Mexico City when it collided with a trolley car. A metal handrail pierced her abdomen and exited through her vagina. Her injuries were quite devastating: "[A] streetcar crashed into the fragile bus she was riding, broke her spinal column, her collarbone, her ribs, her pelvis.... The impact of the crash left Frida naked and bloodied, but covered with gold dust" (Fuentes, 11,12). After a month in the hospital, Frida returned home with a bleak prognosis and a broken body encased in plaster casts. Shortly after the accident, Frida began painting. Her work depicts the totality of her bodily experience, from anguish to sensuality. Kahlo said, "I never painted dreams, I painted my own reality." This visionary gift ultimately earned her a place among the renowned surrealists.

Although Kahlo had briefly met Rivera as a teenager, it was not until 1928 that the artists met again, thanks to the photographer, film star and revolutionary Tina Modotti. When Modotti reintroduced them Rivera was no longer married to his first wife. It was during this encounter that Diego pulled his pistol and shot the phonograph, a move that captured Kahlo's interest and at the same time causing fear. In August 1929, as the political climate was worsening in Mexico, Frieda Kahlo and Diego Rivera exchanged marriage vows.

During that year, Rivera's artistic career expanded on an international level. In 1930 the couple relocated to San Francisco, where he thrived and she pined for familiar female companionship. A year later they were off to New York and Detroit. Although the couple arrived in the United States at the beginning of the Great Depression, financing was available for murals and lavish welcoming parties.

Up until that time, Kahlo was best known as Rivera's charming wife and was not yet appreciated as an influential artist. This would change in 1932, when Kahlo experienced a devastating miscarriage. While she was recovering, Kahlo, known for her very personal and intimate style, painted a self-portrait aptly entitled *Miscarriage in Detroit*.

Rivera had fallen in love with the United States, while Kahlo desperately wanted to return to Mexico. Rivera relented and the couple returned home in 1935. After the move, they took up residence in two International Style houses built for them in San Angel—a large pink cube for Rivera and a small blue one for Kahlo. The houses were linked by a bridge.

Soon after their return home, Rivera began an affair with Kahlo's younger sister, Christina. Kahlo was completely devastated by this dual betrayal of trust. Although the couple finally reconciled, Rivera's transgression marked a turning point in their relationship and both partners would subsequently

Frida. Red and yellow paper flowers surround a self-portrait of the Mexican artist Frida Kahlo. The artist's tools—a palette, brushes and tubes of paint—are found throughout the display.

yield to infidelity and betrayal. In 1939 the couple divorced but they still frequently appeared in public together. That same year Frida went to live in Paris for a time. Not only did she exhibit some of her paintings, she developed friendships with two major artists,

Marcel Duchamp and Pablo Picasso. It was here that she painted one of her most famous works, *The Two Fridas.*

Despite their volatile marriage, Kahlo and Rivera did not stay divorced for long. They remarried in 1940. Although they continued to lead largely separate lives and over the course of the next decade, both artists engaged in extramarital relationships.

Kahlo's health deteriorated for the remainder of her life. It has been suggested that she used her failing health as a means to hold Rivera's interest, but, despite these rumors, it could not be denied that when Frieda Kahlo was near death her husband was there for her. Art historians suggest that Kahlo never fully recovered physically or emotionally following the amputation of part of her right leg several months prior to her death.

Despite their infidelities and their passionate disputes, Frida Kahlo and Diego Rivera's love endured. In 1954, when Frida passed away at the age of 47, Diego was by her side. At his insistence, no autopsy was performed, and so the cause of death was not determined. Although a pulmonary embolism was suspected, suicide remained a possibility. Rivera, who married Emma Hurtado, his art dealer and publicist, in 1955, died of heart failure in 1957 following a battle with cancer.

Diego Rivera stipulated a period of 50 years from the time of Frida's death until her bathroom/dressing room in their residence, Casa Azul, could be opened. His request was honored by Dolores Olmedo Patiño, director for life of the Anahuacalli and Frida Kahlo museums, who skillfully oversaw both institutions, often at her own expense.

In April 2004, Carlos Phillips Olmedo, the director of Casa Azul, now the Museo Frida Kahlo, and several bank trustees opened Frida's bathroom and retrieved the objects inside:

> The lock securing the door was removed, and in our capacity as restorers we were summoned to assess the condition of Frida's belongings. Even though we knew what awaited us, it was a very emotional experience to step into this space that had lain undisturbed for so many years. Inside, a strong smell, half acrid, half sweet, pervaded the air, a mixture of dampness, medicines, dust, and time. Once the window was opened, we began to make sense of the scene, the shapes of objects now distinguishable in the light (Rosenzweig, 13).

Among the items currently on exhibit at the museum are two hundred garments belonging to Frida, as well as corsets, medicines, jewelry and other articles. A new dimension of the artist emerged with the discovery of these items. Frida had reclaimed Mexico's past through an array of indigenous costumes. The colorful attire served to camouflage her orthopedic shoes, her wasted right leg and the corsets that braced her damaged spine.

Frida's manner of dressing became a large part of her personality and provided an avenue to affirm her independent, creative nature. These fashions can be seen in a beautiful monograph titled *Self-Portrait in a Velvet Dress: Frida's Wardrobe,* edited by Denise and Magdalena Rosenweig. In this text, ninety-five original and brilliantly staged photographs of Kahlo's newly restored clothing are paired with notable photos of the artist wearing them and the paintings in which the garments appeared.

The Rosenzweigs, both textile restorers, chronicled the restoration process used with the stash of clothing housed at Casa Azul:

> The work of preserving all the materials and items found in Frida's bathroom was laborious. First, we made a general evaluation of the collection. We unfolded it piece by piece to assess each item's condition and to register and photograph them all. During this initial inspection, we planned the process of conserving, or, where necessary, restoring the objects. When everything was laid out before us, we were able to appreciate the respository's great value, not only because it had belonged to Frida, but also as an ethnographic and historical collection (Rosenzweig, 175).

The garments were first aired out, then either brushed softly by hand or vacuumed to eliminate dust, cobwebs, or insect droppings. Then the items were either washed or dry cleaned, at which time they could be properly assessed as to the work each required. The restoration process for the wardrobe remains unfinished as some pieces require much time and labor.

The Rosenzweigs' monograph is invaluable. Within its pages a story of culture and couture unfolds to reveal the character, travails, preferences and personality of Frida Kahlo. The book serves to remind us that even a hundred years after her birth, the artist remains an inexhaustible source of interest and study.

Haden Herrera, biographer of Frida Kahlo, writes poignantly about the artist's reality in her book, *Frida Kahlo: The Paintings:* " She painted herself cracked open, weeping beside her extracted heart, hemorrhaging during a miscarriage, anesthetized on a hospital trolley, sleeping with a skeleton, and always—even when she appears beside her pets or her husband, the muralist, Diego Rivera—she looks fearfully alone" (Herrera 3).

Both Frida *Kahlo* and Diego Rivera are recognized worldwide for their contributions to the evolution of art. This vibrant pair was not only known for their immense talent and vision, but also for their tempestuous love affair that spanned thirty years. Theirs was a love inspired by shared beliefs and undeniable passions.

Credits

On a crisp autumn afternoon in the middle–1990s, I had the good fortune to find myself in a charming independent bookstore in mid–Manhattan. As I browsed the nonfiction titles, I found the newly published *Diary of Frida Kahlo: An Intimate Self-Portrait* by Carlos Fuentes. Although I was familiar with the artist's work, I was intrigued with the contents of this diary. Entwined within the journal pages were colored-ink entries and haunting self-portraits, sketches, doodles and paintings. Passionate entries and love letters revealed Frida's fanatical devotion to her philandering husband. Irony, black humor and gaiety are interspersed throughout the entries along with translations, commentaries and photographs which pay tribute to the resilience and courage which defined her.

Reading the diary was a surreal experience that expanded my understanding of the art of Frida Kahlo and the machinations of her complex interior world. This journal was the catalyst for my interest in the artist as a woman and the life and times of the prolific final decade (1944–1954) of her life.

Assembling the Display

1. The background of the display was created using red felt. The black poster board was sized at 27"h × 21½"w. The green poster board measured 21"h × 13"w. The self-portrait of Frida Kahlo was found through a Google image search, printed on card stock and glued to the center of the poster board. The eleven paper flowers were reused from the Cinco de Mayo display (page 23) They can be created using 6" sheets of red and yellow tissue paper and green pipe cleaners. For easy written instructions on how to make tissue paper flowers visit *http://www.azcentral.com/ent/ dead/articles/dead-crafts_paperflowers.html.* For video instructions visit *http://www.won derhowto.com/how-to/video/how-to-make-giant-tissue-paper-flowers-31/.* The flowers were attached with pins. Under that was a colorful artist's palette anchored to the background with pins. The brushes were affixed with rolled tape.

Books displayed on the top shelf were *The Diary of Frida Kahlo: An Intimate Portrait* by Carlos Fuentes, *Frida's Fiestas: Recipes and Remembrances of Life with Frida Kahlo* by Guadalupe Rivera and Marie-Pierre Colle, and *Frida Kahlo* by Sarah M. Lowe. A paper flower, small paint brushes and tubes of acrylic paints along with tropical silk greens were placed among the books.

2. On the top left was information taken from this text on the relationship of Diego Rivera and Frida Kahlo. A black and white photo of the couple was glued above the document. Under that was a picture of the artist painting. Both photos were found using Google images searches. Next was a quote by Frida Kahlo: "I never painted dreams, I painted my own reality." Last was information titled "Frida and the Trolley Accident" taken from this text.

Items on the left were printed on card stock and attached to green or black poster board.

3. On the top right was a picture of *The

Two Fridas and under that information about Frida's motivation for painting it. For more information visit *http://www.smc.edu/voices /forerunner/fall2001/directories/focuson smc/lasdosfridas.htm.* Next was this quote by Frida about her husband that introduced this display.

Under that was this quote by Honoré de Balzac:

> One's wardrobe reveals one's poli-
> tics;It is the story one lives by; It is
> one's symbolic self.

Last was a copy of one of Frida's skirts and corsets found through a Google image search using the term *Self Portrait in a Velvet Dress.*

Items on the right were printed and mounted like those on the left.

4. On the base of the display was the book titled *Frida Kahlo* by Frida Kahlo. It was open to reveal two of Frida's paintings: *Self-Portrait with Red and Gold* and *Me and My Parrots.* Acryllic paints and silk greens framed the open book.

Bigger and Better

Should your space be larger, include some tropical plants, a parrot, pots of silk flowers, and a colorful map of Mexico along with the country's flag. Incorporate the colors of the flag—red, white and green—into your display. Include some fruit symbolizing the many still life paintings created by the artist. Add a sombrero, maracas, guitars, drums and serapes. Enlarge a photo and place it on an easel. Hang colorful Mexican cutout banners or lanterns available at party or dollar stores or online at reasonable prices.

Dedicate the display to the art of both Frida Kahlo and her husband, Diego Rivera. Include one of his many murals, available online. Feature the portrait she painted of her husband title *Portrait of Diego Rivera.* Mount this display around Cinco de Mayo (May 5th), or the Day of the Dead, November 1 and 2, to celebrate the Mexican culture.

For another display related to Mexico, see page 81 of my first book, *Great Displays for Your Library Step by Step*, where the tradition of the Day of the Dead is celebrated.

Ladies of the Court

At first I was disappointed, as were most of those who saw her for the first time, after having heard so much about her. She played with marvelous ease the simplest strokes in the world. It was only after several games that I understood what harmony was concealed by her simplicity, what wonderful mental and physical balance was hidden by the facility of her play.
—Tennis player René Lacoste on Suzanne Lenglen

When Major Walter Clopton Wingfield invented the game of lawn tennis in 1873, the sport was enthusiastically embraced by the upper class. Tennis was initially considered a man's sport. The newest afternoon pastime was not immediately popular with the Victorian women. Many felt it to be far too strenuous for the "weaker sex." There was also the concern that it would compromise their femininity as well as some debate about it's overall propriety. Others felt that serious athletic competition among women was inadvisable. The idea of keeping active and staying fit was foreign to the genteel, finely dressed ladies of the period.

However, the lure of the game prevailed.

Women, dressed for garden parties in all their finest clothing, ultimately picked up heavy wooden racquets and made their way to the court. It wouldn't take long for the players to become competitive. The first ladies' championship tournament in the world was held in Dublin, Ireland, in 1879.

A careful review of the fashion prevalent at the century's end gives us great insight into both culture and community. The prevailing mores dictated fashion as well as morality. Women's tennis clothing of this period was extremely cumbersome. It included long skirts and dresses, bustles, ties, hats and veils, steel-boned corsets, stockings, petticoats and gloves. Heavy material such as flannel and

Ladies of the Court. Women playing tennis in period costumes are captured in this framed poster of *The Tennis Party*. Vintage wooden racquets flank a silver loving cup atop a sea of tennis balls.

serge, and accessories including scarves and fur trims were responsible for much of the discomfort experienced by the pioneers of women's tennis. Happily, these restrictive ensembles ceased with the century's end. Heavy fabrics were replaced by lighter textiles and more pliant fabrics. White remained the norm for the practical reason that it didn't show perspiration.

One of the first important innovations in tennis apparel was India rubber-soled shoes that appeared around 1878. The soles were black so grass stains weren't visible. The women players added a feminine touch by choosing laces of pink or blue.

Maud Watson won the 1884 inaugural Wimbledon Ladies' Singles Championship, in an arduous three-set match, wearing an all-white, ankle-length dress. Tennis sensation Charlotte "Lottie" Dod challenged convention by wearing mid-calf skirts throughout her Wimbledon matches in the late 1880s. The outfit she was wearing was actually part of her school uniform, so officials didn't hold her to the accepted standard. By the early 1900s hats and bustles had disappeared and

tennis aprons became the fashion. This continued until pockets were sewn into women's apparel. Other trends such as bloomer outfits, stiff collars, leg-o'-mutton sleeves and sailor hats came and went.

In 1905, Californian May Sutton became the first American, male or female, to win Wimbledon. She made headlines by rolling up her sleeves during the match. She later played a match in a sleeveless, calf-length ensemble. May again challenged convention by donning one of her father's shirts during a match, claiming it provided her more freedom to move around the court. The heavy boning that reinforced the corsets often gouged the players. This was so commonplace that there was a rack in the Wimbledon dressing room, as late as 1914, where the blood-stained corsets could be hung up to dry.

Six-time Wimbledon champion Suzanne Lenglen generated a lot of press relative to her playing as well as her wardrobe choices for the court. She was keen on "spectacle" and helped to advance the popularity of the women's game. Her unorthodox behavior on and off the court made her a magnet for gossip, while her wardrobe often shocked the tennis world. Lenglen played a match in 1919 sans stockings and a petticoat. The absence of stockings had a surprising effect on the fashion of the sport. When the tops of the stocking no longer determined the length of the garment, tennis designers were free to experiment with the length of the skirts.

In 1920 Lenglen boldly appeared without a corset. Two years later she donned a low cut sleeveless dress made of silk,—clingy and filmy—closer to a ballet costume than athletic wear. She was the first to introduce brightly colored cardigans and hair bandeaus fastened with jeweled pins. Lenglen never failed to embellish her tennis ensembles with a fur coat, despite the soaring temperatures of summer! Lenglen's close friend and fellow player, Elizabeth Ryan, was quoted as saying "All women players should go to their knees in thankfulness to Suzanne for delivering them from the tyranny of corsets."

Helen Wills brought the golf-style visor to the game along with knee-length pleated skirts and stockings held up by garters. She credited her signature red sweater with giving her additional confidence. She wore two pairs of socks along with an extra layer of face powder to help with facial perspiration. In 1929 Billie Tapscott was the first player to forgo stockings at Wimbledon. Once hosiery was no longer an issue, skirts morphed into shorts, a much more reasonable wardrobe alternative for active players. Alice Marble's style created controversy when she introduced boyish shorts. She also debuted the jockey cap.

Wartime had an effect on the world of tennis. During World War II the matches that were played were mostly for exhibition, with proceeds going toward the war effort. There were restrictions on the amount of yardage allowed for clothing in general, and sportswear availability was limited in both the United States and Great Britain.

Couturier Theodore Tinling wore many hats in the sport of tennis. His most famous role, that of designer to the top female players of the "Golden Age of Tennis," overshadowed his contributions as player, umpire, commentator and historian of the game:

> Tinling experimented with fabric,
> color and form while outfitting the

most glamorous figures in women's tennis. He designed a dress with a colored border for Joy Gannon in her debut in 1947 at Wimbledon. This clearly violated the all-white dress rule and created a stir.

> A combination of short skirts and lace panties designed for California native Gertrude "Gussy" Moran in 1949 resulted in Tinling's being banned from the game. He was accused of putting vulgarity and sin into tennis. Following the incident, lace became a fashion staple in every aspect of the sport (Phillips D 254).

It took 33 years for Tinling to be reinstated as a liaison to the players at Wimbledon. His contribution to the tennis fashion revolution made him a highly influential force in the history of the sport.

Gussie Moran added gold braid to a dress she wore on the tournament held at Madison Square Garden in the 1950s. Pauline Betz sported a gold lamé tunic and apricot fur panties at that same event. Nancy Chaffee will be remembered for her divided skirts and shocking sharkskin ensemble she wore during that decade. Warm-up suits became fashionable in the mid–1960s. Prior to that, there had been no way to keep the legs warm before a match. Short socks were marketed to players at this time, but were not immediately popular. Many players felt the longer socks were more practical when playing on clay surfaces.

The last decades of the century saw the introduction of lace and nylon tennis dresses, polyester knits, stretch woven fabrics and kilted skirts as well as colorful outfits adorned with embroidery and rhinestones. Chris Evert was quite the trendsetter during the 1970s, wearing halter and sarong style dresses which included brilliantly colored geometric and floral patterns. By the 1980s tennis fashions included lycra body suits and backless tank tops. Hair beads, short shorts, denim bodysuits, and knee high boots pushed the clothing to the limit at the century's end.

By 2007, metallic gold dresses and leopard print ensembles no longer shocked the tennis community. Clothes had become news in the sport. Maria Sharapova called a news conference to announce her wardrobe prior to the U.S. Open that year. Separate outfits were created for her and unveiled in dramatic style on the rooftop of Rockefeller Center. These player endorsements translated into lucrative sales for the manufacturers.

The evolution of fashion in tennis was largely the result of innovations within the fabric industry coupled with creative designers and fearless players who were willing to test the limits of the tennis establishment. Today, the women's designer tennis apparel industry is a multimillion dollar business.

Credits

My husband's latest book, *Women Tennis Stars: Biographies and Records of Champions, 1800s to Today,* was published by Mc-Farland in 2009. This sourcebook includes career milestones and biographies of three dozen women who won Grand Slam events and achieved a certain level of prominence in the sport of tennis. He included women from the early years of the game as well as current players.

Since fashion was not his area of expertise, my husband asked if I would edit a chapter within his book titled "A Brief History of Women's Tennis Fashion." It was through this process that I learned the evolution of women in the sport and the important part that fashion played in this transition. The irony of attempting to play the sport in the clothing prevalent in Victorian times was not lost on me. I became fascinated with the many players who challenged the dictates of existing mores, took bold chances, and advanced the cause for women athletes.

This display is dedicated to the lady pioneers of the game of tennis.

Assembling the Display

1. The background of the display was lined with a forest green felt. The framed poster of *The Tennis Party* by Sir John Lavery was positioned in the center of the case. This is available at http://www.allposters.com. The font Century School sized at 375 was used for the word *Ladies.* MS Mincho sized at 250 bold was used for the other three words. The *o* in court was a tennis ball sliced in half.

2. On the top left of the display was a document containing a synopsis of the history of women's tennis from 1873 to 1950 taken from the introduction to this display. Under that was this quote by Martina Navratilova: "I think the key is for women not to set any limits."

These were printed on off white card stock and mounted on gold poster board

3. On the top right was series of photos of top female players: Justine Henin, Monica Seles, Chris Evert and Serena Williams. The text continued the fashion retrospective from 1950 up to the present day.

Items on the right were printed and mounted like those on the left.

4. On the base of the display was a rectangular block of Styrofoam covered in green felt. A loving cup was centered on the form. Two vintage tennis racquets and yellow silk flowers flanked the cup. The book *Tennis: Nostalgia* by Christopher Dunkley was open to a photo of Suzanne Lenglen. On top of that was a postcard with a photo of 19th century players at the Staten Island Cricket & Tennis Club circa 1885. To the right of that is an antique racquet cover and a can of tennis balls. Loose balls were interspersed throughout the books.

Books featured in the display are *We Have Come a Long Way: The Story of Women's Tennis* by Billy Jean King with Cynthia Starr, *Venus and Serena Williams: A Biography* by Jacqueline Edmondson, *Top 10 Women Tennis Players* by Denis J. Harrington, *Beyond Center Court: My Story* by Tracy Austin with Christine Brennan, *Martina: The Lives and Times of Martina Navratilova* by Adrianne Blue, *Tennis: Playing the Game* by Christopher Dunkley.

Bigger and Better

In my first book, *Great Displays for Your Library Step by Step,*

I mounted a display titled "Game, Set, Match." This arrangement would work for women's tennis as well, with a few additions, such as a ladies' visor, clothing, photos or shoes.

Line your case with green fabric, the color associated with the sport. If your space permits, place a sports net on the base or pinned to the background to add some texture. Stack some tennis ball cans to create a focal point, or fill a caddie and use that, on its side if need be. Select a poster or magazine cover featuring one of the early players of the sport. You can purchase these types of items from Websites such as http://store.tennisfame.com/store/xcart/customer/home.php; *http://www.1920s-fashions.co.uk/tennis.htm*; *http://www.gasolinealleyantiques.com/sport*

s/sports.htm#TENNIS; or *http://www.all posters.com* (select "tennis art" as your subject).

Feature strawberries in glassware to symbolize the specialty dish at Wimbledon. Add an English flag if you are featuring this British venue, or one of the other country's flags if you are focusing on the French or Australian opens. Use all four flags (U.S. included) if you are doing the entire Grand Slam series.

Gutsy Girls

Cautious, careful people always casting about to preserve their reputation or social standards never can bring about reform. Those who are really in earnest are willing to be anything or nothing in the world's estimation, and publicly and privately, in season and out, avow their sympathies with despised ideas and their advocates and bear the consequences.
—Susan B. Anthony

WANTED: Intelligent, strong-minded females, left or right brained. They may be artistic, athletic, innovative or adventurous. They must be progressive thinkers, industrious and emotionally stable individuals. The task at hand? To move the nation forward in the areas of politics, economics, science, education, sports and the arts.

This display is dedicated to the notable women and gutsy girls who had the right stuff to make history in America by living a courageous life, going the extra mile and truly making a difference in the well-being of society. Many sources were consulted when I was deciding which women to feature in this display that celebrated 19th and 20th century American women of importance. Some names appeared on virtually each and every list on the topic. These names were Susan B. Anthony, Eleanor Roosevelt, Harriet Tubman, Margaret Mead, Elizabeth Cady Stanton, Sojourner Truth, Rachel Carson and Jane Addams. Athletes such as Althea Gibson, Babe Didrickson Zaharias, Billie Jean King and Wilma Rudolph were included on others. Dancer and choreographer Martha Graham and actresses Katharine Hepburn, Helen Hayes and Shirley Temple frequently appeared on lists of outstanding women in the performing arts.

Other notable women worthy of inclusion in a celebration of women follow:

LOUISA MAY ALCOTT (1832–1888)

This Pennsylvania-born author produced the first literature for the mass market of juvenile girls in the 19th century. Her most popular book, *Little Women,* was just one of 270 works that she published during her lifetime. Her informal education was provided first by her father, and then continued by family friends such as Henry David Thoreau, Ralph Waldo Emerson and the Rev. Theodore Parker. Alcott served as a nurse in the Civil War. She parlayed her wartime experiences into a novel titled *Hospital Sketches*, which was published in 1863. Alcott cared for her demanding father throughout her adult life and died two days after his demise.

CLARA BARTON (1821–1912)

Barton got involved with tending to the needy when she treated wounded Union soldiers during the Civil War. She was named the Angel of the Battlefield for the role she played in the Battle of Antietam. She later founded, and was the first president of, the American Red Cross.

ELIZABETH BLACKWELL (1821–1910)

Born in England, Blackwell became a naturalized citizen and the first American woman awarded a medical degree. She attended Geneva Medical College in New York

Gutsy Girls. Install this display in March for Women's History Month. Include those female pioneers who blazed a trail throughout history.

after she was rejected by all the major medical schools in the nation strictly because of her gender. Dr. Blackwell later founded a women's medical college to provide opportunities for other women to become physicians.

ELLA FITZGERALD (1918–1996)

Considered one of the greatest jazz singers of all time, Virginia-born Ella Fitzgerald was the winner of a total of 12 Grammy awards and was awarded the Presidential Medal of Freedom. Her lucid intonation and broad range made her a top jazz singer. Fitzgerald's long battle with diabetes left her blind and resulted in the loss of both of her legs two years prior to her death.

LADONNA HARRIS (BORN 1931)

Harris is the president and founder of Americans for Indian Opportunity, a national multi-tribal organization devoted to developing the economic opportunities and resources of Indians. Raised by her grandparents with traditional Comanche values, Harris was politically active all her life. She crusaded for the rights of children, women and the mentally ill as well as the elimination of poverty and discrimination in the Native American community.

GRACE HOPPER (1906–1992)

A Vassar graduate in mathematics and physics, Hopper went on to earn a masters and a PhD from Yale University while on the faculty at Vassar. A technology trailblazer, she worked on Mark I, which was the first large-scale computer and the precursor of electronic computers. A naval reservist who reached the rank of rear admiral, Hopper designed naval applications for COBOL, one of the first easy-to-use computer languages. She was also instrumental in developing UNIVAC 1, the first electronic computer.

SHIRLEY JACKSON (BORN 1946)

Jackson is the former head of the U.S. Nuclear Regulatory Commission, where she reaffirmed the agency's commitment to public health and safety. She is the first female African American to receive a PhD from MIT. Dr. Jackson's outstanding leadership in education, science, and public policy demonstrates the capability of women to be leaders in the field of science and technology.

HELEN KELLER (1880–1968)

A devastating childhood disease left Keller deaf, mute, and blind. She became an expert author and much sought after lecturer who traveled around the globe educating audiences on behalf of others with disabilities. She raised money for many organizations at home and abroad. Keller received the coveted Presidential Medal of Freedom, America's highest civilian award, in 1964.

ROSA LOUISE MCCAULEY PARKS (1913–2005)

When she refused to give up her seat to a white person on a crowded bus, Rosa Parks set in motion the Montgomery bus boycott, which became a cornerstone of the civil rights movement. She was arrested and fined for violating a city ordinance, but her single act of defiance began a movement that ended legal segregation in America and made her an inspiration to freedom-loving people everywhere. She was a strong advocate for human rights issues and was the recipient of both the Presidential Medal of Freedom (1996) and the Congressional Gold Medal (1999).

SACAGAWEA (1787–1812)

Born to the Shoshone tribe, a pregnant Sacagawea became the interpreter for Lewis and Clark during the U.S. government's first exploration of the Northwest. Lewis and Clark believed that her knowledge of the Shoshone language would be a necessity on their journey. Sacagawea's role was to help negotiate safe and peaceful passages through tribal lands. Her enduring contribution to the nation was noted when she was featured on a highly collectable dollar coin issued by the U.S. Mint 2000.

MARGARET SANGER (1879–1966)

Margaret Louise Higgins Sanger was the founder of the birth control movement in the United States. In her work as a nurse with poor women on the Lower East Side of New York, Sanger became aware of the effects of both unplanned and unwelcome pregnancies. Her mother's health had deteriorated over the years as she bore a total of eleven children. Sanger believed in the availability of birth control and its importance to women's lives and women's health. Birth control is a term she's credited with coining.

In 1927 she helped organize the first World Population Conference in Geneva. In 1942 Sanger helped form what would later be known as the Planned Parenthood Federation of America.

VICTORIA WOODHULL (1838–1927)

Woodhull was the first woman to be nominated and actively campaign for the U.S. presidency, fifty years before women earned the right to vote. She was nominated by the Women's National Equal Rights Party with abolitionist and reformer Frederick Douglass as her running mate. Vilified by many in the 19th century, Woodhull was considered a brilliant orator and ran on a platform of social and political reform while espousing the doctrine of free love. She was among several leaders of the suffrage movement. Woodhull became the lover of widowed railroad magnate Commodore Cornelius Vanderbilt, age 76. As a result of that relationship, Woodhull and her sister gained much financial expertise and became the first two females to establish a banking and brokerage firm on Wall Street.

Credits

Each year someone is certain to remind me that March is Women in History month. Since I have worked at a women's college for twenty plus years, I have given this subject quite a bit of thought and have mounted many displays on notable women. One display, titled "Women Who Dared," included pioneers in many fields and received some positive feedback.

I am always on the lookout for new faces to include in future displays celebrating contemporary women. I keep a file in my desk with possible candidates and go through them every year to see if I can come up with a new angle. I have mounted displays, featuring women titled "Film Legends," "Pioneering Women," "Ladies First (First Ladies)" and "Mothers & Daughters." I have also featured displays on Pocahontas, Mary Shelly, Mary Cassatt, Sylvia Plath, Zelda

Fitzgerald and children's illustrator and Cedar Crest College alum Jane Dyer.

Assembling the Display

1. The black and white font Castellar sized at 425 was used to create the title "Gutsy Girls." This was printed on white card stock and attached to the gray felt with pins and pulled forward.

Above that was this quote by Susan B. Anthony:

> The day will come when men will recognize woman as his peer, not only at the fireside, but in councils of the nation. Then, and not until then, will there be the perfect comradeship, the ideal union between the sexes that shall result in the highest development of the race.

This was printed on white card stock and mounted on black poster board. Above and to the left of the quote was a white dove in flight with a green olive branch. To the right were three symbols of the female. Both of these images were found through Google image searches and were printed on white card stock. The symbol for woman was traced onto black poster board. All were attached with pins and pulled forward. The image of the three women in profile was drawn on black and white poster board with inspiration from silhouettes found online. These were glued together, attached with pins and pulled forward. Black poster board was cut into 18" strips and pinned on the left and right of the background.

2. On the top left was a biography of Anna Eleanor Roosevelt, wife of FDR. This can be found if you visit *http://www.fdrli brary.marist.edu/erbio.html*. Under that was a color photocopy of the April 17, 1939, issue of *Time* magazine on which Eleanor Roosevelt was pictured. This is also available through an online image search. Under that was a quote by Katharine Hepburn:

> Acting is the most minor of gifts. After all, Shirley Temple could do it when she was four.

Items on the left were printed on white card stock and mounted on black and silver poster board.

3. On the top right was a quote by anthropologist Ruth Benedict:

> I long to speak out about the inspiration that comes to me from the lives of strong women. They make of their lives a Great Adventure.

Under that was print of a stained glass window featuring Susan B. Anthony with the inscription *Failure Is Impossible*. To view an image of this window visit *http://winningth evote.org/HJeffreys1-big.html*. Next was a biography of Susan B. Anthony that can be found if you visit *http://www.susanbantho nyhouse.org/biography.shtml*.

Items on the right were printed and mounted as those on the left.

4. On the base of the display was information about the dancer Martha Graham. This can be found if you visit *http://www. pbs.org/wnet/americanmasters/episodes/ martha-graham/about–the-dancer/497/*.

Flanking that were the following quotes. The first is by Rachel Carson:

> We stand now where two roads diverge. But unlike the roads in Robert Frost's familiar poem, they are not equally fair. The road we have long been traveling is deceptively easy, a smooth superhighway on which we progress with great speed, but at its end lies disaster. The other fork of the road—the one "less traveled by"—offers our last, our only chance to reach a destination that assures the preservation of the earth.

The other quote is by the famed anthropologist Margaret Mead:

> Never doubt that a small group of thoughtful committed citizens can change the world. Indeed, it is the only thing that ever has.

Books featured in the display are *Margaret Mead, a Life* by Jane Howard, *Rabble Rousers: Twenty Women Who Made a Difference* by Cheryl Harness, *Eleanor Roosevelt* by Blanche Cook, *So Much to Be Done: Women Settlers on the Mining and Ranching Frontier* by Ruth Moynihan, *Amelia Earhart : A Biography* by Doris Rich, *The Story of Harriet Tubman* by Kate McMullan, *Rachel Carson: Witness for Nature* by Linda J. Lear, The *Education of Jane Addams* by Victoria Bissell

Brown, *Blood Memory* by Martha Graham, and *Katharine Hepburn* by Barbara Leaming.

Yellow silk daisies were interspersed onto the display base, which was lined in gray felt.

Bigger and Better

There are two comprehensive posters titled "Women Who Dared" which are available through the Library of Congress at this site: http://www.loc.gov/shop/index.php?action=cCatalog.showItem&cid=16&scid=234&iid=939.

Either of these would be an easy solution and provide a focal point for your display.

You might decide to focus on "Women in Science," "Women in Flight," "Literary Women," "Women Artists," "Lady Politicians" or "Women in Music." The list and possibilities goes on.

Consider mounting a display on "Women in the Civil War." Unbeknownst to many people, American women served in combat and actually played a much more vital part in this combat than has been recognized historically. Visit these sites for background information of this topic: http://library.duke.edu/specialcollections/bingham/guides/cwdocs.html and http://www.hallrichard.com/civilwomen.htm.

Refer to the book *Women Who Dared* by Alison Auch for comprehensive information on three formidable American women you may want to include in a display of this nature.

4 Pure Whimsy

Shore Summer Reads

Always read something that will make you look good if you die in the middle of it.—P.J. O'Rourke

The books of summer are easy to digest and are calculated to be read while in flight or reclining poolside with beverage in hand. Reassuring, happy endings are preferred for books read on vacation. Couples in summer fiction ultimately find their way to the chapel, despite some doubt created mid–story. Literary classics they are not. The books you tote to the beach aren't the volumes you proudly display on your bookshelves to impress. It's summer time, and it's just too hot for Tolstoy!

Summer readers crave escape. They covet a story that transports them to exotic venues. These readers want to be consoled, moved and entertained, and sometimes even terrified! The authors who pen these novels probably aren't among those whose works are included on the Books of the Century lists. However, they are the writers who have an ease of style and a genuine gift of storytelling. These authors know how to make a connection with readers and have written on relatable topics in language with which the reader can identify. These best-selling writers are capable of pulling more than a few heartstrings, and their bank accounts reflect the mastery of their craft as well as their overall success in the publishing arena.

Popular fiction writers may employ some tricks to keep you reading. James Patterson writes the three-page chapter to insure that his novels become page turners. Recurring characters draw the readers back to the author in many popular serialized works by Agatha Christie and contemporary writers such as Janet Evanovich and Sue Grafton.

Perennial best seller Jodi Picoult creates engrossing family dramas, spiced with her trademark blend of medicine and law with a touch of romance. Mary Higgins Clark begins her story with the crime and entices the reader to care enough to continue reading to discover not only the who but also the why. David Baldacci is popular for his riveting, fast-paced dramas pitting corrupt killers against innocent victims. Stephenie Meyer combined the perennial and disparate interests of the teen reader—romance and the vampire—to create an amazingly popular book series and film franchise.

A relatively new genre with great appeal for beach readers has been termed "chick lit." It originated in Great Britain but found a great following in the United States Some may consider this genre simply "fluff" or vapid prose, but it certainly has a following and is worth considering here. Chick lit is primarily written by women for women and has definitely evolved over time. Main characters range in age from early twenties to late sixties.

Some chick lit authors employ the first person narrative, while others include multiple viewpoints. The plots touch upon commonplace life events, including love, relationships, issues in the workplace and those regarding weight and health, addiction and more. The tone of the book is generally light, personal and entertaining. The addition of humor is really what separates this genre from mainstream women's fiction.

It is relatively common for college students to experience a burnout as they complete the requirements for their undergraduate degree. After years of rigorous demands on their time, reading of any sort has virtually no appeal. There are some actual guidelines, however, that can be followed which will generate a renewed interest in reading.

First, have confidence that a book must win you over. You don't have to give it a chance if you aren't making a connection. Try reading the front and back covers for a

Shore Summer Reads. A brilliant summer sun shines on a host of books destined for the beach. Shells, rocks and a starfish help to create a sense of the ocean's edge

description of plot, genre and some questions that pique your interest. Skim a few pages to assess the writing style and the pace of the story. Evaluate the length of descriptions, the amount of dialogue and narration. Is the language compelling? Does the setting entice? Do you have compassion about the characters? What did reviewers think? Once you have made these assessments, you'll know if this is a good literary fit for you.

Remember that there are comprehensive book reviews online and in newspapers and magazines that help you make good choices. Books, like movies and records, are nominated for awards annually. Visit these sites for award winners that just might fill the bill for summer reading: http://www.indiebook awards.com/2009_winners_and_finalists. php; http://www.ala.org/ala/mgrps/divs/alsc /awardsgrants/bookmedia/2009medaward win.cfm; http://nautilusbookawards.com/ 2009_GOLD_AWARD_WINNERS.html; and http://www.nationalbook.org.

Get a copy of *Between the Covers: The Book Babes' Guide to a Woman's Reading Pleasures* by Margo Hammond and Ellen Heltzel. These authors have compiled a book that has something for every mood and every taste and will be of great help to you in your display about great beach books. Peter Boxall has edited a book entitled *1,000 Books You Must Read Before You Die*. He contends that the compilation of that book taught him how contagious the love of books is, and how much excitement, friendship and pleasure they produce.

J.D. Salinger summed up what comprised a terrific read in *The Catcher in the Rye,* his debut novel about the eternal teenage experience of alienation. Protagonist Holden Caulfield stated that the test of a great book was whether, once you finished it, you wished that the author was a dear friend whom you could call at home. Hopefully, your books of summer will have you reaching for your mobile phone!

Credits

There is a certain mentality prevalent among those of us who live near the coast. We find it imperative to live within striking distance of the ocean. Even if trips to the beach are, in reality, relatively rare we need to know that it is possible to get there within a three-hour time frame.

As a native of Philadelphia, I spent at least a few days each year on the New Jersey Coast—family friendly Ocean City being the resort of choice. When my children were young and we lived in the Annapolis area, it was Ocean City, Maryland, that was our beach destination. In the summer between my freshman and sophomore years of college, and before gambling was legalized, I worked at the Colton Manor Hotel in Atlantic City with some close high school friends. As wait staff we were scheduled for the lunch and dinner shifts, which left the entire afternoon free for relaxing on the beach!

Summer reading was something we savored. Those lightweight novels reigned supreme! With four young adult women packed into a single bedroom in a boardinghouse by the sea, escape (of any kind!) was the operative word! Piles of paperbacks were circulated among us, toted to the beach, and read while impressive tans were being developed.

With fond memories of beaches, boardwalks and the best of times, I give you "Shore Summer Reads!"

Assembling the Display

1. The font Goudy Stout, sized at 200, was selected for the title "Shore Summer Reads." This was printed on card stock and traced onto red poster board then mounted on black felt . The letters were attached with pins and pulled forward. Inspiration for the sun design was found through a Google image search. This was created by using gold poster board for the center circle and silver for the rays. Heat bursts were created using red poster board. The facial features of the sun were drawn on black poster board, cut out and glued in place. The sun was attached with pins and pulled forward.

A beach fence was created using yellow poster board sized at 14"h×1"w. Gray and black chalks were applied to create a weathered effect. A string was woven through and pinned to the background. The sign "To the

Beach" was created in word using the font Comic Sans MS sized at 48. The arrow was found under "shapes" in MS Word and inserted in the document. The background color of the sign was red and the letters and arrow were white. Signs like this can easily be found with an online image search.

2. On the top left was a list of current paperback best sellers which is available online. Under that was a "Danger, Surf at Your Own Risk" sign which can be found at this site: http://hawaiiandays.com/LWS/pix/lws_vintage_tin_signs/surfing_beach/big/V62.gif.

Last was a document titled "Reading for Pleasure" which can be found if you visit http://www.pointsincase.com/articles/non readers_guide.htm. Clip art of a book with sunglasses was inserted in the top of the document.

Items on the left were printed on card stock and attached to red or black poster board.

3. On the top right was a list of hardback bestsellers. Current lists can be found online. Under that was a surfer crossing sign which can be found if you do a Google image search using those terms. Last was a document titled "Beach Books: When It's Too Hot for Dostoevsky." This was an annotated list of beach books that I created from personal favorites.

Items on the right were printed and mounted like those on the left.

4. Rocks of various colors and size, shells and starfish along with a Hawaiian lei were interspersed among the books.

Books featured on the base of the display were *The Divide* by Nicholas Evans, *Beach Road* by James Patterson, *True Believer* by Nicholas Sparks, *Close to Shore: A True Story of Terror in an Age of Innocence* by Michael Capuzzo, *Tangerine Dream* by Ken Douglas and Jack Stewart, *The Big Book of Summer Love* by Red Fox and *Summer Country* by Marcia Willet. Of course, you will want to find more current works by these authors for your current display on "Shore Summer Reads."

Bigger and Better

You might want to add a cooler with additional popular books if your display area permits. If you have the space for a surf or boogie board, include that along with some sea gulls flying among some clouds.

Why not call your display "Just Another Day in Paradise" and frame your signage in colorful leis. Create an alluring beach scene complete with umbrella, bucket, shovel, sand, hammock and palm tree. Add some of the following: a picnic basket, some artificial fruit, beverages, sunglasses, seashells, grasses, sand crabs, beach towel, flip-flops, suntan oil and some popular fiction and you are on your way! If space permits, place a sailboat and a small island in the distance and add a brilliant sun. Be sure to include this quote by Jorge Luis Borges: "I have always imagined that Paradise will be a kind of library."

Get your hands on the July 13, 2009, edition of *Newsweek*. The cover is titled "What to Read Now" and the articles give much insight into the hows and the whys of selecting good reads. One article by David Gates suggests that you find refuge by revisiting comforting, familiar atmospheres by rereading old favorites.

See my first book, *Great Displays for Your Library Step by Step* for instructions on how to create a palm tree (p. 217) for your beach display and another complete idea for summer reading for pleasure titled "Hot Nights, Cool Reads" on page 57. For a related idea for a display by the sea, see page 177 for "Sailor's Tales."

and the Winner is...

Auto racing, bull fighting, and mountain climbing are the only real sports ... all others are games. —Ernest Hemingway

The 19th century was the age of machine tools—tools that made tools—machines able to create parts for other machines. That century saw the invention of the steam engine, usable electricity and the telephone as well as the assembly line, which allowed for the factory production of consumer goods. These technologies had a profound effect on daily life.

Practical inventions such as the stethoscope, telephone, typewriter and sewing machine all came of age during the 19th century. But the invention that ultimately captured the hearts and imagination of a nation was the automobile. Freedom was its promise. In theory, the person behind the wheel of the car could travel anywhere at any time. The love affair born of that invention continues to this day.

To that special breed of automobile enthusiasts, the daredevils and the dreamers, the allure of the car was simple—speed. From the onset of the invention, there were drivers eager and willing to risk their lives pushing these machines to their utmost capacity. Automobile racing dates back to the invention of the first petrol-fuelled autos in the latter part of the 19th century. The Paris magazine *Le Petit Journal* organized the world's first

auto race in 1894. This competition was a reliability test and the course was from Paris to Rouen, a distance of about 80 km (50 miles). The winner clocked an average speed of 24.15 kph. The event was an immediate success and generated a great deal of press.

Although much credit is attributed to Henry Ford for the development of the car in the U.S., the first automobile actually produced here was designed by two brothers with a background in bicycle mechanics and a passion for innovation. Charles and Frank Duryea built and tested their first car on the public streets of Springfield, Massachusetts, in 1893. It was equipped with a one-cylinder gasoline engine and a three-speed transmission mounted on a used horse carriage. The brothers were the first to incorporate an American business for the sole purpose of building automobiles for sale to the public.

The following year, Frank developed a car with an impressive two-cylinder engine. It was this vehicle that took part in America's first automobile race. Sponsored by the *Chicago Times Herald,* the race took place in snowy conditions over a 10 hour period on a 54 mile stretch of road from Chicago to Evanston, Illinois, and back on Thanksgiving Day 1895.

There were five entrants in addition to the Duryea vehicle—two electric cars and three gasoline powered German Benz machines. Frank Duryea won the race and the $2,000 prize, which would be worth about $49,500 in today's economy. His journey included numerous breakdowns and repairs and his average speed was 7.3 mph. The only other car that made it to the finish line was the Benz, sponsored by H. Mueller Company of Decatur, Illinois. It was driven by the race umpire, engineer Charles B. King, as the owner/driver had collapsed from fatigue!

International racing began after James Gordon Bennett, owner of the *New York Herald*, created a competition. He offered a trophy to be competed for annually by national automobile clubs. They would race three cars, each of which would have been built in parts made in the respective countries. The unwillingness of French manufacturers to enter only three vehicles led to their boycott of the Bennett Trophy Race in 1906 and the establishment of the first French Grand Prix Race at Le Mans.

In the early days of racing, both in the U.S. and in Europe, cars in competition were usually prototypes of the upcoming year's models. After World War I, racing became too specialized for the use of production cars, though, on occasion, high-performance cars had their bodies stripped and were outfitted with special seats, fuel tanks and tires. For more information about America's first automobile race visit http://inventors.about.com/od/dstartinventors/a/DuryeaBrothers.htm.

As the sport of auto racing evolved, so too did the vehicle. Automobile designers built lighter, more aerodynamic cars, which were packed with superchargers. The performance of a race car is a function of engine power plus aerodynamics plus tire grip capacity. Modern auto racing encompasses a broad spectrum of vehicles which includes rally cars, stock cars, production cars and funny cars, all of which race under their own unique rules and specifications.

Racing is a thrill: In its simplest form—beating everyone to the finish line—to the more complex question of just how you beat all the other competitors to the finish line. The answers to these and other questions can

be found in Diandra Leslie-Pelecky's book *The Physics of NASCAR: How to Make Steel + Gas + Rubber = Speed.*

and the Winner is... Race cars make their way to the finish line in this display celebrating the evolution of the automobile and the advent of car racing. Automotive cleaning products are interspersed among the books, miniature Corvette and trophy.

Racing

Stock car racing is a form of auto racing found primarily in the United States, Canada, New Zealand, Great Britain and Brazil. Races are run on oval tracks which measure about one quarter mile to 2.66 miles in length. Some take place on road courses. The National Association for Stock Car Auto Racing (NASCAR) is the world's largest governing body for stock car racing. Its Sprint Cup Series is considered the premier series of the sport.

Most of today's stock cars have a superficial resemblance to standard American family sedans. However, they are actually racing machines which must adhere to a strict set of regulations governing the car design. These standards ensure that the chassis, suspension and engine are identical on all vehicles. The result of these regulations is that stock car racers are technologically less sophisticated than standard cars on the road today.

Prior to relocating to Washington, D.C., Bill France, Sr., had owned a service station and promoted, and sometimes drove in, races held on the famed beach-road courses of Daytona Beach. The strong-willed and ambitious France, who had many skeptics, believed that a sanctioning body was critical to the future success of the sport and he founded the family-owned and operated business titled NASCAR in 1947.

Things came together quickly. The first NASCAR-sanctioned race was held on Daytona's beach course on February 15, 1948, just two months after the organizational meeting held at the Streamline Hotel. Red Byron, a stock car legend from Atlanta, won the event in his modified Ford. On February 21, 1948, the National Association for Stock Car Auto Racing was incorporated.

Plans began immediately to find ways to bring bigger, faster races to larger crowds. About a year later, the country's first asphalt superspeedway, Darlington Raceway in South Carolina, opened its doors for the new division. The new racing series was off to a great start and was deemed an instant success. Today, it is one of the most watched television sports.

Indy car racing is sometimes used to describe championship open wheel auto racing in the U.S. The Indy car name was the result of the genre's link to the Indianapolis 500 Mile Race. According to Indy 500 historian Donald Davidson, founder Carl Fisher decided seven hours would be the right amount of time for fans to spend at the speedway and have time to return home.

Given the speeds of the cars at the time, seven hours was in the neighborhood of 500 miles. Entry blanks for the 500-mile race were sent out and Fisher and his partners awaited their response. A total of 46 were received, far more than most races were drawing. Due to eliminations, 40 cars started the race. A multi-car accident on the main straightaway caused the volunteer scoring panel to dash to safety. So, for several laps, no one was scoring the action. Amid protests, a gleeful Ray Harroun was declared the winner. However, due to the circumstances, the results of the race were in question. Harroun had come out of retirement specifically to participate in the Indy 500 and immediately announced his return to retirement upon winning. His legacy in the sport had been established. The Indy 500 race remains the most popular open-wheel competition in North America.

Touring car racing is a general term for a number of distinct auto racing competitions which involve heavily modified street cars. It is notably popular in Britain, Germany, Scandanavia and Australia. Performed by professional drivers, it can be considered a closed-circuit, sponsored, legal form of street racing. Rules vary from country to country. Most series require a standard body shell, but virtually every other component is allowed to be heavily modified for racing. Aerodynamic aids are often added to the front and rear of the cars.

As the automobile continues to morph via modern technology, no doubt the interest in speed and competition will continue to grow. The colorful sport of auto racing, with its bevy of popular drivers and huge fan following, is definitely here to stay.

Credits

My husband's teenage fantasy was fulfilled with the purchase of a 1995 Polo Green Metallic Corvette in the spring of 2007.

Although it was not originally judged a "show car" per se, Denny has effectively labored over the car's interior and exterior for extended periods of time. Consequently, he has entered competitions and managed to acquire a trophy or two as well as some notoriety among fellow members of the Allentown Area Corvette Club. With this recently acquired sports car came a new identity and a renewed interest in everything automotive–especially race car driver Denny Hamlin and NASCAR Sprint Cup Series! All of the items featured in the display are Denny's.

As the spouse of a NASCAR enthusiast, I have learned to ignore the hours of droning that emanates from the TV when a Sprint Cup race is televised. However, come those final laps, I'm there–just waiting for the checkered flag to signal the winning driver and watch as the crowd goes wild!

Assembling the Display

1. The font Cooper Black italicized, sized at 230, was used to create the lower case letters of the title. The word *winner* was created using the same font sized at 250. These words were printed on card stock. The letters were then traced onto white poster board then attached with pins to the red felt background.

The racetrack was inspired by a graphic found online. This was drawn onto black poster board and attached with pins. The race cars were found through a Google image search using "overhead view Porsche." The image was enlarged to three different sizes and traced onto green, yellow and red poster board. The numbers were printed on white card stock and glued to black circles the size of a quarter for the larger cars and a nickel for the smallest one. Windshields were cut from a transparency. Tires and windshield trim were cut from silver poster board. Front headlights were cut from white poster board and back headlights from red or orange poster board. The outline of the interior of the car was traced onto black poster board and glued onto the base of the car. The cars were attached with pins and pulled forward. The finish line was a 1¼" piece of white poster board contoured to fit the track.

A black and white checkered flag design was found through a Google image search using "racing flag" and enlarged on the photocopier. The white checks were traced onto white poster board and glued onto the flag of black poster board. The flag was attached with pins and pulled forward. A 2½" border of black and white checks was made from poster board and glued to the bottom of the racetrack.

On the shelf above the graphic was a Millennium Yellow model C-5 Corvette coupe, a battery charging system, a tin of wadding polish, a wrench and spark plug and a tube of air filter sealing grease. These were grouped on the front of the shelf. Behind were the following books: *Jeff Gordon: Racing Back to the Front–My Memoir* by Jeff Gordon with Steve Eubanks, *Go Ahead–Take the Wheel: Road Racing on Your Budget* and *True Speed: My Racing Life* by Tony Stewart.

2. On the top left was a synopsis of the history of auto racing taken from the information in this chapter. Under that was the quote by Dale Earnhardt, Sr.:

> You win some, lose some, and wreck some.

Next was a document with brief biographies of notable race car drivers. The four drivers included were A.J. Foyt, Mario Andretti, Dale Earnhardt, Sr., and Jeff Gordon. Racing clipart was inserted in the top left of the document.

The last item was a quote by Darrell Waltrip:

> If you don't cheat, you look like an idiot; if you cheat and don't get caught, you look like a hero; if you cheat and get caught, you look like a dope. Put me where I belong.

Items on the left were printed on white card stock and mounted on red, black and/or silver poster board.

3. On the top right was a document titled Racing Flags, which was created using information which is available if you visit http://flagspot.net/flags/xf-auto.html. Images of racing flags found at that site were inserted into the document. Under that was the quote by Ernest Hemingway that introduced this display.

Next was a document titled "Racing," which gave brief descriptions of stock car, NASCAR, Indy and touring car racing. Clipart of a racing flag was inserted on the top right of the document. Last was a pit pass printed on white card stock. This can be found if you visit http://www.nascarpartydecorations.com /balloo16.jpg.

Items on the right were printed and mounted like those on the left.

4. On the base of the display was a trophy from an auto show and a NASCAR cap with the FEDEX logo.

Books featured on the base of the display were *The Driver: My Dangerous Pursuit of Speed and Truth in the Outlaw Racing World* by Alexander Roy, *I Remember Dale Earnhardt* by Tony Gilllispie, *Hard Driving, the Wendell Scott Story: The American Odyssey of NASCAR'S First Black Driver* by Brian Donovan and *The Physics of NASCAR: How to Make Steel + Gas + Rubber = Speed* by Diandra Leslie Pelecky.

Bigger and Better

Should your space be larger, you could make an entire track and add additional cars and other racing flags which can be found if you visit http://www.usflags.com Use real flags if you have access to them. Add oil cans, ratchets, sockets and other auto specialty tools, keys, a license plate, gloves, and specialty towels. A toy racetrack could also be used as the focal point of your display.

Instead of just a racetrack, you could use an eye-catching graphic of a steering wheel made up of racing flags which can be found if you visit http://www.istockphoto.com/file_ thumbview_approve/2442433/2/istockphoto _2442433-auto-racing-flags.jpg. Create a racetrack and place it in front of the wheel. Title your display "Take the Wheel" or "On Course!"

If you are interested in mounting a display strictly on accomplishments of the 19th century, consider including some of the inventions of that era such as the raincoat, modern matches, the battery, gas lighting, the soda fountain, the reaper, rubber vulcanization, the blueprint, the stapler, the bicycle, antisepsis, and Braille printing.

For another sports display idea see "Game, Set, Match!" on page 180 of my first book, *Great Displays for Your Library Step by Step*.

The Jersey Shore

Summer afternoons, summer afternoons ... the two most beautiful words in the English language. – Henry James (1843–1916)

Although modest in size, the state of New Jersey ranks ninth in the nation in population—the highest density of any state. Its proximity to both New York City and Philadelphia account for much of its desirability. New Jersey is a leading industrial center, a key transportation corridor and a major playground for tourists.

The Jersey Shore is a term used in the mid–Atlantic region of the U.S. to refer to both the Atlantic coast of New Jersey and the adjacent resort and residential communities. The shoreline of the New Jersey coast stretches more than 127 miles, with approximately 31 miles of boardwalks lying along this stretch.

The common denominator that connects the string of beach communities in coastal New Jersey is the Atlantic Ocean—with its undulating waves, gently inclined beaches, white sand and balmy breezes. Each resort town has its own particular character, from bustling Atlantic City with its high rise hotels and high rollers to tranquil, noncommercial Spring Lake, which offers an unhurried atmosphere of gracious living.

Ocean City is a popular destination for thousands of vacationers coming to the Garden State each year. Across the bay from Longport, it stands alone on an island eight miles in length. Originally a rugged, sandy clump of earth jutting into the Atlantic with overgrown bayberry, cedar trees and shrubs, it was home to wild cattle and hogs and a

The Jersey Shore. Figures dressed in vintage attire are featured in this display on the history of Ocean City, New Jersey. A lifeguard stand and miniature dock sit atop a base of rocks and sand.

true hunters' haven. Named Peck's Beach, after whaler John Peck, the island was also used by mainland farmers to graze their cattle.

Ocean City was founded in 1879 by Methodist ministers. The clergymen hoped that this would be the site the Lord had chosen for them to establish a Christian seaside resort and camp meeting ground. The founders imagined a colony physically separated from the worldly society of the mainland by nature. The concern for the quality of life possible in this new community was well founded. The wealthy coastal town of Long Branch, New Jersey, less than 80 miles north of Ocean City, had garnered quite a bit of notoriety by permitting gambling halls, a race track and even prostitution.

The Ocean City Association was incorporated in October 1879 and legally acquired title to all of the property on the island. The organization immediately attached its Sabbath and temperance restrictions to the deeds. New and old property owners had to accept restrictions prohibiting the production and sale of alcohol and barring all commercial establishments from operating on Sunday.

The fledgling resort experienced rapid and immediate growth. Within a year three dozen dwellings were built, along with the Brighton Hotel, 10 private stables and 2 public bathhouses. Extensive street and railroad development began, the first newspaper went to press and arrangements were made to establish a post office.

The founding clergymen were well pleased with their venture and attributed much of its success to divine providence. Founder Reverend William B. Wood expressed these sentiments about his hopes for Ocean City: "Our great leading objects have been moral and religious—not secular. If God sends us financial success while maintaining moral integrity, we shall accept it thankfully at His hands.... We have moved forward quietly and without ostentation in the past, so let it be in the future" (Cain, 27).

THE GREAT STORM OF THE JERSEY SHORE

The history of the Jersey Shore would not be complete without a reference to the storms the towns have endured over the centuries. One of the most destructive occurred in March of 1962. The storm gave no warning. It enveloped the Jersey Shore for a span of three days. It wasn't like a hurricane for which advisories could be issued. This storm was equivalent to five high tides, the highest being eight feet six inches—just short of the nine-foot record set in 1944.

Weathermen called it a northeaster more ruinous than any prior storm. Its power demonstrated that nature was a hard mother indeed. It reminded residents that seaside dwellers are but a wave's length from sleeping with the fishes. In actuality it was two storms—one from Iowa and the other from Georgia. By the time they reached the Jersey Shore the winds were traveling at freight train speed. As they neared the beaches the waves soared to the height of a three or four story building.

Meteorologists studying the storm noted that it happened close to the spring equinox, when high tides are at their peak. It also coincided with a new moon, which affects tidal heights known as spring tides. The *New York Times* offered this description of the deadly storm: "A savage gale, with pounding tides, towering seas and heavy snows."

A professional pilot named Captain Paul McGill flew over the shore mid–storm. He likened the devastation to an atomic explosion, the worst storm he had ever seen. Homes, hotels and boardwalks were gradually rebuilt following this dreadful event and comprise the Jersey Shore as we know it today.

Boardwalk Memories

Jersey Shore boardwalks come in all sizes, ranging from a mere 200 feet to a length of 5 miles. Some are made of pine or cedar in herringbone patterns, while others are made from macadam or brick pavers.

Each boardwalk along the coast has its own unique personality that reflects the town it abuts. The 0.7 mile walkway in Ocean Grove reflects the religious tone of that town, which began as a Methodist campground. Fans of heavy decibel, neon-lit, commercial enterprises will savor the boardwalks at Seaside Heights, Ocean City and Wildwood, which have no shortage of movie theatres, arcades, amusement piers, kiddy rides and

souvenir vendors. Known as a "flirtation walk," the pathway in Cape May was erected in 1868. Two years later, the boardwalk as we know it today was created when the first wooden plank was laid in the sand dunes of Atlantic City. Officials adopted the word Boardwalk with a capital *B* as a proper noun in 1896.

The idea of a boardwalk came out of necessity. Most Victorians preferred a leisurely stroll along the beach to an invigorating frolic in the unguarded 19th century surf. Consequently, there was a real need to keep destructive sand out of the fine furnishings and carpets plush hotels were expected to have in order to attract upscale guests to these newfound resorts. First class railroad cars and private residences were also negatively affected by the invasion of sand. Jacob Keim and Alexander Boardman proposed that the city provide a walkway of wood along the dunes to accommodate the people strolling. This would serve to keep sand to a minimum and the hotelier's property in check. The plans for their "board walk" came with a construction budget of $5,000. Nervous hotel owners worried that the view would be adversely affected, so the businessmen included a clause that stated no "bathhouse, shanty or building of any kind" was to be erected within 30 feet of the walkway.

Those of us living within a two-hour commute to the Jersey Shore have our favorite destinations for a myriad of reasons. The diversity of these towns insure that there is some place special for everyone. Whatever your preference, there is a seashore walkway at the ocean's edge certain to entice you at the Jersey Shore. If you haven't experienced the coastal towns of this state, and especially the quaint town of Ocean City, you have a treat awaiting you!

Credits

The Jersey Shore has always had a treasured place in my life. As a youngster, my favorite tradition was our family's annual trek to Ocean City. Limited finances usually permitted a stay of only several days; nonetheless, my sisters and I made the most of this time at the shore. Faded black and white photos stand as a testament to those fond childhood memories we shared.

As luck would have it, my high school friends at Villa Joseph Marie, in Newtown, Pennsylvania, had a preference for this resort town as well! Each summer we would head to the 9th Street Beach after breakfast at the Chatterbox Restaurant, still an Ocean City landmark.

My lifelong friends, Joan and Mike Allen, purchased their first home in Ocean City in the late 1980s. Since that time they have welcomed their family and countless friends to join them in experiencing life at the Jersey Shore. Their eldest daughter, Kimberly, was married in this resort town with a beautiful reception held overlooking the Bay. The younger daughter, Melissa, worked in her uncle's shop, the Cricket Box, throughout her teen and young adult summers. Both daughters now live close enough to this shore point, so the four young grandchildren continue the family tradition of summer fun at the Jersey Shore.

The Allens have had a collection of the Byers' limited edition swimmers, designed for the Ocean City market, on display in their summer home for many years. As you might imagine, I had my eye on them and finally took this opportunity to feature them in a display. It is with great pleasure that I share their collection with you. Thanks, Joan and Mike!

The Byers' Choice, is located in the town of Chalfont, in beautiful Bucks County, Pennsylvania. Since the early 1960s, founder and artist Joyce Byers has overseen the creation of Christmas carolers of every imaginable variety. If you are interested in seeing the many figures currently available in the Byers' collection visit http://www.byerschoice.com/.

Assembling the Display

1. The background of this display was light blue felt. The 10" × 7" flags were cut from red and blue poster board then mounted on black poster board. The letters were created using the font Franklin Gothic Heavy sized at 400. They were printed on card stock and traced onto white poster board, then black poster board and glued to the flags. The flags were pinned to rope and attached to the felt with straight pins. Birds, which were created for the "Going Green" display, were placed among the clouds of fiberfill.

2. On the top left was a document which traced the history of Ocean City. This is available if you visit http://www.oceancitychamber.com/historyofoceancity.asp. Under that was information on the storm of 1962 found in the book *Great Storms of the Jersey Shore* by Larry Savadove and Margaret Thomas Buchholz.

Documents on the left were printed on card stock and mounted on red, blue and black poster board.

3. On the top right was this quote about the storm of 1962, taken from *Great Storms*.

> Never in the memory of anyone living along its 140 mile length of sandy geography had the Jersey shore been dealt a heavier blow. Weathermen were to explain later that the deep low-pressure system alone would have produced a dilly of a northeaster. "We kept waiting for the wind to shift," said the mayor of one tide-battered community. "It always does, you know. As soon as it backs around to the northwest everyone starts to breathe easier. Newspaper editors listening to their reporters' descriptions just didn't believe it all until the photographic evidence came in. Their hard old eyes hadn't seen anything like this in decades (Savadore and Buchholz, 105).

Under that was this famous quote by Herman Melville from *Moby Dick*:

THIS APPALLING OCEAN.

Last was a document which provided an overview of the towns, economy, and entertainment options available at the Jersey Shore. This information can be found if you visit http://www.newjerseyshore.com/.

Items on the right were printed and matted like those on the left.

4. The Byers' Choice swimmers are available at the Cricket Box in Ocean City. These figures, a lifeguard stand, dock, post and lighthouse were placed on the base of the display amid stones and seashells. Coils of ropes were placed on the dock and lifeguard stand.

Other books featured in the display were *Jersey Shore: Vintage Images of Bygone Days* by Emil R. Salvini and *Vacationing on the Jersey Shore: Guide To Beach Resorts Past and Present* by Charles A. Stansfeld, Jr.

Bigger and Better

Byers' carolers are available in retail outlets in all 50 states as well as online. To access this site visit http://www/byerschoice. com.

Chances are you may have access to Byers' carolers dressed in holiday attire. Feature them in a display along with Christmas sheet music, scores and CDs. Title it "Holiday Harmony" and include musical instruments scaled to the size of the display case. Then add holiday greens, ribbons and silk poinsettias.

Byers' has a collection of Dickens carolers, which would be a great way to feature the works of Charles Dickens around the holidays. If you can obtain a few, add some Victorian Christmas ornaments, vintage Christmas cards and postcards and feature the classic *A Christmas Carol*. Add a top hat and cane or a small crutch reminiscent of Tiny Tim.

You may want to feature the history of your favorite coastal town. Include miniatures of the famous attractions found there and include books relevant to the area. Feature postcards which depict the evolution of the architecture of the region. Add some cotton candy, fudge, caramel corn or salt water taffy.

Should you want another idea for a nautical display, see "Manet by the Sea" on page 152 of my first book, *Great Displays for Your Library Step by Step*.

Rock & Roll

I knew the words to 25 rock songs, so I got in the group. "Long Tall Sally" and "Tutti-Frutti," that got me in. That was my audition. — Paul McCartney

Rock and roll can be defined as a style of music that combines the same musical elements (rhythm, pitch, dynamics, form and timbre) present in all styles of music. The way in which these fundamentals are combined, in what proportions and with what characteristics, defines rock as a distinct musical style.

Rock and roll music can trace it roots to the swing bands of the prewar era, music the 1960s kids' parents danced to. Glenn Miller, Benny Goodman, Count Basie, Tom and Jimmy Dorsey and Duke Ellington were among the many who entertained that generation. Nat King Cole had a small jazz combo that became known before he struck out on his own to become a major crooner of his day.

Country and western performers served as early influences on the emerging rock and roll movement which was sometimes called "Texas swing." Bob Wills and the Texas Playboys were hugely popular, along with singer/songwriter Hank Williams, Sr.

In Memphis, Tennessee, during the mid–1950s, Sun Studio record producer Sam Phillips had a sideline business of custom recording, where anyone could go in and make a record for two dollars a side. Shortly after his high school graduation, Elvis Presley arrived at the studio and cut two stylized ballads. Initially Phillips showed little serious interest in the performer; however, he kept his phone number and called Elvis back to try out a demo titled "Without You." Although that ballad met with minimal success, Phillips was convinced Elvis had a certain something. He signed him to his record label along with Jerry Lee Lewis, Carl Perkins, Johnny Cash and Roy Orbison.

A style of music called the blues was highly influential in the evolution of rock music and Chicago, Illinois, was considered its home. It was in that city where the transition from acoustic solo guitar music to electric guitar/electric bass/drums combos first took place. Muddy Waters, Little Milton, B.B. King and Howlin' Wolf were notable Chicago blues artists who regularly brought the house down.

Finally, it was a single man, named Les Paul, who made an enormous contribution to the sound of rock music. He designed the Gibson Les Paul electric guitar and implemented the technique of overdubbing, which allowed a musician to play multiple parts on a recording. Along with his wife and partner, vocalist Mary Ford, Les Paul created recordings that duplicated the sound of an entire band. Robert Palmer's chapter titled "Rock Begins," in *The Rolling Stone Illustrated History of Rock & Roll,* adds this bit of information about the formation of this genre of music:

> Rock & roll was an inevitable out-growth of the social and musical inter-actions between blacks and whites in the South and Southwest. Its roots are a complex tangle. Bedrock black church music influenced blues, rural blues influenced white folk song, and the black popular music of the Northern ghettos-blues and black pop-influenced jazz and so on. But the single most important process was the influence of black music on white. Rock might not have developed out of self-contained African American tradition, but it certainly would not have developed had there been no African-Americans (DeCurtis and Henke, 4).

In the early sixties, pop music gradually became controlled by young vocal groups with charisma, talented songwriters and an expanding production team—working behind the scenes. Rock artists were becoming responsible for writing, producing and creating their own unique sound. In general, East Coast doo-wop and female groups did not write their own material, relying on their handlers to manage and produce the records. The rhythm and blues and soul scene included talented individuals who didn't necessarily receive the notoriety of lesser talented white groups. As the decade progressed, the civil rights movement evolved, and British groups acknowedged the influence of soul music on their sound, these performers received due recognition.

The California scene was marked by instrumental surf groups like the Surfaris, the Crossfires and Dick Dale & the Del-tones.

Dale helped define the sound of the modern rock guitar solo. When the Beach Boys arrived on the scene vocal harmonies defined the surf sound. The fun-in-the-sun sound quickly became a part of pop culture. Brian

Rock & Roll: The Early Years. A colorful jukebox, 45 RPM records, a keyboard, Beatle figurines and a Kiss plaque pay homage to the musical phenomenon known as rock & roll.

Wilson, Phil Spector and the team of Sloan and Barri began the quest for new sounds while turning the studio into their instrument. Back East, Bob Crewe and the team of Burt Bacharach and Hal David were on a similar musical path.

Detroit's Berry Gordy, Jr. demanded total control of the talent on his Motown record label. He dictated their musical styles, clothes and hairdos. He was looking for acceptance among broader audiences. Once he became an established star at Motown, Marvin Gaye demanded artistic control of his recordings. Later, Stevie Wonder and Smokey Robinson proved themselves to be outstanding writers and producers, following Gaye's lead.

The 1960s was a decade fraught with political turmoil that included the assassination of President John Kennedy, the escalation of the United States' involvement in Vietnam, higher taxes and mounting inflation, police action in the streets and a declaration of war on poverty. These policies and programs of President Johnson's Great Society convinced many that the government wasn't committed to protecting the human and constitutional rights of its citizens. As the country's youth began questioning its leaders, a noticeable change became apparent in the popular music of the time. The innocence of the music waned.... And then came the famous British Invasion.

The Beatles were clearly the most famous of the myriad of British music acts which found success in America in the mid–1960s. They hoped to do what no other British group had done: crack the American rock scene. Their debut on the *Ed Sullivan Show*, just months after the nation experienced a presidential assassination, clearly marked the beginning of this new trend in rock music. America need a shot of something fast, loud and superficial during that period and found it in John, Paul, George and Ringo. The "Fab Four" brought the country back together.

The British bands affected U.S. sound and attitudes and influenced everything that came afterwards. Lester Bangs reflects on the transition attributed to these musical groups coming to America in his chapter on the British Invasion:

The British accomplished this in part by resurrecting music we had ignored, forgotten or discarded, recycling it in a shinier, more feckless and yet more raucous form. The fact that much of this music had originally been written and performed by American blacks made it that much more of a sure thing, but this was not a replay of Pat Boone rendering Little Richard palatable to a white audience. In even the limpest, wimpiest Liverpudlian retread of an American R&B oldie, there was at least the promise, the yearning, that both performers and audience might get loose, shake 'em on down and run wild in the streets, as we of course eventually did (DeCurtis & Henke, 199–200).

The Brits succeeded in killing off almost all of the existing American musical groups. Only the Beach Boys, the Four Seasons and the biggest Motown acts survived the invasion.

In 1965 the British group called the Rolling Stones released ("I Can't Get No) Satisfaction," which became their first number one hit in the United States. Many critics consider this rock's greatest song ever. The Rolling Stones were marketed as a group of rebellious, hedonistic rockers, which their lifestyles affirmed.

The following year, the Beatles announced that they would no longer tour and would concentrate on full-time studio recording instead. Shortly thereafter, singer/songwriter Brian Wilson, of the Beach Boys, suffered a breakdown and retreated to the studio where he created what is considered the first rock orchestra. As the decade progressed, Creedence Clearwater Revival appeared on the scene, Led Zeppelin grew out of the ashes of the Yardbirds, and the Black Power movement spurred soul music to new heights in the form of Otis Redding and Aretha Franklin.

The rock festival known as Woodstock took place in August 1969. The hippies had organized a 450,000 person three-day extravaganza with relatively few problems, save of course the incessant rain. In retrospect, it was clear that the miserable weather and overwhelmed facilities symbolized the end of an era, not the dawning of the Age of Aquarius as originally hoped.

Rock and roll has been an important and influential social factor. When historians tally the final figures from the second half of the 20th century, rock will surely prove to be the single most potent economic factor of the multibillion dollar music industry. Rock has influenced the music written for television, films and commercials. In addition, it has affected virtually all musical styles and has influenced hairstyles, clothing, language, lifestyles and politics. For more information of the history of rock and roll visit http://www.spectropop.com/hmadanibrief.html.

Credits

In the summer of 2010 my husband and I saw the Broadway production of *Million Dollar Quartet*. The story took place just before Christmas 1956, when Johnny Cash, Jerry Lee Lewis, Carl Perkins and Elvis Presley gathered at the Sun Record studio in Memphis, Tennessee—the place where their careers had been launched. Word spread about an impromptu jam session and a reporter who was present made the commented "this quartet could sell a million." That was their only performance.

Sam Phillips, owner of Sun Records, discovered and produced members of Million Dollar Quartet. He, along with Presley and Lewis, were among the Rock and Roll Hall of Fame's charter inductees. Perkins and Cash soon followed. Unlike other producers during that era, Phillips took an active role in recording—encouraging and coaxing his young novice artists to reach deep within themselves.

Million Dollar Quartet celebrates the musical session which evolved that evening in Memphis when four giants of the music business came together to play their hearts out. The performances were incredible. The Nederlander Theatre proved to be a perfect and intimate venue. It was impossible NOT to create a display on rock and roll after seeing this production!

Assembling the Display

1. The font used for the title of the display was Anja Elaine bold sized at 375. The ampersand was sized at 350. The letters were printed on card stock and traced onto white poster board. The musical notes were found through a Google image search, printed on card stock and traced onto silver poster board. The three 45 records (two red and one white) were mounted on silver poster board and pinned to the background.

The general design for the jukebox was found through a Google image search and modified to allow the lettering to be incorporated. The perimeter design was created using bright green, yellow, red and silver on a background of black poster board. Many jukebox images were available for inspiration and modification for your display.

The top shelf held a figurine created by the Franklin Mint of the Beatles dressed in costume for the *Sergeant Pepper's Lonely Hearts Club Band* album. This was flanked by a miniature cello and a guitar on individual stands.

Books on the top shelf were *All Shook Up: How Rock & Roll Changed America* by Glenn C. Altschuler, *The Rolling Stone Encyclopedia of Rock & Roll* (third Edition), and *Meet the Beatles* By Steven D. Stark.

2. On the top left of the display was "Time line of Rock & Roll," which can be found if you visit http://pages.prodigy.net/cousinsteve/rock/feat4.htm Under that was this quote by Tina Turner:

> Sometimes you've got to let everything go—purge yourself. If you are unhappy with anything ... whatever is bringing you down, get rid of it. Because you'll find that when you're free, your true creativity, your true self comes out.

Under that was a biography of Chuck Berry from http://www.chuckberry.com/about/bio.htm.

Items on the left were printed on card stock and mounted on green, red or black poster board.

3. On the top right was a biography of Elvis Presley which can be found at http://www.elvis.com/elvisology/bio/elvis_overview.asp. Under that was this quote by Bono:

> As a rock star, I have two instincts: I want to have fun, and I want to change the world. I have a chance to do both.

Next was a miniature reproduction of a

Woodstock poster. Many are available through an online image search. Under that was a biography of the Beatles which can be found if you visit http://www.biography.com/articles/The-Beatles-9203410.

Items on the right were printed and mounted like those on the left.

4. On the base of the display was a small keyboard made from black and white poster board (this was also used on p. 72 in the "Mostly Mozart" display). A figurine of the Beatles dressed for their *Help* album was placed on a Styrofoam disk covered with black velvet. This was elevated on a 3″ disk.

Books featured in the display were *The Beatles in Dreams & History* by Devin McKinney, *Last Train to Memphis: The Rise of Elvis Presley* by Peter Guralnick, *Rock and Roll: A Social History* by Paul Friedlander and *The Beatles, Popular Music and Society* by Ian Inglis.

Bigger and Better

Should your space be larger, include a 45 record player with discs. The dust jackets on 33 records could serve as a background for the display. Include some memorabilia from the 1960s, 1970s, etc. (see the display "Far Out: Surviving the Sixties" on p. 17)

Focus on the British Invasion and include the Rolling Stones, the Beatles, the Moody Blues, the Who, the Dave Clark Five, and the Bee Gees. Visit this site for inspiration: http://www.britishinvasionbands.com/the-bands/. Search online using that subject for some great ideas for backgrounds incorporating the British flag. Include the instruments of rock should you have them available.

Feature Aretha Franklin, Tina Turner, Janis Joplin, Linda Ronstadt, Carole King, Grace Slick and all the other women of the rock and roll movement. For information visit http://www.rockonthenet.com/archive/1999/vh1women.htm. Call it "Girls Rock!"

For another musical theme see page 27 of my first book, *Great Displays for Your Library Step by Step* for a display titled "All That Jazz."

5 In Memory

Mostly Mozart

When I am ... traveling in a carriage, or walking after a good meal, or during the night when I cannot sleep; it is on such occasions that ideas flow best and most abundantly. — Wolfgang Amadeus Mozart

One of the greatest musical geniuses in history, Wolfgang Amadeus Mozart was born in Salzburg, Austria, on January 27, 1756. Although he would have a profound impact on the world of classical music, this child prodigy would not live to see his thirty-sixth birthday.

Mozart was the son of Leopold Mozart—a business-minded composer, violinist and assistant concertmaster at the Salzburg court—and his wife, Anna Maria Pertl. Leopold was considered one of the most distinguished musicians of his time. He had composed the best method for violin playing written up to that period and was an erudite man of sterling character. Leopold recognized the talents of both young Wolfgang and his older sister Maria Anna, and devoted all of his energy and knowledge to their education and development.

Music surrounded Mozart throughout his childhood—both in his actual life and in his world of dreams. At the age of three he devoted whole hours to the piano and soon discovered consonant intervals. By the age of four, under his father's tutelage, he began to receive systematic training in piano playing as well as in the theory of music. By age five Mozart was composing small and beautiful melodious numbers. At the age of six he played piano and his sister accompanied him on the violin in concerts throughout many European courts, including Vienna, Munich, Paris and London. Soon thereafter Mozart wrote and published his first composition.

He was nine years old when he started writing symphonies. High demand forced the family back on yet another tour of Vienna after a mere nine month interlude. The children, especially Mozart, were considered musical wonders of the world.

Despite their frequent travels, and the inherent distractions associated with touring, Mozart continued to make progress in all branches of music. He dedicated himself to the mastery of counterpoint and endeavored to perfect his technique in piano and violin as well as organ playing.

In 1782 Mozart married Constanze Weber, younger sister of his former lover, Aloysia. This was a loving marriage into which six children were born. Two sons survived into their adult years.

In the mid–1780s Mozart received many lucrative opportunities to write and perform his music. Around that time he appeared at public functions, published his work and became involved in music education. In 1787 he was offered a prestigious court position as Kammermusicus, which required that he compose dance music for court balls.

Mozart published beautiful sonatas for violin and piano, wrote music compositions and penned both serious and comic operas. He composed quartets which he dedicated to the composer Joseph Haydn whom he greatly admired. Haydn had recognized Mozart's knowledge of music and his composition talent.

Although a practicing Catholic, Mozart

Mostly Mozart. A musical score, keyboard and portrait of the composer form the background for this display celebrating the musical genius of Wolfgang Amadeus Mozart. A 19th century German violin and bow add dimension and authenticity to the display.

joined a Masonic lodge in Vienna at age 28 and in due course became a master Mason. Mozart's interest in this organization was primarily due to the impressive intellect of its collective members. According to historians he wrote at least eight pieces of music for the Masons. Influences of Masonry are apparent in his famous opera *The Magic Flute*. Mozart joined the organization despite the fact that Pope Clement XII had prohibited membership in 1738. This association did not prevent Mozart from composing some of the most famous Roman Catholic Masses in Western history—a sacred body of work which totaled more than sixty pieces of music. He was devoted to his Catholic faith, which he felt to be a powerful and affirmative force in his life, and found no conflict in his association with Freemasonry.

Mozart gained popularity by managing concerts on his own. He composed the music for the concert and managed the orchestra as well. Mozart was vigorous and productive throughout his life. His income allowed his family to live a comfortable life, but, because of his lack of management skills, he was never able to bank enough earnings to secure the future welfare of his family. Although Mozart gained great recognition for his talent, he frequently needed to borrow money just to make ends meet.

Mozart spent much of his life in Vienna. During the later portion of his life he visited cities such as Salzburg and Berlin to perform in operas, dramas and concerts. This musical genius died on December 5, 1791, in Vienna. The funeral was held two days later in St. Stephen's Cathedral, the site of his marriage to Constanze nine years prior. Although there was no formal autopsy to determine the cause of death, the attending physician, Eduard Guldener von Lobes, found no evidence of foul play. Von Lobes, a municipal health officer in Vienna at the time of Mozart's death, claimed that Mozart succumbed to an epidemic of rheumatic and inflammatory fever and died of a deposit on the brain.

Constanze was unable to afford a first-class funeral, but the modest one she provided for Mozart was commonplace in Vienna at the time. Contrary to popular thought, he was not destitute or ignored in death. Thousands of fans and admirers of the great composer showed up at Wälscher Platz and St. Stephen's to pay their last respects to this accomplished classical musician.

At the time of Mozart's death, medical standards were quite primitive. Now familiar technology such as the thermometer and the stethoscope were not invented until the 19th century. Consequently there was no objective way of measuring a person's vital statistics. A patient's heart and lungs could not be easily or effectively monitored. Observations of a patient's symptoms were purely subjective. Also, the diagnoses of disorders centuries ago may not be considered accurate today. More than 200 years have passed and the cause of Mozart's death remains shrouded in mystery. Despite research conducted by historians, anthropologists, musicologists and doctors, the debate continued. The theories pondered included death by disease or by poison.

In Mozart's case, the greatest obstacle that investigators faced was the lack of a corpse. Even ancient bodily remains give clues to the afflictions which contributed to the cause of death. Mozart's remains were lost to modern researchers thanks to the treatment his body endured during a bare bones funeral that was later followed by exhumation and subsequent moves. What remains are the conflicting testimonies of his doctors and those who surrounded him in death.

All of that changed in the year 2000. A group of experts who researched a variety of notorious case histories convened at the sixth annual Clinical Pathological Conference held at the University of Maryland School of Medicine. This panel included several physicians and one Mozart scholar, Cornell University professor of music Neal Zaslaw. Their conclusion officially ruled out foul play in the death of Mozart. They felt that it was rheumatic fever that extinguished the brilliant life of one of the world's most beloved composers, not poisoning by one of his alleged rivals, as has been suggested. Although modern antibiotics have made rheumatic fever a rare ailment today, this immune system disease occurred frequently in the 18th century.

At the time of his death, Mozart suffered from a high fever, headaches, a rash, pain, and swelling in his arms and legs. He became increasingly agitated and asked that his beloved pet canary be removed from the room because its singing unnerved him. Irritation is a classic symptom of rheumatic fever. Mozart suffered bouts of vomiting and diarrhea, his body became swollen and he was unable to sit upright in bed without assistance. Alert and acutely aware of his impending death, Mozart gave specific instructions as to how to complete the requiem he had been composing. His body lapsed into a coma, followed by death.

Premature death is tragic in any case, but Mozart's demise robbed the world of an incredible talent in his professional prime who surely left this world with many musical compositions still unwritten. His work as a master composer of the opera, the symphony and piano sonata defined musical classicism. For more information and speculation about the reason for Mozart's death visit http://www.bbc.co.uk/dna/h2g2/A1304957 or http://www.news.cornell.edu/chronicle/00/2.17.00/Mozart_death.html.

Credits

My husband, Dennis, and I enjoy a wide variety of musical genres. He remains loyal to a particular surfer group of the 1960s, but appreciates modern alternative music as well. My musical taste is pretty eclectic.

Many years ago we agreed that the music played on the radio or selected on the iPod for those long Sunday drives should be mellow and spiritually uplifting. So Sundays were set aside for classical music, and Mozart's work was a particular favorite. This display is a tribute to the genius that was Wolfgang Amadeus Mozart.

Assembling the Display

1. The font selected for this display was Chopin Script sized at 575. This free font is available at http://www.dafont.com. The letters were printed on card stock, cut and traced onto black poster board. They were attached over a score created by using thin satin

cord which was attached with pins. The letters were pulled forward on pins. The clefts, musical notations and notes were found through a Google image search, enlarged on the photocopier and traced onto black poster board. These were attached with pins to a tan felt background.

The keyboard was created freehand on white poster board using black Magic Marker. The black keys were drawn on black poster board and glued on. The head of Mozart was found through a Google image search, printed on presentation paper, cut into an oval and glued onto black poster board. The keyboard and portrait were attached with pins and pulled forward.

2. On the top left was a document about Wolfgang's wife, Constanze Weber. This information can be found at http://www. geocities.com/mozart_lover83/love.html. Under that was the quote that introduced this display. Lastly was a biography of Mozart found at http://w3.rz-berlin.mpg.de/cmp/mozart.html.

Items on the left were printed on off-white card stock and mounted on black poster board.

3. On the top right was this quote by Mozart:

> I pay no attention whatever to anybody's praise or blame. I simply follow my own feelings.

Under that was an illustration of Constanze Weber Mozart found through a Google image search. Next was another quote by Mozart:

> Music, even in situations of the greatest horror, should never be painful to the ear but should flatter and charm it, and thereby always remain music.

Items on the right were printed and mounted like those on the left.

4. On the base of the display was black velvet fabric on which sat an antique German violin and bow, circa 1895. Books featured in the display were *Mozart: A Life* by Maynard Solomon, *Mozart's Women: His Family, His Friends, His Music* by Jane Glover, *The Mozart Myths: A Critical Reassessment* by William Stafford, *Mozart and His Operas* by David Cairns, *Wolfgang Amadeus Mozart: A Biography* by Piero Melograni and *Wolfgang Amadé Mozart* by Georg Knepler.

Bigger and Better

Your larger display space could include additional instruments used in classical music, such as the flute, viola, cello, the double bass, the clarinet and the trumpet. You could include a period metronome, a quill pen and inkwell, candles and a long-stem red rose.

You could feature a larger image of Mozart, or one of him and his wife, Constanze Weber. You may want to place a larger image of Mozart in the center and surround him with photographs or illustrations of the women in his life: his mother, Maria Anna, his talented sister nicknamed Nannerl, the four Weber sisters (all singers) or the women in his operas and the divas that gave them voice.

Include DVDs, CDs, vinyl records, laser discs, scores and sheet music in your display. You could enlarge the scores and use them as a background. Your display could include images of Handel, Schubert, Bach, Beethoven, Brahms, Chopin, Mahler, Schumann, and others. For more ideas of classical composers to include in your display visit http://www.cl.cam.ac.uk/~mn200/music/composers.html.

If your musical preference is jazz, refer to my first book, *Great Displays for Your Library Step by Step*. You may note that the keyboard shown in "Mostly Mozart" was also featured on page 27 in the display titled "All That Jazz." Don't be afraid to give your graphics a different focus and a new life in a related display.

A Wild Wilde Ride

Always forgive your enemies; nothing annoys them so much. — Oscar Wilde

Oscar Fingal O'Flahertie Wills Wilde was born on October 16, 1854, the middle child of Jane Francesca Agnes Elgee and surgeon William Robert Wills Wilde. An older brother, William, and a younger sister, Isola Francesca, completed the family.

A Wild Wilde Ride. A black top hat is flanked by framed photos of Oscar Wilde, his family and friends. Portraits of the colorful author form a collage on a banner of scrapbook paper on which the catchy title appears.

Oscar's mother was a prominent poet and nationalist who wrote revolutionary Irish verse under the pseudonym "Speranza." His father was a noted ear and eye surgeon, renowned philanthropist and acknowledged expert on Irish antiquities. William Wilde was a gifted author of a variety of books, several of which became standard universal medical textbooks that were used for decades. The senior Wilde was knighted in 1864 for his service to the medical profession and died twelve years later.

Oscar and brother William were educated at Portora Royal School in County Fermanagh, Ireland, beginning in 1864. William was popular with fellow students, but Oscar was more of a loner and had little in common with many boys his age. Although the students at Portora came from relatively wealthy backgrounds, there is evidence to suggest that Wilde felt that the school lacked the level of prestige he would have preferred in his early education. He was awarded scholarships to both Trinity College, Dublin (1871–

74), and Magdalen College, Oxford University (1874–78). Wilde studied the classics at both institutions and developed a keen interest in the Greek philosophers. It was during his years at Oxford that his father died.

In the summer of 1875 Wilde met the first of a series of desirable women with whom he would be associated for the remainder of his bachelor days. Florence Balcombe was the third of five daughters of an English lieutenant colonel. Although she was dowerless, she was generally considered an exquisite beauty. Florence was 17 and Wilde 20 when the romance blossomed. Much to his dismay, Florence broke off the relationship with no explanation and became engaged and then married writer Bram Stoker. Wilde endured greater distress in interpersonal relationships over the years, but he quite enjoyed the drama created by his role as the jilted lover.

From the moment he left Oxford, he was hard at work promoting himself. He made it his business to be present at important social gatherings and premiers, and sought the friendship of popular actresses such as Ellen Terry, Lillie Langtry and Sarah Bernhardt.

During his years at Oxford, he had become markedly more aware of his bisexual tendencies. Wilde received much flack from his conservative peers for his outlandish manner of dress, which was satirized in the cartoons of the day. While at Oxford, he was mentored by writer and critic Walter Pater and helped found the Aesthetic Movement nicknamed "art for art's sake." While at Magdalen, Wilde won many honors, among them the 1878 Oxford's Newdigate Prize for his poem "Ravenna."

Upon graduation, Wilde settled in Chelsea, London, where he pursued his passion for poetry. His first collection, titled *Poems,* was published in 1881 to mixed reviews. It was in London that Wilde entered high society and was recognized for both his literary prowess and his notable wit. He could be considered one of the early celebrities who became "famous for being famous."

In 1881 Wilde traveled throughout Canada and the United States, where he presented lectures on aestheticism. Research has shown that he gave a total of 140 lectures in 260 days prior to the advent of air travel and fast trains. While on tour he had the pleasure of meeting Oliver Wendell Holmes, Walt Whitman and Henry Longfellow. Upon his return to his home in 1883, he moved to Paris and continued to be in demand as a lecturer.

On May 29, 1884, Oscar married Constance Mary Lloyd, the daughter of wealthy queen's counsel Horace Lloyd. During the first two years of their marriage the Wildes had two sons, Cyril and Vyvyan. Cyril died in World War I at the age of 30. Vyvyan pursued a literary career and penned the memoir *Son of Oscar Wilde* in1954. He also published *Oscar Wilde: A Pictorial Biography* in 1960.

To support his family, Wilde accepted a job as the editor of *Woman's World* magazine, where he had earlier worked for several years. In 1888 he published *The Happy Prince and Other Tales,* stories written for his children. *The Picture of Dorian Gray,* his first and only novel, was published in 1892. Initially, it wasn't warmly received due to the novel's homoerotic overtones, which created quite a backlash among Victorian critics.

In 1892, at the premier of Wilde's acclaimed play *Lady Windermere's Fan,* he was introduced to a handsome young Oxford student, Lord Alfred Douglas, son of the marquess of Queensbury. Wilde was smitten by the dashing, self-assured undergraduate nicknamed "Bosie" and began a fervent and stormy relationship which ultimately consumed and then destroyed him. Although Wilde would have preferred a monogamous relationship with his lover, he embraced the promiscuous lifestyle, which included "rent boys," that Bosie found titillating. By choosing this capricious behavior, Wilde neglected Constance and the boys and ultimately suffered great guilt. The marriage ended in 1893.

Following the highly acclaimed openings of *A Woman of No Importance* (1893), *An Ideal Husband* (1895), and *The Importance of Being Earnest* (1895), Wilde was firmly established as a talented playwright. At the opening performance of *Earnest,* the marquess planned to publicly expose Wilde as a homosexual. That action was thwarted when word of it reached Wilde, but the Marquess managed to leave an incriminating accusation four days later at the Albermarle Club, of which Wilde was a member.

At Bosie's urging, Wilde unsuccessfully sued the marquess for libel, which proved a reckless and fatal gesture of bravado. Three trials ensued. Wilde was tried for gross indecency and convicted of the crime of sodomy. He was sentenced to two years hard labor, first at Pentonville, then Wandsworth and finally Reading Goal. That incarceration, which lasted 18 months, left Wilde's health forever compromised. While imprisoned, he wrote *De Profundis,* a dramatic monologue and autobiography dedicated to Bosie. Its title refers to the biblical Psalm 130, and means "From the Depths."

While writing *De Profundis* the prison allotted Wilde but one sheet of paper at a time. During his time at Reading Gaol, the author's mother died, and his humiliated wife officially changed the family surname to Holland. Constance moved around with her sons to several European cities to escape the notoriety Wilde brought upon the family. She died in 1898 following spinal surgery.

Prison regulations forbade writings, other than carefully scrutinized letters, penned during incarceration to leave the institution. However, the governor of Reading Gaol disregarded the rule and returned the manuscript to Wilde, who journeyed to France on the day of the release and never again set foot in England.

Upon his release, Wilde wrote *The Ballad of Reading Gaol*, which exposed his concern for the inhumane prison conditions, the injustice of the death penalty and the hanging of Charles Thomas Wooldridge for the death of his wife:

> Yet each man kill the thing he loves
> By all let this be heard,
> Some do it with a bitter look,
> Some with a flattering word,
> The coward does it with a kiss,
> The brave man with a sword!
> [Wilde, Ballad 42].

In his introduction to *The Ballad of Reading Gaol,* Burton Rascoe states that only rarely did Wilde attempt to express sad, tender or tragic themes in his writings; and when he did he often failed. Wilde did succeed in some of his fairy stories and in the *The Ballad of Reading Gaol,* in which he created a simple theme of a man facing his demise for a crime of passion. In nearly all the verse written by Wilde which included sentiment there is the portrayal of the failure of the man who could think but not feel.

Wilde emerged from prison a disgraced man. He spent his last three years penniless, in self-imposed exile abroad and cut off from society and artistic circles. During this period Wilde was briefly reunited with Bosie. When Wilde realized he could no longer write under his own name, he chose the pseudonym Sebastian Melmoth.

Wilde maintained a lifelong interest in Catholicism, which was fortified as a result of his meeting with Pope Pius IX in 1877. He studied the works of Augustine, Dante and Cardinal Newman while in prison. On his deathbed, in late November 1900, Wilde converted to Catholicism. He received the sacraments of Baptism and extreme unction at his residence in the Hôtel d'Alsace in Paris. He was attended only by his loyal lifelong friend and sometimes lover, Robert "Robbie" Ross.

The cause of the writer's death has been debated. Wilde may have battled syphilis, but the topic would have been taboo for discussion during that period. Documentation verified the fact that he had been suffering from intermittent headaches for several months prior to his death, and they may have been related to syphilis. Wilde's son, Vyvyan Holland, claimed that his father died of cerebral meningitis.

Wilde was buried outside Paris with three friends in attendance. His body was later moved to Père Lachaise Cemetery in Paris. His tomb was designed by sculptor Sir Jacob Epstein at the request of Robert Ross, executor of Wilde's will. Ross requested that a small compartment be made for his own ashes, which were transferred to the tomb in 1950.

Irish writer Oscar Wilde emerged as one of the most iconic figures of the late Victorian period. During his lifetime he enjoyed a meteoric rise to the top echelon of society. He was credited with revolutionizing theme and treatment for the English stage. He opened doors for a brilliant, social-minded successor, George Bernard Shaw. Wilde's genius was for wit and comedy, of the play of the mind upon events and feelings, of commentary that was biting, sophisticated and amusing, of works that inspired the intellect rather than the heart.

The story of Oscar Wilde's life is the one great play he lived but never wrote. It includes all the elements of Greek theatre, which were well-known to him as a student of the classics: the hero in charge of his future, the arrogance, the tragic flaw, and, finally the archenemy. His end was not a quick death but instead a boundless ordeal. Although for many years Wilde's name was synonymous with both shame and scandal, his reputation has improved over time. Twenty-first century reflections are less harsh largely due to the evolution of social attitudes.

Credits

I worked as the first box office manager and publicist for DeSales University's Labuda Center for the Performing Arts in the early 1980s. During my tenure, I was introduced to the works of several Irish playwrights, including Oscar Wilde. One of the early plays produced in the new facility was *The Importance of Being Earnest* by Oscar Wilde. Despite the fact that the play was written during the Victorian period, audiences continued to relate to the playwright's wit and sensibility. The 2002 film *The Importance of Being Earnest* boasts an excellent cast and a fresh look at one of Wilde's most popular works. Over the years, many works by and about Oscar Wilde's made their way to regional and college theatres. Those that debuted as theatrical releases helped to keep his legacy alive.

I have always found Oscar Wilde to be an intriguing figure who lived a very complicated life in a public arena during provincial times. His life and his works were completely intertwined. He was very much a victim of the Victorian morality and paid dearly for his choices.

I mounted a display on this writer many years ago while on the staff at Haas Library, Muhlenberg College. The subject generated much discussion and so I thought I would mount a variation of the original display for inclusion in this book.

Assembling the Display

1. The background of the display was red felt. A wide border was created using 12" × 12" black and silver scrapbook paper with a period handwriting motif which was glued to silver poster board. On the left of this border were five portraits of Oscar Wilde found through a Google image search. Four of these were printed on presentation paper and mounted on red poster board. One was cut into an oval and mounted on silver poster board. The words *A wild* and *ride* were created using Britannic Bold sized at 240, and the word *Wilde* was created using Copperplate Gothic Bold sized at 410. The title signage was printed on card stock and traced onto silver poster board. The photos and lettering were attached with pins.

2. On the top left was a copy of a poster titled *The Trials of Oscar Wilde* found at http://lh3.ggpht.com/_Aq-bEFZKI5w/SpR05nfg RTI/AAAAAAAAAYQ/EbuNNMct3sg/s512/ Poster4.jpg. Next was this quote by Wilde:

Most modern calendars mar the sweet simplicity of our lives by reminding us that each day that passes is the anniversary of some perfectly uninteresting event.

Under that were witticisms of Wilde titled "Phrases and Philosophies for the Use of the Young," which can be found if you visit http://www.law.umkc.edu/faculty/projects/ftri als/wilde/wildeswritings.html.

Items on the left were printed on white card stock and mounted on black or silver poster board.

3. On the top right was a biography of Wilde which can be found if you visit http://www.online-literature.com/wilde/. Next was this quote by Wilde: "Consistency is the last refuge of the unimaginative." Under that was a timeline of the author found on the biography site named above.

Items on the right were printed and mounted like those on the left.

4. The base of the display was lined with black velvet. Metal framed photographs were located through Google image searches. They were of wife Constance and son Cyril Wilde, Wilde as a child, Wilde as an adult, father William Wilde, Lord Alfred Douglas with classmates at Winchester College (1890). The photos were centered on the base of the display around a black top hat. Two vintage sherry glasses, a pair of black leather gloves and wire-rimmed eyeglasses were placed among the picture frames. Styrofoam was placed under the velvet on the left, right and center to provide different elevations for the items in the display.

Books featured in the display were *The Complete Short Stories of Oscar Wilde* and *An Ideal Husband* by Oscar Wilde and *The Complete Fairy Tales of Oscar Wilde, Oscar Wilde* by Richard Ellmann, *The Complete Letters of Oscar Wilde* edited by Merlin Holland and Rupert Hart-Davis, *The Secret Life of Oscar Wilde* by Neil McKenna, *Oscar Wilde: Art and Egotism* by Rodney Shewan, *Built of Books: How Reading Defined the Life of Oscar Wilde* by Thomas Wright and *The Portrait of Dorian Gray* by Oscar Wilde.

Bigger and Better

Should your display be larger, you could

add clothing reminiscent of the late 19th century. Include a cane, a cravat, a cigar, a pocket watch, straw or bowler hats and shoes. Victorian prints or glassware, calling cards, replicas of telegrams, an inkwell and feather pen, period clocks and fans would add to the eye appeal of your display. Check with a local antique shop, museum or costume shop for items that could be lent in exchange for publicity.

You could feature the many letters written by Oscar Wilde during his lifetime, which are available in *The Complete Letters of Oscar Wilde* edited by Merlin Holland and Rupert Hart-Davis. Never meant for publica-

tion, this poignant correspondence reveals the totality of the man.

A poster could anchor your display. There are many posters available on the subject of Oscar Wilde, his works as well as his home in Chelsea. For a large selection visit http://www.allposters.com/-st/Oscar-Wilde-Posters_c9212_.htm.

If you are interested in mounting a display on other Irish writers refer to my first book, *Great Displays for your Library Step by Step*. Check page 9 for "The Life and Times of Bram Stoker" and page 147 for "C.S. Lewis: Into the Wardrobe."

A Brush with History: Portraits of the Presidents

Every man's work, whether it be literature, or music or pictures or architecture or anything else, is always a portrait of himself. — Samuel Butler (1835–1902)

Presidential portraiture has become an important part of our understanding of the country's highest office. It is difficult to imagine that the only way the first citizens of the republic became acquainted with their presidents was through painting, sculpture or prints. Over time, and with the advent of technology, the role of representation broadened to include photography, film, radio, television and evolving media. The depiction of the office of the president and sitting for the portrait have become part of the process by which presidents have affirmed their understanding of that role.

Collections of the presidential portraits are currently housed both in the National Portrait Gallery at the Smithsonian Institution and in the White House. It is interesting to note that for over 50 years the only portrait that hung in the White House was one of George Washington saved by Dolley Madison. In the latter part of the 19 century it became policy for the nation to commission and retain the portraits for the official residence.

Formal presidential portraits tend to adhere to conservative stylistic patterns. Presidential portraiture caters to mainstream tastes, shying away from adventurous extremes. In the broadest sense, portrait paint-

ing became a presentation of interesting lives told well: "The formal likeness of these historic leaders may have lost some relevance in an age inundated by media images, but there remains an enduring fascination with the traditional forms of portraiture and with the chemistry between artist and subject that goes into a painted or sculpted likeness" (Voss, 17). Many portrait painters would have preferred painting landscapes or historical representations. However, the reality was that their clientele were primarily willing to pay for portraits of themselves or their children. Some artists worked miniature landscapes into the background just to satisfy the need to paint them.

One aspect of the business of portrait painting was the making of replicas of the original. Gilbert Stuart's most famous, unfinished portrait of Washington was named the *Athenaeum* after the Boston library that acquired it following the artist's death. Stuart referred to the copies of these portraits of Washington as "hundred dollar bills" because that was his price for a head and shoulders replica of the famous painting. Replicas were usually commissioned by patrons, although there were versions that the artists kept for public exhibition (Carr and Miles, 34–35).

A Brush with History: Portraits of the Presidents. A red, white and blue bunting provides a colorful backdrop for portraits of some of the formidable men who served in the nation's highest office. The artists behind the brush were considered the best artists of their time.

The discovery of the daguerreotype process, and its introduction to the United States in 1839, significantly changed the nature of the art market. Daguerreotype studios were established in many major cities, liberating the portrait painters to paint landscapes or genre subjects. Photography was used by painters to replace the tiresome portrait sittings previously required, or at least to supplement them.

GILBERT CHARLES STUART

Widely regarded as one of America's foremost portraitists, Gilbert Stuart was born in Saunderstown, Rhode Island, in 1755. He was the third son of Gilbert Stewart, a Scottish immigrant involved in the snuff-making business, and Elizabeth Stewart, a member of the landed gentry from Middletown, Rhode Island.

At the age of seven, Stuart moved to Newport, Rhode Island, where his father pursued work as a merchant. It was here that he began to show his ability as a painter. Under the tutelage of Scottish painter Cosmo Alexander, a 12-year-old Stuart created the famous portrait *Dr. Hunter's Spaniels.*

Stuart followed Alexander through the American South and then to Scotland, in 1771, where he completed his studies. Alexander died the following year and Stuart tried unsuccessfully to earn a living as a painter. Working as a sailor, he was able to return to Newport in 1773. With the Revolutionary War on the horizon, Stuart's family, loyal Tory sympathizers, fled to Nova Scotia. In 1775, Stuart sailed to London where he remained for a period of 12 years.

While in London, Stuart was kept afloat financially by the American expatriate painter and mentor Benjamin West. Early on, Stuart showed a particular interest in portraiture and had no inclination to follow West into the branch of history painting West preferred. Following his apprenticeship, Stuart established himself as London's leading portraitist, next to Joshua Reynolds and Thomas Gainsborough, whose style he emulated. Along with those prominent painters, Stuart exhibited his works at the Royal Academy as early as 1777. However, thanks to an extravagant lifestyle and poor business practices, he was mired in debt. In 1792, after a five-year stay in Ireland, Stuart returned to America bent on making his fortune by painting Washington's portrait.

Stuart relocated to Philadelphia, where he opened a studio and gained not only a foothold in the art world but also lasting renown painting portraits of many of its most distinguished citizens. He worked in New York, Philadelphia and Washington until 1805, when he established a studio in Boston.

Stuart set the standard for portrait painting in America in the early decades of the 19th century. All major portrait painters of the time either studied with him, or learned from his works. Stuart's rapid technique provided a legacy of 1,000 portraits he created during his lifetime. His two most famous portraits of Washington, of which he made over 100 copies, are the Vaughan half-length type (1795), which hangs in the Metropolitan Museum, New York City, and the *Athenaeum* portrayal (unfinished; 1796), housed in the Museum of Fine Arts, Boston. It is the latter likeness of Washington that can be found on our one dollar bills. Stuart's portraits depicted Washington as remote and dignified, with a wonderful sense of composure, without insignia suggesting rank. To Stuart's credit, the first six presidents of the United States and several British kings sat for portraits by him.

In 1824 Gilbert Stuart suffered a paralyzing stroke. He struggled to paint for another two years before his death in Boston at age 72. His paintings can be found in art museums throughout the United States as well as the United Kingdom.

Rembrandt Peale

Rembrandt Peale was born in Bucks County, Pennsylvania, on February 22, 1778. The son of renowned artist Charles Willson Peale, he studied first with his father and later with Benjamin West at the turn of the century in London.

While in Paris, in the early part of the 19th century, Peale was named court painter to Napoleon I. He returned to the United States in 1804 and set up a studio in Philadelphia. The next year the artist painted a portrait of Thomas Jefferson, at age 62, that was widely considered his masterpiece. His father had painted a portrait of Jefferson, as secretary of state, in 1791. Peale returned to France in 1808 and again in 1809–1810 armed with letters from Jefferson, a close friend of his father. The young artist studied under Jacques Louis David and John Vanderlyn, famous painters of the day.

Peale and his father founded the Philadelphia Academy of Fine Arts in 1810. The elder Peale was named director. The subject of his first historical painting, featured in the academy's 1812 show, was quite controversial. Titled *The Roman Daughter* it depicted an imprisoned father kept alive by milk from his daughter's breast.

In 1825, Peale was elected president of the American Academy of Fine Arts. Following his father's lead he opened a museum and portrait gallery in Baltimore, where he established the first illuminating gasworks. He then turned to formal pieces before reverting to portraiture and continuing a series of portraits of George Washington. In mid-career Peale taught art in the Philadelphia public schools and published a graphic's instruction book. He died in Philadelphia in 1860.

George Peter Alexander Healy

George P.A. Healy was born in Boston, Massachusetts, in 1813. The son of a ship's captain and the eldest of five children left fatherless early in life, Healy felt honor bound to help support the family. He began drawing at age 16 and, with the help of Gilbert Stuart's daughter, was introduced to the prominent artist Thomas Sully. Healy set up a studio in Boston at the age of seventeen and began painting portraits the following year.

In 1834, Healy went to Europe, where he remained for 16 years. While in France he studied with Baron Gros and under Thomas Couture, who became a lifelong friend. In 1840 Healy won a third class medal in the prestigious Salon. He was awarded second place at the Paris International Exhibit of 1855. That same year he moved back to America and settled in Chicago, where he remained until 1869. He returned to the Continent for 21 years, working primarily in Rome and Paris. His final return to Chicago was in 1892.

Healy was extremely facile, original, courageous and productive. In his charming memoir, *Reminiscences of a Portrait Painter,* he reflected on his years spent as an artist: "All my days are spent in my painting room."

Healy's style was essentially French. His color was considered fine, his drawing accurate and his marriage of light and shade excellent. His likenesses were strong in their outline, firmly painted, and finely finished with layers of glaze. His images were considered definite, rugged, and powerful.

Healy painted more portraits of prominent figures than any other American artist. Among those who sat for portraits were Pius IX, Lincoln, Grant, Hawthorne, Longfellow, Louis Philippe, Liszt and Webster. He died in Chicago in 1894.

JOHN SINGER SARGENT

Sargent's painting would eventually be named the official portrait of President Theodore Roosevelt, but it wasn't the first. In 1902, Theobald Chartran was commissioned to paint portraits of the president and his second wife, Edith. The First Lady was pleased with hers, but her husband abhorred his and finally destroyed it.

Although it was Roosevelt who discovered the talented, burly Sargent, the artist wasn't going to have an easy time with the president. Teddy, having had a negative experience with the first portrait artist, would take no nonsense from the renowned artist. After the two men surveyed the White House, Sargent made sketches of his subject in several rooms, trying to find the most flattering lighting and stance. This tedious approach severely tested the patience of the restless president.

As they mounted the stairs, in an effort to find a better arrangement on the second level, Teddy remarked that he didn't think Sargent had any idea as to what he actually wanted. Sargent retorted that he didn't think Roosevelt knew what was required to pose

for a portrait. Roosevelt had finally reached the landing, where he planted his hand on the balustrade post and turned to the ascending artist bellowing, *"Don't I!"* John Singer Sargent had his pose! The informal portrait that resulted depicted an energetic Roosevelt. It had a modern look, but treated the subject with respect. Surprisingly, the president loved the portrait, which he proudly displayed.

Born in Florence, Italy, to American parents, John Singer Sargent was bright, gifted and diligent. He was considered the last great generalist, as he mastered many different styles of painting. He was an impressionist, a classical portraitist, a landscape artist, a water colorist, a muralist and, in the later days of his life, a sculptor.

Between 1877 and 1925, the prolific Sargent painted over 900 oils and more than 2,000 watercolors along with countless charcoal sketch-portraits and endless pencil drawings.

AARON SHIKLER

Aaron Shikler was born in Brooklyn, New York, in 1922. He studied at the Tyler School of Art in Philadelphia and at the Hans Hofmann School in New York and was primarily known for his landscape and figurative work. He painted portraits of President John F. Kennedy as well as Kennedy's wife, Jacqueline, and their children.

The official portrait of Kennedy was painted posthumously. It is generally considered more of a character study. Unlike most presidential portraits, Kennedy's doesn't reflect his personality. Instead he is shown as pensive, even brooding—eyes downcast and arms folded—a reference to his assassination.

Shikler's works reside in such notable collections as the Brooklyn Museum of Art, the Metropolitan Museum of Art, the Hirshhorn Museum and Sculpture Garden, the New Britain Museum of American Art and the National Academy of Design.

Credits

The walls of the library in our home are lined with portraits of two presidents. George Washington and Thomas Jefferson are well represented in this room, which serves as my husband's sanctuary. Denny has had a great interest in and affection for these men who had the courage to successfully stage a revolution and birth a nation.

The state of Virginia is a goldmine of historical presidential real estate and personal treasures. Our visits to Washington's Mount Vernon and Jefferson's Monticello—as well as his summer home in Poplar Forest—provided many insights into the character, lifestyle, imagination and integrity of these formidable figures.

A retrospective of the Peale family works, from miniatures to still life to tromp l'oeil, was staged at the Philadelphia Museum of Art in the late nineties. Our copy of Rembrandt Peale's portrait of Jefferson was purchased at that exhibit. It was that print which ultimately became the impetus for this display featuring Rembrandt Peale, as well as some of the other artists whose task it was to capture the essence of these giants of history in presidential portraits.

Assembling the Display

1. A red, white and blue bunting was pinned to a background of black felt. Portraits of George Washington and John Adams by Gilbert Stuart, Franklin Pierce and Abraham Lincoln by George P.A. Healy, Theodore Roosevelt by John Singer Sargent and John F. Kennedy by Aaron Shikler were found through Google image searches, printed on card stock and mounted on black, or black and gold poster board. The framed portrait of Thomas Jefferson, by Rembrandt Peale, was placed in the center of the tableau. The title signage was created using Brush Script MT Italic sized at 175. It was printed on off-white card stock and mounted on black and gold poster board. A vintage paint brush was centered about the title. The photocopies and signage were attached with pins and pulled forward.

2. On the top left was a biography of Gilbert Stuart taken from this chapter. Clipart of an artist's brush was inserted in the top left of the document. Under that was this quote by Stuart on the subject of George Washington:

There were features in his face totally different from what I had observed in any other human being. The sockets of the eyes, for instance, were larger than what I ever met with before.... All of his features were indicative of the strongest passions.

Next was a biography of George P.A. Healy, which can be found if you visit http://www.tnportraits.org/artists.htm#George_Peter_Alexander_Healy.

Items on the left were printed on card stock and mounted on black, red, or black and red poster board.

3. On the top right was the biography of Rembrandt Peale from http://biography.yourdictionary.com/rembrandt-peale. Under that was this quote by George P.A. Healy from *Reminisences of a Portrait Painter:*

Fashion changes; the beautiful of yesterday is the grotesque of to-day. What matters it? Each generation as it comes to life does its best, struggles, suffers, hopes or despairs; it adds its little stone to the big edifice which is ever being built; the little stone is lost among others, forgotten, overlooked; but it has helped nevertheless to make the wall solid and beautiful. And that surely is something.

Next was information about the artist John Singer Sargent that provides the backstory on his painting of the portrait of Theodore Roosevelt. This can be found if you visit http://jssgallery.org/paintings/president_theodore_roosevelt.htm.

Items on the right were mounted and framed like those on the left.

4. The base of the display case was covered with black velvet fabric. *Portraits of the Presidents: The National Portrait Gallery* by Frederick S. Voss was open to a portrait of James Madison. A miniature portrait of Thomas Jefferson, by Charles Willson Peale, was placed to the left of the open book. A bust of Jefferson was placed on a Styrofoam form, covered with black velvet, and centered above the open book. Paint brushes flank the pages of the open book.

Books on display were *The Watercolors of John Singer Sargent* by Carl Little, *Gilbert Stuart* by Carrie Rebora Barratt, *Presidential Portraits* by Philip B. Secor, *The Genius of Gilbert Stuart* by Dorinda Evans, *George* and Martha Washington: Portraits of the Presidential Years by Ellen Gross Miles, Reminiscences of a Portrait Painter by George P.A. Healy and Benjamin West: A Biography by Robert C. Alberts.

Bigger and Better

You needn't limit your larger display space to presidential portraits. The catalog A Brush with History: Paintings from the National Portrait Gallery, from a prior exhibit staged at the National Portrait Gallery, includes portraits of people from Benjamin Franklin, Nathaniel Hawthorne, and Mary Cassatt to Michael Jackson and John Updike. It provides comprehensive background information about the subjects of the paintings produced by many great American artists. Teacher resources are available on the Website of the National Portrait Gallery: http://www.npg.si.edu/cexh/brush/activities/index.htm.

You may want to title your display "Art in Letters" and feature literary figures such as Longfellow, T.S. Eliot, Samuel L. Clemens (Mark Twain) and Carl Sandburg.

Should you be interested in a display featuring Thomas Jefferson, titled "The Sage of Monticello," see page 85 of my first book, Great Displays for Your Library Step by Step. "Citizen Ben," a biography of Benjamin Franklin is on page 100. If you would prefer to feature a single artist, a display titled "Manet by the Sea," can be found on page 152. The children's illustrator Ponder Goembel, is the focus of a display on page 109.

Edgar Allan Poe

There is no telling what might happen to a man all alone as I am—I may get sick or worse....—E.A. Poe, "The Light-house"

The story of Edgar Allen Poe begins long before his entry into this world on January 19, 1809, in the city of Boston. The product of two stage actors, Edgar was orphaned at age two. Although his family did not determine his ultimate destiny, they provided the framework from which he would develop.

Edgar Allan Poe was born to a beautiful and petite young British actress named Elizabeth Arnold Hopkins Poe. His father, David Poe, Jr., hailed from Baltimore, Maryland, the son of a prominent craftsman and merchant. The couple had married in Richmond, Virginia, three years prior. Although Elizabeth was highly regarded for her comedic ability, she was also an accomplished singer and dancer. David's theatrical abilities, however, paled in comparison. Consequently, the family faced many financial struggles.

Elizabeth and David had three children, William Henry, Edgar and Rosalie. Hoping for good roles and additional income, the family relocated from Richmond to New York City following the birth of Edgar. After becoming estranged from her husband, Elizabeth died of tuberculosis in Richmond, Virginia, in 1811. (The uncertain time line of David's departure and death leaves questions remaining as to the paternity of Rosalie.)

Upon Elizabeth's death, William Henry was taken in by General Poe, but young Edgar was given to a childless Scottish tobacco exporter and his wife, John and Frances Allan. Although Poe took their surname as his middle name, formal adoption never took place. Rosalie, who remained childlike throughout her life, was adopted by Jane and William Mackenzie of Richmond. Like her brother, Rosalie took their surname as her middle name. The siblings stayed connected throughout their lives. William Henry died at 24 years of age, but Rosalie lived well into her sixties. Edgar was afforded many opportunities with the Allans, including travel and an excellent education. Frances Allan was a devoted Christian who raised her son in the Episcopal faith.

The Allans moved to England in June of 1815 with the hope of expanding the family company. Their business affairs were thwarted, however, by the economic depression which followed the Napoleonic Wars. Frances disliked London and suffered from bouts of ill health. Edgar attended several schools during their five-year residency, concentrating on Latin, French, math and history. These academic experiences were retold in some of his short stories, such as "William Wilson," that the writer crafted later in life.

Upon the family's arrival in Richmond, Edgar returned to his studies and excelled in both sports and academics. He was popular among his peers and well-regarded by his teachers. During those formative years he demonstrated a unique ability to write genuine poetry.

While in Richmond, Edgar developed a friendship with Robert Stanard that would endure through their lifetimes. Edgar adored Robert's mother, Jane, who frequently provided a safe haven when matters became difficult at home. She believed in Edgar's talents as a poet and encouraged him in his early attempts. Her untimely death thrust Edgar in deep depression. Jane Stanard is said to have been the inspiration for the first version of his poem "To Helen."

Around 1825, Edgar fell in love with a pretty neighborhood girl named Elmira Royster. Although he sketched her portrait, there is no evidence that he created poetry for her. Elmira's disapproving father intercepted communiqués between the secretly engaged couple, so the romance was ultimately doomed.

Few who met Poe could forget him, for his keen intellect and distinctive appearance set him apart. He was quiet and shy but handsome. Slightly built, he measured five feet eight inches. Poe's mouth was considered beautiful. His lush eyelashes framed hazel gray eyes. It was said that he generated a visceral reaction among his associates; either they became devoted followers or they were filled with disdain.

Despite the Allan family wealth, Edgar was underfunded when he entered the University of Virginia at age 17. He began drinking and gambling, which caused his expulsion after less than a year. Around this time, Edgar confronted John Allan with regard to marital improprieties. This act would lead Poe's foster father to disown him.

Although beneath the station of a member of the upper class, Edgar went to Boston and enlisted in the U.S. Army in 1827. He used an assumed name, Edgar A. Perry. Only 18 years of age, he published a 40-page collection of his early works titled *Tamerlane and Other Poems* under the name "a Bostonian." This publication was funded by Edgar, but was poorly marketed and yielded little

Edgar Allan Poe. This haunting tribute to the famous author of the macabre features a large raven symbolic of his famous poem. Bats fly above and a skull and bones rest at the foot of his tombstone creating an eerie tableau.

income. Its publication did however, serve to set him apart from other fledgling poets. Today, it is one of the rarest volumes in American literary history, with individual copies selling for $200,000.

In 1829 Frances Allan died and Edgar's relationship with John Allan was temporarily restored. Edgar had earned the rank of sergeant major as an enlisted man, but he was eager to achieve the rank of an officer, which would be more fitting for a gentleman of his social stature. John Allan cooperated by signing his application to West Point. Edgar entered the academy in 1830, but was dishonorably discharged the next year for intentional neglect of his duties. Just before his departure, he had solicited subscriptions for a new collection of poems from his fellow cadets. Surprisingly, 131 of the 232 cadets enrolled at West Point contributed to this effort, thus giving Edgar a real vote of confidence in his literary talent.

In 1830 John Allan married a much younger woman from New Jersey. She had no interest in maintaining harmony between the two men and saw Edgar as a rival to her future inheritance. Edgar moved to Baltimore to live with his aunt Maria Clemm, the mother of Virginia Eliza Clemm, who would become his wife at the age of 13. His brother Henry also resided in the household, but he died of tuberculosis soon after Edgar moved in. In 1833, the *Baltimore Saturday Visiter* published some of Poe's poems and he won the top prize for his story "Manuscript Found in a Bottle." Two years later Edgar became editor and contributor of the *Southern Literary Messenger*. Though he was not without his detractors, this position marked the start of his career as a respected critic and essayist. Other publications to which he contributed were *Burton's Gentleman's Magazine* (1839–1840), *Graham's Magazine* (1841–1842), *Evening Mirror* and *Godey's Lady's Book*.

After Virginia and Edgar married in Richmond in 1836 they moved to New York City. (Marrying one's first cousin was not frowned upon at the time.) Edgar's only completed novel, *The Narrative of Arthur Gordon Pym*, was published in 1838. Poe's contributions to magazines were published as a collection in *Tales of the Grotesque and Arabesque* (1840), which included "The Duc de L'Omelette,"

"Bon-Bon" and "King Pest." Considered by some to be the first detective story, "The Murders in the Rue Morgue" was published in 1841.

Poe's collection of poetry, *The Raven and Other Poems* (1845), which gained him attention at home and abroad, includes the wildly successful trio "The Raven," "Eulalie" and "To Helen."

The Poes resided in a cottage in the Fordham section of the Bronx in New York City, where Virginia died of consumption in 1847. Edgar turned to alcohol and began exhibiting increasingly erratic behavior. The following year he became engaged once again to his teenage sweetheart from Richmond, Elmira Royster. In 1849 he embarked on a tour of poetry readings and lecturing in hopes of raising funds to start a magazine he had named *The Stylus*.

It was surprising to learn that Edgar Allan Poe never wrote his middle name when writing his signature. He used the *A* but refused to acknowledge his spiteful foster father's full surname.

When one reflects on the totality of his life, it is clear that Edgar both embodied and embraced contradiction: "He possessed polished manners, enormous erudition, formidable conversational abilities, and an indescribable personal magnetism; in his better moments he was genial, kind and entirely appealing. At other times he yielded to melancholy and self-pity; when drinking he could be abrasive and combative; when confronted with what he felt to be mediocrity or pretension, he rarely refrained from expressing contempt, either in his book reviews or his conversation" (Thomas and Jackson, x).

There are conflicting accounts surrounding the last days and the circumstances related to the actual death of Edgar Allan Poe. Some say he died from alcoholism and others claim he was murdered. Various other diseases have also been suggested. Most accounts indicate that he was found unconscious on the street and rushed to the Washington College Hospital in Baltimore, Maryland.

Edgar died on October 7, 1849, and was unceremoniously buried in an unmarked grave in the Old Westminster Burying Ground of Baltimore. Word of his passing came days after the funeral, so only ten people attended the service. The infamous and scathing obituary that ran in the *New York Daily Tribune* under the pen name "Ludwig" was in fact written by Rufus Griswold. In one extravagant passage, Griswold created the fictitious figure of a literary madman doomed to eternal hell. Griswold, a failed Baptist minister turned editor, considered himself Edgar's social and moral superior. The two men viewed each other with a certain amount of professional disdain.

Griswold continued his posthumous destruction of Edgar Allan Poe by convincing Mrs. Clemm, his mother-in-law, that it was Edgar's intention that she sign over her power of attorney to him for the entire literary estate. Naively trusting that Griswold was acting in her best interests, Mrs. Clemm acquiesced and never saw a penny of the highly successful four-volume set titled *Works of the Late Edgar Allan Poe.* The final blow to Edgar's memory came when Griswold wrote a fallacious biography which he included in *Works.* Upon its publication, several important literary figures came forth to denounce it and wrote impassioned rebuttals. Others provided original correspondence which refuted the lies Griswold had blatantly manufactured.

Despite Griswold's portrayal of him, Poe amassed a huge literary legacy. Translations of Poe's works were found in Russia in the late 1830s and in France shortly thereafter. Fyodor Dostoevsky found inspiration for *Crime and Punishment* in "The Tell-Tale Heart." Sergei Rachmaninoff used that tale to inspire an orchestral piece titled *The Bells.* Claude Debussy made several attempts to create an opera based on "The Fall of the House of Usher."

On January 19, 1949, 100 years after his death, three red roses and a half a bottle of cognac were placed at the gravesite of Edgar Allan Poe. For decades, a black-clad stranger known as "The Poe Toaster" has visited the grave in the wee hours to mark the birthday and give a graveside tribute to the master storyteller who many consider the father of the modern horror story.

Credits

I have lived near Baltimore, Maryland, and in or near Philadelphia, Pennsylvania, all of my life. Both cities are proud of their association with Edgar Allan Poe and continue to celebrate his life and literary achievements. They offer regular programming which serves to educate those interested in his life and works. Consequently, I have had many reminders of his genius and always planned to celebrate his life and works in a library display.

The year 2009 marked the 200th anniversary of the birth of Edgar Allan Poe and the 160th anniversary of his death. These events did not go unnoticed in the literary world. In October 1849, Poe's burial was hastily arranged by his cousin with no fanfare. Baltimore's Poe House and Museum decided to right this wrong. In October of 2009, they hosted a funeral worthy of the Master of the Macabre. Seven hundred people attended—many dressed as literary figures who held Poe in high regard. They came prepared to deliver proper eulogies. A formidable replica of Poe, in period costume, was placed in a casket and transported by horse-drawn carriage to the Westminster Church, where Poe is buried. This event garnered great press.

Born in Boston and raised in Richmond, Poe also had residences in New York and Philadelphia. So, why the celebration in Baltimore. Though many cities claim an association with him, the body lies in Baltimore.

Assembling the Display

1. Gray felt was pinned to the top of the display back. Black felt was rounded to suggest the shape of a tombstone and attached to the lower half. The image of a raven was found using a Google image search. It was printed on paper, enlarged to 14" on the photocopier and traced onto black poster board. The wings and mouth were outlined using silver poster board. This was attached with pins and pulled forward. The font used for the title was Nightmare sized at 400 for Poe's name and 300 for the dates of his life. This font is available for a free download at http://www.dafont.com. The letters were printed on card stock and traced onto silver poster board. The eye of the raven was cut from red foil wrapping paper. The word *nevermore* was created using the font HamletorNot

sized at 210. This can be downloaded free at http://www.fontstock.net. The letters were printed on card stock, traced onto black poster board and pinned to border the body of the raven.

The 7″ moon was cut from yellow poster board. The bats were recycled from the display "Tales of Horror" created for my first book. Bat graphics can be found online http://www.leehansen.com/clipart/Holi days/Halloween/images/bats-flying.gif. Fiberfill was attached around the moon and bats.

Next was the first paragraph from Poe's obituary, written by Rev. Rufus Wilmot Griswold and published in the October 9, 1849, edition of the *New York Tribune*. It was printed on card stock and mounted on silver poster board then centered under the dates of Poe's life:

> Edgar Allan Poe is dead. He died in Baltimore the day before yesterday. The announcement will startle many, But few will be grieved by it.

A photocopy of a ledger kept by John Allan regarding his stepson's expenses was placed among the books on display. This was available in the book by Harry Lee Poe featured in the display. Animal and human skeletal remains were placed in front of the books.

Books featured on the top shelf were *The Afterlife of Edgar Allan Poe* by Scott Peeples, *The Portable Edgar Allan Poe* edited by J. Gerald Kennedy and *Edgar Allan Poe: An Illustrated Companion to His Tell-Tale Stories* by Harry Lee Poe.

2. On the top left were excerpts from the lengthy obituary referred to above. Under that was a copy of the marriage bond between Edgar and Virginia Clemm. This can be found at http://upload.wikimedia.org/wiki pedia/commons/thumb/a/af/PoeMarriage. JPG/469px-PoeMarriage.JPG.

Next was this quote by Dr. Barbara Cantalupo, associate professor of English, Pennsylvania State University Lehigh Valley Campus and editor of *The Poe Review*:

> Most of us know Edgar Allan Poe as the "master of the macabre," the father of the detective story, the "madman" with his "nevermore," the hoaxer who disdained his readers, the "tomahawk critic," and the storyteller

whose tales keep you up at night. These monikers stand true, but there is another Poe, one who loved beauty and found that beauty not only in nature but in the paintings and sculptures he saw while he lived in New York and Philadelphia as revealed in his domestic tales like "The Domain of Arnheim," for example. These values are truer to Poe's soul than all that make him famous today. Yet few know this Poe. In the letter he wrote to Helen Whitman a year before he died, Poe's "true self" emerges: "'The Domain of Arnheim' expresses much of my soul. This story contains more of myself and of my inherent tastes and habits of thought than anything I have written."

Items on the left were printed on white card stock and mounted on red and black poster board.

3. On the top right was a short biography of Edgar's wife, Virginia Eliza Clemm Poe. This can be found at http://www.eapoe. org/people/poevc.htm. Under that was information about Poe's gravesite which can be found at this site: http://www.eapoe.org/balt/ POEGRAVE.HTM. An image of his grave was inserted into the top of the document. This can be found if you visit http://media.ani mevice.com/uploads/0/193/126953-edgar_ allan_poe_super.jpg. Next was a comprehensive time line of Poe's life found at http://www. poestories.com/time line.php.

Items on the right were printed and mounted like those on the left.

4. Black velvet lined the base of the display. Circular Styrofoam discs were placed under the fabric to elevate the skull and skeleton of the hand. A coccyx was also elevated with a thinner portion of Styrofoam. Fiberfill was placed around the skeletal remains.

Books included on the base of the display were *Edgar Allan Poe: His Life and Legacy* by Jeffrey Meyers, *Edgar Allan Poe: Complete Tales and Poems* by Edgar Allan Poe, *Great Tales and Poems of Edgar Allen Poe* by Edgar Allan Poe, *The Edgar Allan Poe Review* edited by Barbara Cantalupo, *The American Review* dated February 1845 and *The Poe Log: A Documentary Life of Edgar Allan Poe 1809–1940* by Dwight Thomas and David K. Jackson.

Bigger and Better

You may want to install this display in late October, as it could double as an eerie exhibit worthy of Halloween. If your space allows, add seasonal items: pumpkins, haystacks, cornstalks and gourds.

Try to get a copy of *Edgar Allan Poe: An Illustrated Companion to His Tell-Tale Stories* by Harry Lee Poe. It is a beautifully crafted book that includes copies of personal correspondence, Poe's army enlistment document, selected pages from John Allan's account books reflecting the payments he'd made on Edgar's behalf, the cover of the *Baltimore Sunday Visiter* which contains Edgar's "Manuscript Found in a Bottle," the marriage bond between Edgar and his cousin Virginia, selected pages from the first printing of "The Raven," Poe's long and highly judgmental obituary as it appeared in the *New York Daily Tribune* and more.

You might decide to focus on "Poe the Poet" and explore that dimension of this literary figure. Create a seascape and feature the silhouette of a man and a woman suggested in the poem "Annabel Lee."

There is an excellent Website for Poe which provides curriculum materials, photos and comprehensive articles on facets of his life and writings. These were helpful to me for this display. The site offers a club for children as well as online activities. The Edgar Allan Poe Historic Site is located near Seventh and Spring Garden streets in Philadelphia, Pennsylvania. Admission is free and groups are welcome. Special programming is available throughout the year at a nominal fee. For more information please visit http://www.nps.gov/edal/index.htm

Since 1923, the Edgar Allan Poe Society in Baltimore has sponsored an annual commemorative lecture on the life or works (or both) of Poe presented by a noted Poe scholar. Prior to this event, it is traditional for members of the Society to gather at Poe's grave to place flowers on the monument in a brief and informal ceremony to honor Poe's memory. Events are held in the Baltimore area. For information visit http://www.eapoe.org/balt/poehse.htm.

You may want to celebrate the "Man and the Myths." Five popular myths about Poe are explored at this site: http://www.huffingtonpost.com/matthew-pearl/top-five-myths-about–edga_b_334742.html.

For a display on another writer of the macabre, see "Bram Stoker's Dracula" on page 9 of my first book, *Great Displays for Your Library Step by Step*. "Tales of Horror" can be found on page 53 of that text.

Will Power

> The striking feature of Shakespeare's mind was its generic quality, its power of communication with all other minds, – so that it contained a universe of thought and feeling within itself, and had no one particular bias, or exclusive excellence more that another. He was just like any other man, but that he was like all other men. He was the least of an egotist that it was possible to be. He was nothing in himself, but he was all that others were, or that they could become.
>
> —William Hazlitt, *On Shakespeare and Milton*

William Shakespeare's literary accomplishments were so luminous it is hard to fathom that they were created by a mere mortal of simple origins with a modest formal education. When considering his use of language, form and vision, it can be argued that Shakespeare's power has no equal. Through his works it is evident that he created a vast imaginary world inhabited by creditable individuals who mirrored the broadest human experience: "Acknowledged as the greatest English writer, unrivaled in popular and critical acclaim, Shakespeare is also the recognized international master whose universality communicates across cultural divides" (Burt, 1).

How did Shakespeare become Shakespeare? This is the age old question. Born in

Stratford-upon-Avon, a rural community in the geographical center of England, Shakespeare was the son of a prosperous and prominent tradesman, bailiff and alderman named John and his wife, Mary Arden, daughter of wealthy landowners. His birthday is celebrated on April 23, just three days before records of his baptism were filed in the Holy Trinity Church.

Although records have not survived that

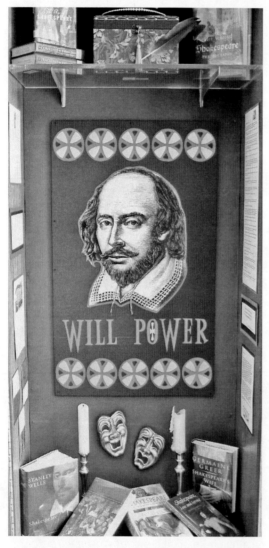

Will Power. A poster was created using a large image of the head of the Bard and edged in a Gaelic cross design. Candles flank the faces of comedy and drama for which Shakespeare was known.

would validate Shakespeare's schooling, it is believed that because of his father's position in the town, young William would have attended the Stratford grammar school free of charge. Both of Shakespeare's parents signed their names with a mark throughout their lifetimes, so there is speculation that they were minimally educated and would have wanted more for their son. The town of Stratford was serious about the education of its male children. In fact, the study and conversing of the Latin language was considered of the utmost importance. Following grammar school there were scholarships available that enabled promising students with financial need to attend the university.

The facts of Shakespeare's life about which we can speculate emanate from very scant records that verify his birth in 1564, his marriage to Anne Hathaway (eight years his senior) in 1582, and the births of his daughter Susanna in 1583 and the twins, Judith and Hamnet, two years later. According to some accounts, Shakespeare's professional career commenced around 1585, when he was believed to have accompanied a troupe of actors and served in the capacity of both playwright and performer.

By 1594 records show that he had become a shareholder in London's most distinguished stage company under the sponsorship of Lord Chamberlain:

> His early plays included comedies, *Comedy of Errors* (1592), *Two Gentlemen of Verona* (1594), *Love's Labour's Lost* (1594), and *A Midsummer Night's Dream* (1595); historical chronicles, *Henry VI* (1590), *Richard III* (1592), and *Richard II* (1595); and the early tragedies, *Titus Andronicus* (1593) and *Romeo and Juliet* (1594). Shakespeare achieved literary distinction as a poet with *Venus and Adonis* (1593) and *The Rape of Lucrece* (1594). He would continue his nondramatic writing with a masterful sonnet cycle that circulated among his friends and was published in 1609. The achievement evident in the sonnets alone would have secured Shakespeare a significant place in English literary history (Burt 2,3).

Shakespeare's literary accomplishments and commercial success allowed for his purchase of a large home, named New Place, in Stratford. He earned the rank of gentleman, which permitted his family's coat of arms to be recognized in 1596.

Construction of the Globe Theatre, in which Shakespeare was a major investor, was completed in 1598. Built by carpenter Peter Smith and his workers, it could hold an audience of several thousand people and was the most magnificent theatre that the city of London had ever seen. This playhouse was located on a venue south of the Thames River in an area called Southwark. The open-air, octagonal amphitheater raised three stories high with a rectangular stage platform 43 feet wide by 28 feet deep. It was the site of the performance of many of Shakespeare's masterpieces.

William Shakespeare lived in the Elizabethan era when bubonic plague, sometimes referred to as the Black Death, was virulent. He was known to have a great fear of the disease and its consequences. The plague touched many areas of Shakespeare's life, including his time as an actor and playwright at the Globe Theatre. Serious outbreaks occurred in 1593, 1603 and 1608, which led to the closure of entertainment venues, including the Globe Theatre. In 1613, the Globe burned to the ground. The following year it was rebuilt on its original foundations. For more information about the history and time line of the Globe visit http://www.william-shakespeare.info/william-shakespeare–old-globe-theatre–history-time line.htm.

In about 1610 Shakespeare retired to Stratford where he penned a series of romances or tragicomedies, the last of which was *The Tempest* in 1611. He died in 1616 at the age of 52, a truly self–made man.

Prior to the Elizabethan dramatists, the English theatre performed primarily religious and allegorical themes. Shakespeare, however, used drama to investigate the secular experience and replicate the actual life of English and world history. He wrote in the four major dramatic categories—tragedy, comedy, history and romance—and turned the limitations of the bare, open stage of Elizabethan theatre into a great power. Shakespeare's expressive language compensated for the limited stage effects used at the time. It was this ability to communicate that defined him, and it is that for which Shakespeare will long be remembered.

Shakespeare never spoke in his own voice about his ideas on writing, or his personal philosophy, but "the things that are said by Hamlet, or Lear, or Macbeth, or just about any other character are so wise and stimulating and eloquently expressed that we are like to imagine that we can hear the author himself. Yet we must be vigilantly aware that each speaker is a narrative voice, even in the Sonnets and other nondramatic poems" (Bevington, 3).

Many have been drawn to the works of Shakespeare. They appeal to both the academic and the unlettered, and to both sophisticated and novice theatergoers. The playwright has the power to bring his audiences to laughter and tears as he effortlessly merges politics with poetry. Shakespeare's characters range from the lively artful jester to the profound worldly philosopher, and his plays were said to have been both *in* the world and *of* the world.

Not only did Shakespeare write and perform in blatantly commercial entertainment projects, he created scripts that were sensitive to the social and political climate of the times. His body of work comprises the most important and imaginative literature of the last thousand years. He understood, and wanted his audiences to comprehend, that the theatre had to have both the visionary flight and the ordinary earthiness for theatergoers to achieve the full experience.

Credits

Many years ago I was hired to be the first box office manager and publicist for the newly constructed Labuda Center for the Performing Arts. It is a beautiful, state-of-the-art facility on the campus of DeSales University, set in the rolling hills in Center Valley, Pennsylvania. The theatre program at DeSales has an excellent reputation and the productions are of the highest caliber. One of the first plays staged at the Labuda Center was Shakespeare's *A Midsummer Night's Dream*. There was a great pool of acting talent in the theatre program that year and the faculty brought with them many and varied valuable professional experiences to inspire the students. Consequently, the production was delightful and very well received. My favorite part of *A Midsummer Night's Dream* occurred in the final moments when Puck asked the audience to forgive the actors if, perchance, they were offended. He then tells the audience that if anyone disliked the play, they should imagine that it was only a dream. A dream indeed, but of the very best kind!

The Labuda Center expanded its horizons when it introduced the Pennsylvania Shakespeare Festival in the summer of 1992. The festival's mission was to enrich, inspire, engage and entertain the widest possible audience through first-rate professional productions of classical and contemporary plays. It included a core commitment to the works of Shakespeare and other master dramatists through an array of educational outreach and mentorship programs. The pre-theatre entertainment at the festival includes court jesters and ladies in waiting intent on entertaining the audience enjoying a pre-theatre outdoor dining experience on the grounds of the facility.

This firsthand exposure to Shakespeare's comedy provided the groundwork for my sustained interest in and appreciation for the Bard's works.

Assembling the Display

1. The font Army of Darkness was sized at 350 for all the letters except the *w* which was sized at 400. This font is available free at http://www.dafont.com. The letters were printed on card stock and traced onto red poster board. An elongated, stylized cross cut from silver poster board was placed in the center of the letter *o*. The letters were glued to a 21" × 37" piece of black poster board which was pinned to a background of red felt and pulled forward.

The image of Shakespeare was cut from a poster titled "Welcome to William's World" obtained free at an ALA convention several years ago. Posters are available for purchase through an online image search, or go to http://www.allposters.com.

The Celtic cross which formed the border was found through an image search and sized at 4.233 in Adobe Photoshop. This was printed on card stock and traced onto red

poster board then glued to a circle of silver poster board. Small black triangular shapes were glued within the points of the cross. This cross can be found at http://www.quil terstreasure.com/productspatternsTSS.html. Under that were the faces of comedy and drama which can be found if you visit https://secure.demonweb.co.uk/veryvenetian/acatalog/cacotra01.jpg.

This was printed on card stock, cut and attached with pins and pulled forward.

On the shelf above the poster was a period wooden box covered with cranberry and gold fabric. A quill pen was attached with rolled tape to the top right of the box. A pearl necklace was attached with pins to a Styrofoam disc covered in black velvet. A pearl encrusted tiara was placed above that. Books featured on the top shelf were *The Age of Shakespeare* by Frank Kermode, *Comedies* and *Tragedies* by William Shakespeare and *Shakespeare: The Biography* by Peter Ackroyd.

2. On the top left was a document titled "The Age of Shakespeare." This can be found if you visit http://www.cummingsstudyguides .net/xAgeof.html. Clip art of a Shakespearean queen was inserted at the top center of the document. Under that was this quote from *As You Like It:*

> All the world's a stage, And all the men and women merely players; They have their exits and their entrances, And one man in his time plays many parts, His acts being seven ages.
>
> Jacques, Act 2, scene 7

Next was a history of the Old Globe Theatre which can be found if you visit http://www.william-shakespeare.info/william -shakespeare–globe-theatre.htm. An image of the theatre, found through a Google image search, was inserted at the top center. Last were descriptions of the culture at the time of Shakespeare that included illustrations of clothing, housework and physicians of the era. This type of information can be found at http://www.brandonsd.mb.ca/crocus/library/s hakespeare.htm.

Items on the left were printed on white card stock and mounted on red and black poster board.

3. On the top right was a time line of Shakespeare which can be found if you visit

http://absoluteshakespeare.com/trivia/time line/time line.htm. Under that was this quote by Duke Orsino:

> If music be the food of love, play on, Give me excess of it; that surfeiting, The appetite may sicken, and so die.
> *Twelfth Night* Act 1, scene 1, 1–3

Last was a document titled "The Black Death." This can be found if you visit http://www.william-shakespeare.info/bubonic-black-plague-elizabethan-era.htm. An illustration of Black Death was inserted at the bottom center of the document. You can find many from which to choose using an image search with the term "black death."

Items on the right were printed and mounted like those on the left.

4. Silver candlesticks were placed on the base of the display flanking the faces of comedy and tragedy. Shakespearean coins were printed on card stock and strewn throughout the books on the velvet covered base of the display. These coins can be found at http://www.matthewgscarsbrook.com-a.googlepages.com/ElizabethanCoins.jpg/ElizabethanCoins-full.jpg. Styroform forms were placed under the velvet to elevate the books.

Books featured in the display were *Shakespeare for All Time* by Stanley Wells, *Shakespeare's Kings* by John Julius Norwich, *Shakespeare: The Invention of the Human* by Harold Bloom, *Shakespeare: Love and Service* by David Schalkwyk and *Shakespeare's Wives* by Germaine Greer.

Bigger and Better

Check with your area college or university theatre department to see if they could provide posters, vintage clothing or jewelry to enhance your larger display on Shakespeare. Costume rental stores may also be willing to lend you items in exchange for advertising.

You might set your Shakespearean display in a theatre. Line the background with a pleated velvet fabric, preferably wine or cranberry. Attach fringe to the bottom of the fabric to suggest a theatre curtain. Add a picture or poster of Shakespeare, call it Shakespeare on Stage and feature only his plays. Visit http://www.weeklyreader.com/readand-writing/content/binary/shakespeare123.jpg for a specific graphic which would help you implement this concept.

If it is Shakespeare's sonnets that you prefer, build your display around them. Visit http://www.shakespeares-sonnets.com/sonn01.htm#anchor001 for access to all of these works. A sonnet written in calligraphy would create an interesting background for your display. Add whatever flowers are mentioned in the sonnet, some candles and pewter goblets. Line the case with fiberfill if winter is suggested in the work. If you limit your selections to sonnets of love you may want to title it "Shakespeare in Love." Remember to include hearts and flowers in various sizes and colors.

FDR Remembered

Let me assert my firm belief that the only thing we have to fear is fear Itself.—Franklin D. Roosevelt

Born at his parents' estate in Hyde Park on January 30, 1882, Franklin Delano Roosevelt was a true American blueblood. Genealogists have found FDR—the only child of James Roosevelt and second wife Sara Delano Roosevelt—to be related, either by blood or through marriage, to 11 former presidents. Although the family was a pillar of society, a portion of their wealth and heritage was somewhat tainted. FDR's maternal grandfather amassed a fortune dealing in tea and opium while living with his young family in Oriental opulence in China. Though legal, the opium trade wasn't considered respectable, so, ultimately, Warren Delano turned to more conventional business opportunities.

FDR Remembered. This large collage of the life and times of Franklin Delano Roosevelt provides a glimpse of the man who served as president during the Great Depression and America's entry into World War II. Authentic rationing books and tokens, along with a draft notice, flank the newspaper headline announcing the declaration of war.

Springwood, home to the Roosevelts, was set in the rolling hills and pastoral splendor of the Hudson Valley. The property offered breathtaking views of the Hudson River and had a special place in FDR's heart throughout his lifetime. He is quoted as saying, "All that is within me cries to go back to my home on the Hudson River." The estate is now a historical site housing the first presidential library, authorized by FDR.

As was the custom of many wealthy New Yorkers, the Roosevelts spent much of the winter in a posh townhouse in New York City. They discovered Campobello Island the year Franklin was born. Located in the Canadian waters in the Bay of Fundy, Sara and James were drawn to the cool summer temperatures and relative isolation the island afforded. When their cottage was complete, Campobello Island became a cherished summer ritual for the family.

As a youngster, FDR prized tales of adventure, especially those dealing with the sea. He learned to fish and ride and grew to love nature and the outdoors. He became an expert swimmer and an accomplished sailor

in the turbulent winds off coastal Maine. Like many offspring of old money, FDR's parents and private tutors were responsible for his formative education. He traveled eight times to Europe as a youngster, each visit lasting for months. This early exposure may account for his unusual, slightly British accent and the comfort level he exuded on the Continent. A natural linguist, Franklin spent enough time in Germany to become proficient in the language, a facility which would be put to good use decades later when he was a U.S. president in the throes of a world at war.

The young and privileged FDR flourished in an environment in which he was the center of his universe. Servants met his every need and indulged his whims. FDR's genteel, sheltered existence had a definite down side, however. This lifestyle meant that he had little contact with microbes at an early age. He endured few illnesses and so he failed to develop a robust immune system. This would prove devastating in his adult years.

At the age of 14, FDR entered the prestigious Groton School in Massachusetts and graduated in 1900, the year his father died.

He then enrolled at Harvard University, where he received a BA degree in history in three years. The newly widowed Sara Roosevelt temporarily moved to Boston to be closer to her son during his undergraduate years. FDR served as editor of the school's newspaper, the *Harvard Crimson*, in 1903. He spent three years studying law at Columbia, but left school before completing his degree. Nonetheless, he passed the bar in 1907. He worked as a clerk for a New York law firm for three years, but showed no real passion for the profession.

In 1903 FDR became engaged to a distant cousin, Anna Eleanor Roosevelt. Certainly he was drawn to her intellect and social consciousness, as she wasn't considered a great beauty. His mother asked that he keep the engagement a secret for a year hoping that her son would tire of Eleanor and that she herself would regain her position in his life. She also sent him on a cruise in hopes that he might change his mind. Despite Sara's objections, Eleanor and Franklin married two years later.

Eleanor's uncle, President Theodore Roosevelt, gave the bride away in the absence of her deceased father. Teddy Roosevelt was an extremely popular figure and his presence caused a stir. A wedding guest was heard to comment that "he is the bride at the wedding and the corpse at the funeral." The marriage of Eleanor and FDR produced six children, five of whom survived infancy. Eleanor felt that the purpose of sex was to produce children. When that phase of her life was over and FDR's transgression with Lucy Mercer became apparent, separate bedrooms were agreed upon.

Sara Roosevelt's meddling existed for many years of the couple's marriage. She handled the family finances and controlled every facet of their lives. Sara built adjoining townhouses with a connecting door for them in the city and adjacent cottages on Campobello Island. Despite the fact that her son was president, Sara never gave up her place at the head of the dining table with her son seated to her right. She often undermined the parents' authority and took pleasure in spoiling the grandchildren.

Eleanor had a testy relationship with her mother, who repeatedly reminded her that she was less than beautiful. Anna Hall Roosevelt died of diphtheria when her Eleanor was only eight years old. Having been raised without benefit of a loving mother, Eleanor initially wanted to establish a close relationship with her new mother-in-law. However, she soon found her completely overbearing and was said to have no feelings upon Sara's death.

FDR has been linked with several women. Lucy Mercer Rutherford was romantically involved with him for many years, despite Eleanor's knowledge and objection. There were also rumors of other dalliances. He had an especially close relationship with his distant cousin Margaret (Daisy) Suckley, which is chronicled in the book *Closest Companion* by Geoffrey Ward. What was known to be true was that the president enjoyed the company of women and sought their uncritical approval; and they in turn found him charming.

When Eleanor was emotionally free of the role of wife, she blossomed in her own right. Her passion was public policy and social injustice. She served as the eyes and ears of the president on her travels around the world. She became a true statesman while keeping check on the progress of the New Deal.

In 1910 FDR won a seat in the New York state senate. Three years later he was appointed assistant secretary of the navy under Woodrow Wilson. He proved to be an effective administrator, particularly in the business dealings of the naval administration. In 1920 he was the vice presidential nominee on the ticket with Governor James M. Cox of Ohio. They were defeated by Republicans Warren G. Harding and Calvin Coolidge, largely as a backlash to former President Wilson's unpopular support of the League of Nations. Despite the loss, FDR had established a national following and was seen as a leader among progressive Democrats and an opponent of "machine politics."

While vacationing at Campobello in the summer of 1921, Roosevelt contracted poliomyelitis. Despite courageous attempts on his part to regain the use of his legs through heavy braces and crutches, he never walked unaided again. He established a foundation at Warm Springs, Georgia, to help fellow polio victims and inspired, as well as directed, the March of Dimes program that eventually funded the research which yielded an effective vaccine.

Roosevelt was elected governor of New York in 1928 and was reelected in 1932. He helped New York weather the depression and won the nomination based on that reputation. Breaking with tradition, Roosevelt accepted the nomination in person in Chicago in 1932. He campaigned on a platform of economic relief, recovery and reform via government intervention. FDR defeated the embattled Herbert Hoover and was sworn in as president in 1933, in the midst of the worst economic crisis in the nation's history.

The American economic system was in a state of shock. The financial downturn had seen more than 11,000 banks close, skyrocketing unemployment figures, a plunging gross national product and a nation heading for an economic abyss that could have ended in chaos. Roosevelt's response was immediate. The "New Deal" was the result of the best available minds—many from academia—who were aptly labeled the "Brains Trust." They were responsible for enacting fifteen major laws during FDR's first hundred days in office. Success could be achieved with the Banking Act of 1933 only if the people would agree to place their faith and money in their local banks once again. The charismatic president turned to the radio for support. He established a series of "fireside chats" to assure the American people that their deposits, now backed by the newly formed Federal Deposit Insurance Corporation, were secure.

FDR established the Social Security Act, the Federal Housing Administraion (FHA), which made home ownership affordable, and the Works Progress Administration (WPA), which employed almost eight million laborers. He established agencies such as the Securities and Exchange Commission (SEC), which was set up to stave off a further crash in the stock market, the Federal Communications Commission (FCC) and the Civil Aeronautics Authority (CAA). While FDR has been credited with reducing the effects of the Great Depression, critics believe his measures were not extensive enough to restore the workforce to full employment. Conservatives argue that FDR went too far and

brought too much government intervention in the economy, while those on the left felt he did not go far enough and that his administration should have implemented a program of direct federal aid to the jobless and the poor.

In June of 1939, the United States, with an army of only 186,000 men, ranked 19th among nations militarily. FDR realized that the American people needed to be educated in the real threats to national security. The existing policy of isolationism would doom the country. With the world on the brink of war, the state of the U.S. armed forces was untenable. Through Roosevelt's efforts, the number of armed forces swelled to 12 million by 1943 and represented the largest and most commanding military force the world had ever seen.

Following the attack on Pearl Harbor by Japan, and America's subsequent entry into the war, FDR gathered an outstanding team of admirals and generals. The president, in concert with Winston Churchill, crafted the "Grand Alliance" that destroyed the evils of German Nazism and Japanese militarism. FDR felt strongly that the U.S. should have a global focus and he committed the country to participation in the International Monetary Fund (IMF) and the World Bank. This action guaranteed America's involvement in a global economy and prevented a return to isolationism.

In the spring of 1945, following a lengthy and exhausting trip to the Crimean Peninsula to meet with Stalin and Churchill, FDR traveled to Warm Springs for rest and recuperation. Although FDR had been an active participant in the suggestions regarding a postwar Europe discussed at the summit, the president's health was clearly deteriorating. Lucy Mercer Rutherford and cousins Margaret Suckley and Laura (Polly) Delano had gathered at Warm Springs to welcome FDR back from the Yalta summit. Upon his arrival his pallor, halting speech and lifeless stare were evidence of his poor health. On April 12, 1945, while posing for a portrait by watercolor artist Elizabeth Shoumatoff, FDR complained of a piercing headache, slumped in his chair, and lost consciousness. Within hours he was pronounced dead of a massive cerebral hemorrhage. The painting remains incomplete and is formally titled *The Unfinished Portrait of FDR*. The news of FDR's passing stunned a nation mired in the final stages of a global struggle.

Upon hearing of the death of FDR, Stalin allowed that news to be the lead story and the president's picture to be printed on front pages of the Russian newspapers—space normally restricted for national stories. Winston Churchill felt as though he had been struck a physical blow and lost his composure when announcing the news to the House of Commons.

The train bearing the president's body departed Warm Springs on April 13. As it journeyed northward to Washington and Hyde Park, throngs of grieving citizens lined the tracks to bear witness to this historic figure. Two days later the body of FDR arrived at Springwood, on the Hudson. The president was home at last.

The policies and personality of Franklin Roosevelt set the tone of the modern presidency. Despite being confined to a wheelchair, he was the most vital figure in the nation, and perhaps the world, throughout his 13 years in the White House. Engendering both respect and disdain, FDR exerted unwavering leadership during the most turbulent period in American history since the Civil War.

For more information about our 32nd president visit http://www.nps.gov/fdrm/fdr/biography.htm, www.feri.org/archives/fdrbio/waryears.cfm or http://www.pbs.org/wgbh/amex/presidents/32_f_roosevelt/f_roosevelt_early.html.

Credits

It was always a good day at the library when the mail included a packet from the History Channel. But when two identical packages inadvertently arrived at our library, I knew for sure that I would mount a display on the subject contained in these packets, Franklin Delano Roosevelt. The information from this organization was comprehensive and the visuals could easily be worked into an effective collage.

Three quarters of a century have passed since Roosevelt was elected president. The challenges he faced were daunting. America was a nation recovering from financial devastation only to then face a vicious attack that debilitated its navy. The decisions required to retaliate and eventually end the war required tremendous courage and tough leadership.

Visit http://www.history.com/classroom/classroom.html for free educational material for your library displays.

Assembling the Display

1. The photos within the History Channel packet were cut, arranged into a collage and glued to a piece of black poster board. A photo of FDR was mounted on red poster board with the quote that introduced the chapter attached below. A 1¼" strip of gold poster board was glued to a 4" strip of black poster board. Stars 2½" in diameter were cut from gold poster board and attached with pins to the red felt background. The collage was pinned to the background and pulled forward.

2. On the top left was an article about the funding of FDR's second election. An image of a presidential campaign button for 1936 was inserted on the top right of the document. This can be found at http://www.buyingofthepresident.org/index.php/the_hanna_project/election_year/1936_roosevelt_vs_landon. Under that was this quote by FDR:

> The truth is found when men are free to pursue it.

On the bottom left was a document titled "Eleanor and Franklin," which chronicled their marriage. This information can be found if you visit http://www.firstladies.org/biographies/firstladies.aspx?biography=33.

Items on the left were printed on off white card stock and mounted on black or red and black poster board.

3. On the top right was a document about the Japanese internment under FDR with an image of a Japanese flag centered under the title. This information can be found at http://www.infoplease.com/spot/internment1.html. Under that was this quotation by FDR:

Democracy cannot succeed unless those who express their choice are prepared to choose wisely. The real safeguard of democracy, therefore, is education.

Last was a FDR time line which can be found if you visit http://www.fdrlibrary.marist.edu/chrono15.html.

Items on the right were printed and mounted like those on the left.

4. A red, white and blue bunting was placed on the base of the display. Styrofoam forms were placed beneath created three elevations. A reprint from the *St. Louis Star Times* about the declaration of war by the U.S. lay in the center. Historical reprints of other newspapers can be found if you visit http://www.anydate.com/products.php?category_id=60.

Books featured in this display were *The Greatest Generation* by Tom Brokaw, *The Privileged Life and Radical Presidency of Franklin Delano Roosevelt* by H.W. Brands, *1942: The Year That Tried Men's Souls* by Winston Groom, *Lindbergh vs. Roosevelt: The Rivalry That Divided America* by James Duffy, *FDR* by Jean Edward Smith, *The Second World War* by Martin Gilbert, *Roosevelt's Secret War* by Joseph E. Persico and *Franklin and Winston: An Intimate Portrait of an Epic Friendship* by Jon Meacham. Gold stars were placed throughout the books.

Bigger and Better

Should your display space be larger, add, if possible, period boots or helmets, World War II uniforms and framed photos. Lots of war posters are available through image searches or through online poster or book vendors. Add a 48-star American flag to your tableau.

You might want to zero in on the complicated marriage/partnership of FDR and Eleanor. Your display could focus on the letters of the former president, which can be found in *FDR: His Personal Letters—Early Years* edited by son Elliot Roosevelt. You might choose FDR's relationship with Winston Churchill, which was well documented. The "Yalta Summit" or the "Fireside Chats" are other subjects you might consider. Use *FDR and His Enemies* by Albert Fried as a source for that fascinating topic. His enemies included such notables as Al Smith, Charles Lindbergh and Senator Huey Long.

Internment of the Japanese in camps in the U.S. during the war was a controversial idea which Eleanor Roosevelt despised. There is a lot of information available on this subject. *Only What We Could Carry: The Japanese American Internment Experience* by Lawson Fusao and *Impounded: Dorothea Lange and the Censored Images of Japanese American Internment* by Dorothy Lange are excellent sources with photos.

The Wright Stuff

Every great architect is necessarily a great poet. He must be a great original interpreter of his time, his day, his age. —Frank Lloyd Wright

Frank Lincoln Wright was born in Richland Center, Wisconsin, on June 8, 1867, to a music teacher/minister father and a homemaker. Welsh-born Anna Lloyd Jones Wright gave birth to two daughters and a son in the course of her marriage to William Russell Wright. Prior to her son's birth, she imagined a career path in architecture for him. Anna provided young Frank with maple wood Froebel kindergarten blocks purchased at the Philadelphia Centennial Exposition. These greatly inspired the future architect.

The family was required to move frequently in order to accommodate the father's position in the ministry. This nomadic existence proved unsettling and William Wright abandoned the family in 1885, never to be seen again. William's relationship with his son was terminated early, but his impact, especially his love of music and the arts, endured. After his parents' divorce, Wright changed his middle name from Lincoln to Lloyd in deference to his mother.

The Wrights settled in Madison, Wisconsin, when Frank was about 12 years old. Summers were spent on his Uncle James' farm in Spring Green, Wisconsin. In 1885, he left Madison prior to graduation from high school to work for the dean of the University of Wisconsin's Engineering department. The decision to leave was prompted by the dramatic change in the family's financial situation. Enrolled as a special student without a diploma, Wright spent two semesters studying drafting and civil engineering before pawning his father's books and relocating to Illinois in 1887. Those semesters were the sum total of his exposure to higher education. By his mid–twenties, Wright had acquired the social acumen and architectural tools necessary for his new life and station in Chicago. He secured a position with the architect Joseph Lyman Silsbee in the new locale. Silsbee's style and preference for residential architecture would inform much of Wright's technique throughout his career. The following year he went to work for the firm of Adler and Sullivan. It was there that Louis Sullivan assumed the role of both supervisor and mentor.

Prior to 21-year-old Wright's marriage to Catherine Lee Tobin, daughter of a prosperous businessman, Sullivan lent him $5,000 to begin building a home in Oak Park, Illinois. This was Wright's wedding gift to his 18-year-old bride. Catherine provided the cultural background that Wright lacked and gave him the social polish as well. The Wrights were well regarded among their neighbors and renowned for the ease with which they entertained.

Wright adapted Sullivan's maxim—"Form follows function." Although he was slow to give credit to mentors in his life, Wright always acknowledged the substantial influence that Sullivan had on his career. In 1893, Sullivan and Wright ended their business arrangement and the latter opened his own firm in Chicago. In 1894 he joined Robert Spencer and Dwight Perkins, among others, to form the Prairie School of Architecture. In 1898 he added a studio to his home in Oak Park. This was the first of many additions to that structure.

Although the egocentric Wright had difficulty relating to his children, the family grew to include six of them, four sons and two daughters. Frank Jr., also known as Lloyd, followed in his father's footsteps and became an architect. He showed such early promise as a draftsman that, at age 19, his father entrusted him with many of the renderings of the renowned prairie houses included in what would be called the Berlin portfolio. Despite their many differences over the years,

The Wright Stuff. A stained glass poster was created in the spirit of the design aesthetic of Frank Lloyd Wright. Colorful geometric shapes surround a biography and photo of the famed architect.

Lloyd never resented his father's place of importance in the profession of architecture.

Wright's early houses exposed his unique talent. They were distinctive in their style, which mimicked that of a horizontal plane absent basement and attics. Built with natural materials, his homes never required paint. Wright incorporated low-pitched rooflines with deep overhangs and continuous walls of windows which fused the horizontal homes into their environment. He included skylights and featured formidable stone or brick fireplaces in the heart of the home. Rooms flowed into one another. His streamlined design served as an inspiration to the Prairie School, a title given to those architects whose style was indigenous of midwestern architects.

Wright's concept of the "prairie house" was considered a functional and aesthetic breakthrough when introduced at the turn of the 20th century. He felt that the boxed-in rooms prevalent in Victorian era homes were confining, so he began to design houses with low horizontal lines and open interior spaces. Rooms were designed to blend in with the flat landscape of the prairie. This concept gained popularity with other architects of the period. Prairie home design carried immense consequences for both national and international architecture.

In 1909, after 18 years in Oak Park, Wright scandalized his family by going to Berlin with Mamah Borthwick Cheney, the wife of a neighbor and client and the mother of two small children. They spent almost two years in Europe, where he worked on the Wasmuth Portfolio, a book dedicated to his work. Upon his return to the U.S., Wright began planning and building a home for himself and his soul mate, Mamah. It was built in Spring Green on ancestral land provided by his mother. The house was named Taliesin, which means "shining brow" in Welsh. Wright carefully situated the house just below the top of the hill so that the house was "of the hill" and not simply "on the hill."

Wright divided his time between Chicago and Taliesen. He and Mamah shocked the town by their bold cohabitation. They lived there until 1914, when a crazed household servant, Julian Carleton, locked all but one door to the sprawling home and set it ablaze.

Carleton axed Mamah, her two visiting children and four workmen to death and injured several others. Many thought that this tragedy would mark the end of the architect's career. Wright was personally devastated by it, received much negative press and experienced a financial downturn as a result. A true survivor, he threw himself into important work at hand such as the final drawings of Chicago's Midway Gardens and the rebuilding of his beloved Taliesin.

Catherine Wright knew the difficulty she would have procuring child and spousal support from her parsimonious husband and had no interest in terminating the marriage despite the circumstances. She would not agree to a divorce until 1922. The existing law required that divorced individuals wait one year before remarrying.

A southern-born divorcee and mother of three, Miriam Noel, wrote a letter of condolence to Wright following the heartbreak in Wisconsin. As a result of this communiqué, a relationship was formed and a romance developed quickly. Miriam was soon living with Wright at Taliesin. After seven years Wright was finally free to marry. The slender, heroin addicted sculptress became wife number two, in a romantic midnight wedding ceremony which took place in the middle of a bridge that spanned the Wisconsin River, upstream from Taliesin. Their marriage was short-lived, however. The couple separated after a matter of months, most certainly as a result of her addiction. After much very public acrimony, Miriam was granted a settlement, which included alimony, and a divorce in 1927.

While still married to Miriam, Frank was introduced to former ballerina Olga Milanoff Hinzenberg at the Petrograd Ballet in Chicago in 1924. They became involved immediately and began living together with both her daughter and their own infant, Iovanna Lazovich Lloyd Wright, who was born in late 1925. When it was legally possible, Wright married the much younger, Hungarian-born divorcee in 1928 at midnight in Rancho Santa Fe near La Jolla, California. This marriage proved to be quite harmonious and lasted until Wright's death in 1959.

In 1991, the American Institute of Architects named Frank Lloyd Wright the greatest architect of all time. At the turn of the century the *Architectural Record* published a list of the 100 most important designs of the 20th century. Twelve of Wright's buildings appeared on that list including: Fallingwater, the Robie and Jacobs houses, Taliesin and Taliesin West.

Frank Lloyd Wright's important designs, such as the Guggenheim Museum in New York, the Marin Civic Center in San Rafael, California, and Tokyo's Imperial Hotel, continue to amaze and influence generations of designers. However, his true architectural legacy remains the nearly 600 residences that he designed and built for upper middle class Americans during his remarkable 72-year career.

Credits

I am a member of a book club, so I am always on the lookout for new and interesting titles that I might suggest for a group read. In 2007, I read *Loving Frank,* Nancy Horan's fictionalized account of the liaison between Frank Lloyd Wright and Mamah Borthwick Cheney. At the time of this affair, Wright was still very married to his first wife, Catherine. The scandal shocked straight-laced, early 20th century America, and the tragic ending was incomprehensible.

I later read a nonfiction account of the tragedy at Taliesin titled *Death in a Prairie House* by William R. Drennan, which substantiated Horan's account of the incident. This glimpse into the life and genius of Wright the architect and his independent, erudite Mamah left me wanting more. I have since read, and thoroughly enjoyed, *The Women* by T.C. Boyle, which is a fictionalized account of Wright's love affair with Mamah, as well as the other women who bore his name. The book club certainly enjoyed *Loving Frank* and the animated discussion that ensued was memorable!

Assembling the Display

1. The font selected for this display was Reynold Art Deco, Regular, sized at 375. This can be found on page 14 if you visit http://www.abstractfonts.com/category/57/art+deco. There were many similar fonts that would

work well located on that site. The letters were printed on white card stock and glued to black poster board. The poster was inspired by a stained glass window found online. If you use the term "Frank Lloyd Wright stained glass window" in a Google image search you will find this design and many more from which to choose. The colors in the poster were red, green, blue, black and silver on a background of white poster board. Above the poster was this quote by Frank Lloyd Wright:

> Buildings, too, are children of Earth and Sun.

Under the poster was a photograph of Wright in profile and an excerpt from a speech he gave to the people of Marin County in July 1975. This can be found if you do a Google image search using the terms "Frank Lloyd Wright address."

Circles and squares were cut from the same colors as those used in the poster and randomly placed to frame the portrait of Wright. The quote and portrait were printed on white card stock and mounted on black poster board. All items were attached with pins and pulled forward on the background of black felt.

2. On the top right was a humorous quote by Wright:

> A doctor can bury his mistakes but an architect can only advise his clients to plant vines.

Under that was a color photograph of Fallingwater that was found through a Google image search. Next was a biography of Wright which can be found at http://www.oprf.com/flw/bio/.

Information about the prairie house, with an image of the Frederick C. Robie house in Chicago, was next. This can be found if you visit http://www.wrightplus.org/robiehouse/robiehouse.html.

Information on the left was printed on white card stock and mounted on blue or black poster board.

3. On the top right was this quote by Wright:

> Organic buildings are the strength and lightness of the spiders' spinning, buildings qualified by light, bred by native character to environment, married to the ground.

Under that was a color print of Taliesin in Spring Green, Wisconsin.

Next was a document titled The Legacy of Frank Lloyd Wright compiled from information that can be found if you visit http://www.pbs.org/flw/ A stained glass image was inserted into the top center of the document.

Last was a color print of Unity Temple. Built in 1906, it is located in Oak Park, Illinois.

Images on the right were found through Google image searches and mounted like those on the left.

Quotes and documents were printed on white card stock and mounted like the images.

Books on display were *Frank Lloyd Wright: The Houses* by Alan Hess, *Loving Frank: A Novel* by Nancy Horan, *Fallingwater Rising: Frank Lloyd Wright, E. J. Kaufmann, and America's Most Extraordinary House* by Franklin Toker, *Frank Lloyd Wright's Interiors* by Thomas Heinz, *Frank Lloyd Wright's Prairie Houses* by Carla Lind, *Apprentice to Genius: Years with Frank Lloyd Wright* by Edgar Tafel and *An Autobiography* by Frank Lloyd Wright.

Red, green, blue and silver poster board squares were interspersed among the books to tie in the colors of the stained glass.

Bigger and Better

Add some tools of the profession if your space permits. A compass, slide rule, drawing instruments, blueprints and some models would add great interest to a display on architecture. The blueprint could also serve as a background in lieu of the stained glass window.

You might want to focus on Wright's distinctively personal Prairie style homes. For information on that visit http://www.delmars.com/wright/flw2.htm.

Should you want to feature the furniture he designed, get a copy of the book *Frank Lloyd Wright: Interiors and Furniture* by Thomas Heinz. Your display may focus on Wright's beloved home in Wisconsin, Taliesin I. This information can be found if you visit http://www.taliesinpreservation.org/.

You may decide to feature the women in his life. Include T.C. Boyle's *The Women*, which covers the four main relationships in his life. You might also focus on his mother, Anna Lloyd Jones, who greatly influenced her son and often alienated his partners. Photos of these women are available online.

Should you decide to feature a number of the great architects, be sure to include I.M. Pei, Le Corbusier, DaVinci, Frank Furness, Antoni Gaudi, Frank Gehry, Walter Gropius, and the like. For a complete list visit http://architecture.about.com/od/architectsaz/Great_Architects_AZ.htm

For another idea related to architecture titled "Skyscrapers of Manhattan," see page 116 of my first book, *Great Displays for Your Library Step by Step*.

6 Moments in Time

Titanic

We do not care anything for the heaviest storms in these big ships. It is fog that we fear. The big icebergs that drift into warmer water melt much more rapidly under water than on the surface, and sometimes a sharp, low reef extending two or three hundred feet beneath the sea is formed. If a vessel should run on one of these reefs half her bottom might be torn away.
—Captain Edward J. Smith, Commander of *Titanic*

Graceful, dramatic, and powerful, the sailing ships of the 18th and 19th centuries were also known as tall ships and traveled between continents over a period of weeks or months. Passengers were far more likely to contract a deadly disease than to be a party to a shipwreck or the victim of a drowning. During the mid 18th century shipyards produced bigger and faster passenger ships named liners, after the shipping lines for whom they were built. In order to attract first-class passengers, these steam powered vessels were built with a host of amenities and included state of the art safety features. The luxurious furniture and fittings rivaled accommodations in the finest hotels of the era.

Construction of the R.M.S. *Titanic* began on March 31, 1909, at a shipyard in Belfast, Northern Ireland. The *Titanic* wasn't just a ship, however, she was a symbol. Her name, from the Greek word "Titan," translated to mean something huge. The construction cost totaled $7.5 million, about $123 million in today's currency. Throughout the 19th century, people had developed a certain sense of security. By 1912, the world had witnessed nearly 100 years of peace and steady industrial growth. Tragically, all that was about to change.

The concept for this vessel was a joint venture conceived by J. Bruce Ismay, managing director of the White Star Line shipping company, and Lord Pirrie, chairman of the board of shipbuilders Harland and Wolff. The White Star Line grew from a bankrupt fleet of clipper ships operating between Britain and Australia. White Star had a 40-year association with this shipyard and was quite confident in the quality of its workmanship.

U.S. banker, industrialist, steel magnate and railroad tycoon John Pierpont Morgan was one of the richest men of his time. He purchased White Star in 1903 along with several competitors hoping to profit from the Atlantic passenger trade, since the only way to cross the ocean at that time was by ship. Morgan's shipping conglomerate reigned supreme. He was a guest of honor at the ship's launch and originally booked passage on *Titanic*'s maiden voyage, but business affairs forced him to cancel his plans.

The design of the *Titanic* was considered sleek and her scale impressive. The ship's power came from three huge steam engines nearly 40 feet tall that required the labor of 200 men when cruising speed was reached. Six hundred tons of coal were used over a 24-hour period. The fourth funnel was mainly aesthetic and served as a giant ventilation shaft while giving balance to the overall design. The two masts were relics from the days of sail and were used only as flagpoles for the ensigns and support for the wireless antenna. Known as the "triple screw steamer" because it was driven by three cast steel and bronze propellers, the *Titanic* featured

Titanic. A model of the *Titanic*, built by Dr. Allen Richardson, anchors this display chronicling the famous 1912 maritime disaster. The interior grid, which hangs above, provides explicit detail about each deck. Telegrams, a *Titanic* postcard signed by five survivors, a boarding pass and second class ticket for the White Star Line and a newspaper masthead lie at the base of the model.

gigantic wing propellers that spanned more than 16 feet.

When viewing the plans for the ship's interior, J. Bruce Ismay was disappointed with the design of the main staircase, which he felt lacked the necessary size and elegance. That design, however, was consistent with shipbuilding safety standards. The change that would be made compromised that standard and would be a contributing factor to the ship's quick demise.

Passenger accommodations on board this floating palace were divided into three classes. Each class occupied separate areas of the vessel and each had its own facilities. First class staterooms numbered 416 and included lavish use of hardwoods, marble and gilt. These passengers enjoyed Turkish and electric baths, a swimming pool, gymnasium,

squash court, bar, darkroom, library and a barbershop. There were rooms dedicated to smoking, reading and writing and an opulent à la carte restaurant run by master chef Luigi Gatti. A glassed-in promenade on deck A provided protection from the elements and three electric elevators allowed passengers to move with ease about the ship. The stateroom cost was equivalent to $4,500 in today's currency, although standard first-class rooms could be had for about $3,700 for a one-way crossing.

Second class was anything but second rate onboard the *Titanic*. The amenities surpassed those of first class facilities on most rival liners. Second class passengers on the *Titanic* had access to a single electric elevator, a promenade on the boat deck, a large dining saloon on D deck, a smoking room, bars and lounges as well as a library. There were

162 staterooms that were considered comfortable and compact. Second class passage for a one-way crossing could be purchased for about $1,700.

Third class included 262 staterooms plus an additional 40 open berth areas. Passengers in this class were segregated from other classes and had few amenities. Passengers in third class were required to be examined by a doctor before boarding. They could use the promenade on the poop deck, and had access to a smoking room, a general room and a dining saloon on F deck that served the numerous passengers in shifts. More than 100 of the 710 third class passengers were Irish who had left their troubled island with mixed emotions to start a new life in America. The average working man earned £1 a week, and one-way passage cost £870, or today's equivalent of $4,350.

The engines were tested and an emergency stop was conducted during the sea trials of the *Titanic* in early April 1912. On April 10, amid much fanfare, the *Titanic* set sail from the port of Southampton, England, with 2,200 aboard. The 899 crew members included Captain Edward J. Smith and his senior officers, who were responsible for every aspect of life onboard the ship. Included were people of all ages, nationalities and economic stations—a true microcosm of society—excited at the prospect of being part of this historical venture. Captain Smith, known as the "Millionaire's Captain" was an ocean voyage away from retirement.

As the *Titanic* sped across the North Atlantic on April 14, cautionary messages came across the wireless from ships in the area regarding the presence of ice. Captain Smith was firm in his belief that his ship was not in danger. He was under pressure from Bruce Ismay, the ship's owner and a passenger onboard the ship, to arrive in New York Harbor not just on time but ahead of schedule, thus proving the vessel's speed and reliability. The captain altered his course slightly in reaction to the warnings, but then proceeded "full speed ahead" toward the U.S. One of the messages read, "Captain, *Titanic*—Westbound steamers report bergs, growlers, and field ice in 42°N, from 49° to 51°W, April 12". (Capt. Barr of the *Caronia*)

The night of April 14, 1914, was clear,

though bitterly cold, on the North Atlantic. Although there was no moon, the cloudless sky was full of stars. The gentle waves belied the danger lurking ahead. Because of the clarity of the night, everyone thought there would be plenty of time to react to obstacles in the sea. Frederick Fleet, the ship's lookout, was not in possession of his field glasses, which had been locked up. By 11:40 P.M., the time he spotted the iceberg, the disaster could not be averted.

At 12:05 A.M. Captain Smith assessed the extent of the damage to the vessel and ordered that the lifeboats be uncovered and preparations made to abandon ship. No lifeboat drills had been ordered previously, so pandemonium reigned among passengers and crew. The prevailing thought was that it was better to remain on deck than to be lowered into the frigid ocean aboard a lifeboat. Officers were ignorant of the fact that the lifeboats could be lowered while fully loaded. So, instead of saving 1,178 passengers, only 706 were ultimately rescued from the small crafts. Despite the fact that there weren't enough lifeboats for all aboard the ship, the *Titanic* surpassed the existing safety requirements by 17 percent. While the lifeboats were being loaded, the radio operators sent out distress signals. Morse code messages were flashed by officers on the bridge. Rockets pierced the night sky in an attempt to attract the attention of ships in the area. At 12:45 A.M. wireless operator Jack Phillips ceased sending the standard CQD signal and changed to the new SOS signal—the first SOS to be transmitted from a sinking ship. Although the *Californian* was situated nearby on that fateful night, their wireless operator was asleep and the Marconi machine was turned off.

At 12:35 A.M. the wireless operator on board the RMS *Carpathia* received a distress message from the *Titanic*. The ship aborted its New York to Mediterranean run and traveled quickly to the distressed liner. Captain Rostron prepared his ship to receive the survivors. Doctors on board were put on standby, stewards and cooks prepared accommodations and food and rockets were fired announcing the ship's approach. Rostron's immediate concern was ice. The same iceberg that sunk the *Titanic* could easily sink his ship (Adams, 44).

The damage to the *Titanic* caused by the collision allowed water to flood six of the sixteen major watertight compartments. As the reality of the ship's demise became apparent, those still onboard tried to make rafts out of deck chairs and other furniture, while others prayed for rescue and comforted their loved ones. During this time the two bands onboard assembled in the first class lounge and played various ragtime selections until the ship sank and the ocean swallowed them. The *Titanic* sank at 2:20 A.M. on April 15, 1912.

Although much has been written about the reasons for the rapid sinking of the *Titanic*, only in the past decade has the quality of the rivets been seen as a contributing factor. It has been documented that the builder of the *Titanic* and her two sisters, *Olympic* and *Britannic,* struggled for years to obtain enough good rivets and riveters and finally settled for substandard materials, which ultimately doomed the ship. The archives of the shipbuilder are full of references to the quality of the rivets and the workmen involved. Because three million rivets were needed per vessel, the builder was forced to turn to small forges which tended to have less skilled and experienced laborers. Also, records indicated that the shipbuilder ordered #3 iron bars, rated as "best," rather than #4, considered "best-best," for the rivets. The latter was the standard used by those competitors still using iron.

Metallurgists knew that good riveting required great skill. The iron had to be heated to a precise cherry red color and beaten by the right combinations of hammer blows. Mediocre work could hide potential problems. Studies show that the rival Cunard line had abandoned iron and switched to steel rivets, which were stronger and required machine installation that improved workmanship. Many of the rivets recovered from the vessel and reviewed by scientists were found to be corroded with high concentrations of slag, a glassy residue of smelting. The presence of slag can make the rivets brittle and thus prone to fracture. The final concensus was that poor quality material coupled with inexperienced laborers were contributing factors to the *Titanic*'s quick demise.

When the *Titanic* struck an iceberg, it was not a foregone conclusion that the ship would sink. The liner was designed to stay afloat if up to four of its sealed compartments were flooded. So many of the rivets popped along the starboard side of the ship that a fifth compartment filled up, condemning the vessel to the depths and dooming the fate of 1,500 souls. For more information about the rivets visit http://www.guardian.co.uk/uk/2008/apr/16/usa.

There are many stories by and about the survivors of the *Titanic*. Women and children were loaded into the lifeboats first and the great majority survived thanks to the excellent care provided onboard the *Carpathia*. There were disputes, however, among the passengers in the lifeboats. Some thought the boats should return to retrieve possible survivors, others felt that the sheer numbers of bodies in the water would swamp the boats. Many of the women in the lifeboats didn't seem to realize that it was their husbands and sons who were among those struggling to survive in their life jackets. Some lifeboats did manage to return to search for survivors but precious few were saved. Many succumbed to hypothermia in the ocean's frigid 28° temperatures. Ironically the ship's designer, J. Bruce Ismay, survived.

Some blame can be attributed to the men working the wireless, who felt that their primary responsibility was sending messages written by their wealthy passengers. So when additional warning messages regarding the iceberg sightings were received, they were not necessarily conveyed in a timely fashion to the ship's officers, who could have responded, and, perhaps, changed the course of history.

Popular opinion suggests that the glamour associated with the maiden voyage of the R.M.S. *Titanic,* combined with its list of notable passengers, magnified the tragedy. Heroes and heroines were created that night and widely celebrated in the press. The totality of the disaster and the mythology that has surrounded it have continued to captivate millions a hundred years hence.

As a result of the disaster, the first International Convention for Safety of Life at Sea was called in London in 1913. Rules were drawn up that required every ship to have lifeboat space for each person onboard, lifeboat drills to be required on each voyage, and all ships to maintain a 24-hour radio watch. Also established at the convention was the International Ice Patrol, whose purpose is to warn ships of icebergs in the shipping lanes of the North Atlantic.

For some excellent resources you may want to tap into for your display visit http://www.historyonthenet.com/Titanic/titanic_time line.htm, http://www.britannica.com/titanic/03_SINK/pict_17.html or http://www.nytimes.com/2008/04/15/science/15titanic.html? r=1.

Credits

The hundredth anniversary of the *Titanic* disaster will be marked in 2012. The research and recovery efforts surrounding the remains of the ship in the late 20th century served to refresh the legend and rekindle the interest in the doomed vessel. The journey below the oceans surface made possible both scientific and historic discoveries of objects lying in chaotic disarray on the ocean floor. These expeditions, especially that of American Robert Ballard, in conjunction with the French oceanographic institute IFREMER, permitted the focus to shift from the totality of loss caused by the maritime disaster to the retrieval of the many artifacts that have since found their way to public exhibits and museums on both sides of the Atlantic. Not only do the objects retrieved from the wreck of the *Titanic* inform our assessment of the events, they also pay homage to those who perished aboard that fateful ship.

According to IMBD, the 1997 movie *Titanic* grossed over $600 million and is the second most lucrative film of all time. This production created a renewed interest in the voyage and dozens of publications emerged as a result. I'm sure that the centennial will see a similar surge of interest, so Titanic should be a relevant display for you to mount around this anniversary.

Orlando, Florida, has a popular attraction titled "Titanic—The Experience." It offers visitors the opportunity to follow a timeless story in a way it has never before been experienced. The attraction features a 20,000 square foot interactive museum, full scale recreations of *Titanic*'s Grand Staircase, the Verandah Café and other rooms. Tourists have the opportunity to view authentic artifacts and historical treasures. Trained actors in period attire portray famous *Titanic* notables throughout the guided tour. A popular feature of the exhibit is the Promenade Deck, where you can actually walk out and feel the chill of the cold Atlantic air as you gaze at the stars.

The model ship featured in the Cressman Library display was crafted by Dr. Allen Richardson, professor of religious studies at Cedar Crest College, who also supplied the interior grid poster and the *Titanic* postcard. An avid collector with many and varied interests, Dr. Richardson has generously supplied numerous items that have been the focal points of displays for this book. I remain in his debt.

Assembling the Display

1. The font Bernard MT sized at 450 was used to create the word *Titanic*. This was printed on card stock and traced onto gold poster board. The letters were attached with pins and pulled forward. Flanking the title were red flags with white stars. This image, representing the White Star Lines, was found through a Google image search, sized to about 5" x 9" in Adobe Photoshop, printed on card stock and traced onto red poster board. The 3 ½" star was cutout and then traced onto white poster board and attached.

An illustration of the interior of the *Titanic* postcard was mounted on black and gold poster board, attached with pins, pulled forward and centered under the display title. Thin strips of red and gold poster board flanked the poster and were attached with pins.

2. On the top left was a document on the "Unsinkable Molly Brown," which can be found if you visit http://www.encyclopedia-titanica.org/titanic-biography/molly-brown.html Under that was a quote by Captain Edward Smith:

> I cannot imagine any condition which would cause a ship to founder. I cannot conceive of any vital disaster happening to this vessel. Modern ship building has gone beyond that.

Next was a document titled "Inside the Titanic," which described some of the special features of the ship's interior. This can be found at http://www.titanicandco.com/inside.html.

All items on the left were printed on off white card stock and mounted on black and gold poster board.

3. On the top right was a list of facts about the *Titanic* which were taken from the book *882 ½ Amazing Answers to Your Questions About the Titanic* by Hugh Brewster and Laurie Coulter. Under that was a telegram from Capt. Barr of the *Caronia* warning of the presence of icebergs in the area of the *Titanic:*

> Captain, *Titanic,* westbound steamers report bergs, growlers, and field Ice in 42°N, from 49° to 51°W, April 12.

Next was a copy of a telegram from Bruce Ismay on board the *Carpathia* to the owners of the White Star Lines informing them of the disaster. This can be found at http://www.liverpoolmuseums.org.uk/maritime/archive/top10treasures/titanic_telegram.aspx.

Items on the right were printed and mounted like those on the left.

4. On the base of the display was a model of the *Titanic*, which was elevated on Styrofoam covered in black velvet. Centered in front of that was a framed vintage postcard of the *Titanic* with signatures of 5 survivors on the verso of the card. Also included on the base was a mint tin with an image of the ship, a photo of a pocket watch stopped at the time the ship sank, an article about the band on the ship playing until the end, a masthead from the *London Herald* announcing the disaster, another telegraph message from Bruce Ismay announcing that 675 passengers had survived, a White Star boarding pass and a second class ticket for the *Titanic*. All of these items were found through Google image searches.

Books featured in the display were *The Complete "Titanic": From the Ship's Earliest Blueprints to the Epic Film* by Stephen J. Spignesi, *The "Titanic" Disaster: As Reported in the British National Press April-July 1912* by Dave Bryceson, *What Really Sank the "Titanic": New Forensic Evidence* by Jennifer Hooper McCarthy and Tim Foecke, *Last Dinner on the Titanic* by Rick Archbold and Dana McCauley, *"Titanic" Survivor* by Violet Jessup and *"Titanic's" Last Secrets* by Brad Matsen.

Bigger and Better

Many posters of the *Titanic* are available online. There are some books with great photographs and illustrations that could be reproduced or enlarged for a background should your space be larger. There is a good illustration of the interior of the ship in the book *On Board the "Titanic": What It Was Like When the Great Liner Sank* by Shelley Tanaka. A collage of these images would work well. You may want to focus on the discovery of the remains of the ship. Line your case with sand and stones to suggest the ocean floor. Cracked china, vintage shoes, and aged pewter are but a few of the items that could be seen peeking out of the sand.

It shouldn't be too difficult to find patrons who are into ship model building and have models that could be used in your exhibit space. Depending on which ships are available, customize your display to that topic. Possibilities are: "Tall Ships," "Ghost Ships" or "Shipwrecks." You may want to check out page 177 of my first book, which features a pond boat in a display titled "Sailors' Tales" and contains fiction and nonfiction books about sailing.

1776

> *The die is now cast; the colonies must either submit or triumph ... we must not retreat.* — King George III, in a letter to Lord North, 1774
>
> *Nothing short of independence, it appears to me, can possibly do. A peace on other terms would ... be a peace of war.* — George Washington, in a letter to John Banister, 1778

Although the colonists had made it abundantly clear that they no longer wished to live under English rule, the British were clearly divided as to their response. Their views on the possibility of an American revolution were in constant flux from 1763 to 1783. There was no universal conviction about the correct course of action—regarding the restless colonists—among the Tories, Whigs, radicals and British citizenry.

Britain held dominion over the colonies because they were settled under English protection, were constituted by an English charter and had been defended by British rule. But by the middle of the 18th century, differences in life, thought, and interests had developed between the thirteen colonies and the mother country. Colonial political institutions and practices differed significantly from those of the English. Disparate social mores, religious traditions and economic interests added to the potential for turmoil.

The issue of sovereign rights was precipitated when the Stamp Act was passed in 1765, followed by its repeal and the passage of the Townsend Act two years later. That piece of legislation levied taxes on colonists on the sale of glass, paint, oil, lead, paper and tea. The Americans resisted, thus forcing a resolution of sovereignty. One possible response was to grant the colonies outright independence, another was to compel colonial obedience to Parliament through force, and a third was to pacify the colonies by granting each colonial assembly considerable autonomy over its internal affairs, including the right of taxation, while still maintaining British imperial sovereignty. The vast range of opinions regarding the revolution was not surprising. They paralleled the common perceptions men held during that period about complex social, political, religious and economic problems in general.

King George III was the ruling monarch in Britain during this period. He ascended to the throne of England in 1760 at the age of 22. Born in London on June 4, 1738, he was the son of Frederick, Prince of Wales, and the grandson of George II. The first of the House of Hanover to be educated as an Englishman, George had high but impractical ideas of kingship.

George III was an uncompromising

1776. A replica of a British redcoat jacket is flanked by two handmade British Revolutionary swords, a copperplate image of King George III, and two English pair-case watches. The top shelf features a hand forged mattock, a naval cannon ball with chains, an 18th century rifleman's powder horn, a pay receipt from the quartermaster, a miniature locket with a head of a British Revolutionary officer and hand forged leg irons and shackles.

monarch which ultimately led to the loss of the American colonies, a blame he shared with his chief minister, Lord North. The minister's handling of the East India Tea Company's impending bankruptcy, which led to additional taxes being levied upon the colonists, created great animosity. In addition, the colonists were resentful that they were not permitted to choose a representative to the British Parliament, even though it was that legislative body which passed the laws under which they were taxed. This injustice, coupled with the widespread unrest incited by the tea tax, prompted the heated response "taxation without representation is tyranny."

King George was a passionate force in politics in 18th century England. He was a strong supporter of the war against America, and he viewed the concession of independence in 1783 with disdain and even contemplated abdicating his throne. He fought a bitter feud with the Whig leader Charles James Fox. This led to the fall of the Fox-North ministry in 1783. The king then prudently placed the newly formed government into the hands of the young prime minister, William Pitt, who restored stability for the remainder of the century.

On April 19, 1775, British general Thomas Gage ordered 700 British troops to be dispatched by Lt. Col. Francis Smith to Concord, Massachusetts, 16 miles northwest of Boston. Their order was to confiscate weapons which the patriots had been stockpiling. News of the British exodus from Boston was quickly spread by Paul Revere on his famous ride. By the time the British reached the village of Lexington, through which they had to pass, they found 70 Minutemen under the command of Capt. John Parker waiting for them. When the colonist were ordered by the British to disperse, the "shot heard round the world" was fired and the American War of Independence was begun in earnest. The British retaliated and fired upon the Minutemen, killing eight and wounding ten. The British suffered only a single injury.

The colonies comprised both British Loyalists and colonial revolutionists. It was an indecisive time. Loyalists were plentiful and could be found in every colony. They included small farmers as well as large landowners, royal officeholders and professionals. A large portion of the population chose a neutral stance, swaying to one point of view or the other or remaining inert in the struggle, which was viewed, to some extent, as a civil war.

In January 1776, Thomas Paine wrote a pamphlet entitled *Common Sense* in which he voiced his support for the colonial cause. He praised the good of society, and warned of the necessity for government as well as the inherent problems in the complex British system. He was especially opposed to the continuation of royal succession. Paine felt that the colonies lacked respectability and were perceived as rebels, incapable of forming alliances with other nations. He urged the colonists to declare freedom, thereby insuring foreign support in the struggle against Britain.

This influential document was widely distributed and enthusiastically received. Still, when Congress decided to declare the independence of the thirteen colonies, support for a military undertaking was not widespread. To read Paine's powerful treatise visit http://www.earlyamerica.com/earlyamerica/milestones/commonsense/text.html.

The war officially ended eight and a half years later on September 3, 1783, with the signing of the Treaty of Paris. The three American negotiators of the treaty, John Adams, Benjamin Franklin and John Jay, clung fiercely to the points of national interest that guaranteed a future for the United States. Some critical provisions of the treaty were British recognition of U.S. independence, the precise delineation of boundaries that would permit fishing off the coast of Newfoundland, British and American access to the navigation of the Mississippi, and most important, allowance for an American expansion west. Other treaties were signed by the British with American allies France and Spain, as well as Holland. The Treaty of Paris was a coup for the patriots involved in the dialogue. Their achievement has been labeled the greatest triumph in the history of American diplomacy. For more information about the Treaty of Paris visit http://www.state.gov/r/pa/ho/time/ar/14313.htm.

The Americans won their independence from Britain, but only just. They were indebted to foreign intervention and dependent upon a relatively small number of young, ill-trained and poorly armed volunteer soldiers and, happily, some particularly zealous patriots. George III reigned until 1820, the longest tenure of the male British monarchs. After 1801 the king was increasingly incapacitated by porphyry, an illness causing blindness and senility. His recurring bouts of insanity were problematic and compelled him to submit to the establishment of a formal Regency in 1811. His oldest son, George IV, was named regent.

Britain lost her colonies, but many of the issues between them and their ex-mother country remained unresolved. The two nations took up arms once again in 1812 when Britain attempted to reestablish control over the new nation but was ultimately defeated. Since that time these great nations have found a way to become staunch allies rather than enemies.

Credits

Dr. Allen Richardson is a published author and professor of religious studies at Cedar Crest College. His name may sound familiar to you, as parts of his collection have been featured in several other displays within this text. A visit to his departmental office is an experience without equal and leaves each visitor transformed. Within these four walls cultures collide while religious artifacts peacefully coexist. Each acquisition has a unique and fascinating backstory.

Among other things, Dr. Richardson is a collector of British Revolutionary War memorabilia which includes clothing, artillery, timepieces, coins, swords and more. Many of those items are featured in this display. The British redcoat was authenticated as a reproduction probably made for the centennial celebration in England in 1876.

Assembling the Display

1. The top shelf housed a hand forged mattock used for cutting roots and breaking soil packing, an 18th century rifleman's powder horn, a pay receipt of the quartermaster dated May 16, 1783, a naval cannon ball with chains (used for breaking masts), a wooden case housing a miniature locket painted with a head of a British Revolutionary War officer, coins predating the Revolutionary War and hand forged leg irons and shackles. The books included were *Year of the Hangman* by George Blackwood and *George III* by Christopher Hibbert.

2. On the left was one of the quotes by George Washington which Introduced the display. Under that was a document titled "The British Army in North America" (May, 3–5). Next was an image of the coat of arms of George III, which was easily found through a Google image search. Finally, there was a document about King George III which can be found if you visit http://www.britannia.com/history/monarchs/mon55.html.

Clip art of the British flag was inserted in the top center of this document.

Items on the left were printed on off white card stock and mounted on silver and/or black poster board.

3. On the top right was a quote by Horace Walpole, Whig Party member:

> The tocsin seems to be sounded in America. That continent ... is growing too mighty to be kept in subjection to half a dozen exhausted nations in Europe.

Next was the summation of a document titled "British Views of the American Revolution" (Stanlis, 191–200). Following that was the quotation by George III that introduced the display. Lastly was a document on the Treaty of Paris which can be found if you visit http://www.state.gov/r/pa/ho/time/ar/14313.htm.

Items on the right were mounted like those on the left.

4. The font Grange was sized at 150 and bolded to create "1776." This can be downloaded if you visit http://www.dafont.com. The numerals were printed on buff card stock and mounted on black poster board. The sign was attached with pins and pulled forward.

Above the signage was an old, but undated, copperplate image of King George III matted in cranberry and framed in gold. Two English pair-case watches hung below on pins and flanked the sign. Two handmade British Revolutionary swords flanked the uniform jacket. The sword on the left, with lion's head pommel, is the type carried both during the French and Indian War and during the

American Revolution. The English small sword on the right is the type carried by British officers during the American Revolution. The light weight of the swords allowed them to be attached with pins. A 19th century copy of a British red coat is draped on a bust dressed in a period white shirt, ascot and black vest. Books, covered with black felt, were stacked to elevate the bust.

Books featured in the display were *American Creation: Triumph and Tragedies at the Founding of the Republic* by Joseph Ellis, *George III: America's Last King* by Jeremy Block, *Fusiliers: The Saga of a British Redcoat Regiment in the American Revolution* by Mark Urban and *Washington's Crossing* by David Hackett Fischer.

Bigger and Better

If you have problems locating an article of clothing for your Revolutionary War display check with the costume department of a college in your area. A costume rental store might be willing to lend some of their inventory in return for free advertising in your library

If you are fortunate enough to have items dating back to the American Revolution or have access to reproductions of the Liberty Bell, The Declaration of Independence, *Poor Richard's Almanac*, a period flag, miniature soldiers, maps, posters, tricorn hats, utensils, brass post or powder horns, a fife, lanterns, medals, "join or die" graphic, and the like, you could mount a display on the War of Independence from the American point of view.

Feature color photocopies of the signers of the Declaration and title it "Founding Fathers". Include a short biography and, for added interest, list their occupations under their portraits, i.e., "Lawyer," "Plantation Owner," "Musician," etc. For this type of information on those patriots please visit http://www.usconstitution.net/declarsigndata.html.

Consider a display on flags of the American Revolution. Not only are they colorful, they also symbolize a people, convey a shared history and represent national pride. If actual flags are unavailable, these can be made from poster board at little cost. Add a little background history and this would make an informative exhibit for the 4th of July. There are many and varied examples to be found if you visit http://americanrevwar.homestead.com/files/flags.htm or http://www.crwflags.com/fotw/flags/us percent5Erv.html.

Focus on General George Washington and the many paintings of him that exist. Call the display "Portraits of a President" and hang the color photocopies, which have been mounted on poster board, on a vintage flag or red, white and blue bunting. Install this in February for President's Day.

Feature Betsy Ross, Abigal Adams, Martha Washington, Hannah Arnett, Prudence Wright and other women who were involved in the Amerlican Revolution. Call the display "Dames for Independence." For background on these ladies visit http://americanrevolution.org/women/women.html.

Check my first book, *Great Displays for Your Library Step by Step*, for exhibits on Thomas Jefferson, titled "The Sage of Monticello" on page 85, and one on Benjamin Franklin called "Citizen Ben" on page 100. Both would tie into the subject of the American Revolution.

The Great War, 1914–1918

President Wilson believed that if the United States could stay out of the war, that we could be the great reconciler, the great mediator.—John Milton Cooper, historian

World War I began suddenly in July 1914 as the result of the assassination of Archduke Francis Ferdinand, heir to the throne of Austria-Hungary. The attack took place on June 28 in Sarajevo, Bosnia. A popular explanation for going to war was that there were economic jealousies and competing imperialisms. Some historians take exception to that theory and are still debating the underlying issues. They hypothesize that it was

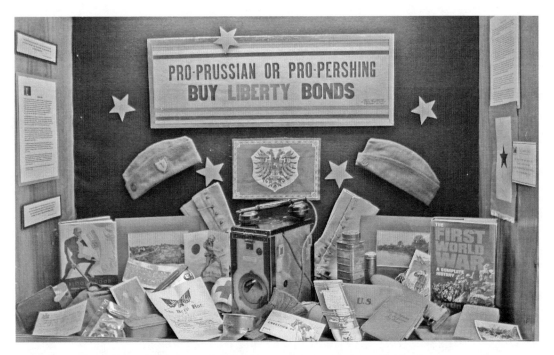

The Great War 1914–1918. Among the memorabilia featured in this display is an authentic 1916 field telephone. Items from the Mark Scasny collection are a war bonds poster, caps, chaps, a service flag, a draft notice, fingerless gloves, troop photos, a New Testament, GI issued pouches, tin mess kit, a Red Cross armband and a diary.

the quest for greater territory, and others conjecture that social turmoil and shifting artistic sensibilities brought about by the industrial revolution led to the outbreak. Others suggest that the arms race was a factor; it was simply a miscalculation by the ruling powers.

Democratic president Woodrow Wilson was elected to the country's highest office in 1912. He spent the early part of his administration developing a program of progressive reform in the United States. He much preferred dealing with domestic matters and had hoped not to be called upon to devote too much time to foreign affairs.

Wilson believed in neutrality and his secretary of state, William Jennings Bryan, was a passionate pacifist. The sinking of the *Lusitania* enraged public opinion in the United States, causing Wilson to craft a strong protest to the Germans and prompting Bryan to resign. The seeds of American hostility toward Germany were sown.

Built as a luxury liner in 1907, the *Lusitania* was dubbed the "Greyhound of the Seas."

She was soon known for the fastest Atlantic crossing. The British Admiralty had secretly underwritten her construction and she was built to government specifications with the understanding that the ship would be drafted into active service at the onset of the war. The *Lusitania* was secretly fitted for military action in 1913 as the winds of war became apparent.

When the *Lusitania* departed New York City on May 1, 1915, bound for Liverpool she carried a total of 1,924 passengers, among them noted Americans Alfred Vanderbilt, one of the world's richest men, and playwright Carl Froman. The possibility of a submarine attack had reduced the number of passengers willing to make the crossing. The hidden cargo onboard consisted of munitions and contraband designated for the British war effort. Although the passengers were totally unaware of this fact, it was no secret to the Germans. The sinking of the *Lusitania* on May 7, 1915, by a German U-boat took the lives of 1,119 souls; of those, 114 were Americans.

A note, the Zimmermann Telegram sent

in 1917 from the German foreign minister to his ambassador in Mexico, contained details of a proposed alliance against Americans. If Mexico agreed to join Germany in a war against the U.S. they would be rewarded with monetary support and reconquered land in 3 southwestern states. When word of this telegram became known, the situation was no longer tolerable and America declared war on Germany on April 6, 1917.

The United States reluctantly intervened in the Great War. Woodrow Wilson was elected to a second term on the slogan "he kept us out of war." He had tried to mediate the conflict to no avail. When he finally joined forces with the Allies, it was so that he could direct the postwar settlement to all the warring nations.

World War I began in Europe and was fought primarily on that continent but eventually involved all the continents of the world. For the first time, all of the world powers were engaged. This included Austria-Hungary, France, Germany, Great Britain, Italy, Russia, Japan and the United States. A huge effort by American forces tipped the scales in favor of the Allies. Wilson appeared before Congress in early 1918 to clarify America's war aims. The speech he gave would later be referred to as his Fourteen Points. The final statement proposed to establish a general association of nations affording mutual guarantees of political independence and territorial integrity to all states great and small.

After the armistice was signed by Germany in November 1918, President Wilson went to Paris to try to establish a lasting peace. He later presented to the U.S. Senate the Versailles Treaty containing the Covenant of the League of Nations. However, the elections of 1918 had shifted the power in Congress to the Republicans and the Versailles Treaty failed to pass in the Senate by a mere seven votes.

The Great War left massive economic burdens on all of the European countries. European victors collectively owed ten billion dollars to the U.S. The economic burdens of the European governments included the rehabilitation of devastated areas, pensions which needed to be paid to both the wounded and relatives of the deceased, and the payment of the interest due on the public and foreign debts. Trade and industry were not immediately revived, complicating the economy even further. By war's end unemployment permeated Italy, Germany, Britain and France. The result was the overthrow of the government in Italy and the establishment of high tariffs for imports throughout Europe that would insure economic self-sufficiency. This attempt at fiscal independence within the European nations did not bode well for a lasting and future peace.

John Keegan has characterized the First World War as a tragic and unnecessary conflict in his 1999 publication *The First World War* — tragic because the consequences of that first clash ended the lives of 10 million people and affected the emotional well-being of millions more, unnecessary because the train of events that led to its outbreak might have been broken at any point during the five weeks of crisis that preceded the first clash of arms had prudence or common goodwill found a voice (3).

Historians believe that the Second World War, which was five times more destructive in terms of casualties and far more costly financially, was the direct result of the First. For more information about the Great War go to http://www.worldwar1.com/ and http://www.pbs.org/greatwar/ or http://www.thecorner.org/hist/wwi/results.htm.

Credits

Several years ago my friend JoEllen Christensen generously offered to share some basement storage space with her brother, history buff Mark Scasny of Staten Island, New York. She agreed to store his assortment of war memorabilia and recently shared the scope of his collection with me. Of course I jumped at the prospect of exhibiting authentic items from that momentous period of history and am grateful to Mark for providing the opportunity. His knowledge of and record keeping for each item in the collection were impressive. Mark's meticulous research added to the experience of mounting this exhibit. One of the photos in the display was taken at the Naval Air Station USS Aghada in Queenstown, Ireland, where Mark and

JoEllen's grandfather, John Joseph Shea, served his country and met his future bride. As I handled the leggings, Bibles, hats, mess kits and diaries of these brave soldiers, a feeling of reverence overwhelmed me. I vowed to create a fitting memorial to these men for the sacrifices they made to maintain a secure homeland.

The field telephone at the center of the display was lent by Dr. Allen Richardson, a Cedar Crest professor of religious studies and collector of note. This model was manufactured in Germany by Siemans-Halske and was the type used on the front line by soldiers responsible for communications. It is extremely heavy, with a beautiful wood patina and a piercing ring. I was pleased to be able to incorporate this vintage phone into the Scasny collection.

I am anticipating a wealth of interest and information surfacing in the year 2014, the centennial of the commencement of the Great War. No doubt new questions will arise as to the reason for this conflict and the motivation of the early powers who sought to involve huge numbers of the world's population in their quest for global supremacy.

Assembling the Display

1 A silver 10" × 30" framed poster, which was advertising for one of the Liberty Loan Campaign Drives in support of General Pershing, hung at the top center on the background of black felt. Below that was a red and gold flag with the imperial Russian crest. During the early part of the century flags from all existing countries were included in boxes of cigars and were collectibles during the war years. Flanking the flag were two caps with the Engineer Corps insignia. Red stars made from poster board framed the liberty bonds print.

2. On the top left is the quote that introduced this display. Under that was a passage titled "America at War". This information can be found at http://www.pbs.org/wgbh/amex/wilson/portrait/wp_war.html. A photo of Woodrow Wilson, found through a Google image search, was inserted into the top left of the document. Next was a quote by David Kennedy:

In Wilson's mind, if the sacrifices of blood that Americans had to pay were ever going to be justified, it had to be with an outcome that didn't simply end the fighting, but created a new international order.

Items on the left were printed on card stock and mounted on red or black poster board.

3. On the top right was a summation of the introduction to this display. Under that was an actual Blue Service Star flag, frequently called "Sons in Service" star, adopted shortly after America's entry into the war in 1917. This was issued by the Department of Defense to families who had members serving in the armed forces during the war. If their soldier died in service, one gold star would replace the blue star to denote this passage.

> The Service Flag
> Dear little flag in the window there,
> Hung with a tear and a womans prayer;
> Child of Old Glory, born with a star—
> Oh, what a wonderful flag you are!

Items on the right were printed and mounted like those on the left.

4. On the base of the display case were a metal trench mirror and leatherette case, a notice of enrollment for a physician from Brooklyn, New York, nine olive drab buttons on the original cardboard packaging, and a khaki-colored painted metal tin marked "Military Button Polish Kit," an American Red Cross canvas "ditty bag," "Trench Art" of an officer's cap made from brass shell casings on which the names of France, America and Roisel 1918 were inscribed, the field telephone flanked by olive drab canvas leggings with brass eyelets and laces manufactured by Rosenwasser Brothers in 1918, various photos of the troops, fingerless gloves which kept the hands warm while keeping the fingers unencumbered, a Bible marked to its owner, khaki cotton pouches with rubberized interiors, a USS Aghada Naval Air Station—Queenstown, Ireland, *newsletter* dated December 21, 1918, a card imprinted with a soldier and gun which would have housed war bonds, an aluminum mess kit dated 1918, prints of the ruins of war from the John Joseph Shea collection (one labeled Comines, a town on the border of France and Belgium),

a souvenir Thanksgiving menu from Camp Wadsworth in Spartanburg, South Carolina (1918), a postcard depicting a dog wearing Red Cross insignia, a Metal Bolo knife sheath which held a heavy duty knife called a bolo which was similar to a small machete, a metal condiment can which had compartments for flour, salt and pepper, a diary, a Colgate Handy Grip Shaving Stick marked September 4, 1917, and a soldier's dispatch to his sister dated 3/13/1918.

Books featured in the display were *Bloody Good: Chivalry, Sacrifice and the Great War* and *The First World War: A Complete Story* by Martin Gilbert.

Bigger and Better

You could choose themes such as "Art of the First World War" for your larger space. For colorful posters of this period go to http://library.georgetown.edu/dept/speccoll/ampposter.htm.

World War I correspondence would be an interesting subject. For a lengthy archive of personal accounts, go to http://www.war-letters.com/0009/0002.html. "Military Commanders and the First World War," "Women, War and Work," "First World War Poetry," "The Last Kaiser," "Nurses at the Trenches," or "Books of the Great War" are all ideas upon which you could expand. For detailed information about those topics go to http://www.spartacus.schoolnet.co.uk/FWWchronoloty.co.uk/FWWchronology.htm.

Your display could focus on one specific battle, such as the Battle of the Somme, the First Battle of the Marne or the Battle of Verdun. For information on these specific battles visit http://www.firstworldwar.com/battles/all.htm.

Feature Woodrow Wilson and his Fourteen Points, or the Treaty of Versailles. Be sure to check the PBS Website for a thorough overview of the Great War.

Far Out! Surviving the Sixties

We don't like their sound. Groups of guitars are on the way out. —Decca executive, 1962, after turning down the Beatles

The conservative 1950s gave rise to scores of teenagers eager to sow the seeds of rebellion by the decade's end. It seemed inevitable that greater numbers would arise in the 1960s and that a movement toward a radical change in the cultural fabric of American life would ensue. The storm was brewing. Free love, flower power, hippies, psychedelic drugs and political mayhem—these were the trends of a decade that observed the turbulent upheaval of traditional social mores, the establishment of new cultural behaviors and the shocking assassination of their beloved president.

As the Beatles rocked, Bob Dylan rolled and the Beach Boys harmonized, the world witnessed an altered political climate. The Vietnam War, opposition to nuclear arms, protests in the streets and the sexual revolution combined to define that volatile period. Young people questioned every aspect of the status quo. Their mantra became "never trust anyone over 30!" This burgeoning unrest gave rise to both angry protests and peaceful confrontations that resulted in the civil rights movement—a movement that ultimately affected the entire fabric of American society.

The fashion of the 1960s was a complete departure from the previous decade. Gone were circle and poodle skirts, form fitting dresses with pinched-in waists and high heels. Many of the new style trends were fashioned on the other side of the Atlantic. The shapes created by London designer Mary Quant in the mid–1960s were simple, neat, clean cut, young and extremely short! Quant introduced hot pants and redefined the daring mini-skirt which rose a good seven inches above the knee. Those style trends, which were eventually dubbed the "Chelsea Look," quickly found a niche in the global fashion market. White patent leather go-go boots became the fashion accessory of choice for young women during this period.

Far Out! Surviving the 1960s. The display title, ensconced in a comical burst with a background of polka dots, was a phrase that aptly described the decade. Barbie and Ken dolls, a pair of trolls, a peace sign and a lava lamp are nostalgic reminders of this period that also witnessed war and rampant social unrest.

Gaunt British model Twiggy skyrocketed to superstardom in the 1960s. Born Lesley Hornby, she became internationally known as the world's first supermodel. Her photographic modeling success epitomized the look of the age. Clothing during this decade was just as likely to be purchased at surplus stores as at boutiques. Unisex attire was very trendy, especially bell bottomed jeans, love beads, and tie-dyed and embellished T-shirts. Men's neckties were boldly patterned and ultimately reached a width of five inches.

Long flowing hair or big frizzy styles became the standard for women and men in the 1960s. Guys sported moustaches and beards. Many African Americans wore their hair in Afros. This image of the decade was memorialized by producer Joseph Papp in the spring of 1968. Titled *Hair*, it was the first true rock musical to make its debut on Broadway and shocked many with its blatant nudity that brought the first act to a close. Mainly just a musical revue with very little story line, *Hair* celebrated the counterculture in Washington Square and closely mirrored the spirit of the times. It featured songs such as "Aquarius" and "Hair" and continues to enjoy numerous revivals throughout the country.

The most popular films of the 1960s included children's favorites such as *101 Dalmatians*, *Mary Poppins* and *The Jungle Book*. Three of Ian Fleming's books went from page to screen during this period. *Thunderball*, *Goldfinger* and *You Only Live Twice* all scored big numbers at the box office with Sean Connery starring as the formidable James Bond. Other films classics from the top ten list of the decade were *Doctor Zhivago*, *The Graduate*, *The Sound of Music* and *Butch Cassidy and the Sundance Kid*.

The music of the 1960s exemplified the revolution of the decade. Artists such as Miles Davis, Jimi Hendrix, James Brown, Aretha Franklin and Ray Charles topped the record charts. Elvis Presley enjoyed continued success during this decade but took issue with the mounting influence that foreign bands and their lifestyle choices had on America's youth. Eventually he met with President Richard Nixon and offered his services as a "Federal Agent at Large." Elvis wanted to discourage drug use among youth and support the war effort. He suggested that the president should ban certain overseas rock groups from entering the country. Given the circumstances of his untimely death, there is much irony in the stance he openly articulated on illegal drug use during the 1960s.

The famous British Invasion came about mid–decade. The Beatles' innovative rock sound had a special appeal to teenagers, who broke all box office records for both attendance and enthusiasm. This crowd fever was ultimately dubbed Beatlemania. The lads from Liverpool overcame humble beginnings to become amazingly self assured, accomplished musicians. The Beatles soon emerged as the most popular and commercially successful band—possibly of all time. John Lennon created quite a controversy when he was quoted as saying that the group was more popular than Jesus. This remark caused some to boycott the purchase of Beatles albums and others to burn them. Overall, the conflict had little effect on the success of that phenomenal rock group. In their quest for truth and meaning, the Beatles made their way to the Far East and brought the poetry, music and messages of India to receptive audiences around the globe.

The Rolling Stones' 1965 single "(I Can't Get No) Satisfaction" established this group as a premier rock and roll act who continue to attract huge audiences to this day. The Who and the Animals made important creative contributions to the decade and were also considered part of the British Invasion. Bob Dylan was an informal raconteur and a tentative figurehead of the American turmoil of the 1960s. Born Robert Allen Zimmerman, he was a much admired poet, musician, songwriter, social activist and folk singer. Dylan was one of the singers who performed at the 1963 March on Washington where Martin Luther King, Jr. addressed the crowd in his immortalized speech. Dylan continues to enjoy a strong musical following. Joan Baez, Pete Seeger and Peter, Paul and Mary added to the folk music revival of this period.

Woodstock took place in mid–August 1969 and came to be known as the "Summer of Peace and Love." This event, which took place on a dairy farm in Bethel, New York, drew over a half million people who gathered to hear Janis Joplin, the Who, Jimi Hendrix, the Grateful Dead and Creedence Clearwater Revival. Woodstock enabled hordes of young people to have their first communal spirit experience. The festival was the symbolic conclusion of a volatile decade of social reform and political unrest. For more information in the music of the 1960s visit http://www.the peoplehistory.com/60smusic.html.

The 1960s marked the rise of many unorthodox forms of artistic expression. Never before had there been such acceptance, or such diversification, both in style and in what was considered permissible art practice. New York had taken the place of Paris and was now considered the art capital of the world. Because of the common language bond, London soon followed New York's lead. As the decade evolved, the cosmic art of Peter Max emerged as the transcendental imagery which captured the imagination of the generation. Andy Warhol, Roy Lichtenstein and David Hockney also gained great recognition as "pop" artists.

Prominent sculptor Alexander Calder was born into a family celebrated, classically trained artist. Although he had trained to become a professional engineer he ultimately found his way into the family business. He created innovative mobiles and sculptures by bending and twisting wire. Calder essentially "drew" three-dimensional figures in space. He is renowned for the invention of the mobile, whose suspended, abstract elements shift and balance in changing harmony. Assemblage art, optical art and environmental art were other forms of expression which evolved throughout the decade.

The literary world examined the turmoil of race relations through Harper Lee's Pulitzer Prize–winning *To Kill a Mockingbird*. Sylvia Plath (*The Bell Jar*) and Mary McCarthy (*The Group*) addressed the lives of post–1950 non-stereotypical women. Feminism was discussed and analyzed by authors Betty Friedan and Gloria Steinem. Disillusionment with the system is thinly veiled in both *Catch-22* by Joseph Heller and *One Flew Over the Cuckoo's Nest* by Ken Kesey. Other significant books of the decade were *The Silent Spring* by Rachel Carson, *In Cold Blood* by Truman Capote, *Unsafe at Any Speed* by Ralph Nader, *The Electric Kool-Aid Acid Test* by Tom Wolfe and *The Valley of the Dolls* by Jacqueline Susann.

Television offered a highly popular prime time cartoon show, *The Flintstones,* in 1960. *The Andy Griffith Show* had a ten-year run and was the epitome of wholesome family television. *The Beverly Hillbillies* signaled the rise of the sitcom. The paranormal combined with science fiction was apparent in many popular shows, including *Bewitched, The Addams Family, My Favorite Martian, I Dream of Jeannie, Star Trek* and *Twilight Zone.* At the close of the decade a new and offbeat humor was revealed in a show called *Rowan and Martin's Laugh-In,* where many regular performers and celebrity guests became part of an instant television classic.

People primarily listened to music on AM radio during the 1960s. This was supplemented by *American Bandstand,* a television show that enjoyed phenomenal success with teens throughout the country. Bandstand played the latest music and showed the newest dance crazes as well. When Chubby Checker introduced the Twist on the show in 1961, dancing became a solo activity. The Mashed Potato, the Swim, the Watusi, the Monkey and the Jerk followed. For those who favored observing the performers, go-go girls, poised on stages or in bird cages, danced above the crowd.

In the early 1960s the surgeon general's findings were published when it was determined that smoking was hazardous to health. By 1965 tobacco companies were mandated to add a warning to both their packages and their advertisements.

Pioneering heart surgeon Dr. Denton Cooley performed the first successful human heart transplant in the U.S. in 1968. He made history the following year when he implanted the first artificial heart in a human. The patient lived for three days, until a human heart could be transplanted. Cooley and his associates have since performed more than 100,000 open heart operations—more than any other group in the world.

In the 1930s the "American Dream" morphed into an economic nightmare as the land of opportunity experienced a decade of financial desperation. The nation was expected to sacrifice and practice frugality. The 1940s required them to endure market scarcities, government rationing and the reality of a world at war. That decade witnessed the annihilation of a despot and the horror of genocide. In contrast, the 1950s and the return to peacetime offered a time of unquestioned respect for authority in all aspects of society. Its nostalgic innocence led to the decade that experienced an affluence unprecedented in our history. People have strong reactions to the memories conjured up by the 1960s. Songs and images of the period fueled emotions and continue to flood the media and the marketplace in deference to the "monster demographic," those baby boomers who came of age during these tumultuous times.

For a comprehensive overview of the era visit http://kclibrary.lonestar.edu/decade60.html.

Credits

I am a child of the sixties, so creating this display conjured up some happy and poignant memories of my coming of age. Milestones were made then. I graduated from high school, received my college degree, married, entered the teaching profession and welcomed my first child during that decade. When reflecting on this period, it is hard to ignore the dramatic difference in the economy of the times. This change has been dramatic. My first job at age 15 was as a kitchen aide earning a whopping $1.00 an hour! My first teaching position in Anne Arundel County, Maryland, offered an annual salary of just over $5,000. The average home cost about $14,000. Waterfront homes overlooking the Severn River could be had for under $40,000! In 1966, our brand new Mustang 2-door hardtop commanded a mere $2,368. The gas it required averaged about 28¢ a gallon! U.S. postage stamps sold for a mere four cents in the early 1960s. In terms of the economy, those were indeed the "good old days!"

Television recently offered a glimpse into the sixties with the sexy, stylized and provocative *Mad Men* series on the AMC network. The show chronicles the ruthlessly competitive world of Madison Avenue advertising, an ego-driven world where key characters make an art of the sell. This highly successful award winning show created a renewed interest in the decade.

Assembling the Display

1. The background of the display was gold felt with black circles cut from poster board. The title signage, "Far Out," was created using the font Bell Bottom Laser sized at 500 and enlarged 200 percent on the photocopier. This font can be found free of charge if you visit www.dafont.com. The title was printed on card stock, enlarged on the photocopier and traced onto black poster board. The background burst was cut from red and framed in black poster board. The title signage was attached with pins and pulled forward, as were the black circles.

2. On the top left was a list of best selling fiction books from the 1960s. This is available if you visit http://www.caderbooks.com/best60.html. Under that was a quote from Paul Kanter:

> If you can remember anything about the sixties, you weren't really there.

Next was a history of fashion from 1960 to 1970 which can be found if you visit http://www.vintageblues.com/history6a.htm.

All items on the left were printed on white card stock and mounted on red or black poster board.

3. On the top right is the quote by a Decca record executive which introduced this display. Under that was a list of the top record albums of the 1960s which can be found if you visit http://www.shakingthrough.net/music/features/bestof/station_music_top_10_1960s.html. Next was a list of "Eight Groovy Fads of the 1960s" which can be found at http://people.howstuffworks.com/8-groovy-fads-of-the-1960s.htm. An image of go-go boots, found through a Google image search, was inserted into the top right of the document.

Items on the right were printed and mounted like those on the left. Green flowers of the '60s, found through a Google image search, were printed on card stock and taped around the documents on both sides of the display case.

4. On the base of the display were vintage Barbie and Ken dolls, two trolls, a 1960s floral purse, a lava lamp with a tie-dyed shirt wrapped around the base, a peace symbol made from red poster board, and a Richard Nixon election pin.

There were three record albums of the period featured in the display. They were *December's Children and Everybody's* by the Rolling Stones, *Revolver* by the Beatles and *Smiley Smile* by The Beach Boys. This quote by John Lennon was printed on white card stock and mounted on black poster board:

> If someone thinks that love and peace is a cliché that must have been left behind in the Sixties, that's his problem. Love and peace are eternal.

Books included in the display were *The Sixties: Cultural Revolution in Britain, France, Italy and the United States* by Arthur Marwick, *Boom! Voices of the Sixties, Personal Reflections on the '60s and Today* by Tom Brokaw, *American Cars of the 1960s* by Craig Cheetham, *Decade of Nightmares* by Philip Jenkins, *Years of Discord: American Politics and Society 1961–1974* by John Blum, *The Movement and the Sixties* by Terry H. Anderson, *Warhol* by Victor Bockris and *Pop Dreams* by Archie Loss.

Bigger and Better

You may want to add other fads of the sixties to your exhibit: Platform shoes, the game Twister, Ouija boards, mood rings, granny glasses, G.I. Joe, hula hoops and bell-bottomed pants. Memorabilia reminiscent of the television shows *American Bandstand* or *The Mickey Mouse Club* would be viable options for inclusion in your display. Visit this site for additional ideas: http://www.crazyfads.com/60s.htm.

Zero in on one phase of the decade such as the British Invasion, the first American in space or the first Americans to walk on the surface of the moon. Feature Woodstock, the development of the birth control pill and its ramifications for women, or Rachel Carson's *Silent Spring*—still timely since it represents the awakening of the environmental movement.

For a display idea celebrating the "The Awesome 80s," see page 39 of my first book, *Great Displays for Your Library Step by Step*.

7 Festivities

Cinco de Mayo

I was taken in by the bravado and the sounds of Mexico ... not so much the music, but the spirit.—Herb Alpert

Cinco de Mayo, the 5th of May, marks the victory of the Mexican militia over the French army at the Battle of Puebla in 1862. This date is of great importance for the Mexican and Chicano communities. In Mexico, the 5th of May is mainly celebrated in the city of Puebla, with some recognition in nearby areas.

U.S. cities with large Mexican populations celebrate Cinco de Mayo. Lately this holiday has been adopted by many cities on and north of the border, regardless of the ethnic demographics. Cinco de Mayo continues to grow in popularity and has become a cause for celebration among Latinos and others.

Many people wrongly equate Cinco de Mayo with Mexican Independence from Spain, which occurred decades earlier. That holiday is celebrated each year on September 16. The battle of Puebla occurred during a violent and frenzied time in the history of Mexico. Spain had granted Mexico its independence in 1821, following a difficult struggle which involved various political takeovers and wars. The cost of these conflicts resulted in the collapse of Mexico's national economy.

During these turbulent times, Mexico became indebted to Spain, England and France—all of whom sought repayment. Mexican president Benito Juarez issued a moratorium on all foreign debt payments for a two-year period, after which time payments would be resumed. Spain and England attempted to negotiate with the president, but eventually acquiesced and withdrew their demands. France, however, had other motives. Its leader, Napoleon III, wanted to expand his empire at that time and used the issue of debt and America's involvement in a civil war to advance his goals of installing his own emissary as a leader of Mexico.

The highly disciplined enemy troops arrived in Mexico sporting the finest and most modern equipment and with a newly reconstituted French army. The invasion began at the Gulf coast of Mexico along the state of Veracruz and continued its march 600 miles inland toward Mexico City. As they advanced toward Mexico City, the French army encountered strong resistance near Puebla at the Mexican forts of Loreto and Guadalupe. Statistics vary as to the size of armies, but the Mexicans were clearly in the minority.

Under the leadership of Mexican general Ignacio Zaragoza Seguin, a poorly armed militia of approximately 4,500 men managed to halt the well equipped French soldiers, who outnumbered them by 2,000 troops. The invasion was stopped after one day of battle and the French troops were forced to retreat. This conquest came to represent a symbol of Mexican unity and patriotism, which was especially savored by the Mexican patriots.

The Mexican army's victory over the French was short lived, however. Napoleon III, nephew of the famous Napoléon Bonaparte, opted to ignore the wishes of his people and organized a second invasion of Mexico. He knew the American Civil War would prevent the U.S. from intervening and thought it was an opportunity to conquer Mexico.

Cinco de Mayo. The celebration marks the 1862 triumph of the Mexican militia over the French army at the Battle of Puebla in 1862. A sombrero filled with colorful paper flowers anchors this confetti-filled display featuring items from the collection of Dr. and Mrs. Arturo James.

Both angry and embarrassed by the defeat, Napoleon ordered 30,000 more troops to Mexico. These forces were able to depose the Mexican army, take over Mexico City and install Archduke Ferdinand Maximilian as emperor of Mexico.

Upon the cessation of the American Civil War the Americans were finally in a position to provide financial, political and military assistance to Mexico. Years earlier President James Monroe had made a statement vowing to prohibit Europeans from gaining power in the Americas. Eventually, this became a longstanding principle of U.S. foreign policy. This display of support by the Americans was in line with the philosophy espoused in the Monroe Doctrine.

Archduke Maximilian's rule lasted from 1864 to 1867. Ultimately, he was executed by the Mexicans. Today the tattered shirt he wore when he was executed hangs in the Museum at Chapultepec Castle, in Mexico City. Despite the French occupation of Mexico City, Cinco de Mayo served to honor the bravery and victory of General Zaragoza's scrappy and outnumbered militia at the Battle of Puebla in 1862.

Latinos are the largest minority population in the U.S. today, numbering approximately 40 million people. Cinco de Mayo rivals St. Patrick's Day in popularity throughout the U.S. It is celebrated in many states but primarily in California, Arizona, New Mexico and Texas. The city of Los Angeles boasts a large celebration on the renowned Olvera Street. The festivities include piñata and Mexican flag making, pinata breaking, storytelling about the Battle of Puebla, mariachi music, costumes and folk dancing, as well as workshops for children. For more information visit http://www.olvera-street.com/html/fiestas.html.

Credits

My niece, Carol, is married to a native of Mexico. Dr. José Arturo James is an erudite, sophisticated man who quickly endeared himself to all of our family. Known to us by his middle name, Arturo has introduced us to his culture in the most subtle ways. Genuine and soft-spoken, he has shared stories of his childhood growing up in a large and loving family in León, located in the state of Guanajuato. Arturo became a U.S. citizen in 1996 and also holds citizenship in France, the birthplace of his father, as well as Mexico. The collage in the display features the many faces and activities of young Arturo at play in the 1950s.

Arturo's parents shared a long and loving marriage which lasted sixty years. Their family included ten children; Arturo was the third. The wedding photograph of his parents, Maria Luisa Marti and José Lorenzo James, is featured in the display. The pottery figure and plate are part of the James family collection.

Arturo has practiced orthodontics in both countries during the last decade, allowing him to stay connected to both his American and Mexican families.

Assembling the Display

1. The font El Rio Lobo was sized at 750 for the words *Cinco* and *Mayo* and at 350 for the word *de*. This was printed on card stock and traced onto blue, red, green, yellow and pink poster board. The font is free under the category Mexican and can be downloaded if you visit http://www.dafont.com.

These letters were then reduced on the photocopier and traced onto contrasting colored poster board. The letters were glued together and designs of contrasting colors were cut out and glued on the two-toned letters. These letters were attached with pins and pulled forward. One inch square confetti was cut from colored poster board and attached with pins and pulled forward.

A sombrero was pinned under the lettering. Paper tissue flowers of yellow, red, and a combination of the colors were pinned around the brim of the hat. For easy written instructions on how to make tissue paper flowers visit http://www.azcentral.com/ent/dead/articles/dead-crafts_paperflowers.html. For video instructions visit http://www.wonderhowto.com/how-to/video/how-to-make-giant-tissue-paper-flowers-31/.

2. On the top left was a collage of photographs of young Arturo as a child. The photographs were scanned and then similarly sized in Adobe Photoshop. They were printed on presentation paper and framed with red or green poster board, then arranged and glued onto black poster board that was framed in red poster board. The letters for the word Mexico were found online at http://www.cptm.com.mx/index.jsp. They were printed on card stock, cut and then glued above the collage. Under that was the quote by Herb Alpert that introduced the display. This was printed on white card stock and framed in red poster board

3. On the top right was an article about Cinco de Mayo taken from the Information found in the text of this display. Clip art of a Mexican flag was inserted on the top right. For additional information on this significant event in Mexico's history visit http://www.houstonculture.org/mexico/cincodemayo.html.

Under that was information gathered from local sources regarding Cinco de Mayo events that were scheduled for this region. An image of a festival was inserted on the top center. Many such graphics are available online through an image search using "Cinco de Mayo."

Items on the right were printed on card stock and mounted on red and black poster board.

4. On the base of the display was a large flag of Mexico. In the center was a wedding photograph of Maria Luisa Marti and José Lorenzo James. Red and yellow paper flowers were spread throughout the base. The ceramic female figure on the left was balanced by the antique bell on the right. The plate on the extreme right is the handiwork of Carlos James, brother of Arturo. The scene was painted on the dish with a toothpick.

In front of the photograph was a tiny ceramic head found at the Aztec site of Xico, probably from the Teotihuacán culture which flourished between 150 CE and 450 CE. Maracas and Mayan chess figures flanked the head.

Books featured in the display are *The Hummingbird's Daughter* by Luis Alberto Urrea, *Chicano Folklore* by Rafaela G. Castro, *Borderlands: La Frontera* by Gloria Anzaldúa, *Drink Cultura: Chicanismo* by Jose Antonio Burciaga, *So Far from God: A Novel* by Ana Castillo and *From Indians to Chicanos* by James Diego Vigil.

Bigger and Better

Food is a significant part of any Latin festival and Cinco de Mayo is certainly no exception. If your display space is larger, you may want to incorporate some of these recipes into your display. For information on foods commonly found at Cinco de Mayo celebrations, be sure to visit http://home-cooking.about.com/od/holidayandpartyrecipes/a/cincodemayo.htm for ideas. Scatter Mexican candies on the base or shelves of your display. To acquire lollipops frequently seen at these fiestas visit http://www.mexgrocer.com/catagories-mexican-candy-lollipops.html. For the Tamarindo candy which is so popular in Mexico visit http://www.mexgrocer.com/best-sellers.html. Add a piñata and some Mexican banners to your larger display space. These are available online if you visit http://www.pinatas.com/SearchResults.asp?Search=mexican&Search.x=27&Search.y=7.

For traditional Papel Picado Banners used in many Latin celebrations visit http://www.mexicansugarskull.com/mexicansugarskull/PapelBanners.htm. These can be hung and crisscrossed from the top of the display space for a festive look.

Mount the Mexican flag as a backdrop to your display and offer a paper flower-making session to your patrons around Cinco de Mayo. Tissue paper and pipe cleaners are the only necessities for this project and they can be found at your local dollar or party store.

Line the base of your case with a serape, or mount it as a backdrop. A poncho would also work. Add an array of Mexican pottery or include art from some of the popular artists such as Frida Kahlo, Diego Rivera or Pedro Friedeberg. For a comprehensive list of Mexican artists visit http://www.artcyclo-pedia.com/nationalities/Mexican.html.

For children's activities and craft projects related to this national holiday visit http://www.kaboose.com/HideTheseForNow?cinco–print.html.

If you are interested in creating a different display on Mexican festivals, see the "Day of the Dead" exhibit on page 81 of my first book, *Great Displays for Your Library Step by Step*.

Bastille Day

The longer we dwell on our misfortunes the greater is their power to harm us.—Voltaire, French philosopher (1694–1778)

On the 14th of July, the French celebrate the Fête Nationale, or Bastille Day. It commemorates the storming of a Paris royal fortress by a group of angry and rebellious citizens on July 14, 1789. The celebration includes a grand military parade up the Champs Elysées, arts festivals and more.

Historians have pondered the causes of the French Revolution for centuries. Many interrelated political and socioeconomic factors contributed to the restless mood of the Parisian people in the late 18th century.

France was unable to repay debts incurred by King Louis XV and the deficit that was created by the monetary support lent to the American colonies, primarily for guns and gunpowder, during their War of Independence. The Ideas of the Enlightenment greatly influenced the citizens of France and its European neighbors. These ideas included an aspiration towards governmental consolidation, nation-creation and increased rights for common people. The Enlightenment has been characterized as an age not simply defined by new ideas, but rather one which espoused altered attitudes. At the core of the conflict was a crucial questioning of traditional institutions, customs and morals.

Prior to 1789, the people of France were faced with an overbearing regime and outrageous taxes that fueled the lifestyles of the landed gentry. After a succession of poor harvests, the peasants were anticipating food shortages, high unemployment and impending bankruptcies. There was rising resentment of noble privilege and religious intolerance. Most important, there was an aspiration for both liberty and the formation of a republic which would insure that power could be held by ordinary citizens rather than by royalty or a supreme being.

Fifteen-year-old Louis XVI, aka Louis-Auguste, and Maria Antonia Josepha Joanna, the 14-year-old Austrian archduchess of the house of Habsburg were betrothed in February 1770. The youngest daughter of Marie Térèse, empress of Austria, Maria enjoyed a special relationship with her mother. The countess took great pleasure in having arranged marriages that were of strategic importance to the future of the Austrian empire for all of her children. The marriage of her young attractive daughter to Louis XVI was an effort to improve Austria's relations with France, which was considered the most powerful nation in the world at the time.

The fetching teenager was first married in a lavish proxy ceremony in her homeland in April of 1770. Her brother, Archduke Ferdinand, stood in for the groom. The magnificent ceremony was unmatched in royal pageantry. There was a huge procession requiring thousands of horses which wound its way through Austria and to the French border where the princess was taken to an uninhabited island on the Rhine, stripped of her clothing and re-dressed with garments that were fashionable at the French court. She was then renamed Marie Antoinette.

Marie's first impressions of the dauphin were disappointing. At 15, the crown prince's sullen temperament, homeliness and uncouth body left something to be desired. Louis had lost both of his parents by the age of 13 and was placed in the care of the arrogant Duc de la Vauguyon. This upbringing did little to foster positive self esteem. Despite

her initial impressions, Marie would eventually discover that Louis was a good and worthy man.

The official wedding took place at the palace of Versailles in late May. This event created much excitement among the citizens. Sadly, during the fireworks that followed the

Bastille Day. This display celebrates the Fête Nationale held on July 14 in France. Fireworks surround the Eiffel Tower and a red, white and blue bunting support books, swords and fleur de lis.

ceremony, many subjects died from being trampled. After learning of the tragedy, and despite their relative immaturity, the royal couple decided to give up all of their private spending money for a year to help relieve the hardship on the families of the victims. This gesture began a practice of almsgiving that Louis and Marie Antoinette maintained throughout their marriage.

In the early years of her marriage, Marie Antoinette loved to entertain and planned wonderful parties. She enjoyed gambling and nightlife and basically lived a frivolous lifestyle. Marie was renowned for her passion for high fashion and had an elegant sense of style. She habitually exceeded the clothing allowance established by the king. Her preference for large headdresses, colorful plumes and voluminous gowns was subject to public comment, even ridicule. Marie's overt spending on her small court circle was despised by the citizens. They strongly resented her efforts to promote Austrian causes. Her sexual activities, real or imagined, were the subject of much discussion and disdain.

Marie spent lavishly on furnishings for her private residence on the palace grounds. The chateau was originally built by the order of Louis XV for his long-time mistress, Madame Pompadour. Named the Petit Trianon, the residence was a wedding gift to Marie Antoinette from her husband, who needed an invitation to visit or spend any time there. Marie Antoinette also built, at great expense, a Viennese retreat where she entertained her coterie of friends.

Although some of the criticism directed at the queen was justified, much of it was unwarranted. She was a teetotaler who ate frugally. She was modest, kind, caring and thoughtful with members of her staff. She challenged the existing protocol and dined alongside her husband and his friends. She eliminated a tax called "The Queen's Belt," which she viewed as a burden on the peasants. Her carefree life reached its apex when Louis XV died and her husband assumed the throne in 1774.

Many years following the wedding, in a poignant letter to her mother, Marie wrote that the consummation of their marriage did not take place until August 1777, seven years after their wedding. Legend has it that Marie's brother ultimately had to have a "man to man" talk with Louis to insure the continuation of the monarchy. Nonetheless, Louis' inability to produce an heir during that period subjected the couple to much ridicule.

Following the consummation of their marriage, Marie gave birth to four children, two daughters and two sons. Sadly, only the oldest daughter, Marie Thérèse Charlotte, lived to old age, exiled to Austria. Louis Joseph Xavier François lived to the age of seven when he succumbed to consumption. Louis Charles, aka Louis XVII, died at the age of ten, the result of neglect while alone and in prison. Sophie Béatrix died in infancy.

Marie became bored with the royal life and constantly being on display. The endless court rituals were tedious so she directed her anger toward the members of the high nobility. Marie began to assert herself as queen and found herself immersed in indiscretions and scandals. Her negative tone directed toward the older members of the nobility was noted and discussed.

A scandal involving the purchase of an expensive diamond necklace ultimately made its way to the French courts. The trial fused three disparate situations and included the queen, a prostitute/queen look alike, and the highest nobles and clergy, coupled with a few charlatans. The French people were riveted to the news regarding the progress of the trial. Following a not guilty verdict, Marie Antoinette fled the opera house amid the jeers and disdain of the crowd.

The French citizens were cognizant and resentful of the power wielded by Marie Antoinette as a result of her husband's inability to govern effectively. The death of their second child did not serve to make the couple sympathetic to the masses. Aware of the mood of the peasants, Louis XVI decided to give a public hearing to the citizens' complaints and convened the council of the king's vassals called the Etats Généraux. The legislative body was immediately transformed into the Assemblée Nationale to include representatives of the working class. This angered the queen, who was eager to maintain an absolute monarchy. Unfortunately for the monarchy, Louis lacked the determination to repress the insurgency.

The peasants viewed the ancient Bastille

as a symbol of the hypocrisy and fraud inherent in the government, which was controlled mainly by the nobility and members of the clergy. The outraged group of Parisians involved hoped to capture sufficient ammunition to accomplish their revolution. Lawlessness had been established and no royal response was apparent. The storming of the prison disturbed many nobles, who feared mob impulses. Many leaders of the royal court fled the country. The royal couple were entrenched at Versailles, twenty miles from the battlefield Paris had become. At Marie's urging, Louis increased the troops in the surrounding provinces. Still, there were no assurances that their loyalty to the crown would remain. The queen's action was interpreted as arrogance and she became the object of vilification by the revolutionaries.

In the period of summer called the "Great Fear" peasants traveled the countryside in fear that the king would succumb to the pressure from his wife and members of her "Austrian committee" and squelch the revolution. By August, the Declaration of the Rights of Man became public. Noble titles were renounced and the people continued to seek equal rights and the elimination of an absolute monarchy. The republic had emerged.

When food shortages became intolerable, the throngs, mainly Parisian women, marched toward Versailles demanding an end to the "orgies" and pleading for bread. Marie barely escaped losing her life to the knife-wielding peasants. In fact, two of her bodyguards were martyred thereby allowing her to flee. The revolutionaries demanded that Marie and Louis return to Paris, where they were imprisoned in the decaying Tuileries palace. By 1791 the revolution seemed to have stabilized. The assembly provided broad rights to the people at the expense of the clergy and nobles. Reforms became law despite the king's veto.

With the aid of Axel Fersen, rumored lover of the queen and friend to Louis, the royal family fled the palace disguised as common travelers. Because their new coach was laden with all their creature comforts it demanded undue attention as it made its way to the border. An Austrian rescue party was unable to provide the royals safe passage to Marie's homeland, and so the family, filthy from the attempt, returned to Paris in disgrace. Legend has it that Marie's hair turned completely white as a result of this aborted flight for freedom.

The royal family was forced to live minimally within the walls of the Tuileries under close watch. Meanwhile, the imprisoned aristocracy met their deaths in brutal fashion. In December 1792, King Louis XVI was tried for treason, convicted and sentenced to death. A month later he faced the guillotine at the Place de la Concorde, the largest square in Paris. His body was taken to the cemetery at the Church of the Madeleine, put into a large pit and then smothered in quicklime.

The young dauphin was taken from the family against the queen's wishes. In September 1793, Marie was placed in solitary confinement in Conciergerie prison. Following a late night "Revolutionary Tribunal," where her own son was forced to testify to her sexual abuse, the "Widow Capet," as she was now known, faced her final hour. With shorn locks, tattered clothes and hands tied tight, Marie sat erect atop a garbage cart attempting to gather the regal bearing she exhibited throughout her adult life. At noon on October 16, 1793, just shy of her 38th birthday, Marie was beheaded before a throng of cheering revolutionaries. Her body was unceremoniously dumped into an unmarked grave.

For information related to Bastille Day and the last of the French monarchs, go to http://www.france.com/docs/63.html#storming or http://www.marie-antoinette.org and select "Articles," or http://www.pbs.org/marie antoinette.

Credits

In 2008, a long awaited trip to Paris became a reality for me and members of my family. We spent time in the city of Paris and experienced the mesmerizing effect of the Eiffel Tower firsthand. Each evening the imposing structure was bathed in a sea of blue with flashing lights twinkling on the hour. The city and its treasures were true inspirations and I knew I would try to find a way to celebrate the majesty of Paris in a library display upon my return.

The Eastern State Penitentiary in Philadelphia was the world's first true penitentiary, a prison designed to inspire penitence in the hearts of the criminals. A real design wonder conceived by British architect John Haviland, Eastern State was the model for 300 other prisons worldwide. The original seven cell blocks spread like the spokes of a wheel and allowed for no interaction among the residents and staff. Today it stands as a ruin, a decaying, eerie coupling of cell blocks and serenity.

Eastern State Penitentiary would make a great display for its architectural importance, harsh punitive philosophy and some of the notorious criminals such as Al Capone and Willie Sutton who served time in this facility. For information visit http://www.easternstate.org/events/bastille.php. The prison hosts an annual Bastille Day celebration on or around July 14. It has become a popular event attracting thousands of visitors each year to commemorate the raid on the Bastille by French revolutionaries. Armed with muskets and cannons they storm the walls of the penitentiary and drag Marie Antoinette to a real, functioning guillotine, built for the occasion. But, happily, her life is spared and the party begins!

The air is permeated with live music and choruses of "La Marseillaise." Tours of the facility are offered along with kids' activities, including a pet parade. There is an exhibit tent which features wine, cheese and even a lesson in the French language! The party spills into the surrounding Fairmont neighborhood where restaurants and bars continue the alfresco gala throughout the evening. Whether you are a revolutionary or a royalist, you can't help but get caught up in the festive atmosphere of Bastille Day!

Assembling the Display

1. The black felt background provided a contrast to the royal blue poster board, which was framed in red and white poster board. The font for the title signage was Civitype FG sized at 350. This was printed on card stock and traced onto white card stock.

The fireworks were drawn onto silver and red poster board and attached with pins and pulled forward around the Eiffel Tower (Phillips, S 219).

The quote at the top of the display is by Voltaire:

> The longer we dwell on our misfortunes the greater is their power to harm us.

The signage under the poster, "Bastille Day, July 14th," was created using French Script MT sized at 90.

2. On the top left was this quote by Victor Hugo:

> Justice has its anger, my lord Bishop, and the wrath of justice is an element of progress. Whatever else may be said of it, the French Revolution was the greatest step forward by mankind since the coming of Christ. It was unfinished, I agree, but still it was sublime. It released the untapped springs of society; it softened hearts, appeased, tranquilized, enlightened, and set flowing through the world the tides of civilization. It was good. The French Revolution was the anointing of humanity.

Under that was a history of Bastille Day which can be found if you visit http://www.france.com/docs/63.html. A French flag from clip art was inserted at the top right of the document. Next was a photograph of the Louvre and under that a picture of the type a guillotine used in 18th century France, which was found through a Google image search. Under that was a passage on the death of Louis XVI found at http://www.eyewitnesstohistory.com/louis.htm.

Documents on the left were printed and white card stock and mounted on red or blue poster board.

3. On the top right was a quotation from Napoleon Bonaparte:

> Vanity made the French Revolution; liberty was only a pretext.

Under that was a photo of the Place de la Concorde. Next was a brief biography of Marie Antoinette taken from the above text. A red fleur de lis, found in clip art, was inserted at the top right of the document.

Next was a graphic of the Bastille found

through a Google image search. Finally there was a quote from Marie Antoinette:

> I was a queen, and you took away my crown; a wife, and you killed my husband; a mother, and you deprived me of my children. My blood alone remains: take it, but do not make me suffer long.

Items on the right were printed and mounted like those on the left.

4. Levels of Styrofoam were placed on the base of the display to provide different elevations for the books on display. This was covered in a red, white and blue bunting. Swords were cut from silver poster board outlined in black poster board. A Google image search provided a design, which was enlarged on the photocopier. Fleur de lis were found in the same manner and constructed the same way. These were pinned to the Styrofoam and pulled forward.

Books featured in the display were *Marie Antoinette* by Joan Haslip, *French Revolution* by Sylvia Neely, *Citizens: A Chronicle of the French Revolution* by Simon Scham, *The French Revolution and Human Rights* by Lynn Hunt, *The French Revolution: A History* by Thomas Carlyle and *Louis and Antoinette* by Vincent Cronin.

Bigger and Better

Should your space be larger, you could highlight several attractions in the city of Paris. Graphics of the Arc de Triomphe or the Bastille are easily found through an image search. Project your selection on the wall with a data projector and trace the contours onto silver or gray poster board with black markers. If you use the Bastille itself as a graphic, use fiberfill that has been darkened with gray, black, red and brown chalks or paint to suggest the inferno. A very simple graphic that you could use for Bastille Day can be found if you visit http://www.broadwaytovegas.com/bastilledayportland.jpg.

A large firecracker could also be the symbol of choice should you want a simpler design. Many posters are also available for this event and would effectively anchor your display. A simple flag of France, enlarged to fit the space, would also work as a background. Remember to add some big bold fireworks!

Another idea for a display on France, titled "Paris, City of Lights," can be found on page 130 of my first book, *Great Displays for Your Library Step by Step.*

Lovers in History

She press'd his hand in slumber; so once more He could not help but kiss her and adore. — John Keats

The subject of love is complicated. Some have suggested that love is friendship set on fire. Perhaps it is a bit like luck—you have to go to great measures to find it! Love has been defined as a profoundly tender and passionate affection for another person. The triangular theory of love suggests that this emotion has three different components: intimacy, commitment and passion. An ancient proverb suggests, and philosophers agree, that it can be defined as a high form of tolerance. Love in its various forms acts as a major facilitator of interpersonal relationships and is one of the most common themes in the creative arts. However you experience it, it is the eternal truth in the history of mankind.

Although there are many kinds and levels of love, the type that brings men and women together is among the strongest. Love can be established when you are able to focus on the decency and positive aspects of the other person. So powerful is this emotion that it has both started and ended wars.

The search for significant lovers in history yields some interesting results. Some, however, are clearly more notorious than noteworthy. King Solomon was said to have literally hundreds of wives and mistresses. Sixth century Byzantine Empress Theodora entertained dozens of lovers during her wayward youth while still a commoner. Seventeenth century Angolan Queen Zingua was said to have a huge harem of men and often ordered her lovers to be killed in the morning when she was finished with them! The infamous librarian Giovana Giacomo Cassanova recorded over 100 sexual liaisons but is rumored to have actually seduced thousands of women. It has been written that Catherine the Great had many liaisons throughout her reign. Legend has it that Don Juan was destroyed by his obsessive and reckless search for the ideal woman. The Marquis de Sade was put in an asylum as a result of his many and deviant sexual activities.

After a failed marriage, Dutch-born Margaretha Zelle made her way to Paris on the eve of World War I. She became an exotic dancer and adopted the stage name of Mata Hari. As such, she performed in many European capitals and attracted a number of highly placed aristocratic lovers who paid her handsomely for the pleasure of her company. Her involvement with German officers during wartime brought her to the attention of the French Secret Police who ultimately convicted her of being a double agent and sentenced her to death by firing squad. French film actress Brigitte Bardot, the eternal sex kitten, is still considered by some to be the primary symbol of the postwar sexual revolution of the fifties. A ballet dancer who turned to modeling in her teens Bardot once claimed that she must have a man every night.

While these sexual escapades are titillating, it is the royal couples in history that capture our imagination. Napoleon Bonaparte was smitten with his older, fashionable mistress Josephine, much to the dismay of his family. To the surprise of many, he fell deeply in love with her and vowed that he would take this widow as his wife. Although the future empress initially found the diminutive Napoleon a bit droll, Josephine was captivated by his self-confidence and saw many benefits for both her and her children in accepting his proposal. Once crowned empress, however, she spent lavishly. Considered a diva of fashion, it was rumored that at one time Josephine had 1,000 dresses and spent copious amounts of money redecorating. But, it was the mutual Infidelities and the lack of an heir that ultimately caused the demise of the union of Napoleon and Josephine after 13 years of marriage. Following the divorce Napoleon married Marie-Louise of Austria, who bore a son within a year. He wrote, however, of Josephine: "She had something, I don't know what, that attracted me. She was a real woman."

Some royal coupling ended tragically.

Lovers in History. The simple line graphic is the focal point of a romantic display filled with fruit, pewter martini glasses and hearts of gold. Mount this display around Valentine's Day.

Had commoner Anne Boleyn's pregnancies produced the required male heir, her marriage to King Henry VIII might have survived, for Henry had indeed moved heaven and earth to marry her. Their union came on the heels of his divorce from the Spanish-born princess Catherine of Aragon, who had been wed to Henry's brother Arthur for six months, until his death. Although she had many pregnancies, only one daughter, Mary, survived. The divorce was a true act of defiance of church law and brought shame to the crown and ultimately scandalized all of Europe. With several unsuccessful pregnancies and the birth of a daughter during his three year marriage to Anne Boleyn, Henry still had no successor to the throne. As a result, Henry's eye began to wander to Jane Seymour, the rather plain lady-in-waiting to Anne Boleyn. So that he might take another wife, Anne was unjustly accused of adultery with her own brother, among others, and sentenced to death by beheading. Bravely she accepted her fate, pleading at that dire time for the assembled throng to remain loyal to their king. Anne Boleyn's tragic final words were "oh God, have pity on my soul." Days later Henry took Jane Seymour as his bride. Sadly, Jane died just two weeks after giving birth to Prince Edward, the future male heir to the British throne. She is the only wife of Henry VIII to be buried by his side (Haynie, 56).

Queen Victoria found happiness with husband and soul mate Prince Albert, whom she considered to be strikingly handsome. Her love for him embodied mental, physical, and emotional aspects and never waned. After his untimely death in 1861, Victoria insisted that his clothes be laid out daily. She and her servants wore only black and mourned his passing for the next 40 years.

Who could forget King Edward VIII and the much married Mrs. Wallis Warfield Simpson of Baltimore, Maryland, for whom he renounced the crown of England to assume the title of Duke of Windsor? In 1936, the king spoke to his subjects and rejected his crown for himself and his heirs via this radio announcement, which began as follows: "You must believe me when I tell you that I have found it impossible to carry the heavy burden of responsibility and to discharge my duties as King, as I wish to do, without the help and support of the woman I love." For more interesting facts about the royals visit http://morticom.com/royaltytriviaqueens.htm.

Other famous couples that come to mind when considering the topic of lovers in history are purely fictional. Famous lovers in literature include Romeo and Juliet, Arthur and Guinevere, Scarlett and Rhett, Fitzwilliam Darcy and Elizabeth Bennet, Tristan and Isolde, Gatsby and Daisy, Jane Eyre and Edward Rochester, Catherine and Heathcliff and Odysseus and Penelope—to name but a few!

Hollywood has provided a long list of real-life famous couples: Marilyn Monroe and Joe DiMaggio, Katherine Hepburn and Spencer Tracy, Humphrey Bogart and Lauren Bacall, Clark Gable and Jean Harlow, Elizabeth Taylor and Richard Burton and Laurence Olivier and Vivien Leigh. Other couplings were strictly the creation of the film studios. Fred Astaire and Ginger Rogers, Rock Hudson and Doris Day, John Wayne and Maureen O'Hara, Elvis Presley and Ann-Margret and Gregory Peck and Audrey Hepburn created cinematic chemistry during the so-called studio era.

Television has offered us some real-life couples over the decades such as George Burns and Gracie Allen, Ozzie and Harriet Nelson and Lucille Ball and Desi Arnaz. Screenwriters have created many more for the small screen and the chemistry sizzles between characters on shows like *Gray's Anatomy* and *Desperate Housewives.*

Poet and philosopher Kahlil Gibran sums up his thoughts on love with this sentiment: "If you love somebody, let them go, for if they return, they were always yours. And if they don't they never were."

For some good suggestions for romantic couples in history visit http://fun.familyeducation.com/slideshow/love/49015.html?page=13.

Credits

Each year, on Valentine's Day, I observed a number of my students anxiously waiting to see what that certain someone would do to make the day special. I marveled that the idea of a day set aside for lovers is of such great importance to the 18 to 22 year olds in my employ. Many of these students take great care to find the perfect gift or thoughtful gesture that will give pleasure to their significant other. When money isn't available for something more lavish, a greeting card, a hand-knitted scarf or a hand-crafted journal will suffice.

I have created other romantic displays to coordinate with St. Valentine's Day, but I found the content available for "Lovers in History" to be very interesting.

Assembling the Display

1. The poster was inspired by one designed for a production of *Aida*. The design was drawn freehand onto gold and black poster board. The font for the word *Lovers* was Monotype Corsiva sized at 330, and the word *In* was the same font sized at 300. The font choice for the word *History* was Rockwell Extra Bold sized at 350. The cursive letters were printed on card stock and glued to the poster. The word *History* was printed on card stock and traced onto black poster board. A red heart cut from poster board was placed over the *o* in History.

Books on the top shelf were *Napoleon & Josephine: The Improbable Marriage* by Evangeline Bruce, *Katharine and E B. White: An Affectionate Memoir* by Isabel Russell, *Luci & Desi: The Legendary Love Story of Television's Most Famous Couple* by Warren G. Harris and *Dared and Done: The Marriage of Elizabeth Barrett and Robert Browning* by Julia Markus.

2. On the top left was a document on Helen and Paris which can be found at http://www.djmcadam.com/paris-helen.html. Clip art of a Trojan horse was inserted into the bottom center of the document. Under that was an article on Leonardo da Vinci and his model/lover Gian Giacomo Caprotti di Oreno. Clip art of a hand painting was inserted into the top right of the document. Information regarding Da Vinci's lovers can be found at http://www.crystalinks.com/davinci.html The love story of Marie and Pierre Curie was next. For this information visit http://www.pbs.org/wnet/hawking/cosmostar/html/cstars_curies.html. Last was a quote by Thoreau:

> There is no remedy for love but to love more.

All items on the left were printed on card stock and mounted on gold and black poster board.

3. On the top right was a synopsis of the relationship between Antony and Cleopatra. Clip art of the head of a Roman soldier was inserted to the right of the title of this document. Information on Cleopatra can be found at http://www.eyewitnesstohistory.com/cleopatra.htm. Under that was the story of John Alden and Priscilla Mullins, which can be found at http://www.pilgrimhall.org/aldenjohn.htm. Clip art of the ship *Mayflower* was inserted in the bottom of the document.

A summary of the romance of Elizabeth Barrett and Robert Browning was next. Clip art of a hand in the writing position with a vintage pen was inserted in the top center of the document. Information on the Brownings can be found if you visit http://www.victorianweb.org/authors/ebb/ebbio1.html. Last was a quote by Robert A. Heinlein from *Time Enough for Love*:

> May you live as long as you wish and love as long as you live.

All items on the right were printed and mounted like those on the left.

4. On the base of the display were two pewter glasses set atop a 10 inch Styrofoam disk covered in black velvet. Cranberry colored grapes, gold and green pears, yellow apples and green limes were placed around the glasses. Wire-rimmed red ribbon was strewn throughout the fruit and books.

Book featured on the base were *The Book of Abigail and John: Selected Letters of the Adams Family, 1762–1784* by Abigail Adams, *Art and The Crisis of Marriage: Edward Hopper and Georgia O'Keeffe* by Vivian Green Fryd, *Marriage: A History, from Obedience to Intimacy* and *Christo and Jeanne Claude: A Biography* by Burt Chernow.

Bigger and Better

Should your space be larger you may want to include images of the lovers whose story you feature. Set them in hearts cut from poster board or purchased from a party/

dollar store. If you have some angel cut-outs add them and tuck some roses around and through the books. Heart or candy boxes and vintage Valentine cards, as well as candy hearts, could also be worked into your arrangement.

Many books include romantic correspondence that could be the focal point of your display. *Love Letters of Great Men* by John C. Kirkland and *Love Letters of Great Men and Women from the Eighteenth Century to the Present Day* by C.H. Charles are two excellent sources for a display on famous lovers. Enlarge and mount one poignant letter and have that as your primary graphic for the display.

Feature Olivia Langdon and Samuel Clemens (Mark Twain), who shared a glorious love throughout their marriage in your display titled Literary Lovers in History. The story of George Sand and Frederic Chopin and Agatha Christie and Max Mallowan as well as the Brownings would all work well. Include quill and vintage pens and old ink bottles if possible. *Great Lovers and Couples: History's and Hollywood's Most Passionate Pairs* by Elizabeth Haynie and *Historic Lovers* by W.L. George will be great resources for these displays.

Consider a display featuring biblical couples. *Great Couples of the Bible* by Herbert Haag has beautiful illustrations that could serve as a colorful background. Feature Adam and Eve, Abraham and Hagar, David and Bathsheba, Samson and Delilah, or oth-

ers. Create the Garden of Eden with silk tree branches with apples attached. Add some silk flowers and a rubber snake.

You may want to feature specific types of lovers such as "Famous Fictional Couples" or "Political Power Couples." The latter could include people such as Dolley and James Madison, John and Abigail Adams, Edith Bolling Galt and Woodrow Wilson, Eleanor and Franklin Roosevelt, Jacqueline and John Kennedy, Hillary and Bill Clinton and Michelle and Barack Obama.

Leading Couples: The Most Unforgettable Screen Romances of the Studio Era by Frank Miller is an excellent source for a display on "Film Duos." Include film legends who teased, fought, loved, laughed, sang or danced together and created enduring footage that captivated moviegoers throughout the studio era. An online search for free film fonts will give you some excellent alternatives for signage. Consider using the free font Movie Time, which can be downloaded at http://www.1001freefonts.com/movietimes.php.

You may want to include information on the history of Valentine's Day. Set up and decorate a mailbox well in advance of the holiday. Have it positioned outside the display and solicit Valentine cards that could be sent to the children's ward of a hospital or nursing home. To assure a healthy response, make certain that you create signage well in advance of February 14 that indicates a deadline as well as the destination of the cards.

Season's Readings

I am not alone at all, I thought. I was never alone at all. And that, of course, is the message of Christmas. We are never alone. Not when the night is darkest, the wind coldest, the world seemingly most indifferent. For this is still the time God chooses.

—Taylor Caldwell

The traditions of Christmas have captured the imagination of writers, poets and storytellers for centuries. The Yuletide can be defined by these stories in which the magic and mysteries of the season unfold. These tales underscore the realization that belief is still a possibility and reindeers really can fly!

Publishers regularly repackage popular

Christmas classics to entice a new and eager group of shoppers. They bring original seasonal manuscripts to press, making customers' last-minute purchasing decisions less burdensome. Noted authors such as Anton Chekhov, Jane Austen, Hans Christian Andersen, Charles Dickens, O. Henry, Agatha Christie, Pearl Buck, Truman Capote, John

Grisham, Dr. Seuss, David Baldacci, Richard Paul Evans, Maeve Binchy, Jan Karon, Debbie Macomber and countless others have contributed to the wealth of literature on the season of Christmas.

Charles Dickens penned perhaps the most familiar of the tales of Christmas. The second of nine children, he struggled with

Season's Readings. An asymmetrical Christmas tree is flanked by holiday themed books in this display case housing nutcrackers, stars, pinecones and other seasonal objects.

poor health and few resources during his formative years. A formal education was not a possibility, so Dickens sought his own course of study. He read widely, with a particular affinity for fairy tales and stories of adventure. Forced into the workplace at the age of twelve, Dickens drew on those hardships throughout his lifetime. His literary contributions remained true to the problems plaguing the unfortunate and marginalized souls in Victorian society.

Charles Dickens' work *A Christmas Carol in Prose, Being a Ghost Story of Christmas* (commonly known as *A Christmas Carol*) was published in December 1843. This was the first of his five "Christmas books" and was considered an instant success, selling over 6,000 copies in one week. Dickens originally crafted this narrative to repay some financial obligations, but the tale has remained the most successful Christmas literary publication to date. His contemporaries noted that *A Christmas Carol* was written during a decline in the old traditions surrounding the holiday. They felt that the popularity of the book helped to redefine the significance of the sentiments of Christmas.

A Christmas Carol was the subject of Dickens' first public reading, which was given in Birmingham Town Hall to the Industrial and Literary Institute after Christmas 1852. A repeat performance to a working class audience a few days later yielded rave reviews. Over the years Dickens edited the narrative and adapted it for a listening audience. Excerpts from this text remained part of his public readings until his death. The work has been adapted innumerable times for theatre, opera, film, radio and television.

A Christmas Memory debuted as a feature in the popular women's magazine *Mademoiselle* in 1956 and was reprinted in *The Selected Writings of Truman Capote* in 1963. This frankly autobiographical short story was released as a monograph in 1966 during the holiday season. The publishers were attempting to capitalize on Capote's newly created genre in the publishing world–the hugely popular nonfiction "novel" *In Cold Blood*. Set in the Deep South, *A Christmas Memory* tells the tale of a seven-year-old boy named Buddy and his significantly older cousin's holiday preparations for what is ultimately their final Christmas together. It is with this novel that Capote mastered the world of fantasy. The Christmas fruitcakes these characters created contain the essence of the magical world of childhood.

Capote could write with credibility about these atypical family dynamics since he was essentially abandoned by his mother and neglected by his father as a young child. His reality was an unorthodox upbringing under the supervision of aunts and cousins in Alabama during his formative years. Capote longed to be a part of the world of his attractive mother and new stepfather when they took up residence in Manhattan. He finally had that opportunity when his mother regained custody of him when he was nine. The troubled nature of the mother-son relationship continued, however, throughout his lifetime. Her criticism of his lifestyle and sexual preferences remained constant. The openly gay, genuinely flamboyant and successful writer spent his final years in an unproductive manner. Largely unfocused, he lived as a recluse addicted to drugs and alcohol.

John Grisham proposed that the Kranks ignore the holiday altogether in his novel *Skipping Christmas*. The tight-knit neighborhood has some contrary thoughts on that decision, however, and the family finds themselves under increasing pressure to conform. This work is a departure from the drama inherent in Grisham's many legal thrillers and it provides a funny poke at the madness surrounding the holidays.

Debbie Macomber parodies the first Christmas with a pregnant protagonist, her three "wise" brothers and a local inn with no vacancies. The kindness of Christmas is manifested in an offer by the innkeeper to the mother-to-be to provide a room over the stable which housed the animals that were to participate in the Nativity pageant. *A Cedar Cove Christmas* is sure to touch readers and add a little warmth to the holiday season.

The diminutive work by Jason Wright entitled *Christmas Jars* deals with the concept of paying it forward. Hope, a young journalist grieving the loss of her mother, discovers the kindness of a stranger in the form of a jar filled with coins left at her door on Christmas Eve. This novella tells a heartwarming tale of basic human kindness that will surely inspire.

Merry Christmas: Celebrating America's Greatest Holiday by historian Karal Ann Marling is strewn with surprising details that chronicle the rise of consumerism surrounding the Yule season. The author provides an imaginative and well-researched cultural history of the evolution of the holiday traditions as they affect our Christmas expenditures. There are many other holiday books that you could include in your display. For a list of seasonal books you may want to consider for your display visit either http://www.dmoz.org /Society/Holidays/Christmas/Literature/; http://www.ucalgary.ca/~dKbrown/christmas.html; or http://classiclit.about.com/od/christmas literature.

Credits

There is something emotionally invigorating about the nearby, not-so-little town of Bethlehem, Pennsylvania, in the days which precede Christmas. The allure has a special appeal after sunset when white Moravian stars come to life on scattered porches and windows in historic 18th century homes illuminated by the single light of an electric candle. The Central Moravian Church, dating back to 1806, attracts thousands of visitors seeking a spiritual connection to the holiday. During the Great Depression residents of Christmas City, USA, as Bethlehem has been billed since 1937, were enticed to decorate their homes by a city-sponsored lighting contest. In fact, the real motivation of the city leaders was to lure holiday shoppers to the economically challenged downtown.

These days, 200,000 visitors make the pilgrimage to Bethlehem during the weeks preceding Christmas. The jingle of horse-drawn carriages on cobblestone streets is quite a draw, as are the charming shops and boutiques that line the well-kept streets of this historic city. But, the endearing Christmas tradition is an elaborate, multi-scene Nativity or putz that are set up in private homes with free admission. Years ago a red light on the porch signified that the family's religious display was available for public viewing. The authentic attraction to Bethlehem is not commercial, but rather the simplicity and sense of community offered by the Moravians to visitors each Christmas. This Christmas display is a homage to those values.

Assembling the Display

1. The font Christbaumkugln was selected for the title font. It was sized at 350 and printed on white card stock. This font can be downloaded free at http://www.fontspace.com. These letters were attached with pins and pulled forward.

The Christmas tree was found through a Google image search, drawn freehand onto bright green poster board and embellished with colorful Christmas lights and strings of colored beads. A gold star was drawn onto gold poster board and placed at the apex of the tree. The entire tree was attached with pins and pulled forward.

On the shelf above the display was a 10 inch artificial tree, 3 nutcrackers (2 red, 1 blue) a red Christmas ball, a string of silver beads, 2 gold star ornaments, pine cones, Christmas greens and fiberfill.

2. On the top left was an essay entitled "Who Is St. Nicholas?" This Information can be found if you visit http://www.stnicholascenter.org/Brix?pageID=38. Clip art of St. Nicholas was inserted on the top left of the document. Under that was a document titled "The Origin of Santa Claus," which can be found at the same website. Clip art of Santa Claus was inserted on the top right. Below that was a quote by President Calvin Coolidge:

> Christmas is not a time nor a season, but a state of mind. To cherish peace and goodwill, to be plenteous in mercy, is to have the right spirit of Christmas.

All items on the left were printed on card stock and mounted on red, gold, black and green poster board.

3. On the top right was a document entitled "St. Nicholas Day." This can be found if you visit the St. Nicholas URL listed previously. Seasonal clip art was inserted above and below the text. Under that was the quote by Taylor Caldwell which introduced this display.

On the lower right was an article titled "O Little Town of Bethlehem," which can be found on the *Los Angeles Times* Website: http://travel.latimes.com/articles/la-trw-sns-trvmain3-wk33–2008dec03.

All items on the right were printed and mounted as those on the left.

4. On the base of the display were 3 gold star ornaments, candy canes, red Christmas balls, a stuffed red and white felt Santa embroidered with the word *Believe*, a stuffed green and white felt snowman, a tall resin carved red Santa, a cylindrical forest green replica of an early 20th century box adorned with images of children. Also on the base were large and small pine cones, artificial red berries and fiberfill.

Books featured in the display were *A Christmas Carol* by Charles Dickens, *Merry Christmas* by Karal Ann Marling, *An Old-Fashioned Christmas* and *Christmas Jars* by Jason F. Wright, *A Cedar Cove Christmas* by Debbie Macomber, *Skipping Christmas* by John Grisham and *A Christmas Memory* by Truman Capote.

Bigger and Better

If your space allows, use some 2'–3' artificial trees with real ornaments. Add some of the great holiday CDs and DVDs in your library. Include collections of snowmen, Santas, angels, reindeer, holiday cookie jars, etc. Have students, volunteers or young patrons create a colorful paper or popcorn chain to adorn your trees or branches.

You may want to design your display around white birch branches available at craft stores. Drape the branches in colored beads. Use this as a backdrop for storytelling if the space allows. As a craft project, public or school librarians could create a gingerbread house to anchor the display and salt-dough ornaments to adorn the tree. For ideas on specific crafts that could be included in the display visit http://www.enchantedlearning.com/crafts/christmas/ http://www.daniellesplace.com/HTML/christmas.html or http://www.kidsturncentral.com/holidays/christmas/ccrafts.htm.

See page 73 of my first book, *Great Displays for Your Library Step by Step,* for a Christmas display entitled "Santa Blue: The Legend Begins."

8 Newsworthy

When We're Gone

The firmament is blue forever, and the Earth/ Will long stand firm and bloom in spring/ But, man, how long will you live!—Li-Tai-Po

It's eerie to fathom the notion of an eco-apocalypse—where nonhuman nature retakes the globe following the total extinction of homo sapiens. Alan Wiseman explores this concept in his best selling tome, *The World Without Us,* a work that straddles science and speculation. Wiseman, a science journalist and member of the faculty at the University of Arizona, offered a unique approach to the questions of man's impact on the planet. The author certainly did his research. Wiseman drew on the resources of engineers, atmospheric scientists, art conservators, zoologists, oil refiners, marine biologists, astrophysicists, paleontologists and religious leaders ranging from rabbis to the Dalai Lama.

Wiseman illustrated what the planet might be like if humans vanished. According to the author, large parts of our physical infrastructure would begin to crumble almost immediately. Without street cleaners and road crews, our boulevards and highways would begin to crack and buckle in a matter of months. Over the subsequent decades, homes and office buildings would crumple, but some ordinary items would resist decay for extremely long periods of time. Stainless steel pots would last for a millennia if they were buried in the weed-covered mounds that were formerly kitchens. Certain ordinary plastic might endure for hundreds of thousands of years until microbes evolved the ability to consume them.

The author described the collapse of iconic structures and the enormous infrastructure which were so highly dependent on human involvement. Wiseman explains why some of our earliest buildings might be the last remaining architecture, how copper pipes and wiring would be crushed into mere seams of reddish rock; and how plastic, bronze sculptures, radio waves and some man-made molecules might indeed be our legacy to the universe.

The World Without Us suggests that just days after humans disappear, floods in New York's subway system would start eroding the city's foundations. After one week, nuclear reactors would burn or melt down as their water systems fail. At the end of year one, the street pavements would split and buckle as water in the cracks freeze and thaw. Within two to four years cracked streets would become covered with weeds followed by colonizing trees whose roots upheave sidewalks and wreak havoc with severely damaged sewers.

In five years, large parts of New York would have burned due to lightning strikes on dead branches throughout Central Park. After 20 years, dozens of streams and marshes would form in Manhattan as collapsed streets fill with water. By year 100, the roofs of nearly all houses would have caved in. In 300 years, New York City's suspension bridges would have fallen. Structurally more sound, arched railroad bridges are projected to last several hundred years longer.

By 500 years, mature forests would cover the New York metropolitan area. After 5,000 years the casings of nuclear warheads would

When We're Gone. A cityscape on the brink of extinction sits beneath an ominous sky. The diminishing title hints of a world without people.

corrode, releasing radioactive plutonium 239 into the atmosphere. The last remnants of stone buildings in Manhattan would fall to advancing glaciers as the new ice age begins in 15,000 years. In 35,000 years, the lead deposited in the soil from automobile emissions would dissipate. In 10,000,000 years bronze sculptures would continue to survive as historic relics of the human age. After five billion years the earth would vaporize as the dying sun expands and consumes all the inner planets.

Wiseman describes the fate of the flora and fauna that remained when we're gone. With humans extinct, animals inherit the places where we once lived. Although the concept of a world without people is bleak—fear not! Here is some encouraging speculation:

BIRDS: Without skyscrapers and power lines to fly into, at least a billion birds a year would avoid breaking their necks.

TREES: In New York City, oaks and maples along with the invasive Chinese Ailanthus would claim the city.

MOSQUITOES: As extermination efforts cease and wetlands rebound, great clouds of the insects would feed on other wildlife.

FERAL DOMESTIC CATS: They would probably do well dining on small mammals and birds in the posthuman world.

In a world without people the losers would be:

DOMESTICATED CATTLE: They would become a delicious meal for mountain lions, coyotes and other predators.

RATS: Minus our garbage, rats

would either starve or be eaten by raptors nesting in fallen buildings.

COCKROACHES: Without heated buildings cockroaches would disappear from temperate regions.

HEAD LICE: Because these insects are so specifically adapted to humans, our demise would lead to their extinction.

In *The World Without Us* Weisman references the Korean DMZ as a place devoid of humans. The demilitarized area between North and South Korea is about 150 miles long and 2.5 wide. Although it has two of world's biggest armed forces facing off against each other, the area in between has reverted to an amazing and unexpected wildlife preserve. Species that would otherwise become extinct thrive in this region.

The last remaining portion of primeval wilderness, a half million acres of woods which span the border between Poland and Belarus, is called the Bialowieza. It provides another glimpse of how the world would look if we were gone. In this forest, huge ash and linden trees rise 138 feet above an understory of hornbeams, ferns, swamp alders, massive birches and oversized fungi. Norway spruces and five-century-old oaks grow taller still. Pigmy owl whistles, nutcracker croaks and wolf howls combine to create the musical harmony audible within the forest.

The Chernobyl disaster took place in 1986 in northern Ukraine, near the border with Belarus. At the time of the nuclear meltdown, the area's population was estimated to be 50,000 people. Today, the city stands in great decay. The only residents in the zone of alienation are deer and wolves and one single guard. Once tall buildings are now dwarfed by towering trees. To view photos of the aftermath of that disaster and its effects on the city 25-years later visit http://village-ofjoy.com/chernobyl-today-a-creepy-story-told-in-pictures/.

Weisman describes at length the earth's abundant capacity for self-healing. While showing which human devastations are indelible and which fragments of art and culture would endure the longest, Weisman's sobering, cautionary tale drives toward a far-reaching but convincing solution that needn't depend on the absolute extinction of man.

Weisman gently unfolds his restrained and cautionary tale, permitting us to determine what we may about the delicate balancing act that nature and humans need to establish to assure continued survival.

Credits

In February of 2010 my husband and I took a vacation to Florida to visit family and friends. The "in-season" trip was a rarity for us, so you can imagine our dismay when we encountered sustained, unseasonably cold temperatures throughout our stay. The rainy, cold weather precluded many of the usual outdoor activities available in the Sunshine State. One morning, under a gray and ominous cloud cover, we made our way to the Orlando Museum of Art where it was certain to be warm and dry.

It was at this museum that I saw the exhibit which depicted the aftermath of something going terribly amiss on planet Earth. The devastating result was a world without people. The provocative display was titled "Without a Trace: Artists Imagine a World Without Us." The inspiration for this came largely from the *New York Times* best seller list book titled *The World Without Us*.

The Orlando exhibit explored the ways in which nature would go about undoing what civilization has wrought. At times frightening and sometimes encouraging, the exhibit provided an objective look at how the natural world could encroach on our man-made landscape and the human will to both survive and leave a mark.

The contemporary works in the exhibit were on loan from local collections. One of the most compelling items on display was a series of miniature sculptures depicting some of the disasters and acts of terror that have occurred during the past 35-years. The 1979 accident at Three Mile Island, the Chernobyl disaster of 1986, the 1995 Oklahoma City bombing, and 9/11 were some of the ominous events carved in clay.

This exhibit proved quite powerful and provided much food for thought. I was confident that the topic would create some interesting conversation and visceral reactions at our library—and it did.

Assembling the Display

1. This cityscape image was found through a Google search using the terms "sky-line silhouette." It was enlarged on the photo-copier in sections, taped together, then used as a template and traced onto black poster board. The tallest building in the image was 12" high, about ⅓ the height of the display case (this would not be difficult to create free-hand). The image was attached with pins and pulled forward.

The background material was a murky gray felt. The moon was an 8" circle cut from gold poster board. It was attached with pins and pulled forward. Polyester fiberfill clouds were painted with dark blue acrylic and at-tached with pins.

The font used for the title signage was called Megaton and can be downloaded free at http://www.dafont.com. The letters were sized at 300, 250 and 200, printed on card stock and traced onto black, royal blue and silver poster board.

2. On the top left was an imagined time line for the future of the earth taken from an article in *Scientific American* (Mirsky, 76–81). Under that was a document titled "A World Without People, the Winners and the Losers." All of this information can be found in the text introducing this display.

Items on the left were printed on white card stock and mounted on black and blue poster board.

3. On the top right was this quote:

> If all human beings vanished, Man-hattan would eventually revert to a forested island. Many skyscrapers would topple within decades, under-mined by waterlogged foundations; stone buildings such as St. Patrick's Cathedral would survive longer. Weeds and colonizing trees would take root in the cracked pavement, while raptors nested in the ruins and foxes roamed the streets.
> —An Interview with Alan Weisman, *Scientific American,* 2007

Under that was a list of books on the apocalypse which can be found if you visit http://www.goodreads.com/shelf/show/apocalypse. Last was the quote from *The Chinese Flute* which introduced this display.

Items on the right were printed and mounted like those on the left.

4. The books were elevated on Styro-foam and covered with black fabric. The base of the display was then lined with artificial greens and plastic bottles.

Books featured in the display were *The World Without Us* by Alan Weisman, *On the Beach* by Nevil Shute, *The Plague* by Albert Camus, *Field Notes from a Catastrophe: Man, Nature and Climate Change* by Elizabeth Kolbert and *Riddley Walker* by Russell Hoban.

Bigger and Better

Should your space be larger, you could feature miniatures of some iconic structures such as the Statue of Liberty and the Liberty Bell. Have them toppled over on the base of the display. Make sure that you create the ap-propriate skyline for the iconic structures you are featuring. You could also intersperse miniature domesticated and wild animal figures, upended cars and toy planes.

The History Channel featured the topic of the apocalypse in their series titled *Life After People*, which first aired in 2008 and was repeated in 2010. They have also pro-duced two other series dealing with the de-mise of civilization, titled *Armageddon* and *The Nostradamus Effect*. Several years ago *National Geographic* produced a speculative documentary titled *Aftermath: Population Zero*. So, clearly, this subject is of interest to many people and very topical.

Be sure to view these Websites for ideas you could use in your display: http://www.history.com/shows/life-after-people/articles/about–life-after-people and http://channel.nationalgeographic.com/episode/aftermath-population-zero-3225.

Fit or Fat: Are You Fed Up?

One who knows "enough is enough" always has enough. — Tao Te Ching

The problem of obesity is expanding in America. The number of people considered overweight or obese is formidable. Among men there was an increase in obesity prevalence between 1999 and 2006. Since 1999 there appears to have been a leveling off in obesity among women. Well over 30 percent of U.S. adults fit this category. With regard to education levels of men, obesity prevalence was lowest among college graduates (22.1 percent) and highest among those with some college (29.1 percent). For women, obesity prevalence was lowest among college graduates (17.9 percent) and highest among those with less than a high school diploma (32.6 percent), according the Centers for Disease Control report issued in November of 2007. The South, especially Mississippi, Alabama and Tennessee, have the highest percentages of obesity in the nation, with Colorado the lowest.

Obesity is a huge health-risk factor and a real cause for medical concern. Statistics show that almost a half million deaths a year can be directly or indirectly tied to this condition. Seriously overweight Americans spend approximately 100 billion dollars a year on doctors, hospital stays, and work-related accidents. The number of American deaths linked to obesity is rising and rival those fatalities which result from tobacco use (Montignac, 16).

While many governments struggle to keep their citizens nourished, the leaders of wealthy nations are attempting to educate theirs to eat less. Japanese citizens over the age of 40 have their waistlines measured by health officials. Those considered too large must seek nutrition counseling. Fines are imposed on those who fail to slim down. New Zealand has taken it to a new level and actually bars people deemed too fat from immigrating!

In Great Britain residents of some cities are asked to wear electronic tracking tags to calculate their movement and the number of calories burned. Officials estimate that 60 percent of men and 50 percent of women will be considered obese by mid–century. Rewards for lost poundage range from awarding store coupons to days off from work. Currently Great Britain's National Health Service is paying for at least 30,000 people to take weight-loss classes. Germany has allotted $47 million for health and nutrition education and new sports programs. They intend to set strict nutritional standards for school lunches. The government is asking candy manufacturers not to target young children via their advertising and software companies to develop games requiring movement.

When did the problem of overeating begin? The early 20th century experienced a huge shift to industrialization and motorization. Far less energy was needed to travel to work and reduced labor was demanded while on the job. More energy-saving innovations continued to evolve over the succeeding decades, but eating habits weren't modified to conform and so those unused calories were stored in the body as fat. Convenience foods and fast-food restaurant options served only to complicate the issue of maintaining a healthy weight through discerning eating.

Dr. Ancel Keys was a Minnesota physiologist who put saturated fat on the map as a major factor in the development of the most devastating epidemic in the industrialized world, coronary heart disease. His landmark epidemiological study involved 12,000 healthy middle-aged men and was conducted over several decades beginning in 1958. Keys compared the rate of cardiovascular deaths in seven countries: Italy, the Greek Islands, Yugoslavia, the Netherlands, Finland, Japan and the U.S. He discovered that people who consumed fewer saturated fats and whole milk products and who ate more vegetables, fresh fruit and nuts seemed to have lower cardiovascular death rates. These findings were supported by the American Heart Association, whose dietary recommendations influenced millions of Americans to follow a low-fat, high carbohydrate diet. Keys was the first scientist to promote the health value of a Mediterranean style diet. It is interesting to note that he worked in conjunction with the War Department during the World War II. His experiments at high altitudes led to the development of the infamous pocket-sized food portions named K rations, initially created for use at high altitudes by paratroopers. Keys was living proof of the validity of his dietary research and philosophy, as he died in

Fit or Fat: Are You Fed Up? The contrasting fonts set the tone for this display on diet and nutrition. French fries sit front and center ensconced in a tape measure as a reminder of this dietary taboo.

Naples, Italy, in 2004 at the age of 100 (Montignac, 17).

DEFINITION

Overweight people are defined as those having extra body weight from muscle, bone, fat and/or water. Obesity is having a high amount of extra body fat. The most useful gauge for determining which label fits is the body mass index, or BMI. This tool is based on height and weight and applies to people of all ages. To calculate your BMI multiply your weight in pounds by 705; divide by your height in inches; divide this number by your height in inches a second time. For an online BMI calculator visit the National Heart, Lung and Blood Institute Website at http://www.nhibisupport.com/bmi/.

CAUSES

For most people, being overweight and obesity are the result of a lack of energy balance. Weight is balanced by the amount of energy or calories you get from food and drinks (energy IN) equaling the energy your body uses for things like breathing, digesting, and physical activity (energy OUT). Balancing the IN and OUT helps you maintain a healthy weight. The lure of technology is the major reason Americans have adopted a sedentary lifestyle. Extended computer use burns few calories and TV viewing coupled with high calorie snacks has proven to be disastrous to the expanding national waistline.

Decades ago people walked—to school, to shopping, to church. Modern suburban neighborhoods have fewer sidewalks, which contribute to the problem of lack of exercise. America's dependence on the automobile added to its relative inactivity. More office and sedentary jobs are another topic in the conversation about obesity.

Supersized portions at home and at restaurants create too much energy IN. Lack of access to healthy foods such as fresh fruit and vegetables, or their prohibitive cost, contribute to poor food selections. Food advertising directed at children touting high calorie, high fat snacks and sugary drinks have successfully lured our youngsters to select food devoid of healthy nutrients. In the 1950s, kids had three cups of milk for every cup of soda. Today the reverse is true. Children are getting all of the calories and none of the nutrients, a deadly combination.

Genes have a strong influence on a person's weight and body structure. Studies of identical twins raised apart showed the apparent connection, since being overweight and obesity tend to run in families. Odds of becoming overweight increased if one or both parents were overweight. Genes may also affect the level and positioning of fat throughout the body.

An underactive thyroid (hypothyroidism), Cushing's syndrome (where the body's adrenal glands overproduce the hormone cortisol) and Polycystic Ovarian Syndrome (in which high levels of androgens are produced) are examples of hormone imbalances that contribute to the problem of obesity.

RISKS

There are many dangers associated with obesity. Physical consequences include an increased risk of heart disease, stroke, diabetes, high blood pressure, breathing problems and difficulty sleeping. Being overweight or obese raises the risk of colon, breast, endometrial and gallbladder cancers. It also contributes to joint problems and osteoarthritis, infertility, the formation of gallstones and psychosocial disability.

Child and adolescent obesity includes an increased risk of emotional problems. Overweight teens often have low self-esteem and are frequently less popular with their peers and sometimes bullied. As a result they may also experience depression, anxiety and obsessive compulsive disorder.

DIAGNOSIS

A physical examination, including a measurement of height and weight, is usually all that is needed to diagnose obesity. A thorough medical history which includes age of onset, family background, eating and exercise patterns, behavior, alcohol and tobacco use and previous weight loss experiences are all essential. Blood tests may be ordered to determine any existing obesity-related conditions.

TREATMENT

Successful programs for weight loss reduction and maintenance should be undertaken under the care of a physician or a nutritionist or both. An effective weight loss program may include exercise and a low-fat, high-complex carbohydrate and high fiber diet. Behavior modification should be used to alter eating habits. A support network needs to be established for effective long-term weight loss and medications may also have a place in obesity treatment. In extreme situations surgery such as gastric bypass may be indicated.

The primary reason for dietary success is that fewer calories are consumed than are expended. There are numerous Websites dedicated to the topic of obesity in America. For information that will aid you in your display visit http://www.mayoclinic.com/health/childhood-obesity/DS00698, http://www.obesity.org/, http://www.nhlbi.nih.gov/health/dci/Diseases/obe/obe_whatare.html or http://www.obesityinamerica.org/causes.html.

Consumers spend billions of dollars a year on books, DVDs, dieting programs, drugs and fitness club memberships—all in an effort to slim down. In addition, billions more are spent on "lite" or "low-fat" items. One would think that with this amount of money and dedication being spent dieting, exercising and eating mindfully, that the world would be getting thinner. Unfortunately, the opposite is true.

Hopefully you will determine which foods are processed most effectively for you to maintain a healthy mind and body and achieve the equilibrium that will sustain you for life. For information on obesity from the National Center for Health Statistics visit http://www.cdc.gov/nchs/PRESSROOM/07newsreleases/obesity.htm.

Credits

Cedar Crest College has a "Healthy U" program designed to encourage students to confront their weight issues and to provide them with the tools to both eat healthily and maintain fitness. There are incentives such as cash prizes and merchandise that are awarded at the end of each semester. A good percentage of students, staff and faculty have participated in the program with impressive results. The pounds lost, trimmed waistlines and positive outlooks are testimony to the program's success. Increased self-esteem has certainly been a positive by-product of Healthy U. The college food service has cooperated by offering fewer fried foods and adding more fresh fruits, vegetables and vegetarian options to the menu. Organic fruit-based drinks are now an option along with fresh juices.

It was my hope that the display "Fit or Fat" would serve to remind people about the Healthy U program on our campus and increase awareness of alternatives that will result in an improved body and mind.

Assembling the Display

A shelf was added to the top of the display case featuring these books: *Fat Land* by Greg Critser, *Fat: The Anthropology of an Obsession* by Don Kulick and Anne Meneley, *One Bowl: A Guide to Eating for Body and Spirit* by Don Gerrard, *Big Fat Lies: The Truth About Your Weight and Your Health* by Glenn A. Gaesser and *Fat Is a Family Affair: A Frank Discussion of Eating Disorders and the Family's Involvement* by Judi Hollis.

1. The background was black felt. The word *FIT* was created using the font Ariel sized at 96 and then enlarged in WordArt. This was printed on white card stock, traced onto white poster board. The word was then mounted on black, silver and white poster board. It was attached with pins and pulled forward. The word *or* was created using the font Cabrini Body italicized and sized at 200. This was printed on white poster board and traced onto white poster board and attached with pins and pulled forward. The word *FAT* was created using a font named Font, which was available for download at http://www.freefont.com. This was printed on card stock and traced onto black poster board then mounted on white, black and silver poster board. It was attached with pins and pulled forward.

The scale was created using 24"h white poster board framed in black and silver poster board. A small coffee table was used to create the circle. The font for the numbers was PTF Nordic Rnd sized at 80. These were printed on white card stock and cut out as a rectangle then glued to the scale. The ques-

tion "are you fed up?" used the font named Font sized at 200. This can be found free at http://www.fontspace.com/prismtone. The arrow was found through a Google image search and was printed on card stock then traced onto red and black poster board and glued.

2. On the top left of the display was a quote by Fritz Perls:

Awareness Cures.

Under that was a document on childhood obesity which can be found at http://www.mayoclinic.com/health/childhood-obesity/DS00698. Clip art of food figures were inserted at the top right of the title. Under that was a clip art image of an overweight teen sitting on a bench. Next came this passage:

Fat is a three-letter word (Kulick and Meneley, 1).

Under that was a document on obesity bias and stigmatization which can be found if you visit http://www.obesity.org/information/weight_bias.asp.

All items on the left were printed on white card stock and mounted on red, silver and black poster board.

3. On the top right was the quotation that introduced this display. Under that was a BMI chart that can be found if you visit http://www.consumer.gov/weightloss/bmi.htm. Below that was a document which included the medical problems associated with obesity (Kulick and Meneley, 2–3). Next was a food guide pyramid found through a Google image search. Last was this quotation by Plato:

Lack of activity destroys the good condition of every human being, while movement and methodical physical exercise save it and preserve it.

All items on the right were printed and mounted like those on the left.

4. At the base of the display Styrofoam blocks were stacked and covered with black and white dotted Swiss fabric. On top of that was a French fry holder made from four sheets of red 8½" × 11" copy paper taped together. This was attached to a book stand with tape. The French fries were found through an online image search and then enlarged on the photocopier. Four different shapes were traced onto yellow construction

paper and shaded with brown crayon. A mock logo could be cut out and glued to the French fry holder. A yellow tape measure was placed around the fry holder.

Books featured on the base of the display were *Generation Extra Large: Rescuing Our Children from the Epidemic of Obesity* by Lisa Tartamella, Elaine Herscher and Chris Woolston, *Rethinking Thin* by Gina Kolata, *The Way We Eat: Why Our Food Choices Matter* by Peter Singer and Jim Mason, *Super Sized Kids* by Walt Larimore, Sherri Flynt and Steve Halliday, *The Zen of Eating* by Donna Kabatznick, *Food Marketing to Children and Youth* by Michael McGinnis and Jennifer Appleton Gootman.

Bigger and Better

Should your display space be larger, you could create a bigger table and add images such as soda, hamburgers, pie wedges, cook-ies, dishes, cups, etc. You could enlarge the scale to a full size with a floor stand or use an actual scale.

You could feature a color coded map of the U.S. indicating obesity rates nationwide. This is available if you visit http://www.epi demiologic.org/obesity/obesity-epidemic 2004-msn-small.JPG. You could use a PC and a data projector to enlarge the image and trace it onto poster board. The same could be done with the food pyramid.

Create a silhouette of a slender individual on red poster board and outline it in an obese shape on black poster board and use that as your eye-catching graphic. For online templates visit http://content.answers.com/main/content/wp/en-commons/thumb/c/c9/190px-Obesity-waist_circumference.PNG.

Lots of posters are available on the subject are available on this subject. For free posters visit http://www.totallyfreestuff.com/index.asp?ID=9096&m=39&sb=1.

Autism Aware

The real voyage of discovery consists not in seeking new landscapes but in having new eyes. — Marcel Proust

Every 21 minutes a child is diagnosed with autism. This epidemic is so rampant that approximately 67 children will be labeled as such each day. In the late 1980s the incidence rate for those diagnosed with this disorder was 1 to 2 per 10,000. Today autism affects 1 in 150 children, making it more common than pediatric cancer, diabetes and AIDS combined. This condition is a complex neurobiological disorder that typically lasts throughout a lifetime. Sometimes referred to as classic autism, it is part of a larger group of disorders known as ASD, autism spectrum disorders, and the most widespread. As many as one million Americans are currently living with some form of this disorder. It is our nation's most prevalent childhood developmental disorder.

Autism is present in all racial, ethnic and social groups and boys are four times more likely to be diagnosed with it. Simply put, the hallmark characteristic of autism is that it impairs a person's ability to communicate both verbally and nonverbally and to relate to others. The disorder also includes rigid routines and unusual, repetitive or limited activities. The thinking and learning abilities and behaviors of people with ASDs can vary—from gifted to severely challenged.

Autism was first identified in 1943 by Dr. Leo Kanner of Johns Hopkins Hospital in Baltimore, Maryland. The following year Dr. Hans Asperger, a German scientist, described a milder form of the disorder that today bears his name. Both of these disorders fall under the autism spectrum umbrella along with Rett syndrome, pervasive developmental disorder and childhood disintegration disorder. The common link among these disorders is that they involve varying degrees of impairment of communication skills and social abilities. Parents are normally the first to notice signs of impaired social interaction in their child. As early as infancy, a baby with autism may fail to react to people or achieve developmental milestones. The child may become fixated on one item to the exclusion of others for prolonged periods. Some children with autism may initially appear to develop normally and then withdraw, lose abil-

Autism Aware. Art therapy has been used as an effective tool in the treatment of autism. Colorful puzzle pieces serve as an identifiable graphic for this disorder. Artwork was created by Mike Frederick.

ities and become indifferent to social interaction.

Children with autism often fail to respond to their name and avoid eye contact. Many engage in repetitive movements such as rocking and twirling or self-abusive behavior such as biting or head-banging. They are unable to interpret thoughts and emotions because they can't recognize social cues such as tone of voice or facial expressions. These children ignore clues that would inform their social behavior and typically lack empathy. Interactive play is a challenge for them. Some converse in a sing-song voice about a narrow range of topics, with little or no regard for the interests of the person with whom they are conversing. Many children with autism are relatively indifferent to levels of pain, but have a heightened sensitivity to sound, touch or other sensory stimulation. Often they resist being cuddled or hugged.

Asperger syndrome, which also falls under the ASD, is usually regarded as a high functioning form of autism. People identified with this disorder have impaired social interactions and limited repetitive patterns of behavior. Since motor development may be delayed, victims are often clumsy. While people with Asperger syndrome are frequently socially inept, many have above-average intelligence and they may even excel in areas such as computer programming and science. There is no apparent delay in cognitive growth or in development of age-appropriate self-help skills.

Rett syndrome is a childhood neurodevelopmental disorder characterized by normal early development that is followed by loss of purposeful use of the hands, distinctive hand movements, slowed brain and head growth, gait abnormalities, seizures, and mental retardation. Unlike classic autism it affects females almost exclusively. The disorder was identified by Austrian physician Dr. Andreas Rett, who first described it in a journal article in 1966. However, it was not until after a second article about the disorder was published in 1983 that the syndrome became widely recognized.

The course of Rett syndrome varies. The age of onset can be sudden and the severity of symptoms varies. Before the symptoms appear, the child seems to be developing normally. Gradually, mental and physical symptoms present. Early on, loss of muscle tone becomes apparent. As the syndrome progresses, the child's hand use and the ability to speak are affected and compulsive hand movements such as wringing and washing appear. Other early symptoms may include trouble crawling or walking and diminished meaningful eye contact. Apraxia—the inability to perform motor functions—is perhaps the most severely disabling feature of Rett syndrome. It hinders every body movement, including eye gaze and speech. Persons with Rett syndrome often exhibit autistic-like behaviors in the early stages. Other characteristics include toe walking, problems with sleep, wide-based gait, teeth grinding, difficulty chewing, slowed growth, seizures, cognitive disabilities, and breathing difficulties while awake such as hyperventilation, apnea (breath holding), and air swallowing.

Pervasive developmental disorders (PDD) refers to a group of disorders characterized by delays in the development of socialization and communication skills. Parents may note symptoms in infancy, although age of onset is typically before three years of age. Symptoms may include problems with using and understanding language as well as trouble relating to people, objects, and events. Children may demonstrate unusual play with toys and other objects, difficulty with changes in schedule, and repetitive body movements or behavior patterns. Children with PDD vary widely in abilities, intelligence and conduct. Some children lack speech, others speak in limited levels of conversation, and some are not impaired with respect to language. Repetitive play and limited social skills are apparent. Atypical responses to sensory information, such as loud noises and lights, are also common.

Childhood disintegration disorder (CDD) is a developmental disorder characterized by a loss of thinking, communication, and language skills. This usually occurs sometime between ages two and four. Normal development is seen until then. The cause of childhood disintegrative disorder is unknown. Symptoms include poor social skills and lack of bowel and bladder control. Children with CDD have impaired language and motor skills and difficulties forming relationships. The condition is very similar to autism in its more severe forms. CDD affects girls and boys in equal numbers. More research is needed to determine how many children are affected by childhood disintegrative disorder, but it is much less common than autism.

As a result of new research methods, disorders within the autism spectrum have been diagnosed in infants as young as six months old. Typically, however, a child reaches the age of three before autism appears conclusive. Early intervention is critical if benefits from existing therapies are to be gained. Programs which focus on developing communication, social and cognitive skills yield the best results. However, at present, there are no means to prevent autism, no fully effective treatments and no cure.

There is a book by Ellen Notbohm titled *Ten Things Every Child with Autism Wishes You Knew*. These pointers are listed below and are poignant reminders for the people involved with a special needs autistic child:

1. I am first and foremost a child. I have autism. I am not primarily "autistic."

2. My sensory perceptions are disordered.

3. Please remember to distinguish between won't (I choose not to) and can't (I am not able to).

4. I am a concrete thinker. This means I interpret language very literally.

5. Please be patient with my limited vocabulary.

6. Because language is so difficult for me, I am very visually oriented.

7. Please focus and build on what I can do rather than what I can't do.

8. Help me with social interactions.

9. Try to identify what triggers my meltdowns.

10. If you are a family member, please love me unconditionally.

Much has been written about the importance of diet with special needs children. Some studies show that mild to dramatic improvements in speech or behavior or both and overall health had been noted after gluten and casein have been removed from the child's diet. Autistic author and consultant Donna Williams claims that she has been helped by nutritional supplements together with a dairy and gluten-free and low salicy-late diet. Salicylates can be found in very high amounts in many fruits, including apri-cots, cherries, oranges, strawberries and grapes. It is also found in foods such as cu-cumbers, radishes, almonds and honey, as well as peppermints and chewing gum. Some people report no significant benefits from the gluten-free, casein free (GFCF) regimen; oth-ers have found that the diet eases gastroin-testinal problems, food allergies and sensi-tivities.

Glutens are found in wheat and other grains, including oats, rye, barley, bulgar, durum, kamut and spelt and foods made from those grains. They are also found in food starches, semolina, couscous, malt, some vinegars, soy sauce, flavorings, artificial colors and hydrolyzed vegetable proteins. Casein is a protein found in milk and foods containing milk, such as cheese, butter, yo-gurt, ice cream, whey and even some brands of margarine. It may also be found as an ad-ditive in non-milk products such as soy cheese and in hot dogs in the form of ca-seinate.

The authors of *The Kid-Friendly ADHD & Autism Cookbook* wrote the following: "An optimized diet, along with nutritional sup-plements, provides nutrients that are essential for body and brain functioning. In addition, breakdown products from certain foods (par-ticularly dairy and glutens) can interfere with brain functioning" (Compart and Laake, 7). For more information about proper nutrition with respect to children with autism visit http://www.autismweb.com/diet.htm, which also has links to relevant cookbooks.

In February 2010 the British journal *Lancet* retracted a flawed study that linked the measles, mumps, rubella vaccine to autism and bowel disease. Medical researcher An-drew Wakefield took blood samples from children at his son's birthday party, paying them £5 ($8) for their contributions and later making light of the incident. Subsequent studies found no proof that the vaccine is connected to autism, though some parents remain wary of the shot.

In April 2009 a breakthrough discovery which involved nearly 11,000 families showed the strongest genetic link to autism thus far. A gene mutation was found to be present in two-thirds of children with autism. Using the world's largest DNA database, researchers discovered a defect that disrupts synapses—the way brain cells communicate with each other. Without that communication, it is difficult to carry out complex social behaviors such as understanding language and inter-preting gestures and facial expressions.

Medical research is just part of the puz-zle, but a significant part nonetheless. It is important to remember that many factors, in-cluding environmental issues, contribute to the development of autism. However, re-searchers are optimistic that this break-through will lead to treatment in the future.

ART THERAPY

The first stage in art therapy is the build-ing of trust and empathy between artist and pupil. The goal is to enlarge vocabulary through the introduction of new materials. Trained art therapists are also artists who focus on feelings and sensations that children experience in their use of materials, i.e., wet-ness, sharpness, textures. The new shared vo-cabulary helps the therapist to understand the level of the child's self awareness. Creat-ing art is a meaningful and therapeutic ac-tivity for children with ASD due to their intense sensory needs and reduced commu-nication skills. Art provides visual, concrete, and hands-on therapy. This tangible, creative activity offers a myriad of possibilities for per-sonal expression through an interpretive process. The extent of the body of literature in the field of art therapy demonstrates that it is an effectual, clinically sound treatment alternative.

Once a person with autism reaches adulthood, the cost to provide the necessary educational and social services, including supervised living, amounts to more than $100,000 per year. Currently over $90 billion is spent annually on treating individuals with this disorder. The figure is projected to in-crease to $400 billion a year by 2015.

Credits

My daughter-in-law, Mary, spent many years working with autistic children, one on one. She went to their homes and often escorted them on purposeful ventures in the community. Over the years I marveled at the patience she extended to each of her clients. Mary is a positive, determined and resilient young woman who sees a rainbow of possibilities in her students and never gives up. Her graduate work in school counseling comes into play as she comforts and sometimes cautions families struggling to cope with the chaos created by their special needs child. Observing Mary finding joy in the tiniest improvements of those entrusted to her was heartwarming.

One of Mary's students was Mike Frederick, a 14-year-old Lehigh Valley youngster living with autism. His art therapy began several years ago and it is obvious that this medium is helping him to communicate his thoughts and feelings. Some of his artwork is featured in this display.

It is my hope that autism awareness will be achieved and that progress in finding a cause and a cure will be identified—hopefully, sooner rather than later. This display was installed in April, which is Autism Awareness month, as a tribute to those educators and parents who face the daily challenges autism presents.

Assembling the Display

These books were featured on the top of the display: *Somebody Somewhere: Breaking Free from the World of Autism* and *Art Therapy with Children on the Autistic Spectrum* by Kathy Evans and Janek Dubowski, *The Way I See It: A Personal Look at Autism and Asperger's* by Temple Grandin and *Mother Warriors* by Jenny McCarthy. The Play-Doh flower and containers were placed in the center front of the shelf along with a tin of crayons, some colored markers and a card designed to distribute to curious onlookers, titled "My Child Has Autism," which gives a brief explanation of the child's behavior. The verso of the card defines the disorder. To order this type of card go to the Website http://www.talkaboutcuringautism.org, which also offers a host of products of interest to families dealing with autism.

1. The background of the display was black felt. The puzzle design was found through a Google image search. The pieces were approximately 6" square and were cut from yellow, green and blue poster board and pinned to the felt. The title was created using the font Berlin Sans FB Demi. The A was sized at 850 and the lower case letters at 310. The letters were yellow with blue dots created with a hole punch.

Three works of art by Mike Frederick were mounted on black and yellow poster board and pinned to the black velvet. The words *Art by* were created using the font Harlow Solid Italic sized at 28. The font Gill Sans Ultra Bold Condensed sized at 72 was used for the artist's name.

2. On the top left was a document titled "Ten Things Every Child with Autism Wishes You Knew," taken from the book by the same name by Ellen Notbohm. Under that was the quote by Marcel Proust that introduced this display. Next was a graphic titled "Major Brain Structures Implicated by Autism," easily found through Google image search using those terms. Last was this quote by Ellen Notbohm found in her book *Ten Things Every Child with Autism Wishes You Knew:*

> Work to view my autism as a different ability rather than a disability. Look past what you may see as limitations and see the gifts autism has given me. I may not be good at eye contact or conversation, but have you noticed I don't lie, cheat at games, tattle on my classmates, or pass judgment on other people?

Items on the left were printed on white card stock and mounted on yellow and/or blue poster board.

3. On the top right was a document on "Autism Spectrum Disorders" which can be found if you visit http://www.kennedykrieger.org/kki_diag.jsp?pid=1072. Under that was a drawing by a child with autism, found through a Google image search. Last was a document describing Asperger syndrome, which can be found if you visit http://assets.aarp.org/external_sites/adam/html/1/001549.html.

Items on the right were printed and mounted like those on the left.

4. On the base of the display were sign language flash cards, a small puzzle, tubes of paints and brushes and a variety of Picture

Exchange Communication System squares commonly known as pecs.

Books featured on the base of the display were *1001 Great Ideas for Teaching and Raising Children with Autism Spectrum Disorders* by Ellen Notbohm and Veronica Zysk, *The Kid-Friendly ADHD & Autism Cookbook* by Pamela J. Compart and Dana Laake, *Art as Therapy* by Edith Kramer, *Jonathan Lerman: Drawings by an Artist with Autism* by Lyle Rexer and *Ten Things Every Child with Autism Wishes You Knew* by Ellen Notbohm.

Bigger and Better

Should your space be bigger you could include artwork done by several autistic children. Contact your local intermediate unit or activity center for their cooperation in this venture. Have a theme such as "Art with Heart" and include a photo of the artist encased in a heart and add a few sentences about their artwork. Emphasize the part that art therapy plays in the recovery of autistic children.

Use the source *Jonathan Lerman: Drawings by an Artist with Autism,* text by Lyle Rexer, as an inspiration for the healing possibilities attainable through art therapy. A chance encounter with charcoal and pastels at the age of ten helped to reveal the latent talent in Jonathan. Up until that point there was no discerning his private thoughts and feelings. Jonathan was a youngster whose emotions were being held hostage. His early doodling of cartoon-like figures morphed into expressive drawings which gave those around him a window into his heart. His drawings illustrate the loneliness and isolation of those who are different, and they will serve you well in a display on art therapy and autism. For more information on this topic, visit http://www.arttherapyblog.com/c/autism or http://autism.healingthresholds.com/tags/art-therapy.

Mount your display in conjunction with an ASD fund-raiser or Valentine's Day. Your focus could be on the larger spectrum of the "Exceptional Child." The Council for Exceptional Children offers some easy graphics which can be found through an online search and would make an effective focal point for your display. Include other exceptionalities such as children with learning disabilities, ADHD, the hearing or visually impaired and children with physical handicaps. SEN Teacher provides cost-free teaching & learning resources for students with special needs and learning disabilities. These can be incorporated into your display. To view them visit http://www.senteacher.org.

Invite students from your area colleges who are majoring in special education to come to your library and mount a display on current trends in the field. Coordinate this with a story hour and have a student read *Susan Laughs* by Jeanne Willis and Tony Ross, *My Friend Isabelle* by Eliza Woloson, or *Rolling Along: The Story of Taylor and His Wheelchair* by Jamee Riggio Heelan. Encourage a discussion among the children about special needs children and tolerance.

Gallery of Rogues

I am like any other man. All I do is supply a demand. — Al Capone

Few criminals achieved the level of adoration and publicity afforded true mobsters of the tumultuous 1920s and 1930s. During that period gangsters were revered, feared and despised simultaneously. The legends that surround the notorious men of the era, like Al Capone and "Bugs" Moran, were born of prohibition. Gangsters found it very profitable to buck the system and reject the rules of society. Those were the glory days of bootleg booze, easy women, crime and corruption.

The gangster represented urban life: the streetwise, self-made man, a small guy destined to make big headlines. Considered as modern day Robin Hoods by some, these gangsters were really outright criminals. During the twenties and thirties, the public's appetite for more information was insatiable.

Gallery of Rogues. Bullet holes puncture the poster featuring seven of the most notorious criminals of the 1930s and 1940s. Wool pinned to the display background suggests a prison wall of blocks. Vintage beer bottles, a sack of money, playing cards and dice were tools of the underground gambling world prevalent during Prohibition.

Darlings of the media, these outlaws were treated like today's celebrities. Prior to the advent of television, newspapers trumpeted the headlines. The public yearned for more press and the journalists were happy to oblige. In the twenties, New York and Chicago were the centers of both American society and organized crime. Both cities encompassed the economic extremes within their population. Their citizens ran the gamut from excessively wealthy to abjectly poverty stricken and the result proved to be a volatile combination.

The gangster business was thriving in the Roaring Twenties. Al Capone and other bootleggers wielded absolute control over their cities. The notoriety Capone achieved in capitalistic Chicago during those early years was a novelty in American culture. He was the true paparazzi poster boy, who clearly savored the spotlight. He was a real rags to riches story, and his reputation and influence were largely due to his own style of handling the press during the era of Prohibition. Dressed in classic gangster garb, Capone could be spotted in expensively tailored pin-striped suits sporting a huge diamond ring and a felt fedora. Articulate, but with an edge, the media could count on him for colorful quotes to caption their plethora of photographs.

Gangsters in New York ran the streets and clubs of the city like the kings of mythical Gotham. They boldly paraded through Broadway shows and gambling joints in Harlem. Much of their business was negotiated in the recesses of popular eating establishments throughout Manhattan and the boroughs. The activities of men like Dutch Schultz and Jack "Legs" Diamond contributed to the increased awareness of the bright lights and big cities known today as the Big Apple and Second City. Although these men were all-around bad guys, kidnappers and known killers, the public simply couldn't get enough.

THE FBIS MOST WANTED

JOHN DILLINGER (1903–1934)

Dillinger was the son of a grocer who was widowed when John was three years old. His childhood was dysfunctional and discipline was harsh. Dillinger was a dangerous criminal who was responsible for the murder of several police officers, robbed at least two dozen banks and four police stations, and escaped from jail twice. He was nicknamed the "Jackrabbit" for his graceful movements during heists, such as leaping over counters, and his many narrow getaways from police. For more information about Dillinger visit http://www.thebiographychannel.co.uk/biography_story/835:451/1/John_Dillinger.htm.

BONNIE PARKER (1910–1934)

Intelligent and personable, yet strong willed, petite Bonnie Parker was a comely 19-year-old whose husband was serving a 99-year jail sentence for murder when she met Clyde Barrow. She had been less than faithful to her husband since his incarceration and she was immediately smitten. Most historians believe Bonnie joined Clyde because she was in love and accepted the inevitability of their violent demise. Her fondness for creative writing found expression in poems such as "The Story of Suicide Sal" and "The Trail's End" (aka "The Story of Bonnie and Clyde").

CLYDE BARROW (1909–1934)

Clyde Champion Barrow was born in Ellis County, Texas. Although he held legitimate jobs during the years 1927 through 1929, he also had a sideline. He cracked safes, robbed stores, and stole cars. Primarily known for robbing banks, Clyde also focused on smaller jobs, robbing grocery stores and gas stations at a rate which far outpaced the 10 to 15 bank robberies attributed to him and his cronies known as the Barrow Gang.

Bonnie and Clyde were killed in a roadblock ambush near Gibland, Louisiana. Texas Ranger Frank Hamer and his posse

fired 187 shells into the couple, killing them instantly—Clyde in his socks and Bonnie with a sandwich in her mouth. For more information on Bonnie and Clyde visit http://www.thebiographychannel.co.uk/biography_home/460:0/Bonnie_and_Clyde_.htm.

AL CAPONE (1899–1947)

Al "Scarface" Capone was a notorious American gangster and the leader of a crime syndicate dedicated to smuggling and bootlegging of liquor and other illegal activities during the Prohibition Era. Capone began his career in Brooklyn before relocating to Chicago and becoming the boss of the criminal organization known as the Chicago Outfit. Although the authorities were never able to convict him of racketeering charges, Capone's criminal career ended in 1931 when he was indicted, then convicted by the federal government of income-tax evasion. He served a total of eight years at Leavenworth and Alcatraz and was paroled in 1939.

In his role as Mafia boss, Capone ordered the deaths of 500 men in Chicago. More than a thousand others met their demise in his bootleg wars. The high living he enjoyed early in his career had taken a damaging toll on his body. Capone died at age 48 of bronchial pneumonia and a brain hemorrhage at his estate in Palm Island, Florida, in 1947. For more information on Al Capone visit http://www.angelfire.com/co/pscst/capone.html.

JOE BONANNO (1905–2002)

Joe Bonanno was a Sicilian-born American who founded one of the nation's most enduring Mafia families and rose to the pinnacle of organized crime in the U.S. Sometimes referred to as "the boss of all bosses," he was nicknamed "Joe Bananas"—a name he despised—because it implied he was crazy. Early in his career Bonanno was recognized by his Brooklyn accomplices as a fearless figure with superior organizational skills and quick instincts. At age 26, he became one of the youngest bosses of a crime family. In 1983 Bonanno wrote a candid autobiography in which he listed both the regrets and accomplishments of his life and affirmed his disdain for modern organized crime's involvement in drug trafficking. He died in Tucson at the age of 97. For more information on Joe Bonanno visit http://gangstersinc.tri-pod.com/JoeBon.html.

CHARLES "LUCKY" LUCIANO (1897–1962)

Charles Luciano was a Sicilian-born American mobster who was credited with turning syndicated crime into a nationwide organization based on legitimate business models. The avant-garde Luciano was considered the father of modern organized crime and is credited with being the mastermind behind the massive postwar expansion of the international heroin trade. He was the first official boss of the modern Genovese crime family. Luciano became a celebrity, living in high style and having celebrity pals such as actor George Raft and singer Frank Sinatra.

His mobster fame caught up with him in 1936, when special prosecutor (and soon-to-be New York governor) Thomas E. Dewey charged Luciano with 62 counts of compulsory prostitution. He was convicted and sentenced to a minimum of 30 years in prison. In February of 1946 Governor Dewey struck a deal that released Luciano from prison with the provision that he be deported to Italy. It was rumored that during World War II Luciano used his contacts to help the U.S. government fight the Nazis. Luciano, who maintained his position as crime boss, even when serving time in prison, surfaced in Cuba in 1947 and was deported a second time to Italy by U.S. officials.

Luciano died of a heart attack at the age of 65 in Capodichino airport in Naples. Eventually, his body was returned to the U.S. where he was entombed at St. John's cemetery in New York City. For additional information on Lucky Luciano visit http://people.famouswhy.com/lucky_luciano.

"MACHINE GUN" KELLY (1895–1954)

George Kelly Barnes was a notorious American criminal who gained a reputation during the Prohibition era. A college dropout and father of two, Kelly was struggling financially when he turned to a life of crime which included bootlegging, armed robbery and, most prominent, kidnapping. Kelly savored the financial rewards of his new trade as well as the notoriety.

On 22 July 1933, Kelly and his gang kidnapped Oklahoma oilman Charles F. Urschel. They held him for nine days before he was released upon receipt of a ransom totaling $200,000. Although the victim had been blindfolded through the entire nightmare, he had listened carefully to his captors' discussions and was able to provide numerous clues to the FBI. This information lead to Kelly's arrest shortly after the crime. Kelly and his wife were sentenced to life in prison. It is interesting to note that during his years at Alcatraz and Leavenworth he became pen pals with his victim. Kathryn Kelly's sentence was commuted in 1958, four years after her husband's death. For additional information about Machine Gun Kelly visit http://www.biography.com/articles/George-Machine-Gun-Kelly-235983.

Credits

Bad guys make good press. In the summer of 2009, Johnny Depp traded his mangy pirate persona for that of a notorious gangster in the film *Public Enemies*. The movie opened to positive reviews that credited Depp with a competent and technically impressive portrayal of the brooding gangster John Dillinger. Depp's charismatic performance served to introduce this Depression Era outlaw to a whole new generation.

Dillinger robbed major banks, escaped from two prisons and frequently associated with known scumbags throughout his lifetime. He boasted that he liked baseball, movies, fine clothing, whiskey, fast cars and beautiful women. Dillinger didn't like the Federal Bureau of Investigation or its chief, Melvin Purvis. It is the FBI that is credited with Dillinger's demise in Chicago as he exited a movie house (featuring a Clark Gable film) with two women companions in July of 1934. Twenty-three people died of the heat on that infamous summer day, but the death that drew the most attention was that of 31-year-old Indiana born John Dillinger, who had been declared Public Enemy No. 1 by the FBI the month prior.

Dillinger's Remington .41-caliber double Derringer was sold at a Dallas auction for $95,600 during the summer of 2009. The small two-shot pistol was a favorite among riverboat gamblers and commanded twice the pre-auction estimate. The weapon's price certainly reinforced the concept that John Dillinger's legacy will continue. All of this attention being paid to 1930s era gangsters assured me that there would be some keen interest in a display involving other infamous people of the period.

Assembling the Display

1. The background of this display was gray felt. Black yarn was attached with pins to suggest jail cell blocks. An image of the machine gun was found through a Google image search. This was printed on copy paper, enlarged in sections on the photocopier, and traced onto black poster board. This image was then mounted on red poster board.

Under that was a 37" × 16" sheet of black poster board. The title font, Grenadier, was sized at 350, printed on card stock and traced onto red poster board. The letters were glued onto the poster board. This font is available to download free at http://www.dafont.com.

Mug shots and photos of the criminals were found through Google image searches. These were printed on white card stock, framed in red poster board, and glued onto the black poster board. The names were printed on card stock and affixed to the photos. Gunshots, found through a Google image search, were saved and edited in Adobe Photoshop. They were sized in Adobe Photoshop at 1" and 1" in diameter, printed on paper and glued in the *o* of the word *of*, and randomly place around the poster. Photos were of Machine Gun Kelly, Clyde Barrow, Bonnie Parker, Al Capone, Charles "Lucky" Luciano, Joe Bonanno and John Dillinger.

2. On the top left was a brief biography of the criminals pictured. This information can be found if you visit http://www.biography.com. Under that was a document on the history of the FBI, which can be found at this site: http://www.policyalmanac.org/crime/archive/fbi.shtml.

Items on the left were printed on card stock and framed on red or black poster board.

3. On the top right was the quote that introduced the display. Under that was a time line on Prohibition. This can be found at http://americanhistory.about.com/od/prohibitionera/a/prohibition.htm. Next was this quotation by Canadian humorist Stephen Leacock (1869–1944):

> The attempt to make the consumption of beer criminal is as silly and as futile as if you passed a law to send a man to jail for eating cucumber salad.

Items on the right were printed and mounted like those on the left.

4. On the base of the display was black velvet fabric which covered books that were stacked on the left, center and right to create some elevation. The bag of money was created from a 24" circle of gray felt stuffed with bubble wrap. A rubber band was wrapped around the top and strands of black yarn were tied around it. A dollar sign, made out of red poster board, was attached with tape to the bag. One hundred dollar bills, found through a Google image search, were printed on paper and stuffed in the money bag and throughout the base.

The cubes were created using white construction paper. The instructions for this origami technique are on video and can be found at http://www.metacafe.com/watch/1006984/origami_cube. Dots were cut from black poster board and attached with glue to create the dice. Stacks of poker chips in red, blue and black flanked the moneybag. Red playing cards were taped together and positioned behind the rest of the deck.

Labels were removed from empty beer bottles. Vintage beer bottle labels from the 1930s were printed on paper and attached with rubber cement. These can be found if you use the term "vintage beer labels" in Google image search.

Books featured in the display were *Son of Scarface* by Chris W. Knight, *Murder, Inc: The Story of "The Syndicate"* by Burton Turkus and Sid Feder, *Bad Seeds in the Big Apple: Bandits, Killers, and Chaos in New York City, 1920–1940* by Patrick Downey, *Gangsters, Swindlers, Killers & Thieves: The Lives & Crimes of Fifty American Villains* edited by Lawrence Block, *Dry Manhattan: Prohibition in New York City* by Michael A. Lerner and *Prohibition: Thirteen Years That Changed America* by Edward Behr.

Bigger and Better

You could mount this display in October, which is Crime Prevention Month. Should your space be larger you might include wanted posters which are readily available and reasonably priced. They can be found through an online Google search. Add a fedora, a feather boa, handcuffs, a diamond ring, and wedge heels to suggest the clothes of the era. For more information about fashion of the 1930s visit http://www.fashion-era.com/stylish_thirties.htm or http://www.murrayonhawaii.com/nolan/fashionhistory_1930mens.html.

You may want to focus on criminals of a more modern era, such as Jeffrey Dahmer, Charles Manson, Ted Bundy, John Wayne Gacy. Be sure to refer to *Bloodletters and Badmen* by Jay Robert Nash when mounting a display on the infamous. This comprehensive text was revised in the 1990s and includes criminals from the Pilgrims to 1995.

You could create the feeling of an old speakeasy in your display space. Craft some vintage bottles of gin with period labels, which are available online. These labels can be glued on used liquor bottles. Include the beer bottles created for this display and add glasses, cigarettes, cigars and ashtrays. To obtain a Speakeasy poster to complete the display visit http://www.bonanzle.com/booths/fungus_amungus_com/items/Speak_Easy_Rare_Bally_Pinball_Promo_Poster_Mint.

If the concept of rogues is not of interest to you, focus on positive role models and create a display titled "Heroes and Icons." Check the *Time* magazine annual issue of "Man of the Year" (first issue in January) for ideas as to people who could be featured. Or, visit this site: http://www.time.com/time/time100/leaders/index.html.

Should infamous pirates be your preference see display on the notorious, "The Legend of Blackbeard" on page 143 of my first book, *Great Displays for Your Library Step by Step*.

Election Central

Bad politicians are sent to Washington by good people who don't vote.
—William E. Simon

The very first presidential election in 1789 was really no contest at all. George Washington ran unopposed for the newly created office. He was reelected in 1792, again with no opposition. To date there have been 55 presidential elections in the U.S. and 44 men who have filled this office.

Americans have made a poor showing at the polls in recent decades. Statistics indicate that in general only half of all possible voters exercised their right to vote in presidential elections. Fewer still, 20 to 25 percent, participated in state and local contests. These numbers suggest that our democracy has become dispirited and that the ability to be counted has been devalued. And yet, the global image of a democratic United States is that of a nation with universal suffrage.

Abraham Lincoln coined the phrase "government of the people, by the people, and for the people" in an effort to adequately describe democracy. For that government to be "by the people" suggests that the citizens actually decide who shall be their leaders. Surely, there can be no truly democratic society without free and fair elections. Without the continuous accountability of elected officials, all of our other rights are in question. The right to vote is a vital individual liberty, a cornerstone of free government.

Deciding who should have the right to vote has been a recurrent question since our country's founding. Americans have argued and fought over restrictions on this right since the nation's birth in 1776. Those debates have revealed much about the meaning of democracy in the political life and culture of our country. Framers of the Constitution originally limited the right to vote to white, male property owners.

The history of voting rights for women spanned a period of more than seventy years, eventually spawning the nation's largest mass movement for suffrage. Women enjoyed different relationships with the men who could enfranchise them—unlike other excluded groups such as African Americans, immigrants or those without claim to property. The debate sparked by the prospect of granting

Election Central. The simple message of this display is clear. Get out and vote! Red and blue balloons surround the patriotic poster. An elephant and a donkey, on the display base, represent the two major parties.

women the right to vote involved fears that the female participation in electoral politics would somehow undermine family life and denigrate women themselves (Keyssar, 173).

A convention to discuss the social, civil and religious rights of women gathered in Seneca Falls, New York, in July 1848 thanks to the efforts of Elizabeth Cady Stanton and Lucretia Mott. Stanton was the daughter of a judge and the wife of an important abolitionist. Mott, an eloquent speaker, was a prominent Quaker minister. Three hundred people attended, including many men. After two days, 100 of the participants approved and signed a set of resolutions calling for equal rights for women, including the right to elective franchise. Sadly, the 19th Amendment, granting women the right to vote, would not pass until 1920. Presently the universal franchise applies to every citizen over the age of 18 regardless of race or gender.

Ever since the ratification of the Constitution in 1788, Americans have had the privilege of going to the polls to elect a president every four years. Incredibly, this tradition has survived despite years engulfed in a civil war, periods of domestic unrest and economic depression, and involvements in conflicts abroad. In the early years of the Republic, the decision the electorate faced was between candidates of the Federalists and the Democratic-Republican parties. Later the party names changed to Democrats and Whigs. Currently the two major parties are the Democrats and Republicans. Recent years have seen a rise in membership in other parties such as the Libertarian, the *Green* Party of the U.S., the American Party and the Socialist Party of the U.S. (Not an actual party, the Tea Party movement emerged in the U.S. after the election of President Barack Obama and the disenchantment with Democratic politicians via a series of locally and nationally coordinated protests.) Despite the existence of these alternatives, the United States remains primarily a two-party system.

The electoral college was another tradition that has been sustained since our country's origins. This body remains the legal framework of our presidential elections. The term *electoral college* does not appear in the Constitution, but the 12th Amendment does refer to "electors." The number of electors a state has equals the number of its senators plus the number of U.S. representatives. Each state has two senators, but the number of representatives is determined by the population within the state. The Constitution gives the District of Columbia three electoral votes.

The electoral college was first written into federal law in 1845. The Founding Fathers defined democracy in a somewhat limited way. They felt that the masses should not be trusted with political power, so the members of the electoral college actually elect the new president. Under the electoral college system a candidate can win the most popular votes for president but still lose the election. This has happened four times in history. John Quincy Adams, Rutherford B. Hayes, Benjamin Harrison and George W. Bush all assumed the presidency as a result of the electoral college vote.

With nearly 200 million citizens eligible to vote, many think that their individual vote will not count. The circumstances surrounding the 2000 presidential election serve as a reminder that every vote is critical. The 2008 election saw voters come out in record numbers to elect the first African American president. For more information regarding the electoral college visit http://history.howstuff works.com/american-history/electoral-col lege1.htm.

Money, particularly campaign contributions, influences the process and remains critical to the success of a candidate. To qualify for public monies, presidential candidates and party convention committees must first meet certain eligibility requirements, such as agreeing to limit campaign spending to a specified amount. Once the Federal Election Commission determines that eligibility requirements have been met, it certifies the amount of public funds to which the candidate is entitled. The U.S. Treasury then makes the actual payments from the Presidential Election Campaign Fund. This fund consists of dollars voluntarily contributed by taxpayers via their federal income tax returns.

In the 2008 election John McCain accepted funds from the federal government. Barack Obama initially agreed to accept these funds, but then opted against them. The decision had historic implications. Obama was the first presidential candidate since the public finance system was established in 1971 not to participate in general election public funding. His record for raising money allowed him to solicit and accept campaign donations that totally funded his campaign expenses and permitted him to spend more money as a result.

Political symbols have an interesting history. The famous Democratic donkey was first associated with candidate Andrew Jackson's 1828 presidential campaign. The opposition referred to him as a "jackass" for his populist beliefs and campaign slogan, "Let the people rule." Jackson found this quite amusing and decided to use the image of the strong-willed animal on his campaign posters. Many years later, cartoonist Thomas Nast used the Democratic donkey in newspaper cartoons. The animal often represented an anti–Civil War faction. Today the donkey is thought to be smart and brave, and the rest is, well, history.

Nast also created the other famous political symbol—the Republican elephant. In 1874, his cartoon appeared in *Harper's Weekly*. Nast sketched a donkey dressed in a lion's skin who frightened away all the animals at the zoo. One of those animals, the elephant, was labeled the "Republican Vote." Party loyalists saw the animal as strong and dignified and readily adopted it as the party symbol.

Credits

The election of 2008 made its mark on the American electorate. The crisis of the economy was surely the most pressing issue facing the candidates, Congress and the American public. Enormous bank failures occurred in the weeks preceding the election. Volatile stock fluctuations could not be ignored. In addition, dissatisfaction with the way the war in Iraq was being handled and a desire for change in the health care system were also critical issues in the election. Change was the chant of the masses who made their way to the polls in record numbers on November 4 of that year.

The emphasis in 2008 on registering the vast majority of eligible voters was the impetus for this display. The political parties created a sense of urgency to register, vote and have your opinion count where it mattered. Cedar Crest College set up information booths early in the fall semester to assist students in obtaining absentee ballots. Record numbers of college students filled out the necessary paperwork for these ballots so that their voices were indeed heard on Election Day 2008.

Assembling the Display

1. The flag was fashioned from red, white and blue poster board. The 4" stars were made from silver poster board. This poster was attached with pins and pulled forward. The letters for the word *vote* were created using the font Britannnic Bold sized at 400. They were printed on card stock and traced onto black poster board. The letter *V* was created by drawing a large checkmark onto the same material. Nine inch red and blue balloons were attached with rolled packing tape to frame the top and upper sides of the poster. On the top shelf was a small American flag and two vintage campaign buttons. Red confetti was strewn around the books. The date "Nov 4th" was created using the font Elephant sized at 100. This was printed on white card stock and attached with rolled tape to the glass shelf.

Books featured in the top shelf were *The Presidential Election Game* by Steven J. Brams, *Party Wars: Polarization and Politics of National Policy Making* by Barbara Sinclair, *Parties and Elections in America: The Electoral Process (3rd ed)*, by L. Sandy Maisel, *Steal this Vote: Dirty Elections and the Rotten History of Democracy in America* by Andrew Gumbel.

2. On the top left was a quote by Plato:

> Democracy is a charming form of government, full of variety and disorder, and dispensing a sort of equality to equals and unequals alike.

Under that was a history of the electoral college, which can be found if you visit http://www.archives.gov/federal-register/electoral-college/faq.html. Next was a biography of John McCain, Republican candidate in the 2008 election. Clip art of a naval officer was inserted at the top right of the document. Under that was this quote by Margaret Mead:

> Never doubt that a small group of thoughtful citizens can change the world. Indeed, it is the only thing that ever has.

Items on the left were printed on white card stock and mounted on red and black poster board.

3. On the top right was a graphic of the party registration in the state of Pennsylvania. This can be found through a Google image search. Next was a quote by H.L. Mencken:

> Democracy is the art of running the circus from the monkey cage.

Under that was a biography of Barack Obama, Democratic candidate for President in 2008. Clip art of an American flag was inserted at the bottom center of the document. Next was a short essay by John Adams on suffrage which can be found at http://uninfo.state.gov /products/pubs/rightsof/vote.htm Clip art of a period ballot box, found through a Google image search, was inserted at the top right. Under that was a quote by Abraham Lincoln:

> Elections belong to the people. It is their decision. If they decide to turn their back on the fire and burn their behinds, then they will just have to sit on their blisters.

Items on the right were printed and mounted like those on the left.

4. On the base was a Styrofoam form covered with black felt which served to elevate the book and provide a base for more red and blue balloons. An elephant and a donkey were found through a Google image search, printed on card stock and traced onto red and blue poster board. Small white stars made from card stock were attached. These political symbols were attached with rolled packing tape to the Styrofoam form. Red confetti was strewn throughout the books and balloons featured on the display shelf and base.

Books on the base of the display were *The Presidential Difference Leadership Style from FDR to Clinton* by Fred Greenstein, *Black Box Voting: Ballot Tampering in the 21st Century* by Beverly Harris and David Allen, *Brave New Ballot: the Battle to Safeguard*

Democracy in the Age of Electronic Voting by Aviel D. Rubin and *The Power of the Vote: Electing Presidents, Overthrowing Dictators and Promoting Democracy Around the World* by Douglas Schoen.

Bigger and Better

If your space allows you could expand the display to include information about local and state candidates. Also, items included on the referendum could be featured.

You may decide to feature some of the great political scandals in U.S. history. Tracey Campbell's *Deliver the Vote: A History of Election Fraud, an American Political Tradi-* *tion—1742–2004* would be a great source for material on that subject. Kim Long has authored another valuable resource, *The Almanac of Political Corruption, Scandals and Dirty Politics.* Also, *A Treasury of Great American Scandals: Tantalizing True Tales of Historic Misbehavior by the Founding Fathers and Others Who Let Freedom Swing* by Michael Farquhar covers different political ideologies which have caused rifts over the ages. You could feature landslide elections, either by the popular vote or the electoral college. Elections in which Ronald Reagan, FDR, Abraham Lincoln or Lyndon Johnson won by large majorities would make interesting displays.

Connections: The Social Network

The successful networkers I know, the ones receiving tons of referrals and feeling truly happy about themselves, continually put the other person's needs ahead of their own.

—Bob Burg, Author, *Endless Referrals*

Exactly how, when and where did we begin to become connected in the workplace? Our online connections can be traced to Ray Tomlinson, who devised the first Internet-based e-mail in late 1971. He was employed as a computer engineer for Bolt Beranek and Newman (BBN), the firm hired by the U.S. Defense Department to develop the first Internet in 1968.

Tomlinson was experimenting with a popular program he wrote called SNDMSG, a "local" electronic message program which allowed a person to leave messages on the computer that other people with access to that same computer could read. Tomlinson used a file transfer protocol called CYPNET to adapt the SNDMSG program so it could send electronic messages to any computer on their network.

Tomlinson chose the @ symbol to determine which user was at a particular workstation. The first message he sent was "QWERTYUIOP." It's interesting to note that Tomlinson invented e-mail because it seemed like a neat idea—no one had asked him to do it! And, so, in a manner of speaking, the social network was born.

Social networking can be defined as the assembling of individuals into specific groups, like small rural communities or a suburban subdivision. Although social networking is possible to achieve in person, as well as in the workplace, schools and universities, it is most commonly done online. Unlike most institutions, the Internet is packed with millions of people looking to meet others, to gather and share first-hand experiences about a myriad of topics—from sports, cooking, gardening, music, film, developing friendships and making professional contacts.

Social networks can be traced back to 1995 when a Website named Classmates. com first appeared. Similar to the UK's Friends Reunited, which was founded in 1999, its aim was to stay in contact with old friends from kindergarten through college. This site is generally recognized as the model for the social network sites that followed in its wake.

Social networking sites have morphed into a mainstream medium for both teens and adults. The Websites involved are referred to as social sites which function like an online community of Internet users. Many of

Connections: The Social Network. This display celebrates the way in which we are connected through the sites collectively known as the "Social Network." A large poster features photos of friends, family and a celebrity or two!

these online community members share similar interests in hobbies, religion or politics. Once you register at a social site, you can begin the process of socialization. This may include perusing the profile pages created by fellow members and possibly contacting them.

Social networking sites offer a variety of technical features. Their backbone includes visible profiles that display an articulated list of friends who are users of the system. Profiles are pages on which an individual can actually create a person. Once membership is obtained, forms containing a series of questions such as age, location, interests, and the like need to be completed. Most sites request that users upload a digital photo. Multimedia content can be added to some sites. Many allow for modification of the profile's look and feel. Making friends is just

one benefit to online social networking. Since the Internet gives access to individuals worldwide, there is the added benefit of having the ability to meet diverse people from different cultures.

Clear communication is critical when using the Twitter network. With only 140 characters per message—approximately the length of a news headline- sharing information and ideas can be a challenge. Since Twitter is an opt-in medium, users are advised to contemplate a more entertaining or informative way to give updates about your life. People will be quick to "unfollow" you if the wording of the messages is mundane.

Social networking sites usually have a section dedicated to comments by friends. On Friendster, this section is called "Testimonials." On Facebook it's titled "The Wall."

This feature encourages members to create messages about the person in the profile. Over time, people responded with creative testimonials—and the conversation began.

Some social networking sites are created for the benefit of others, such as the parents' site "Gurgle." This was specifically designed to provide parenting knowledge and tools for discussion about topics such as infertility, pregnancy, childbirth and childrearing. A relatively new site, Formspring.me provides a platform where members can send and receive anonymous questions and learn more about the people they find interesting by following their answers. It can become, in essence, your own personal interview.

Certain social networking sites attract kids as young as five or six. These specialized sites don't allow the same level of communication that teens and adults have, but there are still things that parents can do to guide young children to socialize safely online. The law offers several protections and gives parents some control over the type of information that youngsters are permitted to reveal online. For sites aimed at preteens and for general online locations that know they're attracting this age group, there's the Children's Online Privacy Protection Act (COPPA). Regulations require that these sites secure parental consent before they gather, maintain, or use a youngster's information. COPPA allows and encourages parents to examine their child's online profiles and blog pages.

Various social networks in Asian markets such as India, China, Japan and Korea have large numbers of users and a high level of profitability, setting themselves apart from their western counterparts. In China, the leading publicly traded Web portal, Tencent, earned $1 billion in 2009. It offers its members instant message client, social networking, game developer and more. Their Internet value-added services include avatars, dating services, online memberships, music and community sites.

In 2008 MySpace brought in around $800 million, coming in less than the hoped for $1 billion goal set during a healthier economic market. Facebook earned between 250 and 300 million dollars that year despite their claims that they are not focused on monetization. Both of these companies have minimal virtual goods services, but are able to raise revenue from various forms of online advertising.

While there are many social networking sites that focus on specific interests, many do not. The latter are sometimes referred to as "traditional" Websites and generally have open memberships. Once membership is established, you can create your own network of friends and limit members that do not share a common focus.

So, is social media a fad? Statistics show otherwise. Here are some interesting facts about social networking. One out of eight couples who married in 2009 met on the Internet. If Facebook were a country it would be the fourth largest in the world! The great majority of new Facebook users are women between 55 and 65 years old. In 2010, 80 percent of companies used LinkedIn as their primary tool in finding employees. The Department of Education statistics show that online students outperform students receiving face to face instruction. Social media took over pornography as the #1 activity on the web.

In 2010 Generation Y will outnumber the baby boomers. Ninety-six percent of Gen Y's have joined a social network. Generations Y and Z consider e-mail passé. YouTube is the second largest search engine in the world and boasted a collection of 100,000,000 videos in 2009. Wikipedia has over 13,000,000 articles, and studies show that it is more reliable than the Encyclopædia Britannica as a result of frequent updates.

It took radio 38 years from the time it was invented to reach 50 million people. Television took 13 years to reach that number. The Internet took four years, and the IPod three years. Facebook added 100 million members in less than nine months. IPod application downloads hit the 1 billion mark in just nine months. One in six higher education students are enrolled in online courses. China's QZone has 300 million people using their services.

As of 2010, there were over 200,000,000 people using blogs. Fifty-four percent of bloggers post content or tweet daily. People care more about how their social graph ranks products and services than how Google ranks them. Seventy-eight percent of consumers value peer recommendations, only 14 percent trust advertisements. Seventy percent of 18–34 year-olds have watched TV on the Web while only 33 percent have ever viewed a show on DVR or TiVo. Twenty-five percent of Americans recently polled said they had watched a short video on their phone.

Thirty-five percent of book sales are for the Kindle. Twenty-four of the twenty-five largest newspapers are experiencing record declines in circulation. The reality is that we no longer search for the news, the news finds us. In the near future, we will no longer search for products or services, they will find us through social media. Social media is no longer a fad, it's a fundamental shift in the way we communicate.

More than 1.5 million pieces of content are shared on Facebook alone on a daily basis. Since businesses need to be where the customers are, these social networks are the key to their future success: "Social networks are emerging as a powerful and sophisticated new kind of marketing channel. Marketing is becoming precise, personal, and social: social networking sites are giving marketers new abilities to hypertarget campaigns using profile information, engage community members by tapping into social capital within friend groups, and systematically cultivate word-of-mouth marketing across their existing customer base" (Shih, 81–82). President Barack Obama's successful presidential 2008 campaign is a prime example of the power of social networks. He rallied millions of supporters on social network sites and helped raise nearly $1 billion in grassroots campaign contributions.

The 2010 earthquake in Haiti saw social networking rise to a new humanitarian level. Texts from individuals trapped in the rubble allowed rescuers to locate, and in some cases save, victims of this catastrophic event. In December of 2009 a brawl erupted in the streets of Suffolk, Virginia. Participants had fled and witnessed were not talking. Days later investigators got a break via YouTube. Cellphone videos of the fight had been posted on the Website. The video clearly showed the youth involved. Seven people in the clip went to trial. Police across the country are increasingly using YouTube and other online social networks to apprehend criminals.

There are several myths circulating about the value of social networking for marketing. One such myth is that they are free. It is true that you can set up an account and integrate other services at no charge, but there is a significant cost: your valued time. Also, someone needs to keep the site up to date, respond to queries, post data and monitor activity.

Another myth is that social media sites are a great place to find new customers. However, since many of the users are teenagers, and older members are often mainly concerned about rekindling old relationships, these sites may not be the best places for business owners to invest.

The third myth is that you need to be on all the big sites. To the contrary, successful business owners who have succeeded with social networking usually focus on just a few site rather than spreading themselves too thin.

Myth number four suggests that social networking sites are for marketing when in fact they are really more service oriented. When helpful customer service is provided, loyalty is fostered and satisfaction assured. This could definitely result in future business possibilities.

A final myth about social networking is that the existing sites are a permanent phenomenon. However, the main sites today may not be the primary players of the future. Other customer approaches, such as newsletters, phone calls and seminars may continue to be effectively used in marketing.

There are many videos available on social networking. These two are very well done and would be helpful in your understanding of the concept of social connections. For more information visit http://www.youtube.com/watch?v=6a_KF7TYKVc and http://www.youtube.com/watch?v=sIFYPQjYhv8.

Credits

In October of 2010, a new movie titled *The Social Network* garnered four-star reviews. The public came out in full force to see the fictionalized account of the young man who made claim to the founding of Facebook. The story unfolds on a fall night in 2003 when Harvard undergrad and computer programming genius Mark Zuckerberg sits down at his computer and heatedly begins working on a new idea. The fury of blogging and programming that began in his dorm room soon became a global social network and a revolution in communication was born.

I don't think I really "got" social networks until quite recently. It seems one of my very best student assistants forgot her evening shift at the library. The student waiting to be replaced tried to phone the missing student's cell phone and then her dorm room extension, to no avail. She also tried a quick e-mail—still nothing. *Finally*, she went to the student's FACEBOOK page and reminded her of her shift, and sure enough, the student was soon on her way!

Social networks have forever changed the way in which we communicate. Over the years, many of my students and some family members have suggested that I do a display on this topic. So they weren't surprised when I asked them to send me a headshot for the featured poster. Some of the student faces featured in the "Connections" display are members of the 2009–2010 Cressman Library staff. I thank them for their cooperation!

Assembling the Display

1. The background of the display was lined with red felt. The poster was created using digital headshots printed on presentation paper and glued on black poster board. The photos were sized in Word at a height of three inches. The title signage was created using the font Detonate sized at 260. This font is available for a free download at http://www.dafont.com. The title was printed on white card stock, mounted on red poster board and glued to the center of the poster. Single and double arrows were created from poster board and pinned on three sides of the poster. A 3" by ⅓" strip of silver poster was pinned to the center of the double arrows.

2. On the top left was the a document titled "Social Media Marketing Myths." An image of a globe surrounded by people was inserted at the bottom center. This can be found through a Google image search. The information on social media and marketing can be found if you visit http://www.businessweek.com/print/technology/content/may2009/tc20090522_078978.htm. Under that was the quote that introduced this display. Last was a document describing social networks which can be found if you visit http://en.wikipedia.org/wiki/Social_network_service.

Documents on the left had borders inserted and were printed on white card stock and mounted on red and black poster board.

3. On the top right was a document titled "Seven Facebook and Twitter Security Stories of 2009." Information such as this can be found by searching under the topic "social networking hacks." Clip art of a cell phone was inserted to the left of the title. Under that was this quote by Mark Zuckerberg, founder of Facebook:

> People have really gotten comfortable not only sharing more information and different kinds, but more openly and with more people.

Next was a document titled "The History of e-mail and Roy Tomlinson." This information can be found if you visit http://inventors.about.com/od/estartinventions/a/email.htm.

Items on the right were printed and mounted like those on the left.

4. On the base of the display were the tools of social networking. A laptop with a webcam was placed in the center with cell phones arranged throughout the books.

An image of a search engine screen, found through a Google image search, was printed on paper and affixed to the laptop screen with double sided tape.

Books featured in the display were *My-Space Visual Quick Tips* by Paul McFedries and Sherry Willard Kinkoph, *The Facebook Era: Tapping Online Social Networks to Build Better Products, Reach New Audiences, and Sell More Stuff* by Clara Shih, *YouTube 4 You* by Michael Miller, *Social Media Marketing an Hour a Day* by Dave Evans, *The Social Media Bible: Tactics, Tools & Strategies for Business Success* by Lon Safko and David K. Brake, *How to Really Use LinkedIn* by Jan Vermeiren, *Socialnomics: How Social Media Transforms the Way We Live and Do Business* by Erik

Qualman, *The Rough Guide to MySpace and Online Community* by Peter Buckley, *The Twitter Book* by Tim O'Reilly and Sarah Milstein, and *YouTube: An Insider's Guide to Climbing the Charts* by Alan Lastufka and Michael W. Dean.

Bigger and Better

You may want to feature a globe as your main graphic. Surrounding that image could be figures holding hands. This can be found if you visit http://www.craighighschool.org/Portals/0/people%20around%20the%20globe.gif.

There are many easy, excellent and eye-catching variations of this concept available if you search images using the words "globe with people around it." You could choose to use an actual globe and have the figures surround the three dimensional structure.

For a graphic idea you could use to create a collage of social network logos please visit http://www.tkc.go.th/Sitedirectory/156/2951/3139_Social%20Networking.JPG.

If you choose this graphic, remember to pull a percentage of the images forward on pins to create some dimension. Be sure to choose Websites that your students or patrons are actively using. For information such as charts and graphs regarding the number of users and time spent on social networks internationally, as well as a comparison of the features offered by social networking sites, visit http://www.penn-olson.com/2010/01/27/top-10-social-media-countries/.

Going Green

There is a sufficiency in the world for man's need but not for man's greed. — Mohandas K. Gandhi

People worldwide are much more aware and keenly sensitive to the fragility of the earth's environment as a result of the plethora of information that is available. Many of us are consciously finding ways to lessen our carbon footprint so that future generations may enjoy all of the earth's bountiful resources. These individual cognitive acts, when multiplied, are cumulative. Together our efforts can make a difference that will produce positive results which are beneficial to the planet.

Climate change has been with us since the first microbes, afloat in a prehistoric ocean, noted that the temperature was dropping. Life on planet Earth has had two choices—adapt to climate changes or die. What is new is a rapidly changing climate driven by an enhanced greenhouse effect—man's uncontrolled experiment on the planet whereby we pump enough greenhouse gas into the atmosphere to double or triple its concentration and then see what happens (Reay, xi).

There are countless sources of information about ways to "Go Green." Some sources have even combined the concept of going green with saving money—a win-win situation. Here are some ways to save both energy and money. Set your thermostat a few degrees higher in the summer and lower in the winter. Install compact fluorescent light bulbs. Unplug appliances when not in use. Use cold water for washing. Dry clothes on a clothesline or drying rack. Plant drought resistant native plants in your garden. Take shorter showers and install a low-flow shower head to save money and water. Telecommute when possible. Walk or bike to work to save gas and improve health. Eat one meatless meal per week. Buy locally raised organic meat, eggs and dairy to support the local economy. Buy a water filter and choose reusable water bottles rather than purchase bottled water. Attend garage sales or shop thrift stores. Borrow from the library. Share power tools with neighbors. Buy in bulk. Invest in high-quality, long-lasting products. Keep your cell phones, computers and other electronics as long as possible and donate them when feasible. Ask your local government to set up electronics recycling and hazard waste collection sites.

Going Green. Three large windmills dot the landscape of this topical display on alternative energy sources critical to the future of the health of the planet.

You can make your own environmental friendly cleaning supplies with a few simple ingredients such as baking soda, vinegar, lemon and soap. For more information on specific formulas visit http://www.care2.com /greenliving/make-your-own-non–toxic-cleaning-kit.html. These are surefire ways to lighten your impact on the environment, lessen climate change and improve the quality of life.

Alternative Energy Sources

Ever since fire was discovered we have been burning fuels that release carbon dioxide into the atmosphere. With the onset of the industrial revolution in the 1700s, the use of fossil fuels increased. Unfortunately, this source of energy released large amounts of carbon dioxide when ignited.

As technology has evolved so has the potential for altering our environment. It is now critical that our dependency on fossil fuels be reduced and other sources of energy explored, analyzed and ultimately adopted. Here are some viable alternatives.

Wind Technology: Wind power is defined as the conversion of wind energy into a useful form, such as electricity, using wind turbines. There are vast wind resources in the United States. Wind energy is clean and renewable and reduces greenhouse gas emissions when it displaces electricity derived from fossil fuels. Theoretically, using modern technology, all of our electricity requirements could be met by the wind power flowing across the country. This being said, less than 1 percent of the nation's electricity is currently provided in this manner. Only a fraction of the country's enormous potential will be utilized unless there is a change in our energy policies favoring long-standing support for renewable power development.

The Bush administration estimated that wind energy can provide approximately 20 percent of the country's electrical needs. According to the American Wind Energy Association, this goal is both possible and affordable. Only regulatory barriers exist regarding this technology. The physical challenges of using wind as an energy resource can be overcome. For more information on wind technology visit http://www.thegreenguide.com/.

Solar Energy: The sun has produced energy for billions of years. Solar energy is found in the sun's rays and is one of the most practical sources of energy for the future. It is free and inexhaustible. This vast, clean energy source is a feasible alternative to the fossil fuels currently in use that pollute both air and water, compromise our public health and augment global warming. Failing to utilize this widely available resource would do a disservice to future generations.

Solar power refers to the conversion of sunlight to electricity, either by the combination of photovoltaics and concentrating solar thermal devices, or by thermoelectric converters, solar chimneys and solar ponds. Solar energy can be converted to other forms of energy to directly generate heat, light and electricity. It supports all of the life on the planet and is the basis for almost every energy form.

Solar energy technologies are projected to grow significantly in the 21st century. More architects and contractors are effectively integrating this technology into their building designs. Germany and Japan have become global leaders in solar deployment but the United States is making real strides due to strong state-level policy support. California, Arizona, Colorado, New Jersey and Pennsylvania have specific requirements for solar energy as part of their renewable electricity standards. Solar energy is currently being converted to thermal energy to heat water for homes, buildings and swimming pools and to heat spaces such as greenhouses, homes and buildings. Using solar power will secure a future based on clean and sustainable energy that will run automobiles, power plants and space ships. For more information on solar power visit http://www.ucsusa.org/clean_energy/renewable_energy_basics/how-solar-energy-works.html.

Hydroelectricity: Hydroelectricity pertains to the generation and distribution of electricity derived from the energy of falling water or any other hydraulic source. It is created when rivers are dammed and the potential energy stored in the water is usable. As the water stored behind the dam is released at high pressure, its kinetic energy is transferred onto turbine blades and used to generate electrical power.

Water has been used as a source of energy since the Greeks first designed the waterwheel over 2,000 years ago. For over a century hydropower has been used to generate electricity from falling water. Hydroelectric power is created when the water's energy flows from a higher to a lower elevation and rotates the hydraulic turbines.

Hydroelectric systems are expensive to install, but they have relatively low maintenance costs and provide power quite cheaply once established. In the United States approximately 180,000 megawatts of hydroelectric power potential is available. Only about a third of that is currently being harnessed. For additional information about hydroelectric power visit http://www.enviroliteracy.org/article.php/59.html.

Tidal Power: Tidal power is the only form of energy derived directly from the relative motions of the earth-moon system, and to a somewhat lesser extent from the earth-sun system. The tidal forces by the moon and the sun, in conjunction with earth's rotation, are responsible for the generation of the tides.

The tidal process utilizes the rhythmic motion of the tides to fill reservoirs which are then carefully discharged through electricity producing turbines. These large underwater turbines are placed in sections having high tidal movements and are calculated to capture the kinetic motion of the ocean tides in order to create electricity. Because 70 percent of the earth's surface is covered with water, tidal power has great potential for the generation of future power. This technology is similar to the more conventional hydroelectric dams. The former USSR produced 300 megawatts in its Lumkara plant using this alternative energy method. For additional information on the subject of tidal power visit http://www.alternative-energy-news.info/technology/hydro/tidal-power/.

Geothermal Energy: Although geothermal energy is an alternative energy source, it is not efficient enough to replace more than a relatively small amount of the future's energy needs. Geothermal energy is obtained from the internal heat of the planet and can be used to generate steam to run a steam turbine. This in turn generates electricity, which is a very useful and necessary form of energy.

The radius of the earth is about 4,000 miles, with an internal core temperature of about 4,000 degrees Celsius at the center. The mantle surrounds the outer core and is only about 45 miles below the surface, depending on location. The temperature at the mantle-surface crust boundary is about 375 degrees Celsius. The existing technology cannot reach that deep, but even if drilling goes three miles into the earth's surface, we can reach temperatures of 100 degrees Celsius, enough to boil the water to energize a steam-powered plant. An easier route to generating electricity is referred to as geothermal hotspots, or volcanoes, which exist around the globe.

The climate summit, held in Copenhagen in December of 2009, included 193 nations and yielded a 3-page document titled the "Copenhagen Agreement." The accord mandated that rich nations agree to cut emissions of greenhouse gases, which data suggests cause the earth to warm. These countries will provide ten billion dollars a year over a three-year period to aid third world countries in dealing with climate change. Poorer countries agreed to report on their voluntary actions to reduce emissions biannually. For more information about "Going Green" visit http://www.worldwatch.org/resources/go_green_save_green.

Credits

The idea for creating a display on the subject of "Going Green" began close to home. Our son is a young architect living and working in Philadelphia where he is endeavoring to create "green"—sustainable, earth-friendly, and high-performance designs which will improve the urban environment. These naturally ventilated, daylight flooded working and living spaces are designed to enhance the quality and productivity of employees and residents. As a result of his interest and focus, we have become aware of the significance of erecting high performance buildings.

Even though many Americans support the goals of the environmental movement, in reality, recycling may be their single individual contribution. It is puzzling why there is such a disparity between ecological sentiment and personal actions. In *It's Easy Being Green,* author Crissy Trask suggests that people would make better environmental choices

if the alternatives were apparent to them. Perhaps, in some small way, this display will fill a few informational gaps on the subject and increase awareness of the environmental stewardship inherent in our roles as citizens of the planet Earth.

Assembling the Display

1. The background is divided into light blue felt which indicated the sky and two shades of green felt suggesting rolling hills. Fiberfill is used to create clouds. The windmills were found using a Google image search and enlarged on the photocopier to create a template. They were traced onto white poster board and mounted on black poster board. They were attached with pins and pulled forward. An orange circle outlined in black was placed in the center of the blades on a pin and pulled forward.

The flowers were cut from yellow and orange poster board and pinned on moss that was attached with rubber cement to the green felt. Birds were located through a Google image search, printed on card stock and traced onto black poster board. The birds and flowers were attached with pins and pulled forward.

2. On the top left was a document titled "What Is Your Carbon Footprint?" This can be found if you visit http://www.carbonfootprint.com/. Under that was a quote from 1732 by Thomas Fuller:

> We never know the worth of water till the well is dry.

Under that was information about "Windmill Technology" which can be found if you visit http://www.awea.org/pubs/factsheets/WindPowerToday_2007.pdf. Clip art of a windmill was inserted on the top right of the document.

All items on the left were printed on card stock and mounted on green and/or black poster board.

3. On the top right was a quote from Ansel Adams:

> It is horrifying that we have to fight our own government to save the environment.

Next was a sheet titled "Ten Ways to Go Green and Save Green." Information on this subject can be found if you visit http://www.world watch.org/node/3915?gelid=CKe25OG06pQ CFQSwFQodvicKTA. Under that was a quote from Steve Forbert:

> Don't blow it—good planets are
> hard to find.

Items on the right were printed on card stock and mounted like those on the left.

4. On the base of the display, moss was sprinkled throughout the books and yellow and orange flowers were placed randomly throughout. A Kurt Vonnegut Jr., quote was placed in front of the open book in the center. It was printed on card stock and mounted on black poster board:

> We could have saved the Earth but
> we were too damned cheap.

Books featured in the display were *Greening the Ivory Tower* by Sarah Hammond Creighton, *Environmental Aesthetics* by David Schmidtz and Elizabeth Willott, *It's Easy Being Green* by Crissy Trask, *The Green Book* by Elizabeth Rogers and Thomas Kostigen, *The Collapse of the Kyota Protocol and the Struggle to Slow Global Warming* by David G. Victor, *The Greening of Conservative America* by John R. E. Bliese, *Global Warming: The Science of Climate Change* by Frances Drake, *High Tech Trash* by Elizabeth Grossman, *Green Seduction* by Bill Streever, *1,001 Ways to Save Earth* by Joanna Yarrow, *Understanding Environmental Pollution* by Marquita K. Hill, *Climate Change Begins at Home* by Dave Reay and *The Everything Green Living Book* by Diane Gow McDilda.

Bigger and Better

If your space is bigger, add some solar panels made from black and silver poster board and mount them on a stand. An image search will yield viable results. Add a large sun to the design.

You may want to focus on air pollution and the automobile. Incorporate information on alternative automotive choices highlighting cars that run on hydrogen, ethanol, natural gas and electricity. Draw the front grill of a car with the headlights and title the display "Auto Options."

Create a frame of a garage with the door opened showing the back of a car in one bay and a scooter in the other. Include the phrase "Maybe your second car shouldn't be a car." Add some facts about electric and gas scooters, motorcycles and bicycles (Felton, 18).

Since compact fluorescent light bulbs have a small trace of mercury in them. Your display could focus on the impact of this element on the environment and the importance of proper disposal. The Internet has great graphs and charts relevant to a display on this topic.

For other ideas on the environment visit any of these sites: http://www.msnbc.msn. com/id/3032493/, http://web.worldbank.org/ WBSITE/EXTERNAL/TOPICS/ENVIRONMENT /0,menuPK:176751~pagePK:149018~piPK: 149093~theSitePK:244381,00.html, and http: //environment.about.com/.

9 Books and More

Sci-Fi

Everything is becoming science fiction. From the margins of an almost invisible literature has sprung the intact reality of the 20th century. —J.G. Ballard, American novelist

How can science—the methodical attainment of information resulting in statements that must be checked and verified- be combined with fiction, something invented or imagined that has nothing to do with science or the scientific method whatsoever? It sounds implausible, but, science fiction was created because there exists a marketplace which craves such literature. It is a genre which continues to change and reinvent itself, establishing boundaries that are both tenuous and explicit.

Contemporary science fiction came into existence as a separate literary genre in April 1926, with the publication of *Amazing Stories,* the first magazine to recognize the existence of a marketplace for short stories of this nature. This pioneering periodical was the brainchild of Hugo Gernsback, considered by many to be the "father" of science fiction. He's the man for whom the Hugo awards were named. These awards, given annually since 1955, are science fiction's most prestigious prize. The Hugos are voted on by the thousands of current members of the World Science Fiction Convention, known as Worldcon, which is also responsible for administering them. For detailed information on the Hugos visit http://www.thehugoawards. org/hugo-history.

Since the science fiction genre overlaps other genres, it is difficult to characterize it with a simple, straightforward definition that explains its relation to other types of literature. There is an ongoing debate about the differences and similarities between fantasy and scientific fiction in the literary world.

Fantasy is make-believe. It is a genre that uses magic and other supernatural forms as a primary element of plot, theme, and setting. It could be described as something that contains rudiments that are not realistic, such as talking animals. Fantasy is often characterized by a departure from the accepted rules by which individuals perceive the world around them; it represents that which is impossible or unexplained and outside the parameters of our known reality.

In general it can be said that science fiction explores the question "what if?" It repeatedly investigates ethical, theoretical and technological possibilities by creating new and stimulating realities. Science fiction is frequently recognized for its rich history and intellectual bent, as well as its diversity. Within the sci-fi genre there are great variations in the topics, themes and even the length of the works. Here is a list of themes that can be found in this genre: Hard Science, New Wave, Ecology, Messianic/Religious, Dystopia/Utopia, Apocalypse, Alternate and Parallel Worlds, Time Travel, Time Warp, Lost Worlds, Immortality, Space Opera, Galactic Empires, Militaristic, Space Travel, Alien Beings, Computers, Automation, Cyberpunk, Robots, Androids, Cyborgs, Social Criticism, The Superhuman, Women, Love and Sex, Detectives and Science Fantasy.

Here are the characteristics that are common to all works of science fiction.

STORY LINE: Authors within this genre utilize a location that establishes differences of time or place or both, and employ a setting outside of daily reality to allow the discussion of new, challenging and sometimes divisive issues.

FRAME: One critical part of the frame in science fiction writing is the level of technical and scientific detail. The location and atmosphere of the story set the tone. The tone varies to include both the comic nature of a

Sci-Fi. The red, green, yellow and blue background sets off a large green alien head rising from the clouds in this homage to the science fiction genre.

Douglas Adams, and the more somber atmosphere created by an Ursula LeGuin.

CHARACTERIZATION: Since story line and frame are the focus of this genre, characters are often secondary to the questions that are pursued through the action of the plot. Situations and events are the primary focus. Because many of the characters found within this genre are part of a series, they tend to evolve over the course of time.

PACING: Typically, the action works of science fiction are either Psychological/philosophical (interior), which is generally slower paced, or physical (exterior), which is faster.

It has been said that science fiction is the literature of change. When a culture undergoes dramatic transformations, as a result of scientific evolution and technological developments, it's understandable that stories reflecting these advances find an audience. Some stories present prospective technologies that are somewhat plausible based on existing science. Others dazzle us with future concepts, advanced beyond the current technologies but with some recognizable elements of the world as we know it. Therefore, the possibility of this impending world becoming a reality exists.

The language of science fiction permeates mainstream speech and culture and runs the gamut from apparent computer and aerospace references to drug slang, underground comix and environmentalism. Dictionaries of science fiction terms are available to help the novice reader properly decipher the vocabulary found within this body of literature. Fans of science fiction and fantasy have developed their own jargon referred to as fanspeak, which serves to connect the community and distinguish it from everyday society. Science fiction encompasses a host of writers. Here are a few brief biographies of some of the most popular authors.

ISAAC ASIMOV: Asimov emigrated from Russia to Brooklyn in 1923 at the age of three. He was a gifted student who skipped several grades. In 1934 Asimov published his first story in his high school newspaper. He entered Low Junior College in 1935 and transferred to the main campus of Columbia University the following year, changing his major from biology to chemistry. Asimov's interest in history grew throughout his college years along with his passion for reading and writing science fiction. He received his bachelor's degree from Columbia in 1939.

Asimov was fascinated by the science fiction magazines on sale in his family's candy store. His father frowned upon this interest and relented only when his son was able to convince him that the new magazine, *Science Wonder Stories,* was a serious journal of science.

The 1940s were incredibly productive for Asimov. He earned both a masters degree and a PhD., served as a chemist during World War II at a Naval Air facility in Philadelphia, Pennsylvania, and then assumed a faculty position at Boston University School of Medicine. Stories he wrote at this time, such as *Nightfall* and *The Bicentennial Man,* and novels such as *The Gods Themselves* and *Foundation's Edge* brought him great acclaim and he received numerous literary honors.

Asimov's books about robots—*I, Robot* and *The Caves of Steel* and *The Naked Sun*—used elements of style found in mystery and detective stories and helped gain a broader respect for the genre. In 1966, the World Science Fiction Convention honored Asimov's *Foundation* series, which were written decades earlier, with a special Hugo Award for the best all-time sci-fi series. Asimov went on to write sci-fi for children as well as medical textbooks. He savored his work as an educator. Prior to his death he wrote this: "I'm on fire to explain, and happiest when it's something reasonably intricate which I can make clear step by step. It's the easiest way I clarify things in my own mind."

Asimov married twice during his lifetime and fathered two children with his first wife. He died in 1992 of the complications of AIDS, which he contracted through blood transfusions received during heart by-pass surgery a decade prior. This information was not disclosed at the time of his death due to the fear of prejudice toward his survivors.

ANNE MCCAFFREY: McCaffrey was born to George and Anne McCaffrey in Cambridge, Massachusetts, in 1926. Anne received her BA from Radcliffe College, in 1947, where she majored in Slavonic languages and literature. She worked as a copywriter from 1947 to 1952, studied theatre and voice, and directed operas and operettas. She was married to H. Wright Johnson from 1950 to 1970 and had three children.

Anne's first novel, *Restoree,* was published by Ballantine Books in 1967. It was written as a protest against the absurd portrayals of women in the science fiction novels of the 1950s and early 1960s. Her handling of broader themes and the worlds of her imagination are apparent in the two series which showcase her talents as a storyteller—*The Ship Who Sang* and the fourteen science fiction/fantasy novels about the Dragonriders of Pern.

In August of 1970, McCaffrey filed for a quick divorce in Mexico and moved her mother and younger children to Ireland. Her son, Alec, was enrolled in Stony Brook University and stayed in the U.S. With many financial obligations resulting from the divorce, McCaffrey chose Ireland because of the excellent school system and the fact that Ireland not only welcomes artists and writers but also allows them to live there tax free.

McCaffrey's equine love affair began with the purchase of a horse named Mr. Ed in 1971. She oversees a private livery stable and her horses have successfully competed in horse trials and show jumping. Arthritis has prevented her from riding in recent years, but she takes great pleasure both in her horses and in her self designed house, named Dragonhold-Underhill, in Wicklow County, Ireland.

GEORGE LUCAS—Lucas was born in Modesto, California, in 1944. A near fatal auto accident in a souped-up Fiat during his teen years ended his dreams of becoming a race car driver. During his time at a community college, Lucas developed a passion for cinematography and camera tricks. He transferred to the University of Southern California filmmaking school and produced a short futuristic film called *THX-1138:4EB.* He was mentored by Francis Ford Coppola, who savored new talent. The director urged Warner Brothers to produce this film, which flopped in its 1971 release.

American Graffiti was released in 1973. It cost $780,000 and grossed $50,000,000. Lucas then set out to make a Saturday morning serial type film that would be part fairy tale, part *Flash Gordon* and part fantasy/adventure set in the imaginary frontier of outer space.

In its 1977 release *Star Wars* bombarded audiences with awe-inspiring special effects, imaginative landscapes and captivating characters set in a fairy tale atmosphere. The film was made for $11,000,000 and grossed $513,000,000 worldwide in its first release. Lucas continued the series with *The Empire Strikes Back* (1980) and *The Return of the Jedi* (1983). He created the cutting edge Industrial Light & Magic Co., as well as a sound studio, Skywalker Sound, which permitted him more control over the finished product of his films. Lucas eventually built his own studio in Marin County, California, far from the influence of Hollywood.

Lucas went on to produce three lucrative prequels to the *Star Wars Trilogy*. He also wrote and produced the blockbuster Indiana Jones films and *Willow*.

ARTHUR C. CLARKE: Clarke was born in the seaside town of Minehead, Somerset, England, in 1917. After attending schools in his home county, Clarke moved to London in 1936 and pursued his early interest in space sciences by joining the British Interplanetary Society. He made contributions to the BIS Bulletin and began to create science fiction. In World War II he joined the RAF, where he became the officer in charge of the first radar talk-down equipment during its experimental trials. Later, his only non-science-fiction novel, *Glide Path*, was based on this work. After the war, he returned to London and to the BIS, where he became its president from 1947 to 1950 and again in 1953.

In 1945, a UK magazine, *Wireless World*, published his landmark technical paper "Extra-terrestrial Relays" in which he introduced the principles of satellite communication with satellites in geostationary orbits—a theory realized 25 years later. During the evolution of his discovery, he worked jointly with scientists and engineers in the U.S. on the development of spacecraft and launch systems and addressed the United Nations during their deliberations on the Peaceful Uses of Outer Space.

After leaving the RAF in 1946, he continued his studies and was awarded a Fellowship at King's College, London, where he achieved honors in physics and mathematics in 1948. In 1954, Clarke wrote to Dr. Harry Wexler, then chief of the Scientific Services Division, U.S. Weather Bureau, about satellite applications for weather forecasting. From these exchanges a new branch of meteorology emerged. Dr. Wexler became the driving force in using rockets and satellites for meteorological research and operations.

In 1964, Clarke joined forces with the noted film producer Stanley Kubrick on a science fiction movie script. Four years later, he shared an Oscar nomination with Kubrick for the film version of *2001: A Space Odyssey*. Then, in 1985, he published a sequel, *2010: Odyssey Two*. He and Peter Hyams used a Kaypro computer and a modem, which linked Clarke in Sri Lanka to Hyams in Los Angeles, leading to a book, *The Odyssey File: The Making of 2010*.

Clarke first visited Colombo, Sri Lanka (Ceylon), in 1954 and was smitten. He moved there in 1956 and pursued his passion for underwater exploration along that coast and on the Great Barrier Reef. In later years, he was confined to a wheelchair due to post-polio syndrome but continued his output as a writer. Two of his novels, *Childhood's End* and *The City and the Stars,* regularly appear on the list of top science fiction titles.

In 1998, Clarke was recognized for his body of work by Queen Elizabeth II when he was honored with a knighthood in Sri Lanka. He died there on March 19, 2008. The famed science fiction writer, who once denigrated religion as "a necessary evil in the childhood of our particular species," left written instructions that his funeral be completely secular.

Credits

My son Jeff was introduced to the phenomenon known as *Star Wars* at the tender age of four. Although a timid child in general, he chose to embrace this new intergalactic experience and stoically sat through the two-hour film simply mesmerized. It is no surprise that Jeff soon became an ardent fan and collector. His playroom was replete with miniature figures and spaceships, and his imagination was fueled by the plethora of books and accessories available in the marketplace.

Today my seven-year-old grandson, Gage,

has discovered, and is captivated by, the world of *Star Wars*. It has been fascinating for me to see the staying power of this brand over the last three decades and to know it will continue to engage and intrigue future generations.

The release of the much anticipated film *Avatar,* created by *Titanic* director James Cameron, in late 2009 caused quite a stir among sci-fi aficionados. The massive box-office returns broke all records in the film industry and proved that science fiction will be around for a very long time.

Assembling the Display

1. The background was black felt with red, green and yellow crepe paper. The 20" by 8' crepe paper was folded into fourths and then pressed by hand into 1½" pleats. Heavy books were placed on top to create crisp angles. This was attached with pins. A 1½" strip of black poster board was attached to each side of the crepe paper to give a more even edge.

The font Terminator Real NF1 sized at 210 was used to create the title signage. This font is available for a free download at http://www.dafont.com. The title signage was printed with black ink on white card stock and glued to a burst graphic which was drawn onto white poster board and mounted onto black poster board. Many bursts are available online to give you some ideas. The signage was attached with pins and pulled forward.

Under that was a graphic of an alien. Many line drawings are available online that can be enlarged on the photocopier and trace. The alien was drawn onto white poster board and painted with green and black acrylics. White acrylic was used to highlight the eyes. The head and neck were glued onto both black and white poster board, attached with pins and pulled forward. Fiberfill was placed under the alien head and around the books and media.

Miniature figures from *Star Wars* were placed in front of a larger Darth Maul on the top shelf. Books featured were *Breakfast of Champions* by Kurt Vonnegut, *Women at War* by Lois McMaster Bujold, *Worlds of Wonder: How to Write Science Fiction and*

Fantasy by David Gerrold, *Starfarers* by Poul Anderson and *The Oxford Book of Science Fiction Stories* by Tom Shippey.

2. On the top left was a biography of Isaac Asimov which can be found If you visit http://www.notablebiographies.com/An-Ba/Asimov-Isaac.html. A photo of Asimov was inserted in the top of the document. Under that was a synopsis of the life of Anne McCaffrey. Clip art of the author was inserted at the bottom center of the document. Next was this quote by Asimov:

> The science fiction story does not deal with the restoration of order, but with change and, ideally, with continuing change.... [W]e leave our society and never return to it.

Last was a list of the top forty science fiction titles compiled by Scottish editor David Pringle. The list of the top 100 can be found at http://www.listology.com/list/david-pringles-best-100-science-fiction-novels.

Items on the left were printed on white card stock and mounted on black or red poster board.

3. On the top right was a list of science fiction terms which can be found in *Critical Terms for Science Fiction and Fantasy: A Glossary and Guide to Scholarship* by Gary K. Wolfe. Under that was a biography of Arthur C. Clarke found at http://www.clarke foundation.org/acc/biography.php. A clip art image of the author was inserted on the top left of the document. Next was a quote by Kathryn Cramer:

> Science Fiction allows us to understand and experience our past, present, and future in terms of an imagined future.

Last was a short biography of George Lucas with a Star Wars image inserted in the bottom center of the document. This is available if you visithttp://www.biography.com/articles/George-Lucas-9388168.

Items on the right were printed and mounted like those on the left.

4. On the base of the display was an image of a Dalek on a tin canister and a miniature model of K-9 the dog. Both of these are from the *Dr. Who* television series. Flanking the Dalek were DVDs titled *Resident Evil* and *Signs*. Books featured were *Iron Sunrise*

by Charles Stross, *Dragonseye* by Anne Mc-
Caffrey, *Galactic Suburbia* by Lisa Yaszek and
Red Lightning by John Varley.

Bigger and Better

Should your space be larger, be sure to
hang some spaceships on fishing line from
the top of the display case. Vary the size of
the vehicles and the lengths at which they
hang. Include costume masks of space crea-
tures and arrange them in a cluster. If you do
not have access to a pertinent mask, go online and do an image search using the term
"alien clipart" and some very simple line
drawings will result. Enlarge on the photocopier to a size that corresponds to your
space, trace onto a bright green poster board,
and dab with white and black acrylic paint
to add texture.

If you mount this display around Halloween, you will be able to purchase inexpensive alien masks at your local party or
Halloween store. If you choose a different
time of year, go online and shop for masks.
Here are two sites with a variety of inventory:
http://www.halloweencostumes4u.com/alien

-masks.html and http://www.amazon.com/
Unknown-Alien-Mask/dp/B000VJ5UC8. Use
a globe, or create one, and have the alien
head hovering over and peeping from behind. Line the base with sand and rocks.

Should you be on staff in a school or
public library, you may want to have a workshop or contest to create alien masks from
paper maché. The winning entries could be
featured in your display on science fiction.
Have a sci-fi audiobook playing in the background to set the mood. Take photos and include them on an online exhibition on your
library's Web page. Schedule this at the end
of October.

Great posters are out there and can provide the focal point for your sci-fi exhibit.
You may want to feature the movie *Metropolis,* the first German Expressionist silent science fiction film, produced in 1927. Much
of it has been found and restored on DVD
and many excellent posters are available.

Choose from the over 500 works of
Isaac Asimov and call your display "All Asimov!" Use a black background and enlarge
a portrait of the author. Arrange planets
around him in the universe. Select a big, bold
font for the title signage.

Generations

*Books are the treasured wealth of the world and the fit inheritance of gen-
erations and nations.* — Henry David Thoreau, American essayist, poet and
philosopher (1817–1862)

This exhibit is a tribute to the generations
of women who spent their college years pur-
suing an education at Cedar Crest College.
This single-sex institution is nestled in the
Lehigh Valley, approximately one hour northwest of Philadelphia. Since its founding in
1867, Cedar Crest had taken a bold approach
to education by creating a curriculum designed for women who want to experience
leadership and achieve at the highest levels.
Cedar Crest's mission dates back to the years
following the Civil War. Due to the tremendous loss of lives that conflict incurred, an
urgent void was created. In order to meet the
needs of a growing nation, it became necessary to educate women. As the college

evolved, it continued to place a high priority
on meeting the expanding needs of the country. Today it is fulfilling that mission by chan-
neling much of its energy into educating
young women in the sciences.

In 1983, Cedar Crest established one of
the first undergraduate programs in genetic
engineering and more recently launched a
degree in the neurosciences. As her term
began in 1989, the late Cedar Crest College
president Dorothy Gulbenkian Blaney was
faced with great academic transitions and a
plethora of economic challenges. These were
her thoughts on the direction taken by the
college during her tenure: "I would love to
say that I came here to advance poetry and

comparative literature. But we didn't have enough students interested in those fields to grow. Moreover, the world needs more people who can think about the sciences."

Cedar Crest College is dedicated to the education of the next generation of women leaders by preparing the whole student for life in a global community. Cedar Crest also provides a wealth of opportunity for nontraditional and graduate students. The coeducational School of Adult and Graduate Education demonstrates its commitment to education at all levels. The hope for students attending the college is that they will gather the tools necessary to become leaders for life. Low teacher/student ratios contribute to the sense of caring and sharing experienced by the students at Cedar Crest.

The combined efforts of the enterprising females who, over the years, valued personal growth, excellence, scholarship and leadership comprise the generations we celebrate in this display. For each generation of women, the college experience is fresh and unique. Over the years, going away to college has come to represent a break from parental control to an emerging independence. Insulated from the economic consequences of the adult world, undergraduates enjoy the luxury of a four-year transitional cocoon. During these years the universal need to fit in takes on exaggerated importance. In order to find a place among their peers, college students create a youth-oriented subculture in which its members are united by attitudes and circumstances. In the flush of their newfound autonomy, collegians endeavor to establish a viable life style. This activity is a highly creative process. Unconcerned with the intricacy of self-realization, students seize upon the fashions and fads that guarantee instant transformation and acceptance. When those choices are reinforced by their peer group, students experience a sense of well-being and camaraderie—a common bond that endures beyond graduation.

Over the generations, it has been the continuity of the college experience that has had the most profound impact on these women. If their college years spanned the 1940s, their memories might include the sobering reality of a world at war. Fathers, brothers and boyfriends were deployed in global service to insure the homeland security. Some may recollect the dichotomy of the innocence of the 1950s, a time which also saw the emergence of the Cold War. Later memories included the radical hippie subculture of the revolutionary 1960s and mounting opposition to an increasingly unpopular war. Students in this decade joined together to form a collective voice which served to change the cultural fabric of American life. Those coming of age in the 1970s saw the advances in civil rights and the increased influence of both the women's movement and space exploration.

College life in the awesome 1980s, aka the "decade of plenty," included a setback

Generations. This display is a celebration of the women who spent their years of higher education at Cedar Crest College. Scrapbook pages provide a nostalgic glimpse into the traditions that marked their college years. The books featured were those which they indicated had an impact on their lives.

to our space program which followed the shocking explosion of the *Challenger* space shuttle. That decade also experienced rampant inflation and the tragic loss of many fine talented individuals to the insidious AIDS epidemic. Reflections of college experiences in the 1990s, coined the electronic age, included the reality of the cell phone as a required accessory, and the availability of the World Wide Web—technologies that dramatically changed the way we communicated, managed money and conducted business. The beginning of the twenty-first century found students enmeshed in social networks and absorbed in increasingly divergent tasks, but with a greater sense of the larger community and the awareness of the need to give back.

For this display, alumnae were asked to suggest a favorite book which they read for fun, entertainment or information that was a hallmark of their years at Cedar Crest. Dozens of alums responded to the inquiry and the results were many and varied. This exhibit features many of their suggestions. The formidable list provided by the graduates spanned the literary spectrum and reinforced the concept of the power of the written word. The results included important works of the 20th century such as *Ulysses* by James Joyce as well as the spiritual journey *Siddhartha* by Hermann Hesse. Also suggested were classics of modern American literature such as *Catcher in the Rye* and *East of Eden*. The playfully and painfully moving *Portnoy's Complaint* touched a chord with one alum, as did the commercially successful *Valley of the Dolls*.

Not surprisingly, female-centered tomes such as *The Group* and *The Red Tent* were suggested, as were books which dealt with racial and ethnic issues such as those found in *The Bluest Eye* and *Reading Lolita in Tehran*. Self-help books such as *Everything You Wanted to Know About Sex but Were Afraid to Ask*, *Jane Fonda's Workout Book* and *Who Moved My Cheese?* made the list. Among the hallmark books mentioned was Betty Friedan's *The Feminine Mystique*, which was credited with igniting the contemporary women's movement in 1963.

Pulitzer Prize winner *Advise and Consent* told a compelling story of politics in the late 1950s, and was suggested for the display, along with Rachel Carson's *Silent Spring*, which offered the first shattering look at widespread ecological degradation and touched off an environmental awareness that continues to this day.

More recent graduates mentioned the Harry Potter and Twilight series, as well as books by popular novelists Jodi Picoult and Nicholas Sparks. Some submitted titles that have morphed from page to screen, such as *Divine Secrets of the Ya-Ya Sisterhood*, *Jonathan Livingston Seagull*, *Love Story* and *The Lord of the Rings* trilogy. Other works suggested for inclusion in the display were *Motherhood: The Second Oldest Profession*; *Listen to the Warm*; *Hollywood Wives*; *The Audacity of Hope*, *Dreams of My Father: A Story of Race and Inheritance*; and *Whisper of the River*.

Since the exhibit focused on the college's history, it was decided that creating scrapbook pages depicting the traditions would provide background information while helping to give a nostalgic feel. Some of the customs dated back to the college's founding over 142 years ago, while others have emerged in recent decades. These traditions reflect both the solemn rituals, and the lighter side of college life. Each served to connect students with a living history, important aspects of the academic and social community, and the college's distinguished past. Traditions highlighted in the display were Father-Daughter Weekend, the Wishing Steps, Junior Ring Ceremony, Dink-Donut Night (caps known as dinks) and the highly competitive and much ballyhooed Song Contest. Also included was a colorful page highlighting the ornithology field trip depicting student bird watchers in the early 1980s. For more information about Cedar Crest College visit http://www.cedarcrest.edu/ca/index.shtm.

Credits

In the fall of 2009, students, faculty, staff, board members, alumnae, family members and friends of the Cedar Crest College joined to celebrate the inauguration of the college's thirteenth president. Carmen Twillie Ambar had assumed her role as president the year before, so the preparations for this event were extensive and the celebration long anticipated.

My contribution to the inauguration was to create an exhibit for the display case, located in the college center, which was the site of many of the inaugural festivities. Because of its placement, I realized the exhibit would have a high profile and that I had my work cut out for me! I also knew that I needed the help of my friend and coworker, JoEllen Christensen, administrative assistant to the library director and unofficial assistant to our library archivist. Her interest in and knowledge of the history of the college is extensive. Over the years, JoEllen had crafted dozens of family scrapbooks filled with imagination and creativity. She encouraged and guided me in the early days of my attempts at this craft. JoEllen has spent years digitizing photos, scrapbooks and other information critical to the history of the college. I knew she would be a great partner in this venture, and that she would insure that the display reflected a true sense of the college's history with warmth and cohesiveness.

I hope that together we accomplished that goal!

Assembling the Display

1. The college seal was printed on foam board and attached to the top center of the display case. On the top shelf back were scrapbook pages in shades of taupe and sage depicting the traditions of the Song Contest and the Junior Ring Ceremony. In the center of those was an essay drafted from this chapter on the generations at Cedar Crest. Also included were a teddy bear, two dinks, two college mugs, two college flags, a stuffed falcon, and these books: *The Good Soldier, The Wapshot Chronicle, Portnoy's Complaint, Harry Potter and the Chamber of Secrets* and the *At the Crest: The History of Cedar Crest College from 1867–1988*.

College pins, with various tongue-in-cheek slogans, were placed among the items featured.

2. On the top left and right were quotes from our alums about the hallmark book that they selected. Literary and generational quotes follow:

> Each generation imagines itself to be more intelligent than the one that

went before it, and wiser than the one that comes after it.

> —George Orwell

> A great book should leave you with many experiences, and slightly exhausted. You should live several lives while reading it.

> —William Styron, American author

> What makes a book great, a so-called classic, is its quality of always being modern, of its author, though he be long dead, continuing to speak to each new generation.

> —Clark Powell, American librarian, writer, critic (1906–2001)

> When I look back, I am so impressed again with the life-giving power of literature. If I were a young person today, trying to gain a sense of myself in the world, I would do that again by reading, just as I did when I was young.

> —Maya Angelou

3. On the middle shelf back was an essay on the hallmark books of the generations taken from this chapter. Scrapbook pages with color tones similar to those previously mentioned depicted Father-Daughter Weekend and an ornithology fieldtrip. Framed photos of James Joyce and Edith Wharton were placed among vintage jewelry, a certificate acknowledging the 50th anniversary of an alum's graduation, dance cards from the 1930s, a Cedar Crest clock, a Cedar Crest scarf and a vintage calling card and tray. Books included on this shelf were: *The Movie Goer, Giant, Miss Lonelyhearts & The Day of the Locust, Under the Volcano, A house for Mr. Biswas, The Killer Angels, Ulysses, The Heart Is a Lonely Hunter, Catcher in the Rye* and *The Divine Secrets of the Ya-Ya- Sisterhood.* This Chinese proverb was featured on that shelf:

> If you want happiness for a lifetime, help the next generation.

4. A taupe fabric lined the base of the display case. Included on the lower-level back were scrapbook pages in tones of taupe and sage featuring the traditions known as Dink-Donut Night and the Wishing Steps. An essay

on "Reading Favorites," taken from the text of this chapter, was centered between the scrapbook pages. The trophy was awarded as second prize in a 1959 Song Contest and is surrounded with gold and black pompoms. A vintage floral hat, a dink, and a bud vase with the college flower were interspersed with several college bulletins from 1940s, a program from a 1991 Mom-Daughter weekend, a graduation program from the period when the college was known as Allentown College for Women and a program from 2004 Class Night. Also included was a vintage watch, jeweled eyeglasses and case, a string of pearls and a holiday card from the early 21st century.

The essays featured in the display were printed on white foam board and affixed to black poster board. The quotations were printed on white card stock and mounted on black or gold poster board.

Books featured on the display base were *Who Moved My Cheese. The Audacity of Hope.*

Bigger and Better

If you are mounting a retrospective of photos and memorabilia for your display, be sure to check with the museum and bookstore at your institution. They will probably be happy to lend items for this purpose. The college archives and possibly the theatre prop shop might also be rich resources for you. Include some of the trophies won by your athletic teams or other club or departmental awards (speech, debate, theatre, etc.). Mount this display in conjunction with alumni functions, homecoming, parents' weekend, etc.

If scrapbooking is new to you, be sure to check out some of the many online sites that provide great layouts at no charge. Here are a couple: http://scrapbooking.lovetoknow. com/Main_Page and http://www.smilebox. com/all/scrapbooking/.

Naturally, your customs and traditions will dictate the specifics of your display. Be sure to choose the best photos to use in the scrapbook pages. In the end, it is the quality and content of the photo that makes the greatest impact. Choose one large photo, as opposed to many small ones, which may not be as effective. Be sure to color coordinate the items within your display. Try to stick to three colors, if possible, to create maximum harmony.

Get Lit at the Library

The difficulty of literature is not to write, but to write what you mean; not to affect your reader, but to affect him precisely as you wish.
—Robert Louis Stevenson

What is it about a literary work that makes it outstanding? Answering that question and compiling a list of the top ranked authors of the 20th century could be daunting tasks. However, around the millennium, many such lists were created to identify those writers who made the greatest contributions to 20th century literature.

No one would argue that great literature inspires. It can alter perceptions and change lives. Great writing transforms our thinking and permits us a glimpse into the psyche of the author. Great writers open up the boundaries of the imagination in numerous ways. As the literary critic, Barbara Hardy states,

"Good artists work within their chosen genre, great artists transform it." There is much consensus regarding the importance of innovation in literary influence over the centuries. Revered writers offered ideas that broke with the known and attempted to reconceptualize the world. The literary journey endeavors to take us to new places and often provides keen insight and understanding.

Robert Louis Stevenson said that all speech, written or spoken, is a dead language until it finds a willing and prepared listener. The most basic of all human needs is the need to understand and be understood. The best

Get Lit at the Library. This catchy phrase will be sure to grab your patrons' attention! Most of the books featured made the top 100 lists of the best literature of the 20th century. Framed photos of James Joyce and Edith Wharton flanked the books.

way to value a person is to listen. Author Jeanette Winterson says that everything in writing begins with language and that language begins with listening. Literature is the most durable of durables. The best outlasts its authors and each generation of readers. Here are but a few of the authors whose writings are considered by many to be great literature listed below,

JAMES JOYCE (1882–1941)

Ulysses was published on Joyce's 40th birthday in 1922. It met with a storm of controversy, which surrounded virtually all of his published works. Banned in Great Britain and America as obscene for over ten years, the book asserted its influence in smuggled copies covertly published in France. To this day it remains *the* modernist masterpiece in which the author takes both Celtic lyricism and vulgarity to splendid extremes.

Joyce's stories and novels work on different levels. His most famous work culminates in the extraordinary accomplishments of Ulysses. Joyce attempts nothing less than a complete reconstruction of a day in the life of Dublin, underlaid with correspondence of myth and symbolism borrowed from Homer. *Ulysses* made virtually every list of best literary works of the 20th century on both sides of the Atlantic.

VLADIMIR NABOKOV (1899–1977)

A Russian-born American poet, fiction writer, and butterfly expert, Nabokov is linked to the great figures of the Russian literary tradition that included Pushkin, Tolstoy, Dostoevsky and Gogol. The novel *Lolita,* which many consider the defining American novel of the postwar period, established him as America's dominant creative force. It was first published in Paris in 1955. After its American release in 1958, some U.S. libraries banned it. As is often the case, the negative publicity helped the book become immensely popular.

Nabakov was a master prose stylist with a great facility for language. This may have been the result of growing up in a wealthy multilingual household in St. Petersburg, Russia. In 1964 Nabokov summed up his literary life in an interview with *Life* magazine: "Writing has always been for me a torture and a pastime."

D. H. LAWRENCE (1885–1930)

Lawrence was an English novelist, story writer, critic, poet and painter, and one of the greatest figures in 20th-century English literature. An influential and controversial author, his writing explored human emotions, the psyche, and sexuality in a frank and honest manner while breaking down moral conventions.

Lawrence was haunted by what he felt was the collapse of values in modern life. He was primarily interested in the tension between art and life and not the complete resolution of problems of life within the illusion of art. The novel *Sons and Lovers* is the first of his works to examine the fundamental divisions in the relationships between men and women. Although primarily considered a literary figure, Lawrence also gained posthumous recognition for his expressionistic paintings completed during the 1920s

F. SCOTT FITZGERALD (1896–1940)

Fitzgerald was well known for living life large during a period of time known as the Jazz Age. His passion for writing influenced his character even as a young child. He gained early recognition for his talent when his detective stories were published in his school magazine.

Fitzgerald defined Amercian literature in the important period between the two world wars of the 20th century. *The Great Gatsby,* arguably America's greatest novel, is of interest primarily for its sociological evidence, uniquely capturing the sentiment of the period. The exuberance of youth and its fleeting glamour attracted Fitzgerald and formed the center of his tragic sense of dreams both deferred and betrayed.

Fitzgerald married Zelda Sayre in 1920 and their lives quickly became a classic study of the American Dream in all its highs, lows, excesses and joys. Sadly, Fitzgerald died at the age of 44, with no knowledge of the literary legacy he left behind, and with a sense of failure about the course of his life.

WILLIAM FAULKNER (1897–1962)

Faulkner was born in New Albany, Mississippi, and later moved to Oxford, Mississippi. Faulkner invented a host of literary characters which defined the historical growth and subsequent decadence of the South as he knew it. The human drama in Faulkner's novels was then built on the model of the actual, historical drama which extended over almost a century and a half. Every story and each novel was set in the imaginary Yoknapatawpha County and featured its many colorful citizens.

Faulkner was awarded the Nobel Prize for Literature in 1949. Despite this acclaim he, like many of his peers, turned to writing Hollywood screenplays, which gave him little satisfaction but provided the necessary income. Nobel writer J.M. Coetzee defined Faulkner as "the most radical innovator in the annals of American fiction."

Faulkner was quoted as saying, "I'm trying to say it all in one sentence, between one Cap and one period." Sadly, a fall from a horse led to his early demise.

EDITH WHARTON (1862–1937)

Edith Newbold Jones was born into affluence in New York City. She lived a privileged life both on the Continent and in the States. Her education was overseen by private tutors and encompassed languages, literature, philosophy, science, and art.

On April 29, 1885, Edith married banker Edward "Teddy" Robbins Wharton in Trinity Chapel, New York. It was a sexless, unhappy marriage that ended in 1913. Several years later her poems and short stories were published by *Scribner's* magazine. For the next 40 years or so they, would publish her stories as would other publications including *Atlantic Monthly, Century Magazine, Harper's, Lippincott's* and the *Saturday Evening Post,*

Wharton moved in literary circles and was close friends with Henry James and others. She traveled widely and undertook serious work during World War I, including visiting the front line and working with refugees who in turn inspired her writing. Familiar themes of Wharton's are seen in *Ethan Frome*, including the conflict between societal mores and the pursuit of happiness. Her extensive body of work included the Pulitzer Prize-winning novel *The Age of Innocence*, which she wrote in 1920. She moved to France following an affair and died in 1937 at the age of 75.

ERNEST HEMINGWAY (1899–1961)

The second of six children, Ernest enjoyed an adventurous childhood, fishing and hunting with his father in the northern woods of Michigan. As a high school student, he excelled in his studies and contributed to his school's literary magazine while serving as editor of the school paper. His first position as a reporter was for the *Kansas City Star*. He served as an ambulance driver for the Italian army in World War I and was wounded at Fossalta on the Piave River.

Hemingway married Elizabeth Hadley Richardson in 1921 and lived off of her trust fund in Paris until the demise of the union in 1927. The couple counted F. Scott Fitzgerald and John Dos Passos among their circle of disenchanted literary friends living abroad. Those were highly productive years for Hemingway and he had many works published, including the widely successful breakthrough novel *The Sun Also Rises*. Ernest married Pauline Pfeiffer in 1927 and lived in Key West, Florida. During this period he wrote *A Farewell to Arms* and the love-lost story titled *The Snows of Kilimanjaro*. Papa, as he was known to friends and family, married writer Martha Ellis Gellhorn in 1940, a month after the publication of *For Whom the Bell Tolls*. His final marriage was to Mary Welsh Monks and they resided in San Francisco de Paula, Cuba. It was a short novel, *The Old Man and the Sea*, which earned both the 1953 Pulitzer Prize and the Nobel Prize for Literature the following year. Hemingway was unable to attend the prize ceremonies due to his altered mental state following his involvement in two plane crashes.

Hemingway's sense of writing as competition—with the past and with himself—produced a distinctive style that changed how writers of the American vernacular conceived of the way in which the printed language can work. Hemingway had his own host of influences, both contemporary and past, but he learned to take from them what was useful and fashion it into a style distinctly his own (Wilson, 230). Following his father's lead, Ernest died of a self-inflicted shotgun wound to the head in his home in Ketchum, Idaho, in 1961.

Credits

Several years ago an urban billboard caught my eye. The caption was "Get Lit at the Library." The advertisement was designed to promote the Rosenbach Museum and Library located in a charming 19th century townhouse on Delancey Street in the heart of Philadelphia. I made a mental note of the phrase, thinking it might raise some eyebrows, pique a little interest and also find its way into an effective library display. Years later my college student workers had quite a reaction to this display title, which, after all, was really just a play on words!

The Rosenbach has a particularly literate clientele. They offer reading groups to members who promise to actually finish reading the assigned titles and ultimately understand works such as James Joyce's *Ulysses* and Herman Melville's *Moby Dick*. Patrons can select from various house tours guided by knowledgeable docents through the treasure trove of collections which offer a glimpse into the brothers Rosenbach, their collecting passions and the world their collections chronicled. One of the most interesting tours available at the museum/library explores the works of Maurice Sendak, author and illustrator of more than 100 books over a period of seven decades. The gallery bearing his name is dedicated to showcasing the works and personal collections of this longtime Rosenbach trustee and supporter.

Assembling the Display

1. The font selected for the title was Wide Latin sized at 275. The words *at the* were sized at 225. The letters were printed on card stock and traced onto red poster

board. They were attached with pins to a background of black flannel and pulled forward. The letter *L* in Lit was an image of a candle found through a Google image search using the terms "clipart candle." This was printed on card stock and traced onto gold poster board. The flame was drawn on gold poster and then mounted on red poster board.

The graphic of the books was found through a Google image search using the term "clipart books." The image was enlarged on the photocopier. The pages were traced onto gold or silver poster board and the edging of the books was traced onto black, red and blue poster board. The detail on the pages of the book was created with a black pen and ruler. This image can be found if you visit http://images.google.com/images?hl=en&um=1&q=lamp+of+knowledge&sa=N&start=0&ndsp=20. It was printed on card stock and traced onto gold poster board and framed in red poster board. Details were added with a black Sharpie. Black crayon was used for shading. The image of the books was attached to the background with pins and pulled forward. Elongated diamonds 5½" in length were drawn on red and gold poster board. They were attached with pins to create a border for the signage. The red and gold diamonds were alternated to create the border.

2. On the top left was a document titled "100 Great Books of the Century." Many such lists are available online. Under that was this quote by Maya Angelou:

> When I look back, I am so impressed again with the life-giving power of literature. If I were a young person today, trying to gain a sense of myself in the world, I would do that again by reading, just as I did when I was young.

These items were printed on white card stock and mounted on black and red poster board.

3. On the top right was a quote by 18th century English essayist, poet and politician Joseph Addison:

> Books are the legacies that a great genius leaves to mankind, which are delivered down from generation to generation as presents to the posterity of those who are yet unborn.

Under that was a document titled "Influential Authors" that included information about James Joyce, F. Scott Fitzgerald, Vladimir Nabokov, William Faulkner and D.H. Lawrence. Next was the quote by Robert Louis Stevenson which introduced this display.

Items on the right were printed and mounted like those on the left.

4. Black velvet lined the base of the display. Three large antique brass candle sticks with ecru candles were placed on the bottom right. Books featured in the display were *A Gentle Madness* by Nicholas Basbanes, *Ada* by Vladimir Nabokov, *Ethan Frome* and *Old New York: Four Novellas* by Edith Wharton, *The Great Gatsby* and *Tender Is the Night* by F. Scott Fitzgerald, *The Literary 100* and *The Novel 100* by Daniel S. Burt, *Heart of Darkness* by Joseph Conrad, *A Portrait of the Artist as a Young Man* and *Ulysses* by James Joyce, *Lord of the Flies* by William Golding, *Sister Carrie* by Theodore Drieser, *The Poems of Shakespeare (Shakespeare)*, *1984* by George Orwell, *The Sound and the Fury* by William Faulkner, *On the Road* by Jack Kerouac, and *Animal Farm* by George Orwell. A framed photo print of Edith Wharton was placed to the bottom right along with a pair of reading glasses. This portrait can be found at http://www-tc.pbs.org/wnet/americannovel/timeline/images/wharton_pic.jpg. Flanking the books on the bottom left was a framed print of a photo of James Joyce found at http://www.shejapan.com/www/wquiz/ireland/ireland2.jpg.

Bigger and Better

If your space is larger you may want to include additional portraits of the writers included in the display. Or enlarge a photo of a writer. Keep the left side of the photo intact, then fill the right half with some of the writer's actual text. For an example of this, visit http://www.english.ufl.edu/faculty/publications/2006summer/bryant_photo-textualities.html. Add a quill pen and an inkwell, a vintage typewriter and a pen holder with pens.

If you prefer a different graphic for your display, consider the simple hand with pen which can be found through a Google image search using those terms. You may want to mount this display around National Literacy Day, which is celebrated on July 2nd.

The book *501 Great Writers: A Comprehensive Guide to the Giants of Literature* edited by Julian Patrick will be a very helpful resource for your display. The entries are chronological and run the gamut from Homer to Mark Twain to J.K. Rowling.

For four other ideas on literary displays see the chapter titled "Authors" in my first book, *Great Displays for Your Library Step by Step*. Also included in that book is a display on the writer C.S. Lewis, which can be found on page 147, and one about author/naturalist John Muir (p. 165.)

10 Etcetera

...Isms

*All religions, arts and sciences are branches of the same tree. All these
aspirations are directed toward ennobling man's life, lifting it from the sphere
of mere physical existence and leading the individual towards freedom.*
—Albert Einstein

Religions, like people, have histories. To understand the true philosophy of a religion one needs to research its origins, its leaders and the significant events that led to its development. Historical study of religions reveal the mystery of who, what, where and when. It is not surprising that the origin of many religions can be traced directly to a charismatic leader whose personality and teachings served as a magnet for enthusiastic followers. The status quo continued until the passing of the founder and interpreters inevitably divided over disparities in beliefs and traditions.

Although religion dates back to ancient times, it continues to remain influential today. Three-quarters of the world's population consider that they belong to a religion despite their level of activity or commitment. Although the religions that are featured in this display are not all known as "isms," they can be defined as such in that each religion remains a discrete

...Isms. Symbols of the world's great religions coexist in this display anchored by the magnificent head of Buddha poised in front of a wine and gold brocade thangka from the collection of Dr. Allen Richardson.

and separate world defined by its own beliefs and practices generally agreed upon by a number of persons or sects. The faithful may gather in special buildings for worship or meditation and live in unique ways in the world. Religious scholars have identified seven dimensions that constitute a religion: doctrinal, experimental, ritual, mythological, social, ethical and material (Gabriel, 6).

Every day people are confronted with issues concerning health, safety, morality and mortality. These daily challenges are the very reason that religions exist. Religion is the universal tool for explaining that which we cannot comprehend within the context of the known physical world. Each religion serves the same purpose. It provides answers to the life questions which all human beings ponder.

The concept of being religious can be interpreted in many ways. It can mean believing that God is the source and the goal of life itself, or that this concept is, at best, a childish illusion. It can stress the need to love one's neighbor as oneself, or banish them to a fate worse than death. It can dictate the consultation of witches for wisdom, or burning them alive. It can be the belief in having a soul or not. Being devout can mean obeying a command to bear children or taking a vow of celibacy. It can require withdrawing into silence or speaking in tongues. Being spiritual can involve shaving one's head or never cutting one's hair. It can entail attending a mosque on Friday, a synagogue on Saturday, or a church on Sunday. It can mean praying, meditating, levitating, worshipping, or even entering ecstasy. It can require building a cathedral or temple or pyramid, or it can require crossing oceans and continents to go on pilgrimages to holy places. It can urge the conversion of disbelievers or insist they join a crusade, holy war or *jihad*. Religions have inspired the creation of music, art, icons, symbols and poetry (Bowker, 6).

Religions

JUDAISM

Judaism is not simply a religion but also a way of life, a race and a culture. Diversity defines Judaism, which includes Orthodox and Reformed Jews, Ashkenazi, Sephardic and other ethnically defined groups spread across races and continents. Secular Jews do not adhere to the Jewish code of law known as the Halakah. Approximately half of the Jews living in the U.S. are not members of a synagogue. Some observe certain Jewish celebrations and holy days, although these are not always viewed as religious practices but are seen more as cultural expressions. The origin of the word *Judaism* comes from Judah, the fourth son of Jacob, who fathered 12 sons. Each sibling became a founder of a tribe in ancient Israel. Modern Jews are viewed as the descendants of Jacob, also known as Israel.

Theodore Herzl founded the Zionist movement in 1897. Zionist ideology holds that the Jews are a people or nation like any other and should gather together in a single homeland, the Holy Land. It was believed that the Jews were a people without a country and would remain politically powerless as long as they did not have a national home. Jews would be guests everywhere and at home nowhere, according to Zionist ideology. By the 1980s, some Israeli historians and sociologists began to question facts about the official history of Israel and Zionism, as well as the Zionist principles. They reasoned that Zionism had accomplished its purpose in creating the Jewish state, and that now it was time to move on.

Jews believe that there is only one God as revealed to Abraham, Isaac and Jacob. His commandments were conveyed to Moses, who led Israel out of bondage from Egypt. Those laws form the Torah, the most prominent scripture of Judaism. God is believed to be intangible, omnipotent, omniscient, eternal, holy, merciful and just. The idea of the coming of the Messiah, a descendant of King David, was central to Jewish beliefs. The Messiah would establish the paramount authority of Israel in the world, create a kingdom of peace, and banish wickedness and sin.

Growing in popularity is a form of ancient Jewish mysticism called Kabbalah. The word is derived from the root "to receive, to accept" and is often used synonymously with "tradition." Kabbalah deals with speculation on the nature of divinity, the creation, the origin and fate of the soul, as well as the role of human beings. It includes meditative, devotional, mystical and magical practices which were taught only to a select few. As a result, Kabbalah is considered an esoteric offshoot of Judaism.

Fewer than 20 million Jews are in existence today. Their influence, and that of their ancestors, has been so enormous that Judaism is counted as one of the major world religions. The study of Judaism is critical to understanding the development of Christianity and Islam, whose followers also worship the God of Abraham.

CHRISTIANITY

Followers of Christianity adhere to the precepts and examples of Christ, which literally means "the anointed one." Most Christians view their history as a plan of God that reached its apex in the birth, life, death and resurrection of Jesus as Christ. All events leading up to this were but a preparation for his coming. All events after him are but a realization of God's plan. Early in their separate religions, Christians added to the Jewish concept of their history. Jews were God's chosen people until their leaders rejected Jesus as their Messiah. After that rejection, the old covenant was replaced by a new covenant for the new people of God, those who accepted Jesus as the Messiah. The central person of Christian history is Jesus of Nazareth, who is worshiped as the Christ, the Son of God (Matthews, 326).

Christians believe that Jesus was a human yet divine being who suffered and died on the cross to make amends for the sins of humanity. Those who accepted him as their savior will achieve salvation and eternal life. Jesus was tried by Pontius Pilate at the insistence of Jewish leaders who viewed him as a threat to their authority.

Christianity developed as an interpretation of the life and teachings of Jesus Christ recounted in the New Testament. The second part of the Christian Bible, the New Testament consists of the four gospels, the Acts of the Apostles, the epistles and the Book of Revelation—the "Apocalypse." Modern Christianity has many denominations. The first major schism occurred in 1054 between the eastern and western churches as a result of doctrinal and political differences. German monk Martin Luther embarked on a reform of the Roman Catholic Church in 1517. The three remaining branches of Christianity—Roman Catholicism, Eastern Orthodoxy and Protestantism—are subdivided further.

The Roman Catholic Church is ruled by the pope, who is considered to be a successor of St. Peter and infallible in matters relating to faith and morals. Papal infallibility is one of the great differences between Catholicism and Protestantism. Catholic dogma teaches both Transubstantiation, which means that the bread and wine in the Eucharist are the actual body and blood of Jesus Christ, and the existence of purgatory, a state of suffering inhabited by the souls of sinners who must amend for their wrongdoing before entering heaven. Mary, the Mother of God, is considered to have been born without original sin, which is referred to as the Immaculate Conception. Her body was assumed into heaven upon her death. Catholicism preaches the veneration of Mary. The church maintains strict rulings against contraception, homosexuality and the ordination of women. It promotes the continuation of priestly celibacy. There are 1.086 billion Roman Catholics worldwide.

Protestantism is the generic term that encompasses a wide variety of churches related to the Reformation and it originated in 1517 when Martin Luther, a German monk, posted on the door of his church in Wittenberg his 95 theses critiquing the Roman Catholic Church. Luther's ideology spread throughout Germany and Northern Europe. Other reformers who had a significant impact on the Reformation were Philip Melancthon, John Calvin, John Knox and Ulrich Zwingli. These reformers objected to the practice of granting of indulgences by the Catholic Church. Protestants believed that salvation comes from belief in Christ's act of atonement on the cross and is dependent on God's grace rather than on human enterprise. Scripture is the only absolute doctrine and they reject the authority of bishops, the pope or tradition.

Protestant Churches tend to be far less ornate than Catholic churches. The concept of Transubstantiation has been modified and the bread and wine are merely symbols of the body and blood of Christ. Only in the

High Church, which is closer to the Roman Catholic tradition, will you find statues or incense used during worship. Groups within the Protestant church are Lutherans, Anglicans, Presbyterians, Unitarians, Baptists, Quakers, Congregationalists, Amish, Episcopalians, Methodists, Jehovah's Witnesses, Mormons, Seventh Day Adventists, Christian Scientists, Pentecostalists and the Holy Spirit Association Unificationists. Protestants number about 590 million worldwide.

The Greek Orthodox Church is a branch of the Christian denomination Eastern Orthodox Church which separated from the Church of Rome in 1054 as a result of the Great Schism. The renowned theologian Germanos Strinopoulos was the first Metropolitan bishop in 1922. The Greek Orthodox Church currently totals approximately 350 million followers and has very strong influence in both Greece and Cyprus. London is the seat of the diocese of Thyateira, the headquarters of Greek Orthodox churches in western and central Europe.

Though Mary is a significant figure in their faith, Greek Orthodox churches do not adhere to the Roman Catholic doctrine of the Immaculate Conception. They do believe that Mary remained a virgin and was sinless until death. The faithful celebrate her death, or Dormition, rather than her bodily assumption into Heaven.

By design, Greek Orthodox church buildings are either rectangular, symbolizing Noah's Ark, or in the shape of the cross. Stacidia, or high chairs, are used instead of pews. The use of incense is central to their worship ritual and almost all liturgy is either sung or chanted. The most important celebration in the Greek Orthodox calendar is Easter, followed by Christmas. Neither date concurs with the Roman calendar.

Christianity is the largest religion in the world, with more than two billion followers worldwide. Recently the numbers have been declining in the West, especially in Europe. However, followers are rising in parts of Latin America, Asia and Africa.

ISLAM

Islam is a religion based on belief in Allah and obedience to his revelation contained in the Quran (Koran). Islam is exemplified in the character and behavior of Muhammad, "the final prophet" of God. Followers of Islam are Muslims. A Muslim is one who has attained a state of peace achieved through surrender to God. Muslims dismiss the idea that the religion began with Muhammad in the 7th century, but believe it to be true path that God has provided for humans since the beginning of time.

Muhammed married Khadija, a wealthy widow, and made his living as a trader. In his role as a merchant he was known for his integrity and sense of justice. He first received, via the intervention of the angel Gabriel, the verses of the Quran in a cave located above the city of Mecca in western Saudi Arabia. This revelation continued for 22 years. The purpose of these verses is to bear witness to the oneness of God (tawhid) and believe in the struggle to remain obedient to God's will. Various prophets have exemplified this life of surrender, cautioning the faithful about the consequences of disobedience and preaching future rewards.

Following the persecution of Muhammed by the merchants, he fled to Medina where Islamic leaders had invited him to arbitrate differences between the city's tribes. In this new locale Muhammed was acknowledged as a respected leader who gathered his followers to form the first Muslim community. These new followers of Islam effectively spread the word throughout the Arabian peninsula. When the struggle against the Meccan leaders developed into a full-blown conflict, the Quran's revelations allowed the Muslims to defend their religion through armed struggle.

Muhammed fought against the Meccans until 630, increasing his power as more tribes acknowledged Islam. When the Meccans accepted defeat he declared an amnesty for all except a few of his former enemies. He died at the age of 62 having transmitted the entire revelations of God.

BUDDHISM

Buddhism began in Northern India in the 6th or 5th century BCE. It is a religion based on a path of practice and spiritual development leading to insights into the nature of life. The origins of Buddhism can be found in the teachings of Siddhartha Gautama—

born a member of a minor royal family in Nepal—who achieved enlightenment after a tedious quest for truth.

The saga of Buddha's journey begins when he sees for the first time and on separate occasions, a sick man, an old man, a corpse, and a wandering holy man. Legend has it that Siddhartha's father had attempted to protect him from a prophesy that stated his son would become a world renouncer. When Buddha finally observed the realities of the human condition, he left his wife and family and lived an ascetic, homeless existence which became known as the Great Renunciation. During that period Siddhartha attained all of the goals that extreme discipline can attain, but it was not enough. He still had not escaped from the world of suffering and death. While in despair, sitting under the bohdi tree in Bodh Gaya, he passed through the four stages of meditative trance and finally attained enlightenment (Bowker, 54).

The Buddha's teachings are based on four noble truths. The first is that life is unsatisfactory and filled with suffering (*dukkha*). The remaining three noble truths examine the cause of suffering and its preventions. The second explains that suffering is caused by desire, the third that it can be overcome, and the fourth provides the path by which suffering can be eliminated (Gabriel, 94).

The Buddhist hierarchy is formed first by male and female monks, followed by male and female laity. The two communities are interdependent; the monks serving as spiritual teachers and the laity providing basic needs such as food, shelter and clothing.

HINDUISM

Hinduism is the name given in the 19th century to describe a broad range of religions in India. While offering many striking parallels to other great religions, it cannot easily be compared to any of them. Hinduism comes from the Persian word *hindu,* in Sanskrit *sindhu* which means "river" and refers to the people of the Indus Valley; thus it means Indian. About 80 percent of India's one billion people consider themselves Hindus, and there are about 50 million more dispersed throughout the world, making it the third largest religion in the world (Klostermaier, 1).

Thousands of years old, Hinduism incorporates hundreds of sacred texts. Hindus worship countless gods, from local deities to divine beings such as Vishnu, Shiva and Krishna, and goddesses Durga, Kali and Lakshmi. Although most branches of the religion acknowledge the canon of sacred texts known as the Veda, others do not. Ritual is embraced by some as vital for salvation and denied by others. Millions accept the idea that human society is hierarchically divided into four divinely ordained varnas and subdivided into thousands of castes to which an individual is assigned at birth and cannot leave. Others believe that caste is a human structure and advocate that salvation is universally available.

All Hindus embrace the belief in reincarnation. It is thought that souls migrate through a cycle of birth and death determined by the law of action and its effect until eventual release. However, the means to such a final liberation are disputed among Hinduism's countless sects. In Hinduism, the Supreme Being is Braham, an impersonal power upon which the universe is woven. Braham is the essence of all existence and remains as the ultimate reality when everything else decays and eventually transforms. Its omnipresence within the universe means that it exists within every created being; it is known as Atman (Gabriel, 85).

Although it has no claim to a solitary founder, Hinduism has been created and re-created via the actions of countless saints and sages through the ages. Prominent among these in the modern period are Gandhi, Vivekananda, Ramakrishna, Swami Dayanand and Sri Aurobindo.

Religions encompass nearly all human endeavors. Many students of world religion have gleaned new information about previously unknown faiths, and at the same time found fresh insights and values in the religion to which they belong.

Credits

Throughout my years in academia, I have been witness to true cultural diversity. My student workers have come from all over North America as well as northern Africa, India, the Middle East, Eastern Europe, Puerto

Rico and the Caribbean/Islands. And yet for all their disparate life experiences and all of the obvious and contrasting characteristics these students exhibit, there are far more similarities. On many occasions my students have shared their cultural and religious experiences with me. They have taught me about the riches and rituals of their worlds—worlds I will probably never see. I remain in their debt.

Dr. Allen Richardson is a professor of religious studies at Cedar Crest College. An author, world traveler and avid collector, Dr. Richardson has provided many artifacts for my displays over the years. Most of the religious icons featured in this display are from his extensive collection. I am forever grateful for his generosity.

Assembling the Display

1. A wine and gold brocade thangka was attached to the black felt background with pins. This banner was from Tibet. These are available online for purchase. Surrounding it were various symbols of world religions easily found through a Google image search. These were sized in Word 2007. The symbols were printed on card stock and cut out and traced onto poster board then glued to a 4" gold circle cut from poster board. They were attached with pins and pulled forward.

2. On the top left was a document on Hinduism taken from the text of this display. Clip Art of a goddess was inserted at the top right. Under that was this quote by Gandhi:

> It is easy enough to be friendly to one's friends. But to befriend the one who regards himself as your enemy is the quintessence of true religion. The other is mere business.

Under that was information about Buddhism taken from the text of this display. Clip Art of Buddha was inserted at the top center.

Items on the left were printed on white card stock and mounted on black and/or gold poster board.

3. On the top right was a document on Christianity take from the text of this display. Clip art of a Christian image was placed at the top right. Under that was a quote by Yale University professor David Gelernter:

> If we were forced to choose just one, there would be no way to deny that Judaism is the most important intellectual development in human history.

Under that was a document listing a brief definition of religions not previously mentioned (Taoism, Bahai, Shinto, Sikhism, Janism and Zoroastrianism).

All items on the right were printed and mounted as those on the left.

On the base of the display was Garuda, the bird-like deity associated with the Hindu god Vishnu. Next was a Tibetan/Buddhist prayer wheel. A gold Christian cross, a wooden carved head of the Buddha and the Hindu god Ganesh were elevated on Styrofoam which was draped in black velvet material. A Tibetan Buddhist bell and Vajra were placed next to a Zen Buddhist pillow, gong and striker. Last was a wood carving of the Egyptian God Horus.

Books featured in the display were: *Survey of Hinduism* by Klaus K. Klostermaier, *...Isms: Understanding Religions* by Theodore Gabriel and Ronald Geaves, *Sufis and Saints' Bodies: Mysticism, Corporeality and Sacred Power in Islam* by Scott Kugle and *Islam: The Straight Path* by John L. Esposito.

Bigger and Better

Should your display space be larger you could include some of the less well-known religions mentioned above. The yin-yang symbol of Taoism is a powerful image. Obviously, your display would be based on the artifacts available to you. Contact members of the clergy or religion instructors to see what items they would be willing to lend for a display of this nature.

If celebrating Judaism, choose a time of year that the menorah and dreidel would not be in use. There are some interesting mystical images associated with Kaballah that could easily anchor a display. For a strong Gothic Kabbalah visit http://upload.wikimedia.org/wikipedia/en/7/7e/Gothic_Kabbalah.jpg. Choose a lesser known holiday such as Tu b'-Shevat or the 15th of Av. For information about Jewish holidays and their significance, visit http://www.chabad.org/calendar/holidays_cdo/aid/36263/jewish/Holiday-Schedules.htm.

In Stitches

Sometimes it is hard to find the simple geometry within an ornate piece of embroidery, architectural ornament, or woven rug. That's why I find quilts so exciting—your eye can suddenly catch the bare bones of a quilt's geometry even though it's buzzing with intertwining floral patterns.
—Kate Fassett, *Simple Shapes Spectacular Quilts* (p. 7)

The art of quilting can be traced to early civilizations in the Far East. The ancient Chinese rarely discarded old garments, believing that the fabrics became part of the person wearing them. Instead, pieces of old material were laid upon new silk fabric, edges were frayed to blend the sections together, then rows of running stitches applied to add strength. The word *quilt* comes originally from the Latin word *culcita*, meaning a stuffed sack, mattress, or cushion; it comes into the English language from the French *cuilte*. The word has undergone various spelling changes since the thirteenth century: "cowltes," "qwhiltez," "quildes," and "twilts" have been mentioned in histories, plays and poems (Orlofsky, 11).

Quilting enjoyed popularity during medieval times. Quilted coats were worn under the knights' armor and served to prevent the metal from rusting in the rain and absorbing the heat from the sun. Quilted coverlets were prevalent during the Elizabethan era and upper class men often sported quilted jackets, despite the fact that the bulk prevented ease of movement.

Sixteenth century England is credited with the quilt as we know it, where luxurious whole-cloth and appliquéd quilts enjoyed enormous popularity. Early colonists migrating to the New World arrived with the knowledge of the principles of quilting, which comprised three layers (top, batting and backing) stitched together to form a thick, warm coverlet. Given the scarcity of fabric during colonial times, women pieced their quilts with fabric scraps from other sewing projects. By the early 19th century these pieced quilts had evolved into the block form that is considered the quintessential North American style of quilting. From pieces of cloth, thread, a needle and endless hours of painstaking precision countless quilts have been created which have come to symbolize North American ingenuity and imagination.

The history of patchwork quilting closely parallels the evolution of the United States. For the colonists of New England, as well as the settlers of the West, quilting was a real necessity. It not only provided warmth and a measure of insulation against the elements, it also allowed for the practical recycling of worn clothing. Not so apparent, but equally important, was the solace it provided these pioneering women in their effort to survive their journey West. From these basic human needs and a dearth of textiles came the art of patchwork quilts.

Quilting and quilting bees became popular sometime after 1750. Quilting brought women together as networks were formed by those who regularly met to exchange a new quilt design or a method for achieving the perfect stitch. But quilting and quilting bees were not exclusively women's work. Husbands and sons often helped with the quilt piecing, just as wives and daughters helped with the labors of daily farmwork. Former presidents Dwight Eisenhower and Calvin Coolidge helped their mothers piece together quilt tops, and couples sometimes quilted together. Quilting bees were sometimes organized for philanthropic purposes. Quilts were made as gifts for departing friends, brides, ministers or those in need. The slow pace of the project allowed for women to be able to share their concerns with their fellow quiltmakers. As a result, many fast friendships ensued.

Historians agree that the peak of early American quiltmaking came later, from 1830 to 1870. That coincides with the manufacturing of good quality, affordable cotton from America's own mills and the cult of domesticity within the society that valued fine needlework as the pinnacle of accomplishments among women. Motifs such as log cabins, windmills and covered wagons were commonly found in the early quilts of the pioneers. Sadly, none of the earliest American

In Stitches. A child's quilt serves as a background for this homespun display on the history of quilting in America. The accoutrements of this craft fill and overflow a sewing basket.

quilts were preserved because they were made of fabric already thin with wear.

The informal style of patching was evident during the Victorian era when the crazy quilt, replete with color and texture, became popular. These vibrant quilts were made of exotic materials such as silks, satins, velvets and brocades and were covered with whatever decorative stitching the quilter desired. Appliqué, the art of attaching one fabric on top of another, was known to the ancient Egyptians, the Native Americans and accomplished European needlewoman. In the prerevolutionary American home, the art of appliqué became an inexpensive way to embellish a bed—often the most valued piece of furniture in the home.

AMISH QUILTS

The Amish people led lives separate from society at large, finding meaning in an austere lifestyle within small faith-based communities. They were prohibited by their religion to decorate their houses or their persons with anything purely decorative. Oddly

enough, they were allowed to create quilts using fabrics of vivid colors.

Amish women often shared piecing and quilting patterns among themselves. Sometimes patterns would be distributed to women from different communities thereby spreading the designs across the country. The Amish quilts display some of the boldest designs and creative color combinations—brilliant reds and purples, turquoises and chartreuse greens—hues made more pronounced by the use of wool, which both absorbed the dye and gave the colors a warm glow. Perhaps it took a group of people whose existence was devoid of color in their daily lives to create the color combinations used in their bedroom quilts. The solid fabrics employed in the Amish quilts are free of patterns. But solid needn't denote plain. There are often large open spaces in Amish quilts. Broad, plain borders serve to set off the design, much like a mat surrounding a picture or photograph. These spaces, replete with quilting, draw the eye to the pieced design in the quilt.

In a recent survey it was estimated that there are about twenty million quilters in the United States alone. A journal of their joys and sorrows are sewn into these quilts, which will be passed to future generations to assure that their memories will be kept alive. The needle arts are intrinsic to societies worldwide. Modern England has its smocking, petit point is a delicate specialty of the French and the Scandinavians create beautiful white openwork embroidery. Patchwork quilting, however, is a true American art form. No other needle art symbolized the pioneer virtues of thrift, diligence and initiative that built America.

Credits

Lancaster County, Pennsylvania, is the site of the oldest, continuously occupied Amish settlement in the United States. The families who live there are the descendants of the 18th century immigrants who came to Pennsylvania. Many of the Amish living in Lancaster County live on farms that have been in their families for 200 years.

In the Lancaster community, the traditions of the Pennsylvania Dutch culture and art are intertwined with the Amish way of life. The Amish country remains a popular travel destination in the state of Pennsylvania. Tourists flock to the beautiful countryside to explore the centuries-old lifestyle of the Amish. Visitors savor the peaceful pace and rhythm of Lancaster County, where the horse and buggy remains a primary method of transportation and where windmills dot the landscape providing a nature-harnessed source of energy. The "Plain People," as they have come to be known, are a vital presence here. They are involved in agriculture as well as a host of cottage industries. Amish themed attractions and events, foods and crafts draw thousands of visitors each year.

The Kutztown Folk Festival, in neighboring Berks County, is held in early July each year in Kutztown, Pennsylvania. Over 100,000 attend the country's largest exhibition of authentic Pennsylvania Dutch quilts. Many unique American crafts and folk art such as blacksmithing, redware, chair caning, paper cutting known as *scherenschnitte*, pot-

tery and woodcarving can be found here as 200 craftsmen demonstrate daily. Folklore and folklife programs, six stages of continuous entertainment, music, a wide array of children's activities and the very best Pennsylvania Dutch food account for the continued success of this festival.

But the Quilt Barn at the festival is the main attraction. It features 2,500 locally handmade quilts and wallhangings on display and for sale. A fully stocked quilt shop offers the notions and hard-to-find items quilters need. The famous Quilt Auction of 24 prize-winners is held on the second Saturday of the fair. Quilting demonstrations provide an opportunity for fairgoers to actually try their hand at quilting which results in a festival visitors quilt, created entirely by people attending the show. For more information visit http://www.kutztownfestival.com/about/quilts.html.

As a Pennsylvania native residing on the fringe of Amish country, I have long been fascinated with their peaceful lifestyle, rejection of technology and unwavering commitment to tradition. My early memories of the Kutztown Folk Festival were of delicious foods, puppets in the barnyard theatre and colorful historical reenactments—including an Amish wedding! The Quilt Barn offered a breathtaking array of beautifully crafted quilts which would be a conversation piece in any home. It was there that my appreciation for quilting began. If a visit to Pennsylvania is possible, bring your family to the fair!

Assembling the Display

1. A coral, tan and ecru child's quilt was pinned to the tan felt background of the display case. The title was created using the font Rockwell Condensed sized at 360. This was printed on card stock and glued to black and then gold poster board. One inch lines of stitching were drawn with black Magic Marker above and below the title. The sign was attached with pins and pulled forward. Over the title signage was an antique wooden thread holder which was attached with pins.

2. On the top left was a document titled "America's Quilt Revival & Bicentennial

Quilts: 1960s & 1970s." This can be found if you visit http://www.womenfolk.com/quilt ing_history/bicentennial-quilts.htm. Under that was the quote that introduced this display. Next was a document titled "Depression Era Quilts: Cheer in Fabric and Color" which can be found at http://www.womenfolk.com/quilting_history/depression.htm.

Items on the left were printed on card stock and mounted on gold poster board.

3. On the top right was a copy of an Amish quilt titled "Sunshine and Shadow" made by an Amish woman for her son's wedding circa 1928. Many such Amish quilts can be found through a Google image search. Under that was this anonymous quote:

> Quilters affect eternity; they can never tell where their influence stops.

Last was a document titled "The Amish Quilt" which can be found on pages 29–34 of *The Amish Quilt* by Eve Wheatcroft. For online information please visit http://www.theamish quilt.com/history.html.

Items on the right were printed and mounted like those on the left.

4. On the base of the display was a painted wooden box filled with various color thread, needles, a yellow cloth measuring tape and scissors. Other items featured on the base was a 6" measure, a compass and pencil, a pattern cutter, a thread cutter, a needle and thread and a retractable measuring tape and various sizes and color spools of thread. To the right of the box was a miniature potted silk sunflower, turned on its side.

Books featured in the display were *The Quilter's Catalog: A Comprehensive Resource Guide* by Meg Cox, *Material Obsession: Modern Quilts with Traditional Roots* by Kathy Doughty and Sarah Fielke, *This Old Quilt: A Heartwarming Celebration of Quilts and Quilting* edited by Margret Aldrich, *Crazy Quilting: The Complete Guide* by Marsha Michler, *Stitches from the Soul: Slave Quilts from the Ante-Bellum South* by Marie Fry, PhD, *The Quilt Encyclopedia* illustrated by Carter Hauck and *Kaffe Fassett's Simple Shapes Spectacular Quilts* by Kaffe Fassett with Liza Prior Lucy.

Bigger and Better

If your space permits, consider including an actual quilt form to display your quilt. You could also use a quilt rack, an easel or a rustic ladder which would hold several quilts. You may want to frame your title in a large embroidery frame, which are available in circular, oval, rectangular and square shapes. You could include squares of fabric across the base of the display, or you could create your title signage using lettering cut from patterned fabric.

There are some catchy titles you can use for your display, such as "Material Obsession," "The Art of the Needle," "Sublime Stitching" or "Quilt Classics." You may want to emphasize specific types such as Victorian, patchwork or crazy quilts. Perhaps you could tie this into a program for adults or children on quilt basics. The individual squares could then be sewn into a quilt which could be displayed in the library. Later it could be raffled or given to a local community center, school, or nursing home, etc. to be placed on display. You might decide to have a theme for the quilt, and the story could unfold in the patches. You might decide to feature various needle arts in your display. Staff or community members would be happy to lend their needlepoint, crocheted or knitted items, crewel, cross stitch, etc.

The Great Ships of Sail

Take it all in all, a ship is the most honorable thing a man has ever produced.—John Ruskin, English art critic, poet and social thinker

Ships are among the most influential artifacts crafted by man. Over the centuries they have surpassed sheer practical use and evolved into instruments of immense influence. Ships have been used to exert political and military might as well as for commercial exploitation.

The Great Ships of Sail. A wooden plaque with a sailing ship circa 1861 is the centerpiece of this display featuring a 19th century ship's sextant, an early 20th century brass and wood compass, a 19th century telescope, a nautical guide dated 1791 and a boatswain's whistle—all from the collection of Dr. Allen Richardson.

The history of the ship belongs to the era of our struggle to dominate the world about us, and has become, for better or worse, a tool with which we have shaped our civilization. J.B. Priestly, writing in the mid 20th century, said that the ship was the greatest construction of the age, likening it to the cathedral of the middle ages. Today, like the medieval cathedral, the ship has slipped to the margins of public perception. The wonders of our own age are smaller, more complex and electronic (Woodman, 6).

During the greatest period of world conquest the role of the sailing ships was paramount. Civilizations were destroyed, populations transported, battles fought and continents dominated—all via the great ships of sail.

Today's shipping industry plays a much different role. Modern ships provide for our daily needs by transporting enormous quantities of the world's natural resources and manufactured products around the globe. On a more ominous note, we have witnessed diseases and pollutants spread globally through various methods of transportation, including shipping.

Although there is evidence of boatbuilding dating back 200,000 years, many credit the Chinese for the construction of the first, most efficient and seaworthy sailing ship with the misnamed moniker of junk. These ships were developed during the Han Dynasty (220 B.C.–A.D. 200) and were used as oceangoing vessels as early as the 2nd century A.D. Although this sailboat design originated in ancient times, it is still in use today.

The Viking Age, from 800 to 1100, was the age of the sleek, speedy longship. Without this development in ship technology, the Vikings would never have become a leading force in medieval politics, warfare and trade. For three hundred years, the sight of a square sail and a dragon-headed prow created terror in the hearts of medieval Europeans. For more information about the Viking ships visit http://www.pbs.org/wgbh/nova/vikings/ships.html.

In the 14th century, during the Ming dynasty, a major but unsuccessful effort for the exploration of the western hemisphere was launched by the Chinese. Shortly thereafter, the Portugese sailed around the southern tip of Africa from the opposite direction and established a settlement in Macao. They wanted to establish a sea lane to the trade marts of Asia. The British and other Europeans soon followed.

In the 14th and 15th centuries, European ships varied greatly in construction because each port in every country had its own practice of shipbuilding. Most ships belonged to one of two types. The northern ship was called a cog and was square rigged. This meant it had a single square sail positioned on a central mast. While the square sail helped maneuver well before the wind, when the wind was blowing from the side or when the ship was sailing into the wind, there were problems. The southern or Mediterranean ship was a caravel and lateen-rigged, with big triangular sails on two or three masts. The lateen sail maneuvered well when the wind came from the side, but had problems when the wind came from behind. Increasingly longer voyages required larger ships with more cargo and crew space. Portugese explorer Ferdinand Magellan could not have sailed successfully around the world in a caravel. By the close of the 15th century, this craft was no longer commonly used.

Italian mariner Christopher Columbus, along with many other educated men of the 15th century, believed the earth was round and thought that Asia could be reached by sailing west. While residing in Lisbon, Columbus sought financial backing from King John of Portugal. The monarchy had been supportive of exploratory expeditions down the west coast of Africa for half a century but was unwilling to fund this request. After this rejection Columbus shifted his base of operations to Los Palos de la Frontera in Spain. He did ultimately win sponsorship from King Ferdinand and Queen Isabella, who bestowed on him the title Admiral of the Ocean Sea and named him supreme commander of the exhibition. His flagship, the *Santa Maria*, led two other little caravels, the *Nina* and the *Pinta*, to the west and eternal renown.

It was the enterprising nature of western societies which encouraged Europeans to seek political autonomy and superiority by way of the sea and to play a major role in maritime exploration. Although Great Britain was the original dominant seafaring power, she ultimately lost that position to the United States.

Sailors aboard whaling ships had much free time during the course of their journey. They soon learned that the ivory whale teeth could be carved into various practical and decorative items. The art of scrimshaw was considered by some to be the only art form that originated in America, since it was first practiced by sailors working on ships out of New England. The word actually came from a slang expression that was used to refer to anything that was the product of a seaman's idle time, or items that were produced while engaged in the act of loafing. Sailors practiced this art between whale sightings, which could extend to weeks or even months. The men created items such as umbrella handles, pie crimpers, and ditty boxes. But the most recognized and sought after form of scrimshaw were the ivory whale teeth that had pictures of ships and other scenes etched on the surface of them.

Definition of Sailing Ships

Fully Rigged: At least three masts, all square rigged.

Barque: A minimum of three masts, two of which are square-rigged, except the aft, which is fore and aft rigged.

Barquetine: At least three masts, which are all fore and aft rigged, except the foremast which is fully rigged, including a square forecourse.

Brig: Two masts always, both of which are square-rigged.

Brigantine: Similar to a brig and has two masts, the aft mast fore and aft rigged.

Schooner: A fore and aft rigged vessel which can have between two and six masts. Schooners rigged with three or more masts have spars and rigging of uniform dimensions and scantlings for all masts, except the main boom of the aftermast which is heavier and longer.

Topsail Schooner: Distinguished by square sails on the foremast, but differs from the brigantine and barquetine by having a gaft sail aloft the foremast.

Ketch: Two masts, each carrying a gaff-headed or job-sail. Ketches differ from the two-masted schooner in that the larger mast and sail stand foremost, whereas in the schooner the reverse is true.

Credits

The grounds of an independent school in Severna Park, Maryland, was an idyllic living scenario for my family. Severn School overlooks the scenic Severn River, a finger of the Chesapeake Bay. Severn began as an all-male boarding prep school for the U.S. Naval Academy in 1914. It has since grown into a vital coeducational institution which emphasizes character, conduct, scholarship and leadership. My older son, Brian, was fortunate to attend Severn School, during his junior high school days, where he thrived academically.

During our tenure at Severn, the tall ships visited the port in Baltimore, just 17 miles to the north. This spectacle sponsored by Sail Baltimore, took place during the nation's bicentennial in 1976. It was a highly publicized and well attended event. Since that time, more than 400 international crafts, including military, private, educational and environmental vessels, have provided visitors a thrilling firsthand look at the world's greatest seagoing vessels. These visiting tall ships dock at various locations in Baltimore Harbor for anywhere from one day to several weeks. They open their decks to the public free of charge.

Should you visit Baltimore Harbor when the tall ships are not on display, tours are available on the USS *Constitution,* an 1854 reproduction of the famous frigate built in 1797. This vessel was first restored in 1968 and again in the 1990s and has served as a great tourist attraction for the city. For information about maritime events in Baltimore visit http://www.sailbaltimore.org/about.htm or http://www.history.navy.mil/USSconstitution/index.html.

It is with great fondness that I recall the fireworks display that backlit the parade of tall ships in Baltimore harbor that summer. The sound and spectacle were aptly reflected in the wide eyed looks of my captivated children.

Assembling the Display

1. The background of this display was blue felt. The poster was made using black poster board. The words *The Great* were created using the font Franklin Gothic Heavy which is available in Word. The words "Ships of Sail" were created using the font Androgyne which is available free if you visit http://www.dafont.com. These letters were printed on card stock and traced onto gold poster board then glued to the black poster board.

A nautical compass, which can be found if you search Google images using that term, was printed on card stock and traced onto gold poster board. A light blue diamond cut from poster board was glued to the center of the compass. One was placed at the top of the poster and another at the bottom. They were put on with pins and pulled forward. A 2" strip of gold poster board was cut and pinned to each side of the poster. The plaque was centered on the poster and nailed to the background.

Books displayed here were *The Complete Encyclopedia of Sailing Ships 2000 B.C.–2006 A.D.* by John Batchelor and Christopher Chant, *The Mutiny on the "Bounty" Trilogy* by Charles Nordhoff and James Norman-Hall, *The Art of Rigging* by George Biddlecombe and David Steele and *Sailing: An Informal Primer* by Richard Ulian.

2. On the top left was a document on "Viking Ships." This information can be found if you visit http://www.pbs.org/wgbh/nova/vikings/ships.html. An illustration of that type of craft, found through a Google image search, was inserted in the top center. Under that was this quote by Michael Lille:

> We rest here while we can, but we hear the ocean calling in our dreams, and we know by morning, the wind will fill our sails to test the seams. A calm is on the water and part of us would linger by the shore, for ships are safe at harbor, but that's not what ships are for.

Under that was a document titled "America Discovered" which gives information about Bjarni Herjolfsson, the first white man to sight the coast of North America. An image of the explorer, found through a Google image search, was inserted into the document. Last was a document on the "Art of Scrimshaw" which can be found if you visit http://www.hopscrimshaw.com/about/scrimh istory.htm.

Items on the left had borders inserted, were printed on card stock and mounted on black and/or gold poster board.

3. On the top right was a document titled "Astrolabes and Quadrants" which can be found if you visit http://www.encyclope dia.com/doc/1G2- 2536600157.html. Images of those instruments, found through a Google image search, were inserted in the top center of the document. Under that was a sketch titled "Parts of a Sextant" which can be found if you visit http://www.infovisual. info/05/076_en.html. Next was the quote by John Ruskin that introduced the display. Last was a painting titled "Ships on a Rough Sea" by Johannes Christiaan Shotel. This is available through a Google image search.

Items on the right were printed and mounted like those on the left.

On the base of the display were shells and rocks, an early 20th century brass ship's compass enclosed in a wooden box, an early 19th century sextant and a small, mid–to late 19th century telescope which rests on top of the compass. A World War II boatswain's whistle etched with the name of the ships on which he served was placed over a signed 1791 nautical guide titled *Navigation New Modelled or a Treatise of Geometrical, Trigonometrical, Arithmetical, Instrumental and Practical Navigation Teachers.*

Books featured on the base were *The History of the Ship: The Comprehensive Story of Seafaring from the Earliest Times to the Present Day* by Richard Woodman, *The Annapolis Book of Seamanship* by John Rousmaniere, and *Glory of the Seas* by Michael Jay Mjelde.

Bigger and Better

Should your space be larger, include items such as a searchlight, a globe, some ship models, cannon balls, a ship's bell and a wooden chest. Be sure to provide information about the name and type of model ship displayed and a brief history. If you have access to nautical maps, they could provide an interesting background, or they could be partially opened and featured on the base of the display. Fish net could also serve as a background with shells randomly placed. You may want to use a piece of driftwood as the backing for your title.

You could also enlarge a print of a ship and have that as your focal point. A ship's wheel could take the place of the wooden plaque featured in this display. Add an anchor, some rope, binoculars, a life ring, an hourglass, scrimshaw, lobster buoys, wooden pilings (tie 3 paper towel cardboard center cylinders together to create your own) and a lighthouse or two. You could incorporate a pirate theme and include coins, knives, a pistol, pirate flags, a treasure chest, jewels and hats.

For a nautical display idea titled "Sailor's Tales," see p. 177 of my first book, *Great Displays for Your Library Step by Step.* For a display celebrating the great marine canvasses painted by 19th century French artist Edouard Manet see page 152 for "Manet: By the Sea." For an idea featuring pirates see page 143 for the display "The Legend of Blackbeard."

The Plain People

Migrating, dividing, struggling and standing together, the Amish people have lived a story which is rich and deep. — Steven M. Nolt, *The History of the Amish*

The Amish people in America are an old religious sect descended from the Anabaptists of 16th-century Europe. During the Protestant Reformation, these Anabaptist Christians challenged the reforms of several religious leaders, including Martin Luther, who proposed revolutionary challenges to some of Rome's basic teachings. They rejected the concept of infant baptism in favor of adult baptism by choice. They also favored separation of church and state which was a unique philosophy for the time. Eventually, a large group sought religious refuge in Switzerland and other remote areas of Eu-

The Plain People. A black Amish carriage with the silhouette of the driver tells the story of the simple life lead by the Plain People of Pennsylvania. Garden tools, seed packets, a crock, a horse, a chalkboard and pumpkins sit on a bed of autumn leaves.

rope. These people were known as Mennonites, after leader Menno Simons (1496–1561).

During the late 1600s a group of devout believers, under the leadership of Jakob Ammann, severed ties with the Swiss Mennonites, primarily over the concept of Meidung, or shunning. The followers of Ammann strongly believed in the excommunication of members who were disobedient or negligent. They also took issue with other practices which they felt were falling out of favor and felt that there should be a rigid regulation of costume.

All aspects of Amish life are dictated by Ordnung, a list of written or oral rules which outlined the basics beliefs of the Amish faith and helped to delineate what it means to be Amish. For an Amish person, the Ordnung may dictate all aspects of one's lifestyle, from length of dress and hair, to buggy style—even farming techniques. The Ordnung varies from community to community and order to order, which explains why you may see some Amish riding in automobiles while others don't even accept the use of battery-powered lights.

Amish clothing styles encourage modesty and separation from the world. The Amish dress in a very simple style, with virtually no ornamentation. Clothing is handmade of dark, plain fabrics. Men usually wear straight-cut suits and coats without collars, lapels or pockets. Trousers have no creases or cuffs and are worn with suspenders. Belts, sweaters, neckties and gloves are prohibited. Men's shirts are made with traditional buttons in most orders, while suit coats and vests fasten with hooks and eyes. Single young men are clean shaven, while married men are required to grow beards. Mustaches are banned. Women typically wear solid-color dresses with long sleeves and a full skirt. This is covered with a cape and an apron. Amish women never cut their hair and wear it in a braid or bun on the back of the head covered with either a small white cap or black bonnet. Clothing is secured with straight pins or snaps, stockings are black cotton and shoes are also black. Amish women are not permitted to wear patterned clothing or jewelry. The Ordnung of each Amish order may dictate matters of dress as explicit as the length of a skirt or the width of a seam. Humility, simplicity, sharing and sacrifice for the welfare of the community are emphasized within the group.

The Amish arrived on American shores with other German speaking people in two waves. The first was from about 1727 through 1790, and the second from 1815 to 1860. They originally settled in Berks, Chester and Lancaster counties in southeastern Pennsylvania. The move westward to Ohio occurred in 1808, to Indiana in 1838 and continued to Iowa in 1840. Today Amish people live in at least twenty U.S. states and the Canadian province of Ontario (Hostetler, 2).

The Amish are opposed to any technology which they feel compromises the family structure. The amenities that the rest of us use each day, such as electricity, TV, cars, phones and tractors, are considered to be a temptation that could cause pride, create disparity or lead the Amish away from their close-knit community. Consequently, these amenities are not encouraged or accepted in most orders. Most Amish cultivate their fields with horse-drawn equipment, live in houses without electrical power and are transported in horse-drawn buggies. Traditionally the Amish have relied on wood heat. Today, many homes are equipped with gas stoves situated in the living room. Central heating is regarded as an unnecessary comfort.

It is common for some Amish communities to allow the use of telephones, but not in the home. As an alternative, several Amish families will share a telephone in a wooden shanty between farms. Electricity is sometimes used in specific situations, such as electric fences for cattle, flashing electric lights on buggies, and for warming homes. Windmills are often used as a source of naturally generated electric power in such instances. It is also not unusual to see Amish using such 20th-century technologies as in-line skates, disposable diapers and gas barbecue grills, since they are not specifically banned by the Ordnung.

It is the issue of technology that creates the greatest disparity among Amish orders. The Swartzentruber and Andy Weaver Amish are ultraconservative in their use of technology. The former, for example, do not even allow the use of battery lights. Old Order Amish have little use for modern technology but are allowed to ride in motorized vehicles including planes and automobiles, though they are not allowed to own them. The New Order Amish permit the use of electricity, ownership of automobiles, modern farming machines, and telephones in the home. Amish women enjoy making quilts for their homes and for sale to supplement the income for their large families. These patterns are always geometric and feature bright, strong colors.

Amish education takes place in one-room schoolhouses which encompass all grades from first through eighth. The teacher is a young, unmarried female with an eighth-grade education. Students, referred to as "scholars," are happy to hear the school bells that shift their attention from farm work to school work. The curriculum is basic and includes reading, writing and arithmetic. The importance of religion, community and cooperation are critical elements of an Amish education. Baseball is a favorite outdoor activity for schoolchildren.

Amish children are taught to be God-fearing, hardworking and self-supporting. They are taught not to have selfish needs of privacy, space, recognition, admiration, ambition and other rewards that children in the larger society consider their birthright. Although the Bible is read in the schoolroom, interpretation is encouraged within the structure of the home. The goal is to prepare the children for usefulness by preparing them for eternity. German is the primary language spoken in the Amish home. English is introduced in the schools. Reading is stressed as it is the foundation of every other subject. After the eighth grade, children have a structured learning program conducted by their parents.

The Amish community resembles a little commonwealth. Their members claim to be ruled by the laws of brotherhood and redemption. Numerous social bonds unite them. The Amish migrate readily and, as a result, there are considerable numbers of extinct communities while others are newly formed. Due to a burgeoning birthrate, Amish schools in Lancaster County, Pennsylvania, are being erected at a rate of five per year. Only about 20 percent of the Amish elect to leave the faith altogether and "go English."

Most Amish weddings occur from late October through December in deference to the families' demands during the busy growing season and take place on Tuesdays or Thursdays, which allows for preparation and clean-up. These are joyful occasions that take place at the home of the bride's parents and assure the continuation of both the faith and the community. Parents allow their children to select a partner, but approval must be given and the deacon usually acts as a mediator. Marriage is considered a serious step within the Amish community, since divorce is prohibited and separation rare.

When a couple becomes engaged in the Lancaster region, several hundred celery plants are sown. Later, the leafy stalks will be placed in jars and serve as centerpieces at the wedding reception. The bridal dinner is indeed a feast. It includes "roast," a mixture of bread filling and chicken, mashed potatoes, cole slaw, apple sauce and creamed celery. Desserts include pies, doughnuts, fruit and Pudding and several wedding cakes, which can be homemade or store-bought.

The newlyweds spend their first night at the bride's home but are expected to join in the clean-up following the festivities the next day. Future weekends will be spent visiting relatives, where wedding gifts are usually presented. The couple will set up housekeeping in a home of their own come spring.

In Amish funerals, the bodies are first washed by family members then dressed in long underwear and clad in white clothing. Women often are dressed in their wedding attire. The corpse is then embalmed by the funeral director. Coffins are made so that only the body from the chest up is revealed. A "rough box" is an outer wooden structure into which the coffin is lowered at the gravesite. An obituary appears in the local newspaper and a viewing is held, usually three days following the death. Men and women visitors are clothed in black. A sheet is pulled back to reveal the face of the deceased. No makeup is applied on the face in this ritual.

The church service is held in the home but eulogies are not given nor are references to the deceased made. The minister instead tells the story of the creation. Chalk numbers are written on the buggies proceeding to the cemetery so that priorities are established and order is maintained. A hymn is read rather than sung, and the Lord's Prayer whispered silently. Some of the attendees will return to the home of the deceased for a simple meal.

The Amish are not immune from the tax burden applicable to all U.S. citizens. They pay real estate, income and sales taxes as well as a variety of local and state taxes. The Amish pay school taxes twice, since their real estate contributions underwrite the public schools which they do not utilize. They fully support their own schools. In general, Social Security taxes do not apply to the Amish, who do not collect from the fund.

By comparison, the Mennonites are far more worldly. They have dozens of elementary schools, more than twenty high schools, eleven colleges, and three seminaries sponsored by various Mennonite groups in North America. Higher education became a necessity as Mennonites left the farm for mission work and service opportunities.

Amish and Mennonite people, diverse as they are, have an affinity and respect for each other. They all profess nonresistance in time of war, natural disaster or national crisis. Both groups cooperate in assisting their neighbors, faraway refugees or other people in desperate circumstances. The Amish have always regarded the Mennonites as very deeply involved in higher education and in the organizational scale of modern life. The Mennonites have frequently looked upon the Amish as backward and crude. But despite a kind of love-hate relationship between the Amish and the Mennonites, the Amish people are remarkably free of judgmental attitudes toward those outside their faith (Hostetler, 5).

Additional information for this display topic can be found if you visit http://pittsburgh. about.com/cs/pennsylvania/a/amish_2.htm or http://www.dutchcrafters.com/aboutamish. aspx.

Credits

I have lived in Pennsylvania the great majority of my life. Consequently, I am fairly well acquainted with the Amish way of life.

Settlements of the Plain People encircle me in the Lehigh Valley. I have purchased their produce, admired their fertile farms and their fetching offspring, and followed close behind their horse drawn buggies. Each encounter has given me pause. I wonder how the Amish continue this existence with blatant disregard for modern conveniences. I marvel at the amount of work that goes into survival each and every day. I question how this group manages to keep the majority of their youth returning to the fold generation after generation. And, so, it seemed inevitable that I share these people and this culture with you in a display on "The Plain People of Pennsylvania."

Assembling the Display

1. The background for this display was gray felt. The font chosen for the title "Plain People" was Berlin Sans FB Demi sized at 210. The word *the* was created using Monotype Corsiva sized at 120. These words were printed on card stock and traced onto black poster board. They were then glued to a 13" square of red/orange poster board made to resemble a quilt square. The illustration of the buggy was found through a Google image search and drawn freehand onto black poster board with silver poster board embellishments. Silver and gray chalks were used to add distress to the look of the buggy's tire. Black metal stars were attached with pins.

Books featured in the top of the display were *The Amish Cook* by Elizabeth Coblentz, *Rumspringa: To Be or Not to Be Amish* by Tom Shachtman, and *The Riddle of the Amish Culture* by Donald B. Kraybill. A wooden quilt square and a homespun doll were placed in the left center of the books.

2. On the top left was a document titled "Amish in America." Clip art of a farm was inserted on the top right. This information can be found if you visit http://pittsburgh.about.com/cs/pennsylvania/a/amish.htm. Under that was a quote by Steven M. Nolt from *A History of the Amish* which introduced this display. The next document was a synopsis of the funeral service which can be found if you visit http://www.amishnews.com/amisharticles/religioustraditions.htm#Part%20Six:%20The%20Funeral%20Service.

Last was an overview of the Amish wedding found in the book of the same name by Stephen Scott. Online information can be found if you visit http://www.amishnews.com/amisharticles/religioustraditions.htm#Part%20Seven:%20The%20Amish%20Wedding.

Items on the left were printed on off white card stock and mounted on red and black poster board.

3. On the top right was a document titled "Amish Beliefs and Customs." This information can be found if you visit http://www.squidoo.com/amish-customs. Clip art of Amish images were inserted at the top and bottom of the document. Under that was a quote from an unknown Amish farmer:

> The children are our most important crop.

Last was a document titled "The Amish School." Clip art of an Amish school was inserted in the top of the document. Information on this topic can be obtained if you visit http://www.800padutch.com/amishschools.shtml.

Items on the right were printed and mounted like those on the left.

4. On the base of the display were a canning jar tied with a raffia bow filled with gold and ercu silk flowers, a jug, two resin pumpkins, an iron horse, a spade and clippers, two miniature husks of dried corn, a slate board and seed packets, along with the books *Plain Secrets* by Joe Mackall and *A Day in the Life of the Amish* by Roy Reiman. The seed packets were found through a Google image search, printed on card stock and taped to form packets. Red, yellow and orange silk leaves were spread on the base of the case. The word *pumpkin* was created using the font Anja Eliane sized at 120. This was printed on white card stock using black type and selecting "outline" then glued to the slate.

Bigger and Better

Should your space be larger you might add a haystack, a wooden wagon, rake, watering can, some stalks of corn and various sizes and colors of pumpkins, a basket of apples or eggs, a figure of a rooster or chicken, as well as gourds, corn husks and additional silk flowers. This display would be effective mounted in the fall with real leaves strewn throughout the showcase.

Line the case with an actual quilt should you have one available to you. An Amish hat or bonnet could be included along with horseshoes, primitive candles with stands, Amish dolls, sunflowers, wire rimmed glasses and a Bible. Salt dough or resin pastries and breads could also be included. Create simple silhouettes of an Amish male and female and use them as the focal point of your display.

Appendix: Month by Month Display Ideas

January

"Someday We'll Laugh About This" Week: The first week in January is dedicated to stress management in the form of humor. Statistics show that it usually takes less than seven days for people to violate 90 percent of their New Year's resolutions. This timeframe is dedicated to the art of laughing at ourselves. What a great way to start the new year—laughing out loud at the humorous human condition!

In the late fall, begin preparations for this display. Have students or patrons submit short essays about "that day gone wrong." Select the best, enlarge and mount. Include photos of the authors and offer prizes to encourage participation. Include books on stress management and humor. Feature some tongue-in-cheek lists of New Year's resolutions from staff members. Use bright colors.

Money Matters: As people's lives resume some normalcy after the hectic holiday pace and the tax forms from the IRS arrive in the mail, a display on managing money is sure to attract your patrons. Print bills found through an online image search on white card stock and create a poster background by gluing the bills on black poster board three across and eight to ten down. Choose 3 different denominations. Select a bold font like Impact and create the title of the display. Print it on card stock and trace onto black poster board. Glue the title over the currency.

Feature current money management guides and make up some handouts with quick tips on managing your money. For college libraries visit this site for information to include in your handouts: http://www.getrichslowly.org/blog/2006/08/30/27-money-tips-for-college-students/. Print some bills on paper, cut them out and place them in and around the books. Elevate a piggy bank in the center with coins around the base.

Dalí: The popular artist died on January 23, 1989. For an eye-catching title graphic for the display, visit the Website of the museum in St. Petersburg, FL: http://www.salvadordalimuseum. org/. Feature examples of his art from Cubism, Futurism and Metaphysical painting to Surrealism.

Include information regarding the marriage to wife Gala, who served as his muse and frequent subject. Feature his famous work *The Persistence of Memory*, which is housed in the MoMA in New York City.

Feature *Salvador Dalí 2v* by Robert Descharmes and Gilles Neret; include *The Secret Life of Salvador Dalí* by Salvador Dalí and Haakon M. Chevalier and *Diary of a Genius* by Salvador Dalí and J. G. Ballard.

The 1970s: As the new year begins, reflect on this earlier decade. Use the graphic which incorporates a 331/3 rpm record as the zero in the numeral. This can be found if you visit http://www.inthe70s.com/generated/terms.shtml. Include a tape recorder, perios shoes, sunglasses, hot pants, boots, bell-bottom pants, Silly Putty, Rubic's cube, Batman, GI Joe, slime, Charles Schulz's Peanuts, Swatch watches, Barbie, Atari game system.

Highlight events such as the deaths of Elvis, Chairman Mao, Lyndon Johnson and Charles de Gaulle. *Star Wars* debuted on the big screen during that period, disco emerged as a new dance craze and *Charlie's Angels* dazzled TV audiences. Lance Armstrong, Mariah Carey, Christina Applegate, Ben Affleck, and other stars were born in this decade. For more information on the 1970s visit http://www.kyrene.org/schools/brisas/sunda/decade/1970.htm.

Organize This! The beginning of new year is the perfect time to get organized. Place baskets in the display case filled with like objects. Include a wastebasket with items that should be regularly discarded, like mail and newspapers. Create a poster with tips for getting organized. For ideas visit http://www.webmd.com/balance/guide/how-to-get-organized and http://www.goodhousekeeping.com/home/organizing/how-to-get-organized.

Feature Getting Organized by Stephanie Winston, *Organizing from the Inside Out, Second*

Edition: The Foolproof System For Organizing Your Home, Your Office and Your Life by Julie Morganstern and *Organizing Plain and Simple: A Ready Reference Guide with Hundreds of Solutions to Your Everyday Clutter Challenges* by Donna Smallin.

Mexico: Zapatista Rebellion:—Declaring war against the government of President Carlos Salinas de Gortari, the Zapatista National Liberation Army seized four towns in the state of Chiapas in southern Mexico in January 1994. The rebel group, which took its name from the early 20th century Mexican revolutionary Emiliano Zapata, issued a declaration stating that they were protesting discrimination against the Indian population of the region and against their severe poverty.

For related material feature Lucia St. Clair Robson's *Last Train to Cuernavaca* and *The Mexican Revolution: 1910–1940* by Michael J. Gonzales and Lyman L. Johnson. Include the flag of Mexico along with some cactus and desert flowers. Feature photos of Mexican revolutionaries available through a Google image search.

National Personal Self-Defense Awareness Month: Schedule a self defense program at your library in conjunction with this exhibit. The thrust of this display is to educate women and teens about realistic self defense options that could very well save their lives. Emphasize the importance of becoming physically fit in order to defend themselves.

For an easy and effective graphic for this display, visit http://www.breaking-free.net/products.html.

Feature *Fight Like a Girl ... and Win: Defense Decisions for Women* by Lori Hartman Gervasi, *See Sally Kick Ass: A Woman's Guide to Personal Safety* by Fred Vogt and *Self-Defense for Peaceable People: Defend Yourself Regardless of Size, Gender, Age and Strength* by J.G. Townsend.

February

James Joyce: February 2, 1882, marks the birth of the Irish novelist and poet, in Dublin, Ireland. Considered a formidable author, Joyce's *Ulysses* topped virtually all the literary lists ranking the top 100 books of the 20th century. Joyce died at the age of 58 of peritonitis in Zurich, Switzerland, on January 13, 1941. For biographical information on this controversial literary figure visit http://www.biography.com/articles/James-Joyce-9358676. For the Joyce coat of arms around which you can create this display visit http://www.zazzle.com/joyce_irish_family_heraldic_shield_crest_postage-172249590457700755.

Include literary criticisms of Joyce's work, and his other famous works *Portrait of the Artist as a Young Man, Dubliners* and *Finnegans Wake*.

Have a Heart: Go Red!: Cardiovascular disease kills over 432,000 women each year—about one every minute. However, studies show that only 21 percent of women view heart disease as their greatest threat. February is American Heart Month. Feature the red dress logo found on the American Heart Association web page. You may want to create a poster with the copies of the red dress logo forming a perimeter around your title signage. Include an arrangement of fruits and vegetables among the books on maintaining a healthy heart.

Feature heart healthy cook books, e.g., *The Women's Healthy Heart Program: Lifesaving Strategies for Preventing and Healing Heart Disease* by Nieca Goldberg.

Fat Tuesday: Create a true Mardi Gras on the Tuesday before Ash Wednesday. Feature masks, necklaces, balloons, feathers, confetti, a king's crown and noisemakers from the dollar store. Provide background information about the origin of the celebration and include some photos of Mardi Gras celebrations.

For its unmatched exuberance, lively spirits, and city-wide participation, the Mardi Gras celebration in New Orleans is regarded as the most extravagant of all American festivals. The parades create a sense of community and a bond of frivolity, love and tradition in a city still bent on recovering from the devastation caused by hurricane Katrina. For a graphic idea visit http://www.marinemotorsports.com/poker09.htm.

Feature *Masking and Madness: Mardi Gras in New Orleans* by Kerri McCafferty and Cynthia Reece McCafferty, *Mardi Gras* by Dianne M. MacMillan, *Mardi Gras Mambo* by Greg Herren and *Mardi Gras: A Cajun Country Celebration* by Diane Hoyt-Goldsmith.

Culture and Change: Black History in America: Pay homage to the African American contribution of inventions to the fabric of our culture. Inventions you could include range from developing peanut butter to curing blindness! Throughout history, African Americans have invented some important and amusing devices. Read about ten examples of both men and women and see what they invented. Visit http://teacher scholastic.com/activities/bhistory/inventors/.

Describe the kind of obstacles they may have faced, personally and professionally.

Create a graphic with the words *The Top Ten* in bold lettering emblazoned with the various inventions mentioned in your text. For additional African American inventors visit http://inventors.about.com/od/blackinventors/a/black_inventors.htm.

Feature *African American Inventors* by Otha Richard Sullivan, *African American Inventors* by Stephen Currie and *Black Pioneers of Science and Invention* by Louis Haber.

Honoré Daumier: The Drawings: This 19th century illustrator, painter and sculptor was born and died in the month of February. Daumier was a biting political cartoonist who contributed satirical drawings to various Paris weeklies for most of his career. His illustrations were frequently placed in the windows of newspaper offices so that the illiterate citizens could be informed of newsworthy events happening in their community. Nearly all of Daumier's cartoons were done with lithography. For biographical information of the artist visit http://www.masterworksfineart.com/inventory/daumier/#biography.

Feature one of Daumier's famous 1834 illustrations, a massacre of nineteen people, including women and children, titled "Rue Transnonain." He also created many illustrations of people traveling by rail. Lay a French flag on the base of your display and add some fleur de lis.

Include *Honoré Daumier* by Bruce Laughton, *Daumier: 120 Great Lithographs* by Honoré Daumier and *The Drawings of Daumier* by Honoré Daumier and Stephen Longstreet.

Frank Gehry: Architect: Ephraim Owen Goldberg was born on February 28, 1929, in Toronto, Canada. He moved with his family to Los Angeles in 1947 and later became a naturalized U.S. citizen. His father soon changed the family's name to Gehry. Ephraim adopted the name Frank in his 20s. He took his first architecture course and became enthralled with the possibilities of the art, although he found himself hampered by his lack of skill as a draftsman. Sympathetic teachers and an early encounter with modernist architect Raphael Soriano confirmed his career choice. He won scholarships to the University of Southern California, graduated with a degree in architecture in 1954 and later studied at Harvard.

Gehry's most spectacular design to date was that of the new Guggenheim Museum in Bilbao, Spain, completed in 1997. Gehry first envisioned its form through a simple freestyle hand sketch, but breakthroughs in computer software had enabled him to build in increasingly eccentric shapes, sweeping irregular curves that were the antithesis of the severely rectilinear International Style.

Feature photos of the Bilbao structure, the American Center in Paris and the Walt Disney Concert Hall in Los Angeles, CA. For a list of Gehry's innovative body of work visit http://www.greatbuildings.com/architects/Frank_Gehry.html.

Feature *Conversations with Frank Gehry* by Barbara Isenberg, *Frank O. Gehry: Selected Works, 1969 to Today* by Casey C.W. Mathewson and *Frank O. Gehry: Since 1997* by Germano Celant.

March

Ladies First: March is Women's History Month. Celebrate the country's First Ladies in a display featuring some of the formidable women who supported their husband in the nation's top job. Include Martha Washington,

Dolley Madison, Abigail Adams, Edith Roosevelt, Helen Taft, Eleanor Roosevelt, Mamie Eisenhower, Jacqueline Kennedy, Barbara Bush and Michelle Obama. Cut out and mount some of the portraits in ovals and others in rectangles. Use a red, white and blue motif. For information visit http://www.whitehouse.gov/about/first-ladies.

Include information about the National First Ladies Museum located in Canton, Ohio. The only facility of its kind, the museum serves as a national archive devoted to educating people about the contributions of First Ladies and other notable women in history. For information visit http://www.firstladies.org/default.aspx.

Check out the Smithsonian Website for information about the inaugural gowns worn by these women: http://americanhistory.si.edu/exhibitions/exhibition.cfm?key=38&exkey=1239. Feature First Lady biographies.

Women at War: Much has been written about the involvement of women both as nurses and as soldiers in the Civil War. It has been determined that women bore arms and charged into battle, too. Like the men, there were women who lived in camps, suffered in prisons, and died for their respective causes. The existence of soldier-women was no secret during or after the Civil War. The reading public was well aware that these women rejected Victorian social constraints that confined them to the domestic sphere. Their motives were open to speculation, perhaps, but not their actions, as numerous newspaper stories and obituaries of women soldiers testified.

Feature *Women in the Civil War* by Mary Elizabeth Massey and Jean V. Berlin, *They Fought Like Demons: Women Soldiers in the Civil War* by DeAnne Blanton and Laura M. Cook, *Women in the Civil War: Extraordinary Stories of Soldiers, Spies, Nurses, Doctors, Crusaders and Others* by Larry G. Eggleston, and *I'll Pass for Your Comrade: Women Soldiers in the Civil War* by Anita Silvey.

There are many photos available online and in the books mentioned above that help that tell the story of the women dedicated to combat in this strife. Personal accounts can be enlarged and serve as the focal point of this display. Use red, white and blue for background and include any artifacts you can find from Civil War collectors in your area. Civil War posters are also available online. Include Confederate and Union flags. For online information about female soldiers in the Civil War visit http://americancivilwar.com/women.

Castles of Ireland: Create the simple Irish flag (orange, white and green) which will serve as the background for your display. Feature the castles of Ireland seen in the book *Medieval Castles of*

Ireland by P. David Sweetman. Include an iron pot with gold coins. Make some clover out of various shades of green poster board and place them among the books. Pull some information from the book *I Never Knew That About Ireland* by Christopher Winn and mount it on the sides of the display. Add a kilt, a pint of Guinness, U-2 CDs, DVDs of *Angela's Ashes, The Gangs of New York* and *In the Name of the Father,* Irish dance shoes and a rock symbolizing the Blarney Stone. Feature a bagpipe if you have the luck of the Irish and can locate one!

Feature the books *The "Daily Telegraph" Castles and Ancient Monuments of Ireland: A Unique Guide to More Than 150 Historic Sites* by Damien Noonan and *Castles of Ireland* by Mairéad Fitzgerald.

Ordinary Genius: Born March 14, 1879, Albert Einstein's lived a remarkable life. His theories and research remain critical to this day.

Procure a poster of Einstein. There are many great ones available. Include a time line of his achievements, noting the Nobel Prize for physics in 1921. For this information visit http://www.fortunecity.com/village/montgomery/683/timeline.html.

Feature the many and provocative quotes attributed to him which can be found if you visit http://www.brainyquote.com/quotes/authors/a/albert_einstein.html.

Include information about Einstein's years at Princeton, which is available at http://www.einstein-website.de/z_biography/idwestn-e.html

Display a violin—an instrument Einstein loved—and a compass, which he received as a boy of five, a Princeton University pennant or symbol, and a slide rule and other tools a physicist might use.

Feature *Einstein: His Life and Universe* by Walter Isaacson, *Albert Einstein: A Biography* by Milton Meltzer and *Einstein: A Biography* by Jürgen Neffe.

Disaster!: March is National Red Cross Month. Display photos of the recent disasters such as the earthquake in Haiti, floods and tornadoes in the Midwest, the BP oil spill and hurricane Katrina. In the center of the photo place the symbol of the American Red Cross. Provide information about how this organization was founded and the manner in which it comes to the rescue in all of these disasters.

Feature *The Unthinkable: Who Survives When Disaster Strikes—And How We Can Do Better* by Amanda Ripley, *When All Hell Breaks Loose: Stuff You Need To Survive When Disaster Strikes* by Cody Lundin, Russell Miller, and Christopher Marchetti and *Disasters: Natural and Man-Made Catastrophes Through the Centuries* by Brenda Z. Guiberson.

Eat This, Not That: March is National Nutrition Month. In an effort to educate consumers about the importance of good nutrition, provide the latest information about eating healthily. For information visit http://www.eatright.org. Create handouts for patrons with information from the *Eat This, Not That* series.

Feature a large food pyramid and use a larger font for the words *this* and *that*. Include the popular nutrition series by David Zinczenko and Matt Goulding along with *Nutrition: Concepts and Controversies* by Frances Sizer and Ellie Whitney and *Understanding Nutrition* by Eleanor Noss Whitney.

You Rang: Alexander Graham Bell was born March 3, 1847, in Edinburgh, Scotland. He acquired his interest in the transmission of sound from his father, Melville Bell, a teacher of the deaf. On March 10, 1876, Bell spoke the first intelligible electrically transmitted sentence to his assistant in the next room, "Mr. Watson, come here. I want you." Include a vintage telegraph, princess phones, dial phones, wall phones, period phones, early and later cell phones. Provide a time line of the evolution of the telephone, a biography of the inventor and information on the importance of this invention.

Feature *America Calling: A Social History of the Telephone to 1940* by Claude S. Fischer and *Old-time Telephones!: Design, History, and Restoration* by R.O. Meyer.

April

Ponce de Leon: April 2, 1513, marks the discovery of Florida by explorer Ponce de Leon. He landed at the site that became the city of St. Augustine which he claimed for the king of Spain. However, he didn't realize he had landed in North America. He thought he had landed on an island.

He named his discovery Florida because he saw lots of flowers ("florida" in Spanish means "flowery"). On the return trip he landed on the west coast of Florida where he encountered hostile Native Americans. He was shot by arrows and died in July, 1521.

Create a map of Florida and place de Leon's portrait over the city of St. Augustine. For a map of his route visit http://cheyennelopezwhite.glogster.com/Ponce-de-Leon/.

Include lots of tropical flowers, a pelican and other tropical birds and butterflies.

Feature *Ponce de Leon: Exploring and Puerto Rico* by Rachel Eagen and *Juan Ponce De Leon* by Jane Sutcliffe.

Poetry Speaks: April is National Poetry Month. There is an easy graphic idea available for inspiration for this display if you visit http://readwritepoem.org/blog/2009/10/07/what-is-poetry-featuring-joan-houlihan/. The word *poetry* is positioned off-center and is the largest of the words placed on the background of the display.

Inspirational words are placed both vertically and horizontally around the main word.

Select poems about specific themes such as love, family, happiness, death, etc. For more ideas on particular themes visit http://www.poetryarchive.org/poetryarchive/themes.do.

Scatter silk flowers around the books of poetry, if appropriate to the theme.

Provide some background information about the various types of poetry such as ballad, blank verse, couplet, elegy, etc. For a complete glossary of terms visit http://www.poetryarchive.org/poetry archive/themes.do.

Leonardo: April 15, 1452, marked the birth of Leonardo da Vinci, a master of both the world of art and the world of the sciences. Leonardo was a painter, sculptor, architect, musician, engineer, inventor, and scientist. He is probably the most famous figure from the Renaissance period. He made painstaking observations and carried out research in fields ranging from architecture and civil engineering to astronomy, anatomy, zoology, geography, geology and paleontology.

Choose either da Vinci's artwork, his inventions or his scientific contributions. Should you decide to feature his drawings, they are available for downloading at http://www.drawings ofleonardo.org/. If you decide on his inventions, visit http://www.leonardo-da-vincibiography.com/leonardo-da-vinci-inventions.html. There are a many great Websites with images of his art that will make a compelling display. Line the background with some of these images.

Feature *Leonardo da Vinci: Flights of the Mind* by Charles Nicholl, *Leonardo's Notebooks* edited by H. Anna Suh and *Leonardo da Vinci: The Marvelous Works of Nature and Man* by Martin Kemp.

National Library Week: Check the ALA Website for the actual week in April that this week is celebrated and for posters to purchase for your library display. Include balloons, confetti, current best sellers and award winning books. For information about the value of the library visit http://www.uneca.org/codi/documents/pdf/library%20services%20and%20development.pdf.

Have cupcakes or candy available and tie balloons to the front of the library. Organize a brown bag lunch and obtain a speaker (a local author, or a member of the humanities department) to speak on the topic of the value of the library.

Be sure to include this sentiment in your display: "Long Live Libraries—the places that host the convergence of the Gutenberg and digital technologies of yesterday and today!" Feature *The Most Beautiful Libraries in the World* by Jacques Bosser and *Library: An Unquiet History* by Matthew Battles as well as books on the inventions of the printing press and the birth of virtual libraries.

De-Stress: April is Stress Awareness Month. Mount a display to promote public awareness of what stress is, what causes it to occur and what can be done about it. For information visit http://www.stresscure.com.

For an easy graphic for this display, visit http://52weeksofimpact.org/2010/04/14/april-mic-week-2-%E2%80%93-identify-your-stressors/.

Feature *Finding Serenity in the Age of Anxiety* by Robert Gerzon, *Present Moment Awareness: A Simple, Step-by-Step Guide to Living in the Now* by Shannon Duncan and *Seven Day Stress Buster* by Jenny Alexander.

Washington Irving: Irving was born on April 3, 1783. During his lifetime, he became an acclaimed author both here and abroad. He was also an attorney and one-time minister to Spain. Irving created *Rip Van Winkle* and *The Legend of Sleepy Hollow* and was the author of many historical and biographical works, including *A History of the Life and Voyages of Christopher Columbus* and *The Life of Washington*. Many of Irving's works have inspired adaptations to the stage and film.

Enlarge the cover art on *Rip Van Winkle* and *The Legend of Sleepy Hollow* for the focal point of your display. These can be found if you visit http://scrapetv.com/News/News%20Pages/Health/Pages/Doctor-pioneering-use-of-Comas-on-demand-Scrape-TV-The-World-on-your-side.html and http://www.acmamall.com/children-books-by-washington-irving.html.

Include *Washington Irving: An American Original* by Brian Jay Jones along with the many books by the author. Be sure to include his memorable quotations.

May

The Sporting Life: Celebrate the sport of horseback riding in the month which begins the quest for the Triple Crown in the sport of horse racing. Incorporate an equestrian riding helmet, chaps, spurs, gloves, some blue ribbons and a crop. Add a figurine of a horse. Draw a simple split rail fence and hang the sign from the top rail. Use a cursive font for the title signage. Or, feature an equestrian print, should you have one available.

Feature *Out Stealing Horses: A Novel* by Per Petterson, *Three Horses: A Novel* by Erri De Luca, *Back at the Track* by Martin H. Greenberg and any of the Dick Francis novels.

Action!: The oldest film festival is usually held the third week in May in Cannes, France. This glamorous event attracts global attention to the world of cinema. The Toronto Festival is scheduled for early May and the Sundance Film Festival in September. If your prefer to mount this around a local film festival, check your community arts calendar.

Mount a display celebrating the great film directors of all time. Include Alfred Hitchcock. H.G. Wells, John Huston, Stanley Kubrick, Steven Spielberg, Martin Scorcese, and others. For a full list of the great men behind the scene visit http://digitaldreamdoor.nutsie.com/pages/ movie-pages/movie_directors.html.

There are many easy graphics of the back of a director's chair. For inspiration visit http://www. fotosearch.com/ARP124/hw_director_chair2/. Create this with a megaphone and position it above the chair. Go to http://www.essentialpartyrentals.com for graphic inspiration for a megaphone and place the word *Action!* on it. If possible, add a clapper. Choose award winning films to include in this display and list the top directors and their best work.

Growing Wild!: National Wildflowers Week is the first full week in May. Create a poster using several varieties of silk or dried wildflowers tied together with raffia. Use a graceful, cursive font for the signage. Include biographical information about former first lady Lady Bird Johnson, who worked tirelessly to beautify America throughout her lifetime. Visit http://www.wildflower.org/ for information about wildflowers and the Lady Bird Johnson Wildflower Center at the University of Texas at Austin. Describe the wildflowers native to your area and provide photos. Show photos of wildflower gardens.

Feature *National Wildlife Federation Field Guide to Wildflowers of North America* by David M. Brandenburg and Craig Tuftsby and *National Audubon Society Field Guide to North American Wildflowers* (revised edition) by the National Audubon Society.

Epic Expedition: Lewis & Clark: In May of 1803, Thomas Jefferson sent Meriwether Lewis and William Clark's Corps of Discovery to find a water route to the Pacific and explore the uncharted West. Jefferson believed woolly mammoths, erupting volcanoes, and a mountain of pure salt awaited them. What they found was no less mind-boggling: some 300 species unknown to science, nearly 50 Indian tribes, and the Rockies.

Include portraits of the explorers, Thomas Jefferson and the Native American tour guide Sacagewea. List some of the animal species found on the expedition, and illustrations and descriptions the Native American tribes they encountered. Include excerpts from the journals kept by kept by Lewis and Clark. This information can be found if you visit http://www.nationalgeographic.com/lewisandclark/record_species_090_1.html.

Feature a map of the expedition which can be found at http://www.pbs.org/weta/thewest/places/ trails_ter/lewis.htm.

Include *Undaunted Courage: Meriwether Lewis, Thomas Jefferson, and the Opening of the American West* by Stephen Ambrose and *How We Crossed the West: The Adventures of Lewis and Clark* by Rosalyn Schanzer.

Mom's Favorite: As the title implies, siblings always think that their brother or sister was their mother's favorite. May 2nd is Sibling Appreciation Day. Mount photos of your students, patrons or staff with their siblings and caption them with humorous comments. Don't have a sibling? Consider joining Big Brothers or Big Sisters. Have handouts for that organization available near your display. Ask patrons, staff or students to write a little blurb describing the positive characteristics of their siblings.

Add some famous siblings, such as the Manning brothers (pro quarterbacks) the Osmonds, the Smothers brothers, Kate and Oliver Hudson, Maggie and Jake Gyllenhaal and Serena and Venus Williams.

Feature *Sibling Without Rivalry: How to Help Your Children Live Together So You Can Live Too* by Adele Faber, *Beyond Sibling Rivalry: How to Help Your Children Become Cooperative, Caring and Compassionate* by Peter Goldenthal and *Siblings* by Nick Kelsh and Anna Quindlen.

Wish You Were Here: The first full week in May is National Postcard Week. Have staff or students bring in postcards from their collections. Scan the front and back of the postcards and arrange them in a collage under the title signage. To personalize the display, use a cursive font for the title. Choose from the many books published in the Postcard History Series to feature in this display. Also include *Boring Postcards* by Martin Parr and *Greetings From the Ocean's Sweaty Face: 100 McSweeney's Postcards* by McSweeney's.

Be sure to put up signage several months in advance asking for postcards from your patrons (which will be returned to them).

We Salute...: The third Saturday in May was named Armed Forces Day by presidential proclamation in 1989. Now's the time to acknowledge the men and women who serve in the armed services worldwide. Hang photos and mailing addresses of area men and women who are deployed oversees around the title signage. Set up an area where donations of personal hygiene items can be collected and sent to those being celebrated.

Feature *America's Armed Forces: A History* (2nd edition) by James M. Morris, *U.S.*

Army Special Operations Forces by Jeremy Roberts and *U.S. Armed Forces Survival Guide* by John Boswell.

June

Henry Tudor's Wives: Better known as Henry VIII, Henry Tudor was born June 28, 1491. Since he was the second son and not expected to become king, little is known of his childhood until the death of his older brother Arthur, Prince of Wales. We know that Henry attended the wedding celebrations of Arthur and his bride, Catherine of Aragon, in November 1501 when he was 10 years old. He would later take Catherine as his wife, and the rest is history. Use the graphic available at http://thefastertimes.com/nonfiction/2009/06/23/henry-viii-divorce-letter-unveiled/ for inspiration. Choose an appropriate font for this, such as Cloister Black available for a free download at http://www.dafont.com.

Provide brief biographies of Henry's six wives and the manner of their death or dismissal through divorce. Provide information about Henry's relationship with the church with regard to the dissolution of his marriages. Feature *The Six Wives of Henry VIII* by Alison Weir, *The Children of Henry VIII* by Alison Weir and *The Wives of Henry VIII* by Antonia Fraser.

Include a king's crown, jewels, pewter goblets, grapes, fruit, a cross and the Tudor coat of arms, which is available if you visit http://www. tudorlovers.com/dynasty/dynasty.htm. For comprehensive information about this English royal, visit http://www.tudorhistory.org/wives/.

Dreamcatchers: Dreamcatchers are one of the most fascinating customs of Native Americans. The traditional dream catcher was intended to protect the sleeping individual from negative dreams while letting positive dreams through. The positive dreams would slip through the hole in the center of the dream catcher and glide down the feathers to the sleeping person below. The negative dreams would get caught up in the web and expire when the first rays of the sun struck them. The dream catcher has been a part of Native American culture for generations. One element of Native American dream catchers relates to the tradition of the hoop. Some Native Americans held the hoop in the highest esteem because it symbolized strength and unity. Many symbols started around the hoop, and one of these symbols is the dream catcher.

Use colors of the Southwest for this display. Arrange a program where patrons or students have the opportunity to make dreamcatchers. For an online tutorial visit http://www.freewebs.com/ndnwoman59/craftonedreamcatchers.htm. Hang dreamcatchers at varying heights in the display case. Enlarge and mount on foam or poster board the poem about the meaning of dreamcatchers found at http://www.soultones.com/dream.html. Add some other Native American crafts: beaded jewelry, baskets, turquoise. Line the case with Native American blankets.

Feature *Dreamcatcher* by Lori Byrd, *Indian Handcrafts* (revised edition) by C. Keith Wilbur and *Dreamcatchers: A Journey into Native-American Spirituality* by John James Stewart.

The World's Wonders: Use *1,000 Places to See Before You Die: A Traveler's Life List* by Patricia Schultz as your guide to create a display based on the places you must add to your "bucket list." The urge to travel—to expand horizons and move beyond the familiar—is as old as man himself.

Feature the anonymous quote "Life is not measured by the number of breaths we take but by the places and moments that take our breath away." Use an italic font and print on white card stock. Mount on colored poster board. Use greens and blues and yellows in this display. Attach an atlas to the back of the display. Include a globe, a passport, a compass and sunglasses. Mark the places you are featuring and provide background information. Include photos of such places as Count Dracula's Castle in Romania, Santa's Village in Finland, Stone Town in Zanzibar and New Zealand's Tasman Glacier.

Feature travel guides and also books such as *Sacred Places of a Lifetime: 500 of the World's Most Peaceful and Powerful Destinations* by National Geographic, *Frommer's 500 Places to See Before They Disappear* by Holly Hughes and *1,001 Natural Wonders You Must See Before You Die* by Michael Bright.

Tap Our Talent: Secure artwork from local artists or contact your Art Department for possible student contributions. Add biographies of the artists and a statement of their artistic process. Embellish with flowers. Feature *An Introduction to Acrylics* by Ray Smith, *Imaginative Realism: How to Paint What Doesn't Exist* by James Gurney and *How to Make a Watercolor Paint Itself: Experimental Techniques for Achieving Realistic Effects* by Nita Engle.

Cousteau: Born June 11, 1910, Jacques Cousteau—a French undersea explorer, writer and filmmaker—was born at St. Andres-de-Cubzac, France. He invented the Aqualung, which allowed him and his colleagues to produce more than 80 documentary films about undersea life, two of which won Oscars. This scientist and explorer was awarded the French Legion of Honor for his work in the Resistance in World War II. He died June 25, 1997.

For biographical information visit http://www.cousteau.org/news/anniversary.

Include some shipping ropes, shells, rocks, sand, a compass, a ship's wheel, an anchor and some fishing nets. Scan and enlarge the cover of the March 28, 1960, issue of *Time* magazine with Cousteau on the cover.

Feature *Jacques Cousteau* by Lesley A. Dutemple, *Jacques Cousteau: The Sea King* by Bradford Matsen and *My Father the Captain: My Life with Jacques Cousteau* by Jean-Michel Cousteau.

On Time: Arrange clocks of various dimensions on the background of your display. Provide information on timepieces of old, such as sundials and hourglasses. Include pocket and wrist watches, mantel and miniature clocks.

Feature information on physicist and mathematician Sir Isaac Newton. Also include theoretical physicist Stephen Hawking, a proponent of the possibility of time travel.

Include this oft repeated quote by early science fiction writer, Ray Cummings: "Time ... is what keeps everything from happening at once." Feature books on time travel such as *Faces in Time: A Time Travel Thriller* by Lewis E. Aleman,

The Time Traveler's Wife by Audrey Niffenegger and *The Reluctant Time Traveler* by Lynda Eymann.

July

Battlefield Gettysburg: This significant battle took place on July 1, 1863. After the Southern success at Chancellorsville, Virginia, Confederate General Robert E. Lee led his forces on an invasion of the North, initially targeting Harrisburg, Pennsylvania. As Union forces moved to counter the invasion, the battle lines were eventually formed at Gettysburg, Pennsylvania, in one of the Civil War's most crucial battles. The year 2013 will mark the 150th anniversary of this historic battle where more men fought and died than in any other battle in American history.

For a relatively simple graphic inspiration visit http://www.brettschulte.net/CWBlog/2008/07/22/gettysburg-magazine-issue-39-arrives/. Use the font Heldorado, which can be downloaded free if you visit http://www.dafont.com.

Check with your local American Civil War Society to find out their policies on loaning items for your exhibit. Include Civil War memorabilia such as a miniature canon, drum, tin cup, caps, and Confederate and Union flags. Include maps, photos of the military involved, a time line and books on this battle.

Degas and the Dance: Edgar Degas was born July 19, 1834, and 2017 will mark the centennial of his death. The painter portrayed the Paris Opera-Ballet in more than 1,500 works of art. He greatly admired the young dancers' athleticism and controlled energy. He tried to capture the tension inherent in the life of a working ballerina. Feature *The Dance Lesson*, and *Before the Ballet*. Include a wooden rehearsal chair, pointe shoes, a tutu, a dance bag, a tiara and a single rose. Be sure to include *The Language of Ballet: A Dictionary* by Thalia Mara, which has a Degas painting on the cover. Incorporate black and pink, the colors of dance, into your display. Add some touches of silver for effect.

Le Tour: Every year, the cycling event with the highest profile, the Tour de France, is held in early July in the country for which it is named. The Tour de France has a tradition of discovering wide open spaces that are dear to the hearts of the people of France. Riders set off through the diverse landscape of the country, sometimes crossing the borders with its European neighbors.

Celebrate this exciting sport with a display featuring the Tour de France logo which can be found if you visit http://factsaboutfrance-marjan.blogspot.com/2009/01/tour-de-france-2009-review.html.

Use a black background with white letters and a yellow bicycle wheel. Include information about the town from which it emanates the year you mount the display. Provide a graphic of the tour route and information about the terrain.

Feature a bicycle pump, helmet, cycling shirt, some sunflowers, a miniature flag of France, cycling magazines, sunglasses and a stopwatch. Feature *The Story of the Tour de France* by Bill McGann, *Inside the Tour de France: The Pictures, the Legends, and the Untold Stories of the World's Most Beloved Bicycle Race* by Eric Delanzy and *Lance Armstrong's War: One Man's Battle Against Fate, Fame, Love, Death, Scandal, and a Few Other Rivals on the Road to the Tour de France* by Daniel Coyle.

Armored Knights: Celebrate the Middle Ages as you travel back in time to explore the world of the medieval knight who was clad in protective armor. Our modern day "Renaissance Faires" can serve as inspiration for this display. Include some images of knights, their weaponry and their garb. Feature a flag of the Crusades as your graphic. This would be easy to construct and can be found at http://www. mapsofworld.com/images/world-countries-flags/georgia-flag.gif.

Include pewter tableware, goblets and pitchers. Add some bunches of grapes and other fruit. Feature *Knights in History and Legend* by Constance Brittain Bouchard, *DK Eyewitness Books: Medieval Life* by Andrew Langley, and *Warfare in the Medieval World* by Brian Todd Carey.

Billy the Kid: Reflect on the life of Henry McCarty, better known as Billy the Kid but also known by the aliases Henry Antrim and William H. Bonney He was reportedly born November 23, 1859, and died July 14, 1881. Billy the Kid was a 19th century American frontier outlaw and gunman who participated in the Lincoln County War, New Mexico.

Provide biographical information which can be found if you visit http://www.eyewitness tohistory.com/billythekid.htm. Include wanted posters, a photo of his gravesite, toy guns and holsters, a cowboy hat and a sheriff's badge.

Choose the font Bleeding Cowboys for your title signage, available for a free download if you visit http://www.dafont.com.

Man vs. Machine: The Luddite Rebellion: The Luddites were a social movement of British textile artisans in the 19th century who protested—often by destroying mechanized looms—against the changes produced by the Industrial Revolution, which they felt was leaving them without work and changing their way of life. It took its name from leader Ned Ludd. The movement emerged in the harsh economic climate of the Napoleonic Wars and difficult working conditions in the new textile factories. The principal objection of the Luddites was to the introduction of new wide-framed automated looms that could be operated by cheap, relatively unskilled labor, resulting in the loss of jobs for many skilled textile workers. The movement began in 1811 and 1812, when mills and pieces of factory machinery were burned by handloom weavers. For a short time the movement was so strong that Luddites clashed in battles with the British Army.

Give background information on the movement and its founder. This can be obtained if your visit http://www.lycos.com/info/luddites—ned-ludd.html Mount some illustrations of the early machines against which the Luddites rebelled.

Feature *Against the Machine: The Hidden Luddite Tradition in Literature, Art, and Individual Lives* by Nicols Fox, *Against Technology: From the Luddites to Neo-Luddism* by Steven E. Jones and *The Luddite Rebellion* by Brian J. Bailey.

August

From Vines to Wines: Give an overview of the process of winemaking in your area, or a wine-producing area near you. Provide photos of the grapevines, and the steps involved in producing wine. For a visual tour through the wine-making process visit http://www.winetrail.com/ initial-grapeprocessing.html. To locate the steps for winemaking visit http://ezinearticles.com/?6-Steps-of-Wine-Making&id=1951527.

Hang clusters of grapes with leaves from the top of the display case. Arrange a tableau with a tray, wine bottles and glasses filled with colored water, a French baguette, a round of cheese and some fruit.

Feature *From Vines to Wines: The Complete Guide to Growing Grapes and Making Your Own Wine* by Jeff Cox, *The Grape Grower: A Guide to Organic Viticulture* by Lon J. Rombaugh and *The Backyard Vintner: An Enthusiast's Guide to Growing Grapes and Making Wine at Home* by Jim Law.

A Guiding Light: August 7 is National Lighthouse Day. Historically, the earliest lighthouses were merely hillside bonfires built to warn ships away from the shore. The first lighthouses in North America were built in the North Atlantic to serve the brisk trade brought by clipper ships to the new world.

Place several miniature lighthouses on a bed of sand, rocks and shells. Provide a history of these structures, especially high profile lighthouses of longstanding, such as Boston Lighthouse, Farallon Lighthouse in San Francisco and the Sandy Hook Lighthouse in New Jersey.

Include a compass along with some photos of the interiors of lighthouses. *America's Lighthouses: An Illustrated History* by F. Ross Holland and *Lighthouses of North America* by Barry Pickthall.

Dogs in Art: Include paintings of working dogs, pet dogs and royal canines in a display celebrating man's favorite pet. Include figurines of dogs, plates with dog motifs, leashes and harnesses, a dog bowl and some doggie biscuits. Use blue, brown and gray for the accent colors.

Feature *Dog: 5000 Years of the Dog in Art* by Tamsin Pickeral, *Best in Show: The Dog in Art from the Renaissance to Today* by Peter Bowron, Carolyn Rose Rebbert, Robert Rosenblum and William Secord and *The Artful Dog: Canines from the Metropolitan Museum of Art* by the Metropolitan Museum of Art.

Canine art dating back to the seventeenth century reveals a long tradition of animal imagery and the continuing influence of the early Dutch and Flemish paintings on later artists. Be sure to include the works of Edwin Lanseer.

A T. rex Named Sue: In 2000, the Field Museum in Chicago debuted an exhibit titled *Sue* which celebrated the world's largest, most complete, and best preserved tyrannosaurus rex ever found. Since that time they have replicated the skeleton and several "clones" of the original Sue are currently on tour across the country.

Enlarge the photo of Sue's profile found on the Website of the Field Museum: http://www.field-museum.org/sue/#photo-gallery-special-features.

Include some photos of the excavation. Provide information on the excavation process. Line the display case with sand and rocks. The graphic of the exhibit—large, bold letters with a "triptych" of a T-Rex silhouette—would be easy and effective graphic for this display.

Feature books on archeology and *A T. rex Named Sue: Sue Hendrickson's Huge Discovery* by Natalie Lunis.

Les Belles Maisons: Feature homes such as Fallingwater by Frank Lloyd Wright, the Glass House by Phillip Johnson, Hearst Castle by Julia Morgan, any of the mansons in Newport Rhode Island and Thomas Jefferson's Monticello. Create a poster with the title signage. Use a cursive font such as Monotype Corsiva.

Include information about the homes featured and the trend toward sustainable architecture. Feature *The Green House: New Directions in Sustainable Architecture* by Alanna Stang and Christopher Hawthorne, *The House Book* by the editors of Phaidon Press and *Compact Houses: Architecture for the Environment* by Cristina del Valle.

History of Chocolate: The secret of the cacao tree was discovered 2000 years ago in the tropical rainforests of the Americas, The pods of this tree contain seeds that can be processed into chocolate. Tell the story of how chocolate grew from a local Mesoamerican drink into a desirable global beverage.

Provide information about the harvesting of the seeds, the selling of the product and the processing involved. Have the pictures tell the tale. The Field Museum in Chicago offers educators resources on this topic which can be downloaded. For this information visit http://www.fieldmuseum.org/chocolate/education.html.

Include chocolate molds, a whisk and bowl, cacao beans, and bars of cooking chocolate interspersed with Hershey's Kisses.

Feature *The True History of Chocolate* by Sophie and Michael Coe, *Chocolate: Pathway to the Gods* by Meredith Dreiss and Sharon Greenhill and *Chocolate: A Bittersweet Sage of Dark and Light* by Mort Rosenblum.

September

Digital Magic: How I Spent My Summer: Solicit digital photographs from your students, staff or patrons showing activities in which they engaged last summer, or travel they experienced. If you have a digital photography class at your school or college, ask the instructor for their cooperation. Have a professional photographer serve as a judge and award several top ribbons and lots of honorable mentions. Enlarge the winning photographs and be sure they are captioned. Make a collage of the others. Place a number on the photos within the collage and cross reference the names so the photographers are credited and captions available for those photos. Include books on digital photography and have handouts with photography tips available. Tie it into a program on digital photography.

Good Job!: Mark the unofficial end of summer with a salute to the nation's workers and their achievements. Provide information on the first Labor Day holiday, which was celebrated on Tuesday, September 5, 1882, in New York City in accordance with the plans of the Central Labor Union. In 1884, the first Monday in September was selected as the holiday and other cities were encouraged to follow the example. The idea spread with the growth of organizations and in 1885 Labor Day was celebrated as a "workingmen's holiday" in many industrial centers of the country. Include a hard hat, an array of tools and a lunch box.

For background information visit http://www.dol.gov/opa/aboutdol/laborday.htm.

An easy and colorful graphic can be found at http://rainbowuniverse.org/laborday.htm.

ADHD: Going back to school can be daunting for children affected with this learning disability. Explore the current research, the possibilities of a genetic link, the issue of gender, and the possibilities of both overdiagnosis and overmedication. Provide information about use of meditation as a way of coping with ADHD.

There is a great graphic for this display which can be found if you visit http://adhdadd.org/. It is based on the logo for the rock band AC/DC.

Use white lettering on a black background. Add some student workbooks, pill bottles, crayons and clay. Include some graphics available online of a brain affected by this disorder.

Feature books by noted authorities Edward M. Hallowell, MD, and Russell A. Barkley, PhD. Spell out the common signs of ADHD, which can be found if you visit http://www.hellolife.net/explore/add-adhd/five-surprising-facts-about-adhd/.

Fashion Forward: September marks Fashion Week in New York City. Create the skyline of the city by enlarging an image of the Empire State Building and mounting it on poster board. Cut the other buildings out of bold fabrics, glue them to poster board, and attach them to the background of the display case on either side of the Empire State Building.

For Fashion Week images, go to http://www.wwd.com/fashion-week/spring-ready-to-wear-2011?src=gokw/fashion_week/fashion_week/fashion_week&gclid=CNnHo6L9i6QCFeQD5Qod22m1LA.

Mount the images on a raised runway in the center of your display and label them with the designers. Include Michael Kors, Vera Wang, Donna Karan, Marc Jacobs, and others. Provide some information on the focus of the designers' collections and the importance of Fashion Week to the industry.

Include some images from your fashion design department. *Feature Fashion 101: A Crash Course in Clothing* by Erika Stalder and *The Fashion Designer's Directory of Shape and Style: Over 500 Mix-and-Match Elements for Creative Clothing Design* by Simon Travers-Spencer and Zarida Zaman.

Master and King: Pay homage to master storyteller Stephen King who was born September 21, 1947, in Portland, Maine. Beginning with 1974's *Carrie,* King has published 40 books and more than 200 short stories. The author of *The Shining, Pet Sematary, The Green Mile* and *The Shawshank Redemption* resents being pegged in one genre. Although he is sometimes referred to as a horror writer and sometimes as a suspense writer, he prefers to be labeled an American novelist. For comprehensive biographical information visit http://www.stephenking.com/the_author.html.

Create a poster with the word *Master* over a large kings's crown and the word *King* under it. Attach the three dimensional crown so that it protrudes and gives dimension to the display. Include his books that have been made into movies.

Star Spangled Banner: On the night of September 13, 1814, Francis Scott Key was aboard a ship that was delayed in Baltimore Harbor by the British attack there on Fort Henry. Key had no choice but to anxiously watch the battle. That experience and seeing the American flag still flying over the fort the next morning inspired him to pen the verses that, coupled with a tune of a popular drinking song, became our official national anthem in 1931, which was 117 years after the words were written. Provide a biography of the author, poet and lawyer who penned this anthem. Give some background about the state of the nation at that point in time.

Create a poster by enlarging the score to "The Star-Spangled Banner" framed in a red, white and blue border. Scatter silver stars throughout the border. Place fireworks around the poster. Cover the base of the display with a flag or banner. Include a vintage pen and inkwell, confetti and patriotic songbooks.

National Hispanic Heritage Month: September 15–October 15 was established by presidential proclamation in 1989 as a time to honor Hispanic heritage. Use these weeks to celebrate the impact Hispanics have made on the country. Celebrate Supreme Court justice Sonia Sotomayor, Senator Bill Richardson, writer Isabel Allende, boxer Oscar de la Hoya, actress Cameron Diaz, actor Martin Sheen, and singer Linda Ronstadt. For design inspiration of an historic nature go to http://sf-bart.posterous.com/celebrating-hispanic-heritage-month. To gather ideas for items to include in the display visit http://www.hmsdc. com/ds/.

Include books on famous Hispanics such as *Famous Hispanic Americans* by Wendy Dunn, *Extraordinary Hispanic Americans* by Cesar Alegre and *Famous Mexican Americans* by Janet Nomura Morey.

October

The Art of Chess: President Gerald Ford established October 9 as National Chess Day. Provide some background information on the history of the game, which is really a history of medieval times in miniature. This is available if you visit http://www.essortment.com/all/chesshistory_rmct. htm.

Chess figurines are available in such themes as rock stars, football players, Civil and Revolutionary War figures, cats and dogs, etc. Every culture is represented in chess figures. For examples see http://www.chesshouse.com/theme_chess_sets_s/81.htm Check with staff and patrons for chess sets that could be borrowed for your display.

Create a poster made of the squares of a chess board. Use a cursive font for the title. Red, white, and black embellished with gold would be good color choices for this display.

Vampires: This subject is of great fascination to people of all ages and would be a topical display around Halloween. Visit http://www.dafont. com and download the font Creepsville, which will set the tone for this display. Use the graphic of a full moon with vampire bats flying and position the first letter or two of your title over the moon. This image can be found if you visit http://www.acclaimimages.com/_gallery/_pages/ 0515-0909-1716-1931.html.

Use a purple background with black lettering for this display.

Books on vampires have great covers. Be sure to include Dracula books and those by popular authors such as Anne Rice and Stephenie Meyer.

Jackson and Lee: Jackson Pollock (1912–1956) is regarded as the undisputed leader of the Abstract Expressionist movement. In October 1945, he married fellow artist Lee Krasner (1908–1984) and moved from New York City to Long Island's East End. With a loan from art dealer Peggy Guggenheim, they purchased a small homestead on one-and-a-quarter acres overlooking Accabonac Creek in "The Springs," near East Hampton. Include examples of the Pollocks work, paint splattered cans and shoes and paintbrushes. Feature biographies of both artists which can be found if you visit http://sb.cc.stonybrook. edu/pkhouse/index.shtml.

Display *Jackson Pollock and Lee Krasner* by Ines Engelmann, *Jackson Pollock: 1912–1956* by Leonhard Emmerling, and *Lee Krasner* by Robert Carleton Hobbs.

Wicked!: Create a display in the spirit of the Halloween season. To create the title signage, use the font Bleeding Freaks available for a free download at http://www.dafont.com. Choose books with the word *Wicked* in the title. Include a witch hat, a miniature broom, and some spiders and spider webs. Open a volume of *Man, Myth & Magic* to the page on witchcraft.

Feature *Wicked: The Life and Times of the Wicked Witch of the West* by Gregory Maguire, *Wicked Appetite* by Janet Evanovich, *Wicked: Witch and Curse* by Nancy Holder and Debbie Viguié, *The Wicked Truth* and *Wicked* by Suzanne Ross, *Wicked Intentions* by Elizabeth Hoyt and *Wicked Prey* by John Sandford.

Sylvia Remembered: February 11, 2013, marks the fiftieth anniversary of the tragic suicide of the poet Sylvia Plath. Use *Letters Home,* correspondence between Sylvia and her mother, to discover a different side of the complex, brilliant woman trapped in a troubled marriage to poet Edward James "(Ted)" Hughes, considered one of the best poets of his generation. Sylvia Plath was born on October 27, 1932.

Include the DVD *Sylvia* released in 2001. Frame a photo of the poet to incorporate among the books. Enlarge an image of her gravestone available through an online image search. Print this on card stock and stand it among the books. Include old *Mademoiselle* magazines (she was a contributor), and an insignia from Smith College where she earned her bachelor's degree. Be sure to include a copy of her famous book, *The Bell Jar.*

Oktoberfest: The original Oktoberfest occurred in Munich, on October 12, 1810. It was the public commemoration of a royal marriage that had taken place five days previously. The event was so successful that organizers decided to repeat it in 1811. For a simple and effective graphic to use as a focus of your display, visit http://www. germanstl.org/oktoberfest.html. For information about the history of Oktoberfest visit http:// www. infoplease.com/spot/oktfest1.html.

Include lederhosen, beer bottles, beer steins, German folk music and dolls in folk dress. Add some confetti and balloons.

Feature *Those Crazy Germans! A Lighthearted Guide to Germany* by Steven Somers, *Look What Came from Germany* by Kevin Davis, and German travel guides.

November

JFK—In Memory: November 22, 2013, will be the fiftieth anniversary of the assassination of President John F. Kennedy. He was gunned down in Dallas, Texas, while in a motorcade with his wife, Jacqueline, and the governor and first lady of Texas. Create a collage of photos of the events surrounding this tragedy and the unforgettable funeral orchestrated by Kennedy's widow.

Include in the collage the presidential seal, newspaper headlines, and a photo of his gravesite with the eternal flame. Look for family photos of the president as a child recreating at the family compound in Hyannis Port on Cape Code, Massachusetts. Select from the many poignant photos of JFK with his children, Carolyn and John, Jr. All of these images are available online. Mount some photos on foam board for greater emphasis and visual depth.

Include the source *The Kennedys: Portrait of a Family* by Richard Avedon and Shannon Thomas Perich, which has poignant photos of the First Family. Include the Pulitzer Prize–winning *Profiles in Courage* by JFK and *An Unfinished Life: John F. Kennedy, 1917–1963* by Robert Dallek.

Henri Matisse: This French lawyer turned artist and sculptor died on November 3, 1954, at the age of 84. He was considered one of the great initiators of the modern art movement, which uses the combination of bold primary colors and free, simple forms. Matisse was the most outstanding personality of the first revolution in 20th century art—Fauvism. This is a style of art that uses color and sometimes distorted forms to send its message. The goal of Matisse's art was the portrayal of joyful living in contrast to the stresses of our technological age. The ultimate step in his art was taken in his papiers découpés, abstract cutouts in colored paper, executed in the mid–1940s.

Use the graphic found at http://www.french-centre.com.au/welcome/images/MatisseJazz.jpg for inspiration. Since Matisse created a lot of still life paintings during his lifetime, create a tableau of fruit and pottery in your display. Add some paints and brushes.

Cliffhangers: Who doesn't love a good mystery? Feature the latest mysteries by Janet Evanovich, James Patterson, Carl Hiaasen, Martin Cruz Smith, Stieg Larsson, Daniel Silva and Kathy Reichs. For additional ideas for those who enjoy crime, thriller, spy, and suspense stories, check out the site Stop You're Killing Me! Award winning books of this genre are listed there: http://www.stopyourekillingme. com/.

For a graphic inspiration of the silhouette of a climber dangling from a cliff visit http://blackarrow.clientlisttruestory.com/cliffhangerblackarrow/. Place stones and rocks at the base of the display and position the books on angles among the rocks.

Wild Things: Create a display as a tribute to children's illustrator Maurice Sendak. Enlarge a page, set in the outdoors, from his famous book, *Where the Wild Things Are*. Line the base of the display with moss and rocks. Hang silk branches with green leaves from the top. Include some of the figures from the story, or some paints, brushes and chalks. Provide biographical information and some facts about Sendak's creative process. Give information about the Sendak collection housed in the Rosenbach Museum and Library located in Philadelphia. For information about the artist visit http://www.themorgan.org/exhibitions/exhibition.asp?id=30.

Be sure to include *The Art of Maurice Sendak 1980 to Present* by Tony Kushner, *Making Mischief: A Maurice Sendak Appreciation* by Gregory Maguire, and *Maurice Sendak* by Amy Sondheim, along with his other children's books and the *Where the Wild Things Are* DVD.

Pilgrims at Plymouth: Celebrate the Pilgrims in this Masachusetts town. The first permanent European settlement in New England was founded by the Pilgrims on December 21, 1620. The *Mayflower* began its historic voyage on September 16, 1620, leaving Plymouth, England, with 102 passengers. After a 65-day journey, the Pilgrims anchored on November 21 at Provincetown. The settlers soon discovered Plymouth Harbor, on the western side of Cape Cod Bay, and made their historic Plymouth Rock landing on December 21.

Include an image of the *Mayflower*, which can be found if you visit http://www.bestscalemodels.com/hmsmayflower.html.

For background information on the Pilgrims visit http://homepages.rootsweb.ancestry.com/~homespun/tply.html

Feature information about the English leader William Bradford, the first historian of the settlement, as well as images of the pilgrims in their daily life. Include a replica of the Mayflower Compact available through an online image search.

Display *The Pilgrims at Plymouth* by Lucille Recht Penner, *William Bradford: Plymouth's Faithful Pilgrim* by Gary D, Schmidt and *Plymouth Plantation 1620–1647* by William Bradford.

Claude Monet: This French painter, leader, and unswerving advocate of the Impressionist style was born on November 14, 1840, in Paris, France. He is regarded as the archetypal Impressionist in that his devotion to the ideals of the movement was unwavering throughout his long career, and it is fitting that that one of his pictures *Impression: Sunrise* gave the group its name. He died in Giverny, France, on December 5, 1926. His works are held in prestigious museums throughout the world.

Include examples of his major works such as the *Water Lilies* series, the *Rouen Cathedral* series and the *Haystacks* series. For biographical information visit http://www.ibiblio.org/wm/paint/auth/monet/. For a time line visit http://www.mootnotes.com/art/monet/monet-timeline.html.

Feature biographies and compilations of Monet's works as well as an artist's palette, brushes and oil paints.

December

Imagine: A tribute to John Lennon, who died December 8, 1980, at the hands of an assassin could begin the month. Much of his work suggested not only a profound musical and literary acumen—he was a genius, in short—but a vision of life that was reflective, utopian and poignantly realistic.

There are a wide variety of posters available featuring John Lennon. Or enlarge the score of the song "Imagine" and mount it on poster board. Add some musical notes. Feature photos of the legend along with those of the Beatles.

Include albums, a peace sign, wire-rimmed glasses, musical memorabilia and a guitar. Wonderful photos can be found if you visit http://www.johnlennon.com/html/photos.aspx. Include a time line of his rise to fame and his untimely death. Feature *December 8, 1980: The Day John Lennon Died* by Keith Elliot Greenberg and *John* by Cynthia Lennon.

Steinbeck Country: John Steinback was born in Salinas, California, in 1902 and died on December 20, 1968. He penned some of the most important works of the 20th century and was awarded the Nobel Prize for Literature in 1962 "for his realistic and imaginative writings, combining as they do sympathetic humour and keen social perception."

Use a map of the United States to represent Steinbeck's journey *Travels with Charley: In Search of America.* Charley was his pet poodle and great traveling companion and crossed America with him in 1962. Include movie posters such as *The Grapes of Wrath, The Red Pony, East of Eden* and *Of Mice and Men.* Add a framed photo of the author, a martini glass, period cigarette pack, grapes and a vintage typewriter with a sheet of paper with the first few paragraphs of one of his novels. Print a replica of the Nobel Peace Prize and add some newspaper headlines from the Vietnam War period (he was a correspondent during that time). Feature some of the writings from *Steinbeck: A Life in Letters,* which was published in 1975. Because he left such a long legacy in letters, be sure to include several of his memorable quotes.

Piaf!: Edith Piaf was born December 19, 1915, and died October 11, 1963, and 2013 marks the fiftieth anniversary of the death of this phenomenal French singer. Include sheet music from "*La Vie en Rose,*" a song for which she was well known, and the DVD of the same name, which was released in 2007. Create a Parisian café setting with a tray, bottle of wine, glasses, confetti, a vase with flowers, candles, cheese and crackers. Include *The Wheel of Fortune: The Official Autobiography* by Edith Piaf, and some of her biographies published in 2008. Feature *Piaf: A Biography* by Simone Berteaut which is considered the ultimate, comprehensive account of her life.

John Brown: John Brown was born into a deeply religious family in Torrington, Connecticut, in 1800. Led by a father who was vehemently opposed to slavery, the family moved to northern Ohio, when John was five. They relocated to a district that would become known for its anti-slavery views. John Brown was a man of action—a man who would not be deterred from his mission of abolishing slavery. On October 16, 1859, he led 21 men on a raid of the federal arsenal at Harpers Ferry, Virginia. His plan to arm slaves with the weapons he and his men seized from the arsenal was thwarted, however, by local farmers, militiamen, and Marines led by Robert E. Lee. Within 36 hours of the attack, most of Brown's men had been killed or captured. He was hanged on December 2, 1859.Include information relevant to the raid on Harpers Ferry, which can be found if you visit http://www.wv-culture.org/history/ jnobrown.html.

Feature *John Brown, Abolitionist: The Man Who Killed Slavery, Sparked the Civil War, and Seeded Civil Rights* by David S. Reynolds, *John Brown's Raid on Harper's Ferry: A Brief History* with *Documents* by Jonathan Halperin Earle and *Patriotic Treason: John Brown and the Soul of America* by Evan Carton.

What's Your Sign?: As the year comes to an end, design a display which demands intro-spection. You can create a poster by going to this site for a free download of astrological signs: http://all-silhouettes.com/vectorzodiacsigns/.

Provide information about the characteristics of each sign and their compatibility with other signs in the universe. Use purple, black, yellow, chartreuse and silver in this display. To set the tone for it, download the free font Hellraiser 3, which can be found at http://www.dafont. com.

Incorporate a crystal ball, tarot cards and a Ouija board into the tableau. Feature *The Only Astrology Book You'll Ever Need* by Joanna Martine Woolfolk,

Llewellyn's 2011 Sun Sign Book: Horoscopes for Everyone by Kris Brandt Riske and *Learning Astrology: An Astrology Book for Beginners* by Damian Sharp.

Winter: Cut out tall thin tree trunks of various sizes from black and charcoal poster board. Have them reach the top of the display case, but don't include any upper branches. With gray, white, brown and beige chalk, add some detail to the bark and trunk of the trees. Make some thinner trunks and place them so that they appear to be in the distance. Attach the trunks with pins on a background of camel or gray and pull forward. Take some light chalks and create the illusion of clouds on the felt background.

Select titles such as *Russian Winter: A Novel* by Daphne Kalotay, *Winter's Bone: A Novel* by Daniel Woodrell, *Winter Kiss: A Dragonfire Novel* by Deborah Cooke, *The Winter War: A Novel* by William Durbin, *Ice: A Novel* by Linda Howard, *Cold Mountain: A Novel* by Charles Frazier.

Place fiberfill among the books to represent snow. Add pinecones, twigs and moss. Place a silk bird of winter such as a yellow warbler or a barn swallow in the tableau.

Bibliography

Adams, Ansel, and Elaine M. Bucher, eds. *American Wilderness*. Philadelphia: Courage Books, 1997.

Adams, Hugh. *Art of the Sixties*. Oxford: Phaidon Press, 1978.

Adams, Robert, Carol Di Grappa, et al. *Landscape Theory*. New York: Listrum Press, 1980.

Adams, Simon. *"Titanic."* Rev. ed. New York: DK, 2004.

Albert, Susan, *Eating Mindfully: How to End Mindless Eating and Enjoy a Balanced Relationship with Food*. Oakland, CA: New Harbinger, 2003.

Aldrich, Margret, ed. *This Old Quilt: A Heartwarming Celebration of Quilts and Quilting Memories*. St. Paul, MN: Voyageur Press, 2001.

Alspaugh, Nancy, and Marilyn Kentz. *Fearless Women: Midlife Portraits*. New York: Stewart, Tabori & Chang, 2005.

Alter, Jonathan. *The Defining Moment: FDR's Hundred Days and the Triumph of Hope*. New York: Simon & Schuster, 2006.

Altman, Donald. *Art of the Inner Meal: The Power of Mindful Practices to Heal Our Food Cravings*. Los Angeles: Moon Lake Media, 1998.

Altschuler, Glenn C. *All Shook Up: How Rock 'n' Roll Changed America*. New York: Oxford University Press, 2003.

Anderson, Terry H. *The Movement and the Sixties*. Oxford: Oxford University Press, 1995.

Andrews, Geroge F. *Maya Cities: Placemaking and Urbanization*. Norman: University of Oklahoma Press, 1977

Archbold, Rick, and Dana McCauley. *Last Dinner on the "Titanic."* New York: Hyperion, 1997.

Baldwin, Louis. *Women of Strength: Biographies of 106 Who Have Excelled in Traditionally Male Fields, A.D. 61 to Present*. Jefferson, NC: McFarland, 1996.

Ballard, Robert D. *"Titanic": The Last Great Images*. Philadelphia: Running Press, 2008.

Barratt, Carrie Rebora, and Ellen G. Miles. *Gilbert Stuart*. New York: Metropolitan Museum of Art, 2004.

Barron, Neil. *Anatomy of Wonder: A Critical Guide to Science Fiction*. 5th ed. Westport, CT: Libraries Unlimited, 2004.

Batchelor, John, and Christopher Chant. *The Complete Encyclopedia of Sailing Ships, 2000 B.C.–2006 A.D.*. Edison, NJ: Chartwell Books, 2006.

Behr, Edward. *Prohibition: Thirteen Years That Changed America*. New York: Arcade, 1996.

Beller, Susan Provost. *Yankee Doodle and the Redcoats: Soldiering in the Revolutionary War*. Minneapolis: Twenty First Century Books, 2008.

Bellush, Bernard. *Franklin D. Roosevelt as Governor of New York*. New York: Columbia University Press, 1955.

Benn, James A. *Burning for the Buddha: Self Immolation in Chinese Buddhism*. Honolulu: University of Hawaii Press, 2007.

Benzel, Rick, ed. *Inspiring Creativity: An Anthology of Powerful Insights and Practical Ideas to Guide You to Successful Creating*. Playa del Rey, CA: Creativity Coaching Association Press, 2005.

Berg, Frances M. *Afraid to Eat: Children and Teens in Weight Crisis*. Hettinger, ND: Healthy Weight Journal, 1997.

Bertine, Eleanor, *Human Relationships: In the Family, in Friendships, in Love*. New York: David McKay, 1963.

Bevington, David. *Shakespeare's Ideas: More Things in Heaven and Earth*. Chichester, West Sussex; Malden, MA: Wiley-Blackwell, 2008.

Bial, Raymond. *Amish Home*. Boston: Houghton Mifflin, 1993.

Biddlecombe, George. *The Art of Rigging*. New York: Dover, 1990.

Billings, Andrew C. *Olympic Media: Inside the Biggest Show on Television*. New York: Routledge, 2008.

Black, Jeremy. *George III: America's Last King*. New Haven, CT: Yale University Press, 2006.

Bleiler, Richard, ed. *Science Fiction Writers: Critical Studies of the Major Authors from the Early Nineteenth Century to the Present Day*. 2nd ed. New York: Macmillan, 1999.

Bliese, John R.E. *The Greening of Conservative America*. Boulder, CO: Westview Press, 2001.

Block, Lawrence. *Gangsters, Swindlers, Killers, and Thieves: The Lives and Crimes of Fifty American Villains*. Oxford: Oxford University Press, 2004.

Bockris, Victor. *Warhol*. New York: Da Capo Press, 1997.

Bodnar, Ethan. *Creative Grab Bag: Inspiring Challenges for Designers, Illlustrators and Artists.* Cincinnati: HOW Books, 2009.

Bolch, Oliver, Roland F. Karl, Jörg Berghoff and Jochen Müssig. *Australia: Continent of Contrasts.* Munich: C.J. Bucher, 2007.

Bonanno, Joseph, with Sergio Lalli. *A Man of Honor: The Autobiography of Joseph Bonanno.* New York: St. Martin's Paperbacks, 2003.

Bonanno, Rosalie. *Mafia Marriage: An Unforgettable Look Inside the Godfather's Own House.* New York: St. Martin's Paperbacks, 2003.

Bowker, John. *World Religions: The Great Faiths Explored and Explained.* New York: DK, 1997.

Boxall, Peter, ed. *1001 Books You Must Read Before You Die.* New York: Universe, 2006.

Brader, Ted. *Campaigning for Hearts and Minds: How Emotional Appeals in Political Ads Work.* Chicago: University of Chicago Press, 2006.

Brams, Steven J. *The Presidential Election Game.* Wellesley, MA: A.K. Peters, 2008.

Brandenburg, Frank. *The Making of Modern Mexico.* Englewood Cliffs, NJ: Prentice-Hall, 1964.

Brands, H.W. *Traitor to His Class: The Privileged Life and Radical Presidency of Franklin Delano Roosevelt.* New York: Doubleday, 2008.

Brewster, Hugh. *Inside the "Titanic."* New York: Little, Brown, 1997.

Brewster, Hugh, and Laurie Coulter. *882 Amazing Answers to Your Questions about the "Titanic."* New York: Scholastic Press, 1998.

Brinnin, John Malcolm. *The Sway of the Grand Saloon: A Social History of the North Atlantic.* New York: Delacorte Press, 1971.

Brower, Kenneth. *Yosemite: An American Treasure.* Washington, D.C.: National Geographic Society, 1990.

Browne, Nick, ed. *Refiguring American Film Genres.* Berkeley: University of California Press, 1998.

Brownell, Susan. *Beijing Games: What the Olympics Mean to China.* Lanham, MD: Rowman & Littlefield, 2008.

Bruce, Evangeline. *Napoleon and Josephine.* New York: Scribner, 1995.

Bryceson, Dave. *The "Titanic" Disaster: As Reported in the British National Press April–July 1912.* New York: W.W. Norton, 1997.

Bryson, Bill. *In a Sunburned Country.* New York: Broadway Books, 2000.

Buckley, Peter. *The Rough Guide to My Space.* New York: Rough Guides, distributed by Penguin Books, 2006.

Burns, James MacGregor. *Roosevelt: The Lion and the Fox.* New York: Harcourt, Brace & World, 1956.

Burt, Daniel S. *The Literary 100: A Ranking of the Most Influential Novelists, Playwrights, and Poets of All Time.* New York: Checkmark Books, 2001.

_____. *The Novel 100: A Ranking of the Greatest Novels of All Time.* New York: Checkmark Books, 2004.

Busch, Kurt, with Rick Houston. *Young Gun: In the Driver's Seat with #97.* New York: New American Library, 2003.

Buszek, Maria Elena. *Pin-Up Grrrls: Feminism, Sexuality, Popular Culture.* Durham, NC: Duke University Press, 2006.

Butzer, Karl W., and Thomas J. Abercrombie. *Ancient Egypt: Discovering Its Splendors.* Washington: National Geographic Society, 1978.

Cain, Tim. *Peck's Beach: A Pictorial History of Ocean City, New Jersey.* Harvey Cedars, NJ: Down the Shore, 1988.

Cairns, David. *Mozart and His Operas.* Berkeley: University of California Press, 2006.

Campbell, Tracy. *Deliver the Vote: A History of Election Fraud, an American Political Tradition, 1742–2004.* New York: Carroll & Graf, 2005.

Campos, Paul. *The Obesity Myth: Why America's Obsession with Weight Is Hazardous to Your Health.* New York: Gotham Books, 2004.

Capote, Truman. *A Christmas Memory.* New York: Random House, 1966.

Carlyle, Thomas. *The French Revolution: A History.* New York: Modern Library, 2002.

Carr, Carolyn Kinder, and Ellen G. Miles. *A Brush with History: Paintings from the National Portrait Gallery.* Washington: National Portrait Gallery, Smithsonian Institution, 2001.

Carroll, Andrew. *War Letters: Extraordinary Correspondence from American Wars.* New York: Scribner, 2001.

Castelot, André. *Queen of France: A Biography of Marie Antoinette.* New York: Harper & Brothers, 1957.

Castillo, Ana. *So Far from God.* New York: W.W. Norton, 1993.

Castro, Rafaela G. *Chicano Folklore: A Guide to the Folktales, Traditions, Rituals and Religious Practices of Mexican Americans.* Oxford: Oxford University Press, 2001.

Clancy, Flora S., Clemency C. Coggins and T. Patrick Culbert. *Maya: Treasures of an Ancient Civilization.* New York: Harry N. Abrams, 1985.

Coblentz, Elizabeth, and Kevin Williams. *The Amish Cook: Recollections and Recipes from an Old Order Amish Family.* Berkeley, CA: Ten Speed Press, 2002.

Collins, Max Allan. *American Gangster.* New York: TOR, 2007.

Compart, Pamela J., and Dana Laake. *The Kid-Friendly ADHD and Autism Cookbook.* Gloucester, MA: Fair Winds Press, 2006.

Cook, Bernie, ed. *Thelma & Louise Live! The Cultural Afterlife of an American Film.* Austin: University of Texas Press, 2007.

Cox, Jon. *Digital Photography Closeup.* New York: Amphoto Books, 2005.

Cox, Meg. *The Quilter's Catalog: A Comprehensive Resource Guide. New York: Workman, 2008.

Creighton, Sarah Hammond. *Greening the Ivory Tower: Improving the Environmental Track Record of Universities, Colleges and Other Institutions.* Cambridge: MIT Press, 1998.

Critser, Greg. *Fat Land: How Americans Became the Fattest People in the World.* Boston: Houghton Mifflin, 2003.

Cronin, Vincent. *Louis and Antoinette.* New York: William Morrow, 1975.

Csikszentmihalyi, Mihalyi. *Creativity: Flow and the Psychology of Discovery and Invention.* New York: Harper Collins, 1996.

David, Marc. *The Slow Down Diet: Eating for Pleasure, Energy, and Weight Loss.* Rochester, NY: Healing Arts Press, 2005.

Davies, Robertson. *Selected Works on the Pleasures of Reading.* Toronto: Penguin, 2008.

Davis, Brangien, and Katharine Wroth, eds. *Wake Up and Smell the Planet: The Non-Pompous, Non-Preachy Grist Guide to Greening Your Day.* Seattle: Skipstone, 2007.

Davis, Kenneth C., and Jenny Davis. *Don't Know Much About Literature.* New York: HarperCollins, 2009.

Day, Nancy. *Your Travel Guide to Ancient Mayan Civilization.* Minneapolis: Runestone Press, 2001.

DeCurtis, Anthony, and James Henke, eds. *The Illustrated History of Rock & Roll: The Defensive History of the Most Important Artists and Their Music.* New York: Random House, 1992.

Demerath, N.J., III. *Crossing the Gods: World Religions and Worldly Politics.* New Brunswick, NJ: Rutgers University Press, 2001.

Detz, Joan. *It's Not What You Say, It's How You Say It.* New York: St. Martin's Press, 2000.

Deutsch, Otto Erich. *Mozart: A Documentary Biography.* Stanford, CA: Stanford University Press, 1966.

Dickens, Charles. *A Christmas Carol.* New York: Macmillan, 1963.

Dolbeare, Kenneth M. *American Political Thought.* Chatham, NJ: Chatham House, 1984.

Downer, Patrick. *Bad Seeds in the Big Apple: Bandits, Killers, and Chaos in New York City, 1920–1940.* Nashville, TN: Cumberland House, 2008.

Downs, Robert B. *Books That Changed the World.* New York: Signet Classic, 2004.

Doyle, William. *The Oxford History of the French Revolution.* 2nd ed. Oxford: Oxford University Press, 2002.

Dozois, Gardner, Tina Lee, Stanley Schmidt, Ian Randal Strock and Sheila Williams, eds. *Writing Science Fiction and Fantasy.* New York: St. Martin's Press, 1991.

Drake, Frances. *Global Warming: The Science of Climate Change.* London: Arnold, 2000.

Drees, Ludwig. *Olympia: Gods, Artists, and Athletes.* New York: Frederick A. Praeger, 1968.

Duncan, Dayton, and Ken Burns. *The National Parks: America's Best Idea, an Illustrated History.* New York: Alfred A. Knopf, 2009.

Durant, John, and Alice Durant. *Pictorial History of American Ships: On the High Seas and Inland Waters.* New York: A.S. Barnes, 1953.

Eberwein, Robert, ed. *The War Film.* New Brunswick, NJ: Rutgers University Press, 2005.

Ellis, Jack. E. *A History of Film.* 4th ed. Boston: Allyn and Bacon, 1995.

Esposito, John L. *Islam: The Straight Path.* Rev. 3rd ed. New York: Oxford University Press, 2005.

Evans, Dave. *Social Media Marketing: An Hour a Day.* Indianapolis: Wiley, 2008.

Evans, Dorinda. *The Genius of Gilbert Stuart.* Princeton, NJ: Princeton University Press, 1999.

Evans, Kathy, and Janek Dubowski. *Art Therapy with Children on the Autistic Spectrum.* London: Jessica Kingsley, 2007.

Fair, Ray C. *Predicting Presidential Elections and Other Things.* Stanford, CA: Stanford University Press, 2002.

Farber, David, ed. *The Sixties: From Memory to History.* Chapel Hill: University of North Carolina Press, 1994.

Felton, George. *Advertising Concept and Copy.* New York: W.W. Norton, 2006.

Fisher, Ron. *Wild Shores of Australia.* Washington, D.C.: National Geographic Society, 1996.

Fitzharris, Tim. *National Audubon Society Guide to Landscape Photography.* Richmond Hill, Ontario: Firefly Books, 2007.

Flannery, Tim, ed. *The Explorers: Stories of Discovery and Adventure from the Australian Frontier.* New York: Grove Press, 1998.

_____. *The Future Eaters: An Ecological History of Australasian Lands and People.* New York: Grove Press, 1994.

Flood, Gavin. *An Introduction to Hinduism.* Cambridge: Cambridge University Press, 1996.

Foster, Jack. *How to Get Ideas.* 2nd ed. San Francisco: Berrett-Koehler, 2007.

Fowler, Merv. *Zen Buddhism: Beliefs and Practices.* Portland, OR: Sussex Academic Press, 2005.

Francke, Klaus D. *Australia: Flying High.* Vercell, Exeter: White Star, 2007.

Frantzen, Allen J. *Bloody Good: Chivalry, Sacrifice, and the Great War.* Chicago: University of Chicago Press, 2004.

Freed, Rachael. *Women's Lives, Women's Legacies: Passing Your Beliefs and Blessings to Future Generations.* Minneapolis: Fairview Press, 2003.

Freidel, Frank. *Franklin D. Roosevelt: Launching the New Deal.* Boston: Little, Brown, 1973.

Friedlander, Paul. *Rock & Roll: A Social History.* 2nd ed. Boulder, CO: Westview Press, 2006.

Fuentes, Carlos. *The Diary of Frida Kahlo: An Intimate Self-Portrait.* New York: Harry N. Abrams, 1995.

Gabriel, Theodore, and Ronald Geaves. *...isms: Understanding Religion.* New York: Universe, 2007.

Gaesser, Glenn A., *Big Fat Lies: The Truth About Your Weight and Your Health.* Carlsbad, CA: Gürze Books, 2002.

Garner, Joe. *And the Crowd Goes Wild: Relive the Most Celebrated Sporting Events Ever Broadcast.* Naperville, IL: Sourcebooks, 1999.

Garofalo, Reebee. *Rockin' Out: Popular Music in the USA.* 2nd ed. Upper Saddle River, NJ: Prentice Hall, 2002.

Garrett, Roberta. *Postmodern Chick Flicks: The Return of the Woman's Film.* Basingstoke, NY: Palgrave Macmillan, 2007.

George, W.L. *Historic Lovers.* London: Bracken Books, 1994.

George-Warren, Holly, and Patricia Romanowski, eds. *The Rolling Stone Encyclopedia of Rock & Roll.* Revised and updated for the 21st century. New York: Fireside, 2005.

Gerlach, John, and Barbara Gerlach. *Digital Nature Photography: The Art and the Science.* Amsterdam: Elsevier/Focal Press, 2007.

Gerrard, Don. *One Bowl: A Guide to Eating for Body and Spirit.* New York: Marlowe, 2001.

Gerrold, David. *Worlds of Wonder: How to Write Science Fiction and Fantasy.* Cincinnati: Writer's Digest Books, 2001.

Gilbert, Martin. *The First World War: A Complete History.* New York: H. Holt, 1994.

Gildea, Robert. "The Fall of the French Monarchy: Louis XVI, Marie Antoinette and the Baron de Breuteuil." *Times Literary Supplement* 5193 (2002), 11–12.

Gillispie, Tom. *I Remember Dale Earnhardt.* Nashville: Cumberland House, 2001.

Gipe, Paul. *Wind Energy Basics: A Guide to Small and Micro Wind Systems.* White River Junction, VT: Chelsea Green, 1999.

Gitlin, Todd. *The Sixties: Years of Hope, Days of Rage.* New York: Bantam Books, 1993.

Glick, Aaron S. *The Fortunate Years: An Amish Life.* Intercourse, PA: Good Books, 1994.

Glover, Jane. *Mozart's Women: His Family, His Friends, His Music.* New York: Harper Collins, 2005.

Goldsmith, Becky, and Linda Jenkins. *Amish-Inspired Quilts: Tradition with a Piece o' Cake Twist.* Concord, CA: C & T, 2006.

Goldsmith, Lynn. *Rock & Roll.* New York: Harry N. Abrams, 2007.

Good, Merle, and Phyllis Good. *Twenty Most Asked Questions about the Amish and Mennonites.* Lancaster, PA: Good Books, 1979.

Goodwin, Doris Kearns. *No Ordinary Time.* New York: Simon & Schuster, 1994.

Gordon, Jeff, with Steve Eubanks. *Jeff Gordon: Raging Back to the Front—My Memoir.* New York: Atria Books, 2003.

Gran, Dave. *Go Ahead, Take the Wheel: Road Racing on Your Budget.* Newington, CT: Dragon, 2006.

Grandin, Temple. *Thinking in Pictures and Other Reports from My Life with Autism.* New York: Vintage Books, 1995.

_____. *The Way I See It: A Personal Look at Autism and Asperger's.* Arlington, TX: Future Horizons, 2008.

Grandin, Temple, and Margaret Scariano. *Emergence: Labeled Autistic.* New York: Warner Books, 1996.

Granick, Eve Wheatcroft. *The Amish Quilt.* Intercourse, PA: Good Books, 1989.

Graves, Mark A., and F. Bruce Engle. *Blockbusters: A Reference Guide to Film Genres.* Westport, CT: Greenwood Press, 2006.

Green, Roger Lancelyn, and Heather Copley. *Tales of Ancient Egypt.* London: Puffin Books, 1995.

Greenblatt, Stephen. *Will in the World: How Shakespeare Became Shakespeare.* New York: W.W. Norton, 2004.

Greenstein, Fred I. *The Presidential Difference: Leadership Style from FDR to Clinton.* New York: Martin Kessler Books, 2000.

Gregory, Mollie. *Women Who Run the Show.* New York: St. Martin's Press, 2002.

Grisham, John. *Skipping Christmas.* New York: Doubleday, 2001.

Grossman, Elizabeth. *High Tech Trash: Digital Devices, Hidden Toxics, and Human Health.* Washington, D.C.: Island Press, 2006.

Guinn, Jeff. *Go Down Together: The True, Untold Story of Bonnie and Clyde.* New York: Simon & Schuster, 2009.

Gumbel, Andrew. *Steal This Vote: Dirty Elections and the Rotten History of Democracy in America.* New York: Nation Books, 2005.

Guoqi, Xu. *Olympic Dreams: China and Sports 1895–2008.* Cambridge: Harvard University Press, 2008.

Guralnick, Peter. *Last Train to Memphis: The Rise of Elvis Presley.* Boston: Little, Brown, 1994.

Guyler, Vivian Varney. *Design in Nature.* Worcester, MA: Davis, 1970.

Haag, Herbert. *Great Couples of the Bible.* Minneapolis: Fortress Press, 2006.

Halperin, Mark, and John F. Harris. *The Way to Win: Taking the White House in 2008.* New York: Random House, 2006.

Hammond, Margo, and Ellen Heltzel. *Between the Covers: The Book Babes' Guide to a Woman's Reading Pleasures.* Philadelphia: Da Capo Press, 2008.

Hamnett, Brian. *A Concise History of Mexico.* Cambridge: Cambridge University Press, 1999.

Harrell, Mary Ann. *Surprising Lands Down Under.*

Washington, D.C.: National Geographic Society, 1989.

Harris, Ann G., Esther Tuttle and Sherwood D. Tuttle. *Geology of National Parks.* 5th ed. Dubuque: Kendall/Hunt, 1995.

Harris, Coy F., ed. *Windmill Tales: Stories from the American Wind Power Center.* Lubbock: Texas Tech University Press, 2004.

Harris, Warren G. *Lucy and Desi: The Legendary Love Story of Television's Most Famous Couple.* New York: Simon & Schuster, 1991.

Harrison, Sam. *Ideaspotting: How to Find Your Next Great Idea.* Cincinnati: How Books, 2006.

_____. *Zing: Five Steps and 101 Tips for Creativity on Command.* Highlands, NC: MacHillock, 2004.

Harter, Jim. *Nautical Illustrations: 681 Permission-Free Illustrations from Nineteenth Century Sources.* Mineola, NY: Dover, 2003.

Haslip, Joan. *Marie Antoinette.* New York: Weidenfeld & Nicolson, 1987.

Haynie, Elizabeth. *Great Lovers and Couples: History's and Hollywood's Most Passionate Pairs.* Downers Grove, IL: Kingsley Press, 1994.

Healy, George P.A. *Reminiscences of a Portrait Painter.* Chicago: A.C. McClurg, 1894.

Heinz, Thomas A. *Frank Lloyd Wright's Interiors.* New York: Gramercy, 2002.

Helm, Burt. "The Olympics—Three PR experts give Beijing some free advice." *Business Week,* April 28, 2008, p. 42.

Henderson, John S. *The World of the Ancient Maya.* Ithaca, NY: Cornell University Press, 1981.

Herr, Patricia T. *Amish Quilts of Lancaster County.* Atglen, PA: Schiffer, 2004.

Herrera, Hayden. *Frida Kahlo: The Paintings.* New York: HarperPerennial, 1993.

Hess, Alan. *Frank Lloyd Wright: The Houses.* New York: Rizzoli, 2005.

Hildesheimer, Wolfgang. *Mozart.* New York: Farrar Straus Giroux, 1982.

Hill, Marquita K. *Understanding Environmental Pollution.* Cambridge: Cambridge University Press, 1997.

Hoehling, A.A. *Lost at Sea.* Nashville: Rutledge Hill Press, 1984.

Holland, Vyvyan. *Oscar Wilde: A Pictorial Biography.* New York: Viking Press, 1960.

Hollis, Judi. *Fat Is a Family Affair: A Frank Discussion of Eating Disorders and the Family's Involvement.* San Francisco: Harper & Row, 1985,

Hopfe, Lewis M. *Religions of the World.* 6th ed. New York: Macmillan College Publishing, 1994.

Horan, Nancy. *Loving Frank.* New York: Ballatine Books, 2007.

Horst, Mel. *Among the Amish.* Lebanon, PA: Applied Arts, 1997.

Horton, Roberta. *An Amish Adventure: A Workbook for Color in Quilts.* Lafayette, CA: C & T, 1983.

Hostetler, John A, ed. *Amish Roots: A Treasury of History, Wisdom, and Love.* Baltimore: Johns Hopkins University Press, 1989.

Hunt, Lynn. *The Family Romance of the French Revolution.* Berkeley: University of California Press, 1992.

Hunt, Lynn, ed. *The French Revolution and Human Rights: A Brief Documentary History.* Boston: Bedford Books, 1996.

Hurd, Mary G. *Women Directors and Their Film.* Westport, CT: Praeger, 2007.

Illsley, Linda. *Mexico: Food and Festivals.* Austin, TX: Raintree Steck-Vaughn, 1999.

Innes, Sherrie A., ed. *Action Chicks: New Images of Tough Women in Popular Culture.* New York: Palgrave MacMillan, 2004.

Iversen, Kristen. *Molly Brown: Unraveling the Myth.* Boulder, CO: Johnson Books, 1999.

Jamison, Andrew, and Ron Eyerman. *Seeds of the Sixties.* Berkley: University of California Press, 1994.

Jenkins, Martin, and Brian Sanders. *"Titanic."* Cambridge, MA: Candlewick Press, 2008.

Jessop, Violet. *"Titanic" Survivor: The Newly Discovered Memoirs of Violet Jessop, Who Survived Both the "Titanic" and "Britannic" Disasters.* Dobbs Ferry, NY: Sheridan House, 1997.

Johnson, David. *The Geology of Australia.* Cambridge: Cambridge University Press, 2004.

Jordan, Shirley. *The Mayan Civilization: Moments in History.* Logan, IA: Perfection Learning, 2001.

Kabatznick, Ronna. *The Zen of Eating: Ancient Answers to Modern Weight Problems.* New York: Perigree Books, 1998.

Kalfatovic, Martin R. *Creating a Winning Online Exhibition: A Guide for Libraries, Archives, and Museums.* Chicago: American Library Association, 2002.

Kaplan, E. Ann. *Feminism & Film.* Oxford: Oxford University Press, 2000.

_____. *Women and Film: Both Sides of the Camera.* New York: Methuen, 1983.

_____, ed. *Women in Film Noir.* London: British Film Institute, 1998.

Kaplan, Steven Laurence. *Farewell, Revolution: Disputed Legacies France, 1789/1989.* Ithaca: Cornell University Press, 1995.

_____. *Farewell, Revolution: The Historian's Feud, France, 1789–1989.* Ithaca: Cornell University Press, 1996.

Keegan, John. *The First World War.* New York: A. Knopf, 1999.

Keller, Sean. "Architecture: Sean Keller on the Beijing Olympics." *Artforum International* 46, no. 10 (2008): 137–150.

Kennedy, J. Gerald, ed. *The Portable Edgar Allan Poe.* New York: Penguin Books, 2006.

Kerasote, Ted, ed. *Return of the Wild: The Future*

of Our Natural Lands. Washington, D.C.: Island Press, 2001.

Keyssar, Alexander. *The Right to Vote: The Contested History of Democracy in the United States.* New York: Basic Books, 2000.

Klett, Mark, Rebecca Solnit and Byron White. *Yosemite in Time: Ice Ages, Tree Clocks, Ghost Rivers.* San Antonio, TX: Trinity University Press, 2005.

Klostermaier, Klaus K. *A Survey of Hinduism.* 3rd ed. Albany: State University of New York, 2007.

Kluger, Jeffrey. "How America's Children Packed on the Pounds." *Time,* June 23, 2008, pp. 66–69.

Knepler, Georg. *Wolfgang Amadé Mozart.* Cambridge: Cambridge University Press, 1994.

Knight, Chris W. *Son of Scarface.* New York: New Era, 2008.

Kobal, John. *Film-Star Portraits of the Fifties.* New York: Dover, 1980.

Kolata, Gina. *Rethinking Thin: The New Science of Weight Loss and the Myths and Realities of Dieting.* New York: Picador, 2007.

Kramer, Edith. *Art as Therapy.* London: Jessica Kingsley, 2000.

Kraybill, Donald B. *The Riddle of Amish Culture.* Rev. ed. Baltimore: Johns Hopkins University Press, 2001.

Kraybill, Donald B., and Carl Bowman. *On the Road to Heaven.* Baltimore: Johns Hopkins University Press, 2001.

Kraybill, Donald B., and Steven M. Nolt. *Amish Enterprise: From Plows to Profits.* Baltimore: Johns Hopkins University Press, 1995.

Kraybill, Donald B., Steven Nolt, and David L. Weaver-Zercher. *Amish Grace: How Forgiveness Transcended Tragedy.* San Francisco: John Wiley & Sons, 2007.

Kugle, Scott. *Sufis and Saints Bodies: Mysticism, Corporeality, and Sacred Power in Islam.* Chapel Hill: University of North Carolina Press, 2007.

Kulick, Don, and Anne Meneley. *Fat: The Anthropology of an Obsession.* New York: Jeremy P. Tarcher/Penguin, 2005.

Larimore, Walter, Sherri Flynt and Steve Halliday. *Super Sized Kids: How to Rescue Your Child from the Threat of Obesity.* New York: Center Street, 2005.

Lash, Joseph. *Eleanor and Franklin: The Story of Their Relationship Based on Eleanor Roosevelt's Private Papers.* New York: W.W. Norton, 1971.

Lastufka, Alan, and Michael W. Dean. *YouTube: An Insider's Guide to Climbing the Charts.* Sebastopol, CA: O'Reilly Media, 2009.

Lauzen, Martha M. *The Celluloid Ceiling: Behind the Scenes Employment of Women in the Top 250 Films of 2007.* San Diego: Center for the Study of Women in Television and Film, San Diego State University, 2008.

Leibovitz, Annie. *Olympic Portraits.* Boston: Little, Brown, 1996.

Leon-Portilla, Miguel. *Time and Reality in the Thought of the Maya.* Boston: Beacon Press, 1968.

Lerner, Michael A. *Dry Manhattan: Prohibition in New York City.* Cambridge, MA: Harvard University Press, 2008.

Leslie-Pelecky, Diandra. *The Physics of NASCAR: How to Make Steel+Gas+Rubber=Speed.* New York: Dutton, 2008.

Levick, Myra R. *They Could Not Talk and So They Drew: Children's Styles of Coping and Thinking.* Springfield, IL: Charles C. Thomas, 1983.

Li, Lillian M., Allison J. Dray-Novey and Haili Kong. *Beijing: From Imperial Capital to Olympic City.* New York: Palgrave Macmillan, 2008.

Lichti, Tim. *Amish.* Berrien Center, MI: Penrod/Hiawatha, 1991.

Lind, Carla. *Frank Lloyd Wright's Prairie Houses.* San Francisco: Pomegranate Artbooks, 1994.

Little, Kathleen Anne Crowley. *A History of Women's Tennis Wear from 1873 to 1979 and an Evaluation of Design and Comfort Characteristics.* San Jose, CA: San Jose State University, 1979.

Loewer, Peter. *Gardens by Design: Step by Step Plans for 12 Imaginative Gardens.* Emmaus, PA: Rodale Press, 1986.

Loori, John Daido. *The Zen of Creativity: Cultivating Your Artistic Life.* New York: Ballantine Books, 2005.

Lord, Walter. *A Night to Remember.* New York: Henry Holt, 1955.

Loss, Archie. *Pop Dreams: Music, Movies and the Media in the 1960s.* Fort Worth: Harcourt Brace College Publishers, 1999.

Lovaas, O. Ivar. *The Autistic Child: Language Development through Behavior Modification.* New York: Irvington, 1977.

Lupack, Barbara Tepa, ed. *Vision/Re-Vision: Adapting Contemporary American Fiction by Women to Film.* Bowling Green, OH: Bowling Green State University Popular Press, 1996.

Lynch, Don. *"Titanic": An Illustrated History.* Toronto: Madison Press Books, 1992.

Macksey, Joan, and Kenneth Macksey. *The Book of Women's Achievements.* New York: Stein and Day, 1975.

Mackesy, Piers. *The War for America, 1775–1783.* Cambridge, MA: Harvard University Press, 1964.

Macomber, Debbie. *A Cedar Cove Christmas.* Don Mills, Ontario: Mira, 2008.

Maier, Pauline. *From Resistance to Revolution: Colonial Radicals and the Development of American Opposition to Britain, 1765–1776.* New York: Alfred A. Knopf, 1973.

Maisel, L. Sandy. *Parties and Elections in America: The Electoral Process.* 3rd ed. Lanham, MD: Rowman & Littlefield, 2002.

Maraniss, David. *Rome 1960: The Olympics That Changed the World.* New York: Simon & Schuster, 2008.

Markel, Howard. "King Tutankhamun, Modern Medical Science, and the Expanding Boundaries of Historical Inquiry." *Journal of the American Medical Association* 303, no.7: 667–668.

Markus, Julia. *Dared and Done: The Marriage of Elizabeth Barrett and Robert Browning.* New York: Knopf, 1995.

Marling, Karal Ann. *Merry Christmas: Celebrating America's Greatest Holiday.* Cambridge, MA: Harvard University Press, 2000.

Marschall, Ken, and Hugh Brewster. *Inside the "Titanic."* New York: Little, Brown, 1997.

Marwick, Arthur. *The Sixties: Cultural Revolution in Britain, France, Italy, and the United States, c. 1958–c.1974.* Oxford: Oxford University Press, 1998.

Mason, Laura, and Tracey Rizzo. *The French Revolution: A Document Collection.* Boston: Houghton Mifflin, 1999.

Matsen, Bradford. *Titanic's Last Secrets.* Detroit: Thorndike Press, 2008.

Matthews, Warren. *World Religions.* 4th ed. Belmont, CA: Wadsworth, 2004.

May, Robin. *The British Army in North America, 1775–1783.* London: Osprey, 1997.

McCaffrey, Paul, ed. *U.S. Election System.* New York: H.W. Wilson, 2004.

McCarthy, Jenny. *Mother Warriors: A Nation of Parents Healing Autism Against All Odds.* New York: Penguin Group, 2008.

McCarty, Jennifer Hooper, and Tim Foecke. *What Really Sank the "Titanic": New Forensic Discoveries.* New York: Citadel Press Books, 2008.

McClaren, Norma Fischer. *A History of the Amish People and Their Faith.* New Wilmington, PA: New Horizons, 1994.

McDilda, Diane Gow. *The Everything Green Living Book.* Avon, MA: Adams Media, 2007.

McFedries, Paul, and Sherry Willard Kinkoph. *My Space: Visual Quick Tips.* Hoboken, NJ: Wiley, 2006.

McKenna, Neil. *The Secret Life of Oscar Wilde.* New York: Basic Books, 2005.

McMeekin, Gail. *12 Secrets of Highly Creative Women: A Portable Mentor.* Berkeley, CA: Conari Press, 2000.

Meacham, Jon. *Franklin and Winston: An Intimate Portrait of an Epic Friendship.* New York: Random House, 2003.

Melograni, Piero. *Wolfgang Amadeus Mozart.* Chicago: University of Chicago Press, 2007.

Merton, Thomas. *Peace in the Post Christian Era.* Maryknoll, NY: Orbis Books, 2004.

Mesibov, Gary B., Lynn W. Adams, and Laura G. Klinger. *Autism: Understanding the Disorder.* New York: Plenun Press, 1997.

Meyers, Jeffrey. *Edgar Allan Poe: His Life and Legacy.* New York: Cooper Square Press, 2000.

Michaels, Patrick J. *Meltdown: The Predictable Distortion of Global Warming by Scientists, Politicians, and the Media.* Washington, D.C.: Cato Institute, 2004.

Michalko, Michael. *Cracking Creativity: The Secrets of Creative Genius.* Berkeley, CA: Ten Speed Press, 2001.

Mikulecky, Beatrice S., and Linda Jeffries. *More Reading Power: Reading for Pleasure, Comprehensive Skills, Thinking Skills, Reading Faster.* 2nd ed. White Plains, NY: Pearson Education, 2004.

Miles, Ellen, ed. *Portrait Painting in America.* New York: Main Street/Universe Books, 1977.

Miller, Frank. *Leading Couples: The Most Unforgettable Screen Romances of the Studio Era.* San Francisco: Chronicle Books, 2008.

Miller, John, and Angelica Huston. *Legends: Women Who Have Changed the World.* Novato, CA: New World Library, 1998.

Miller, Michael. *YouTube 4 You.* Indianapolis: Que, 2007.

Miller, Sally M., ed. *John Muir: Life and Work.* Albuquerque: University of New Mexico Press, 1993.

Miller, Susan. *New Jersey's Southern Shore: An Illustrated History from Brigantine to Cape May Point.* Atglen, PA: Schiffer, 2008.

Miller, William H., Jr. *Doomed Ships: Great Ocean Liner Disasters.* Mineola, NY: Dover, 2006.

Mirsky, Steve. "Environment—An Earth Without People: A New Way to Examine Humanity's Impact on the Environment Is to Consider How the World Would Fare if All the People Disappeared." *Scientific American* 297, no. 1 (2007): 76–81.

Mjelde, Michael Jay. *Glory of the Seas.* Middletown, CT: Wesleyan University Press, 1970.

Monaco, Paul. *The Sixties: 1960–1969.* New York: Charles Scribner's Sons, 2001.

Montignac, Michel. *The French Diet: The Secrets of Why French Women Don't Get Fat.* New York: DK, 2005.

Moore, Lorraine A. *Back Roads and Buggy Trails: A Visitor's Guide to Ohio Amish Country.* Millersburg, OH: Bluebird Press, 1998.

Moorhouse, Geoffrey. *Sydney: The Story of a City.* New York: Harcourt, 2000.

Mumaw, Stefan, and Wendy Lee Oldfield. *Caffeine for the Creative Mind: 250 Exercises to Wake Up Your Brain.* Cincinnati: HOW Books, 2006.

Nash, Jay Robert. *Bloodletters and Badmen: A Narrative Encyclopedia of American Criminals from the Pilgrims to the Present.* New York: M. Evans, 1995.

Neely, Sylvia. *A Concise History of the French Revolution.* Lanthan, MD: Rowman & Littlefield, 2008.

Netzley, Patricia D. *Maya Civilization*. San Diego: Lucent Books, 2002.

Nicholson-Lord, David. *Planet Earth: The Making of an Epic Series*. London: BBC Books, 2006.

Nolt, Steven M. *A History of the Amish*. Intercourse, PA: Good Books, 1992.

Notbohm, Ellen. *Ten Things Every Child with Autism Wishes You Knew*. Arlington, TX: Future Horizons, 2005.

Notbohm, Ellen, and Veronica Zysk. *Ten Things Your Student with Autism Wishes You Knew*. Arlington, TX: Future Horizons, 2006.

O'Brien, Bob R. *Our National Parks and the Search for Sustainability*. Austin, TX: University of Texas Press, 1999.

Olsen, Kirsten. *Chronology of Women's History*. Westport, CT: Greenwood Press, 1994.

Olson, Carl. *The Different Paths of Buddhism: A Narrative-Historical Introduction*. New Brunswick, NJ: Rutgers University Press, 2005.

O'Reilly, Tim, and Sarah Milstein. *The Twitter Book*. Sebastopol, CA: O'Reilly Media Inc., 2009.

Orlofsky, Patsy, and Myron Orlofsky. *Quilts in America*. New York: Abbeville Press, 1992.

Ornish, Dean. *Love & Survival: Eight Pathways to Intimacy and Health*. New York: Harper Perennial, 1999.

Ottum, Bob, ed. *A Day in the Life of the Amish*. Greendale, WI: Reiman, 1994.

Oxlade, Chris, and David Ballheimer. *Olympic Games*. New York: Alfred A. Knopf, 1999.

Palmer, R. Barton, ed. *Twentieth-Century American Fiction on Screen*. Cambridge: Cambridge, University Press, 2007.

Palmer, Tim. *The Sierra Nevada: A Mountain Journey*. Washington, D.C.: Island Press, 1988.

Patrick, Julian, ed. *501 Great Writers*. Hauppauge, NY: Baron's Educational Series, 2008.

Pearce, Joseph. *The Unmasking of Oscar Wilde*. San Francisco: Ignatius Press, 2000.

Peeples, Scott. *The Afterlife of Edgar Allan Poe*. Rochester, NY: Camden House, 2004.

Perl, Lila. *The Ancient Maya*. New York: Franklin Watts, 2005.

Perloff, Richard M. *Political Communication: Politics, Press, and Public in America*. Mahwah, NJ: Lawrence Erlbaum Associates Publishers, 1998.

Peters, F.E. *The Children of Abraham: Judaism, Christianity, Islam* . New ed. Princeton: Princeton University Press, 2004.

Pfiffner, James P. *The Modern Presidency*. 5th ed. Belmont, CA: Thompson/Wadsworth, 2008.

Phillips, Dennis J. *Women Tennis Stars: Biographies and Records of Champions from 1800 to Today*. Jefferson, NC: McFarland, 2009.

Phillips, Susan P. *Great Displays for Your Library Step by Step*. Jefferson, NC: McFarland, 2008.

Picken, Stuart D.B. *Essentials of Shinto: An Analytical Guide to Principal Teachings*. Westport, CT: Greenwood Press, 1994.

Poe, Edgar Allan. *Great Tales and Poems of Edgar Allan Poe*. New York: Pocket Books, 2007.

_____. *Tales of Death and Dementia*. Illustrated by Gris Grimly. New York: Atheneum Books for Young Readers, 2009.

_____. *Tales of Mystery and Madness*. Illustrated by Gris Grimly. New York: Atheneum Books for Young Readers, 2004.

Poe, Harry Lee. *Edgar Allan Poe: An Illustrated Companion to His Tell-Tale Stories*. New York: Metro Books, 2008.

Poltarnees, Welleran. *Sharing for Pleasures of Reading*. Western Springs, IL: Darling, 2000.

Pool, Robert. *Fat: Fighting the Obesity Epidemic*. Oxford: Oxford University Press, 2001.

Powell, Jim. *FDR's Folly: How Roosevelt and His New Deal Prolonged the Great Depression*. New York: Three Rivers Press, 2003.

Price, Monroe E., and Daniel Dayan, eds. *Owning the Olympics: Narratives of the New China*. Ann Arbor: University of Michigan Press, 2008.

Prucher, Jeff, ed. *Brave New Words: The Oxford Dictionary of Science Fiction*. Oxford: Oxford University Press, 2007.

Qualman, Erik. *Socialnomics: How Social Media Transforms the Way We Live and Do Business*. Hoboken, NJ: John Wiley & Sons, 2009.

Radanovich, Leroy. *Yosemite Valley*. Charleston, SC: Arcadia, 2004.

Ream, Todd C., and Perry L. Glanzer. "Christian Faith and Scholarship: An Exploration of Contemporary Developments." *ASHE Higher Education Report* 33, no. 2 (2007): 1–139.

Reay, Dave. *Climate Change Begins at Home: Life on the Two-way Street of Global Warming*. London: Macmillan, 2005.

Reid, Stuart, and G.A. Embleton. *Redcoat Officer, 1740–1815*. London: Osprey, 2002.

Reid, Stuart, and Richard Hook. *British Redcoat, 1740–1793*. London: Osprey Military, 1996.

Reilly, Matthew. *Rediscovering Catholicism: Journeying Toward Our Spiritual North Star*. Cincinnati:: Beacon, 2002.

Renou, Louis. *Hinduism*. New York: George Braziller, 1962.

Rexer, Lyle. *Jonathan Lerman: Drawings by an Artist with Autism*. New York: George Braziller, 2002.

Robertson, David. *West of Eden: A History of the Art and Literature of Yosemite*. Berkeley, CA: Wilderness Press, 1984

Rogers, Elizabeth, and Thomas M. Kostigen. *The Green Book: The Everyday Guide to Saving the Planet One Simple Step at a Time*. New York: Three Rivers Press, 2007.

Roosevelt, Elliot, ed. *FDR: His Personal Letters*. New York: Duell, Sloan and Pearce, 1847.

Rose, Gene, and Keith Trexler. *Yosemite's Tioga Country: A History and Appreciation*. Yosemite National Park, CA: Yosemite Association, 2006.

Rosenheim, Shawn, and Stephen Rachman, eds. *The American Face of Edgar Allan Poe.* Baltimore: Johns Hopkins University Press, 1995.

Rosenzweig, Denise, and Magdalena Rosenwieg, eds. *Self Portrait in a Velvet Dress: Frida's Wardrobe.* San Francisco: Chronicle Books, 2007.

Rousmaniere, John. *The Annapolis Book of Seamanship.* Rev. ed. New York: Simon & Schuster, 1999.

Roy, Alexander. *The Driver: My Dangerous Pursuit of Speed and Truth in The Outlaw Racing World.* New York: HarperEntertainment, 2007.

Russell, Edmund. *War and Nature: Fighting Humans and Insects with Chemicals from World War I to Silent Spring.* Cambridge: Cambridge University Press, 2001.

Russell, Isabel. *Katharine and E.B. White : An Affectionate Memoir.* New York: W.W. Norton, 1988.

Safko, Lon, and David K. Brake. *The Social Media Bible: Tactics, Tools and Strategies for Business Success,* Hoboken, NJ: John Wiley & Sons, 2009.

Sagan, Eli. *Citizens and Cannibals: The French Revolution, the Struggle for Modernity, and the Origins of Ideological Terror.* Lanham, MD: Rowman & Littlefield, 2001.

Salmore, Stephen A., and Barbara G. Salmore. *Candidates, Parties, and Campaigns: Electoral Politics in America.* Washington, D.C.: Congressional Quarterly Press, 1985.

Salvivi, Emil R. *Boardwalk Memories: Tales of the Jersey Shore.* Guilford, CT: Glove Pequot Press, 2006.

_____. *Jersey Shore: Vintage Images of Bygone Days.* Guilford, CT: Globe Pequot Press, 2008.

Sands, Emily. *The Egyptology Handbook: A Course in the Wonders of Egypt.* Cambridge, MA: Candlewick Press, 2005.

Sarvady, Andrea Cornell, Frank Miller and Molly Haskell. *Leading Ladies: The 50 Most Unforgettable Actresses of the Studio Era.* San Francisco: Chronicle Books, 2006.

Savadore, Larry, and Margaret Thomas Buchholz. *Great Storms of the Jersey Shore.* Harvey Cedars, NJ: Down the Shore , 1993.

Schaap, Richard. *An Illustrated History of the Olympics.* New York: Alfred. A. Knopf, 1963.

Schama, Simon. *Citizen: A Chronicle of the French Revolution.* New York: Alfred A. Knopf, 1989.

Schele, Linda, and David Freidel. *A Forest of Kings: The Untold Story of the Ancient Maya.* New York: William Morrow, 1990.

Schele, Linda, and Mary Ellen Miller. *The Blood of Kings: Dynasty and Ritual in Maya Art.* New York: George Braziller, 1986.

Scheuren, Fritz. *Elections and Exit Polling.* Hoboken, NJ: John Wiley & Sons, 2008.

Schmidtz, David, and Elizabeth Willot. *Environmental Ethics: What Really Matters, What Really Works.* New York: Oxford University Press, 2002.

Schoen, Douglas E. *The Power of the Vote: Electing Presidents, Overthrowing Dictators, and Promoting Democracy around the World.* New York: William Morrow, 2007.

Schreier, Barbara A. *Fitting In: Four Generations of College Life.* Chicago: Chicago Historical Society, 1991.

Schulz, Donald E., and Edward J. Williams, eds. *Mexico Faces the 21st Century.* Westport, CT: Greenwood Press, 1995.

Schumann, Hans Wolfgang. *Buddhism: An Outline of Its Teachings and Schools.* Wheaton, IL: Theosophical, 1973.

Scott, Stephen. *The Amish Wedding and Other Special Occasions of the Old Order.* Intercourse, PA: Good Books, 1988.

Sharer, Robert J., and Loa P. Traxler. *The Ancient Maya.* Stanford: Stanford University Press, 2006.

Shaw, Ian, ed. *The Oxford History of Ancient Egypt.* Oxford: Oxford University Press, 2000.

Shih, Clara. *The Facebook Era: Tapping Online Social Networks to Build Better Products, Reach New Audiences, and Sell More Stuff.* Boston: Prentice Hall, 2009.

Shmelter, Richard J. *Chicago Assassin: The Life and Legend of "Machine Gun" Jack McGurn and the Chicago Beer Wars of the Roaring Twenties.* Nashville: Cumberland House, 2008.

Shorris, Earl. *The Life and Times of Mexico.* New York: W.W. Norton, 2004.

Silverberg, Robert, ed. *Science Fiction Hall of Fame:1929–1964.* Vol. 1. New York: Tom Doherty Assoc., 1998.

Silverthorne, Elizabeth. *Fiesta! Mexico's Great Celebrations.* Brookfield, CT: Millbrook Press, 1992.

Sinclair, Barbara. *Party Wars: Polarization and the Politics of National Policy.* Norman: University of Oklahoma Press, 2006.

Sloan, Jane. *Reel Women: An International Directory of Contemporary Feature Films about Women.* Lanham, MD: Scarecrow Press, 2007.

Smith, Digby, and Kevin F. Kiley. *An Illustrated Encyclopedia of Uniforms from 1775 to 1783, the American Revolutionary War.* London: Lorenz, 2008.

Smith, Elmer L. *The Amish.* Lebanon, PA: Applied Arts, 1996.

Smith, Jean Edward. *FDR.* New York: Random House, 2008.

Smith-Davies Publishing. *Women Who Changed the World: Fifty Inspirational Women Who Shaped History.* London: Smith-Davies, 2006.

Sobel, Syl J.D. *Presidential Elections and Other Cool Facts.* 2nd ed. Hauppauge: NY: Barron's Educational Series, 2001.

Solomon, Maynard. *Mozart.* New York: HarperCollins, 1995.

Sosin, Jack M. *The Revolutionary Frontier, 1763–1783.* New York: Holt, Rinehart and Winston, 1967.

Spence, Lewis. *The Myths of Mexico and Peru.* New York: Dover, 1994.

Spignesi, Stephen J. *The Complete "Titanic": From the Ship's Earliest Blueprints to the Epic Film.* Secaucus, NJ: Carol, 1998.

Spivey, Nigel. *The Ancient Olympics.* New York: Oxford University Press, 2005.

Stafford, William. *The Mozart Myths: A Critical Reassessment.* Stanford: Stanford University Press, 1991.

Stanlis, Peter J. "British Views of the American Revolution: A Conflict Over Rights of Sovereignty." *Early American Literature* 11 (1976): 191–201.

Starr, Mark. "A Viewers Guide to Beijing." *Newsweek.* August 4, 2008, pp. 42–49.

Start, Steven D. *Meet the Beatles: A Cultural History of the Band That Shook Youth, Gender, and the World.* New York: HarperCollins, 2005.

Steene, Roger. *Coral Seas.* Buffalo, NY: Firefly Books, 1998.

Stephens, Autumn, ed. *Roar Softly and Carry a Great Lipstick.* Maui: Inner Ocean, 2004.

Stevenson, David. *Cataclysm: The First World War as Political Tragedy.* New York: Basic Books, 2004.

Stewart, Mark. *Auto Racing: A History of Fast Cars and Fearless Drivers.* New York: Franklin Watts, 1998.

Stewart, Tony. *True Speed: My Racing Life.* With Bones Bourcier. New York: HarperEntertainment, 2003.

Stoltzfus, Louise. *Amish Women: Lives and Stories.* Intercourse, PA: Good Books, 1994.

Strachan, Hew, ed. *The Oxford Illustrated History of the First World War.* Oxford: Oxford University Press, 1998.

Streever, Bill. *Green Seduction: Money, Business, and the Environment.* Jackson: University Press of Mississippi, 2007.

Stuessy, Joe, and Scott Lipscomb. *Rock & Roll: Its History and Stylish Development.* 6th ed. Upper Saddle River, NJ: Pearson Education, 2009.

Tafel, Edgar. *Years with Frank Lloyd Wright: Apprentice to Genius.* New York: McGraw Hill, 1974.

Tanaka, Shelley. *On Board the "Titanic": What It Was Like When the Great Liner Sank.* New York: Hyperion Madison, 1997.

Tartamella, Lisa, Elaine Herscher, and Chris Woolston. *Generation Extra Large: Rescuing Our Children from the Epidemic of Obesity.* New York: Basic Books, 2004.

Tenneson, Joyce. *Wise Women: A Celebration of Their Insights, Courage and Beauty.* Boston: Little, Brown, 2002.

Testa, Randy-Michael. *In the Valley of the Shadow: An Elegy to Lancaster County.* Hanover, NH: University Press of New England, 1996.

Thelin, John, Alvin P. Sanoff and Welch Suggs. *Meeting the Challenge: America's Independent Colleges and Universities Since 1956.* Washington, D.C.: Council of Independent Colleges, 2006.

Thomas, Dwight, and David K. Jackson. *The Poe Log: A Documentary Life of Edgar Allan Poe, 1809–1849.* Boston: G.K. Hall, 1987.

Thompson, J. Eric S. *Maya Hieroglyphic Writing.* Norman: University of Oklahoma Press, 1971.

Time-Life Books, ed. *The Complete Garden Guide.* Alexandria, VA: Time-Life Books, 2000.

_____, ed. *Photographing Nature.* New York: Time-Life Books, 1971.

Toker, Franklin. *Fallingwater Rising: Frank Lloyd Wright, E.J. Kaufman and America's Most Extraordinary House.* New York: A.A. Knopf, 2003.

Toner, Jules J. *Love and Friendship.* Milwaukee, WI: Marquette University Press, 2003.

Trask, Crissy. *It's Easy Being Green: A Handbook for Earth-Friendly Living.* Salt Lake City: Gibbs Smith, 2006.

Troost, Linda, and Sayre Greenfield, eds. *Jane Austen in Hollywood.* Lexington: University Press of Kentucky, 1998.

Tuchman, Barbara W. *The Guns of August.* New York: Macmillan, 1962.

Turkus, Burton B., and Sid Feder. *Murder, Inc.: The Story of the Syndicate.* 2nd ed. Cambridge, MA: Da Capo Press, 2003.

Unterburger, Amy L. *Women Filmmakers and Their Films.* Detroit: St. James Press, 1998.

Urban, Mark. *Fusiliers: The Saga of a British Redcoat Regiment in the American Revolution.* New York: Walker, 2007.

Urrea, Luis Alberta. *The Hummingbird's Daughter.* New York: Back Bay Books, 2005.

Vermeiren, Jan. *How to Really Use LinkedIn.* Charleston, SC: Booksurge, 2009.

Victor, David G. *The Collapse of the Kyoto Protocol and the Struggle to Slow Global Warming.* Princeton: Princeton University Press, 2001.

Vigil, James Diego. *From Indians to Chicanos: The Dynamics of Mexican-American Culture.* Prospect Heights, IL: Waveland Press, 1998.

Voss, Frederick S. *Portraits of the Presidents: The National Portrait Gallery.* Washington: National Portrait Gallery, Smithsonian Institution, 2000.

Wallenchinsky, David, and Jaime Loucky. *The Complete Book of the Olympics.* London: Aurum Press, 2008.

Wallick, Clair H. *Looking for Ideas: A Display Manual for Libraries and Bookstores.* Metuchen, NJ: Scarecrow Press, 1970.

Ward, David A. *Alcatraz: The Gangster Years.* Berkeley: University of California, 2009.

Ward, Geoffrey C. *Closest Companion: The Unknown Story of the Intimate Friendship between Franklin Roosevelt and Margaret Suckley*. Boston: Houghton Mifflin, 1995.

Warner, Jay. *Notable Moments of Women in Music*. New York: Hal Leonard Books, 2008.

Weisman, Alan. "Earth Without People: What Would Happen to Our Planet if the Mighty Hand of Humanity Simply Disappeared." *Discover* 26, no. 2 (Feb 2005): 60–66.

_____. *The World Without Us*. New York: Thomas Dunn Books, 2007.

Wels, Susan. *"Titanic": Legacy of the World's Greatest Ocean Liner*. Alexandria: Time-Life Books, 1997.

Welsh, Frank. *Australia: A New History of the Great Southern Land*. Woodstock, NY: Overlook Press, 2004.

Wenner, Jann S. *The Rock & Roll Hall of Fame*. New York: Collins Design, 2009.

Wernecke, Herbert H. *Celebrating Christmas around the World*. Philadelphia: Westminster Press, 1962.

Wilde, Oscar. *The Ballad of Reading Gaol*. New York: Heritage Press, 1937.

_____. *Oscar Wilde's Wit and Wisdom: A Book of Quotations*. Mineola, NY: Dover, 1998.

Wilkes, Roger, ed. *The Mammoth Book of Gangs and Gangsters*. New York: Carroll & Graf, 2006.

Williams, Donna. *Autism: An Inside Out Approach*. London: Jessica Kingsley, 1996.

_____. *Somebody Somewhere: Breaking Free from the World of Autism*. New York: Random House, 1995.

Williamson, Kate T. *A Year in Japan*. New York: Princeton Architectural Press, 2006.

Wilson, Erica. *Quilts in America*. Birmingham, AL: Oxmoor House, 1979.

Wilson, R. Andrew. *Write Like Hemingway: Writing Lessons You Can Learn from the Master*. Avon, MA: Adams Media, 2009.

Winchester, Simon. "China: A Love Story." *Parade,* July 20, 2008, pp. 8–11.

Winocour, Jack, ed. *The Story of the "Titanic" as Told by Its Survivors*. New York: Dover, 1997.

Wittmer, Joe. *The Gentle People: An Inside View of Amish Life*. 3rd ed. Washington, IN: Black Buggy Restaurant and General Store, 2007.

Wolanski, Eric. *Oceanographic Processes of Coral Reefs: Physical and Biological Links in the Great Barrier Reef*. Boca Raton, FL: CRC Press, 2001.

Wolff, Alexander. "Let the Show Begin." *Sports Illustrated* 109, no. 3 (July 26, 2008), 46–50.

Woodman, Richard. *The History of the Ship*. Guilford, CT: Lyons Press, 2002

Worden, Minky. *China's Great Leap: The Beijing Games and Olympian Human Rights Challenges*. New York: Seven Stories Press, 2008.

Wright, Frank Lloyd. *An Autobiography*. New York: Horizon Press, 1977.

Wright, Jason F. *Christmas Jars*. Salt Lake City, UT: Shadow Mountain, 2006.

Wright, Thomas. *Built of Books: How Reading Defined the Life of Oscar Wilde*. New York: Henry Holt, 2008.

Yarrow, Joanna. *1,001 Ways to Save the Earth*. San Francisco: Chronicle Books, 2007.

Young, David C. *A Brief History of the Olympic Games*. Malden, MA: Blackwell, 2004.

Zemke, Ron, Claire Raines, and Bob Filipczak. *Generations at Work: Managing the Clash of Veterans, Boomers, Xers, and Nexters in Your Workplace*. New York: American Management Association, 2000.

Index